DAVID BUS
CANON EOS 7D
Mark II
FAST TRACK GUIDE

David D. Busch

Laserfaire Press

Copyright

Library of Congress Control Number:

ISBN-13: 978-1-946488-00-8

ISBN-10:1-946488-00-3

Laserfaire Press

3780 Lake Rockwell Road

Ravenna, OH 44266

Visit our website at dslrguides.com

Other Credits:

www.jelenpub.com

www.cueravenpublishing.com

About the Author

With more than 2 million books in print, David D. Busch is the world's #1 selling author of camera-specific photography books, and the originator of popular series like David Busch's Pro Secrets and David Busch's Quick Snap Guides. He has written more than 200 hugely successful photography guides and camera-specific manuals for Canon, Nikon, Sony, Olympus, Pentax, and Panasonic products, including the all-time bestsellers for the many models, as well as many popular books devoted to dSLRs. As a roving photojournalist for more than 20 years, he illustrated his books, magazine articles, and newspaper reports with award-winning images. He's operated his own commercial studio, suffocated in formal dress while shooting weddings-for-hire, and shot sports for a daily newspaper and upstate New York college. His photos and articles have been published in Popular Photography, Rangefinder, Professional Photographer, and hundreds of other publications. He's also reviewed dozens of digital cameras for Ziff-Davis online and print publications.

When About.com named its top five books on Beginning Digital Photography, debuting at the #1 and #2 slots were Busch's Digital Photography All-In-One Desk Reference for Dummies and Mastering Digital Photography. During the past year, he's had as many as five of his books listed in the Top 20 of Amazon.com's Digital Photography Bestseller list -- simultaneously! Busch's 150-plus other books published since 1983 include bestsellers like David Busch's Quick Snap Guide to Using Digital SLR Lenses. His advice has been featured on National Public Radio's All Tech Considered.

Busch is a member of the Cleveland Photographic Society (www.clevelandphoto.org), which has operated continuously since 1887. Visit his Canon website at http://www.canonguides.com There you'll find news, tips, and an errata page with typo alerts from sharp-eyed readers, along with an E-Mail Me tab you can use to contact him directly.

Preface

If you've invested in a camera as sophisticated as the Canon EOS 7D II, you're looking for more than good pictures -- you demand outstanding photos. After all, the 7D II is the most advanced APS-C format camera that Canon has ever introduced. It boasts 20 megapixels of resolution, blazing-fast automatic focus, and cool features like full high-definition movie shooting. But your gateway to pixel proficiency is dragged down by the slim little book included in the box as a manual. You know everything you need to know is in there, somewhere, but you don't know where to start. In addition, the camera manual doesn't offer much information on photography or digital photography. Nor are you interested in spending hours or days studying a comprehensive book on digital SLR still photography that doesn't necessarily apply directly to your 7D II.

What you need is a guide that explains the purpose and function of the 7D II's basic controls, how you should use them, and why. Ideally, there should be information about file formats, resolution, exposure, and special autofocus modes available, but you'd prefer to read about those topics only after you've had the chance to go out and take a few hundred great pictures with your new camera. Why isn't there a book that summarizes the most important information in its first two or three chapters, with lots of illustrations showing what your results will look like when you use this setting or that?

Now there is such a book. If you want a quick introduction to the 7D II's focus controls, wireless flash synchronization options, how to choose lenses, or which exposure modes are best, this book is for you. If you can't decide on what basic settings to use with your camera because you can't figure out how changing ISO or white balance or focus defaults will affect your pictures, you need this guide.

Table of Contents

Chapter 3
Some Basic Recommended Settings

Chapter 4
Nailing the Right Exposure

Chapter 5
Mastering the Mysteries of Autofocus

Chapter 6
Advanced Shooting

Chapter 7
Working with Lenses

Chapter 8
Customizing with the Shooting Menu

Chapter 9
Fine Tuning with the Autofocus Menu

Chapter 10
Working with the Playback and Set-Up Menus

Chapter 11
Custom Function and My Menus

Chapter 12
Working with Light

Chapter 14
Troubleshooting and Prevention

Introduction

Ack! When my former publisher closed its photo book division in September, 2014, I was in the middle of planning a book for the just-introduced Canon EOS 7D II as an update to my original book on the very first 7D model. The book was cancelled, and by the time I located a new publisher, the 7D II was far along enough in its life-cycle that the new publishing house was wary about taking the risk of issuing a book at such a late date.

What followed was nearly a year of pleas from readers who counted on me to help them learn the ins and outs of each new camera upgrade they acquired. Many had already purchased a third-party book and found it unsatisfactory, while others simply preferred my way of organization and, perhaps the enthusiasm with which I always have for sharing what I've learned how to do (and what not to do) with a spanking new camera. I continued to use my own 7D II with great pleasure until I finally made the decision to put together a guidebook for this camera, as a labor of love even if it might not prove to be a financial boon. This ebook is the result. Not having access or funds to publish a hardcopy version (although I am still working on that) this electronic book is what you see, and what you get from me for the 7D II.

Canon continues to blaze new, exciting trails. With this camera, Canon has packaged up many of the most alluring features found in any digital SLR and stuffed them into a highly affordable professional body called the 7D II. Your new 20-megapixel camera is loaded with capabilities that few would have expected to find in an inexpensive APS-C dSLR. Indeed, the 7D II retains the ease of use that smoothes the transition for those new to digital photography. For those just dipping their toes into the digital pond, the experience is warm and inviting.

Nor will you easily outgrow this camera. It's got enough resolution for the most demanding applications, improved autofocus, and lots of customization options. Canon must love serious photographers, because it seems to work extra hard to give them incredible value for their money.

But once you've confirmed that you made a wise purchase decision, the question comes up, how do I use this thing? All those cool features can be mind numbing to learn, if all you have as a guide is the manual furnished with the camera. Help is on the way. I sincerely believe that this book is your best bet for learning how to use your new camera for still photography, and for learning how to use it well.

If you're a Canon EOS 7D II owner who's looking to learn more about how to use this great camera, you've probably already explored your options. There are YouTube videos -- but who can learn how to use a camera by sitting in front of a television or computer screen? Do you want to watch a movie or click on HTML links, or do you want to go out and take photos with your camera? Videos are fun, but not the best answer.

There's always the manual furnished with the 7D II. It's compact and filled with information, but there's really very little about why you should use particular settings or features, and its organization may make it difficult to find what you need. Multiple cross-references may send you flipping back and forth between two or three sections of the book to find what you want to know. The basic manual is also hobbled by black-and-white line drawings and tiny monochrome pictures that aren't very good examples of what you can do.

I've tried to make David Busch's Canon EOS 7D II Fast Track Guide different from your other 7D II learn-up options. The roadmap sections use large, color pictures to show you where all the buttons and dials are, and the explanations of what they do are longer and more comprehensive. I've tried to avoid overly general advice, including the two-page checklists on how to take a "sports picture" or a "portrait picture" or a "travel picture." Instead, you'll find tips and techniques for using all the features of your Canon EOS 7D II to take any kind of picture you want. If you want to know where you should stand to take a picture of a quarterback dropping back to unleash a pass, there are plenty of books that will tell you that. This one concentrates on teaching you how to select the best autofocus mode, shutter speed, f/stop, or flash capability to take, say, a great sports picture under any conditions.

However, as you explore the pages of this book, you'll see that, in addition to serving as a supplement to the operator's manual furnished with the camera, I attempt to relate every feature, control, and option to actual picture-taking situations, and, still photography in general, at every opportunity. Some readers who visit my blog have told me that the 7D II is such an advanced camera that few people really need the kind of basics that so many camera guides concentrate on. "Leave out all the basic photography information!" On the other hand, I've had many pleas from those who are trying to master digital photography as they learn to use their 7D II, and they've asked me to help them climb the steep learning curve.

Rather than write a book for just one of those two audiences, I've tried to meet the needs of both. You veterans will find plenty of information on getting the most from the camera's features, and may even learn something from an old hand's photo secrets. I'll bet there was a time when you needed a helping hand with some confusing photographic topic. I've tucked most of the really basic material away in the bonus appendices. And those who are looking to learn about photography and their camera will find just what you need in this book, too.

EMPHASIS ON STILL PHOTOGRAPHY

However, if you're looking for extensive and exhaustive coverage of this camera's video capture capabilities, you'll need a full book from another author if you need to explore that aspect. This is primarily a book devoted to still photography, and, given the 7D II's extensive feature set, already runs more than 100 pages longer than most of my other camera guides. I've devoted extra attention to topics that really deserve it, such as autofocus and wireless flash, and I urge budding Spielbergs to explore the mysteries of time codes and codecs in books that can explore their intricacies in depth. I'll get you started, however, with three basic chapters that do look at the basics of live view and movie making.

Who Am I?

After spending years as the world's most successful unknown author, I've become slightly less obscure in the past few years, thanks to a horde of camera guidebooks and other photographically oriented tomes. You may have seen my photography articles in Popular Photography magazine. I've also written about 2,000 articles for magazines like Petersen's PhotoGraphic (which is now defunct through no fault of my own), plus Rangefinder, Professional Photographer, and dozens of other photographic publications. But, first, and foremost, I'm a photojournalist and commercial photographer and made my living in the field until I began devoting most of my time to writing books.

Although I love writing, I'm happiest when I'm out taking pictures, which is why I invariably spend several days each week photographing landscapes, people, close-up subjects, and other things. I spend a month or two each year traveling to events, such as Native American "powwows," Civil War re-enactments, county fairs, ballet, and sports (baseball, basketball, football, and soccer are favorites). Just before beginning work on this book, I took 11 days for a visit to Europe, strictly to shoot photographs of the people, landscapes, and monuments that I've grown to love. I can offer you my personal advice on how to take photos under a variety of conditions because I've had to meet those challenges myself on an ongoing basis.

Like all my digital photography books, this one was written by someone with an incurable photography bug. My first Canon SLR was a Pellix back in the 1960s, and I've used a variety of newer models since then. I've worked as a sports photographer for an Ohio newspaper and for an upstate New York college. I've operated my own commercial studio and photo lab, cranking out product shots on demand and then printing a few hundred glossy 8 x 10s on a tight deadline for a press kit. I've served as a photo-posing instructor for a modeling agency. People have actually paid me to shoot their weddings and immortalize them with portraits. I even prepared press kits and articles on photography as a PR consultant for a large Rochester, N.Y., company, which shall remain nameless. My trials and travails with imaging and computer technology have made their way into print in book form an alarming number of times.

As you can see, like you, I love photography for its own merits, and I view technology as just another tool to help me get the images I see in my mind's eye. But, also like you, I had to master this technology before I could apply it to my work. This book is the result of what I've learned, and I hope it will help you master your Canon digital SLR, too.

In closing, I'd like to ask a special favor: let me know what you think of this book. If you have any recommendations about how I can make it better, visit my website at www.canonguides.com, click on the E-Mail Me tab, and send your comments, suggestions on topics that should be explained in more detail, or, especially, any typos. (The latter will be compiled on the Errata page you'll also find on my website.) I really value your ideas, and appreciate it when you take the time to tell me what you think! Some of the content of the book you hold in your hands came from suggestions I received from readers like yourself. If you found this book especially useful, tell others about it and leave a positive review. Your feedback is what spurs me to make each one of these books better than the last. And if enough of you value this book, I'll be prompted to write another one the next time Canon comes up with another one of its innovations. Thanks!

Chapter 1

Canon EOS 7D Mark II Quick Start

Now it's time to fire up your 7D Mark II and take some photos. The easy part is turning on the power -- that OFF-ON switch on the top-left shoulder of the camera, nestled next to the Mode Dial (see **Figure 1.1**). Turn on the camera, and, if you mounted a lens and inserted a fresh battery and memory card, you're ready to begin. You'll need to select a shooting mode, metering mode, and focus mode.

Selecting a Shooting Mode

You can choose a shooting method from the Mode Dial located on the top-left edge of the 7D Mark II. The camera has one fully automatic mode called Scene Intelligent Auto, which makes virtually all the decisions for you (except when to press the shutter). There are also five semi-automatic/manual modes (what Canon calls Creative Zone on its entry- and mid-level models), including Program, Shutter-priority, Aperture-priority, Manual, and Bulb, which allow you to provide input over the exposure and settings the camera uses. There are also three camera user settings (Custom shooting modes) that can be used to store specific groups of camera settings, which you can then recall quickly by spinning the Mode Dial to C1, C2, or C3. You'll find a complete description of fully automatic and semi-automatic/manual modes in Chapter 4, as well as Custom shooting modes in Chapter 14.

Turn your camera on by flipping the power switch to ON. Next, you need to select which shooting mode to use. If you're very new to digital photography, you might want to set the camera to Auto (the green frame on the Mode Dial) or P (Program mode) and start snapping away. These modes will make all the appropriate settings for you for many shooting situations. Your choices are as follows:

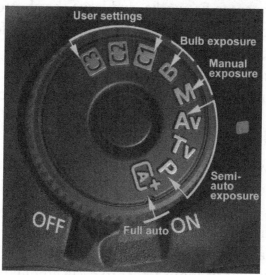

Figure 1.1

The Mode Dial includes both automatic and semi-automatic/manual settings.

- **Scene Intelligent Auto.** In this mode, the EOS 7D Mark II makes all the exposure decisions for you.

- **P (Program).** This semi-automatic mode allows the 7D Mark II to select the basic exposure settings, but you can still override the camera's choices to fine-tune your image.

- **Tv (Shutter-priority).** This mode (Tv stands for *time value*) is useful when you want to use a particular shutter speed to stop action or produce creative blur effects. The 7D Mark II will select the appropriate f/stop for you.

- **Av (Aperture-priority).** Choose when you want to use a particular lens opening, especially to control sharpness or how much of your image is in focus. The 7D Mark II will select the appropriate shutter speed for you. Av stands for *aperture value*.

- **M (Manual).** Select when you want full control over the shutter speed and lens opening, either for creative effects or

25

because you are using a studio flash or other flash unit not compatible with the 7D Mark II's automatic flash metering.

- **B (Bulb).** Choose this mode and the shutter will remain open as long as you hold down the release button. It is useful for making exposures of indeterminate length (say, you want to capture some fireworks, and leave the shutter open until a burst appears, then release the shutter after a few seconds when the light trails have been captured). The B setting can also be used to produce exposures longer than the 30 seconds (maximum) the 7D Mark II can take automatically.

Choosing a Metering Mode

You might want to select a particular metering mode for your first shots, although the default Evaluative metering is probably the best choice as you get to know your camera. To change metering modes, press the Metering-WB button (shown at left in **Figure 1.2**) and spin the Main Dial (one of the basic controls you'll need to learn, shown at right in **Figure 1.2**) to cycle among the choices. A screen like the one in **Figure 1.3** appears. Note: If the screen does not appear, you may have turned the display off. Press the INFO button until the normal display appears.

- **Evaluative metering.** The standard metering mode; the 7D Mark II attempts to intelligently classify your image and choose the best exposure based on readings from 252 different zones in the frame, linked to the autofocus points.

- **Partial metering.** Exposure is based on a central spot, roughly 6 percent of the image area.

- **Spot metering.** Exposure is calculated from a smaller central spot, about 1.8 percent of the image area, located in the center of the frame.

⊙ **Center-weighted averaging metering.** The 7D Mark II meters the entire scene, but gives the most emphasis to the central area of the frame.

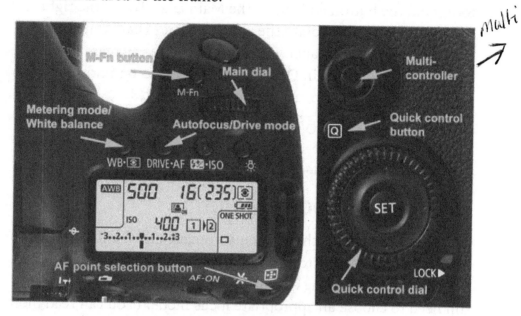

Figure 1.2

Direct access buttons include the Metering-WB button and AF-DRIVE button.

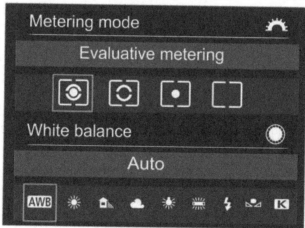

Figure 1.3

Metering modes (left to right, top third of the screen): Evaluative, Partial, Spot, Center-weighted.

You'll find a detailed description of each of these modes in Chapter 4.

Button, Button: Each top-panel button has two functions. To set the left function of each pair (that is AF with the AF-DRIVE button), hold the button and rotate the Main Dial. To set the right function of each pair, rotate the Quick Control Dial located on the right side of the back panel. Each pair of choices appears in a single pop-up screen with Main Dial and QCD icons to remind you which dial sets which function, as you saw in **Figure 1.3**.

Note: If you find the Quick Control Dial is not performing the expected function, make sure the Quick Control Dial LOCK switch, located at the five o'clock position, is moved all the way to the left.

Choosing a Focus Mode

You can easily switch between automatic and manual focus by moving the AF/MF switch on the lens mounted on your camera. However, if you're using a semi-automatic shooting mode, you'll still need to choose an appropriate focus mode. (You can read more on selecting focus parameters in Chapter 5.)

To set the focus mode, press the AF-DRIVE button on the top panel of the camera (see **Figure 1.2**, shown earlier), and spin the Main Dial until the mode you want is shown in the LCD. (See **Figure 1.4**; press INFO if it does not appear.) The three choices are as follows:

- ⊚ **One-Shot**. This mode, sometimes called *single autofocus*, locks in a focus point when the shutter button is pressed down halfway, and the focus confirmation light glows in the viewfinder. The focus will remain locked until you release the button or take the picture. If the camera is unable to achieve sharp focus, the focus confirmation light will blink. This mode is best when your subject is relatively motionless.

- ⊚ **AI Servo**. This mode, sometimes called *continuous autofocus*, sets focus when you partially depress the shutter button, but continues to monitor the frame and refocuses if the camera or subject is moved. This is a useful mode for photographing sports and moving subjects.

● **AI Focus.** In this mode, the 7D Mark II switches between One-Shot and AI Servo as appropriate. That is, it locks in a focus point when you partially depress the shutter button (One-Shot mode), but switches automatically to AI Servo if the subject begins to move. This mode is handy when photographing a subject, such as a child at quiet play, which might move unexpectedly.

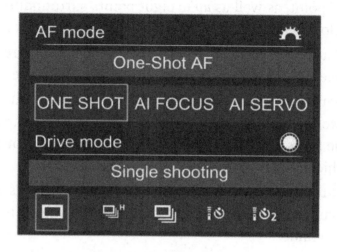

Figure 1.4

Set autofocus mode.

Selecting a Focus Point

The Canon EOS 7D Mark II uses up to 65 different focus points to calculate correct focus. In Full Auto mode, the focus point is selected automatically by the camera. In the other semi-automatic modes, you can allow the camera to select the focus point automatically, or you can specify which focus point should be used.

Your camera has seven different ways of specifying which of the 65 focus points is selected by the camera automatically, or by the user manually. I'll cover each of these in detail, and tell you when you might want to use each of them in Chapter 5 and Chapter 12. The choices are as follows:

◉ **Manual Select:** Spot AF. Allows you to manually select a single, reduced-size AF point.

- ◎ **Manual Selection**: 1 pt AF. For manual selection of a single, slightly larger AF point.
- ◎ **Expand AF Area**: 5 points total. You can manually select a single AF point, as well as the points above, below, and to the left/right of it.
- ◎ **Expand AF Area**: Surround. You can manually select a single AF point, as well as *up to* eight points surrounding it (above, below, left, right, and diagonally from the selected point).
- ◎ **Manual Select**: Zone AF. The AF points are segregated into nine zones, and you can select which zone to use.
- ◎ **Manual Select**: Large Zone AF. The AF points are segregated into three zones, two 20-point zones at the left and right of the focus areas and one center 25-point zone. You may select which of the three large zones you want to use.
- ◎ **Auto Selection**: 65 point AF. The camera selects one or more focus points automatically, and highlights them in red in the viewfinder.

You can access any of these by pressing the AF point selection button to produce the screen shown in **Figure 1.5**. Then, press the M-Fn button or press the lever that rings the multi controller to cycle among the available choices. (The AF point selection button, M-Fn button and multi-controller were shown in **Figure 1.2**.) To get up and running as quickly in this Quick Start, you should choose Manual Select: 1 pt AF (seen in **Figure 1.7**) or Auto Selection: 65 point AF. If you want to learn now about the 7D Mark II's complex autofocus options, skip ahead to Chapter 5.

Once you've chosen your AF point mode, there are several ways to set the focus point in any selection mode. You can press the AF point selection button, and choose a zone or point in any mode other then Auto Selection: 65 point AF from the AF point selection screen that pops up on the LCD monitor. Rotate the the Quick Control dial to move up or down within a column or the front dial to move horizontally. In the manual selection modes, the multi-controller's joystick action is used to highlight the point or zone you want to use. Press the AF point selection button again (or just tap the shutter release button) to confirm your choice and exit.

Or, you can look through the viewfinder, press the AF point selection button, and rotate the Main Dial to move the focus point left/right within its row, or the Quick Control Dial to shift it up or down within its column.

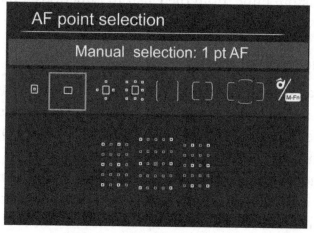

Figure 1.5

Select a focus point and selection mode from the AF point selection screen.

Other Settings

There are a few other options that might interest you, such as white balance, using the self-timer, or working with flash. You use these right away if you're feeling ambitious, but don't feel ashamed if you postpone using these features until you've racked up a little more experience with your EOS 7D Mark II.

Adjusting White Balance and ISO

If you like, you can custom-tailor your white balance (color balance) and ISO sensitivity settings. To start out, it's best to set white balance (WB) to Auto, and ISO to ISO 100 or ISO 200 for daylight photos, and ISO 400 for pictures in dimmer light. You'll find complete recommendations for both these settings in Chapter 4. You can adjust either one now by pressing the Metering-WB button (for white balance) and rotating the Quick Control Dial, or by pressing ISO-Flash exposure compensation button (for ISO sensitivity) and rotating the Main Dial until the setting you want appears on the status LCD. Both buttons were shown earlier in **Figure 1.2**.

If you've been playing with your camera's settings, or your 7D Mark II has been used by someone else, you can restore the factory defaults by selecting Clear Settings from the Set-up 4 menu, and/or Clear All Custom Func, from the Custom Functions 4 menu. I'll show you exactly how to do this in Chapter 14.

Using the Self-Timer

If you want to set a short delay before your picture is taken, you can use the self-timer. Press the AF-DRIVE button (the screen shown earlier in Figure 1.4 will appear) and rotate the Quick Control Dial until the self-timer icon (for a 10-second delay) or the self-timer icon accompanied by the numeral 2 (for a 2-second delay) appear on the status LCD. Canon supplies a rubber eyepiece cover, which attaches to your camera strap and can be slid over the eyepiece in place of the rubber eyecup. This prevents light from entering through the eyepiece, which can confuse the exposure meter. I've found that extraneous light is seldom a problem unless a bright light source is coming from directly behind the camera, in which case I use my hand to shield the viewfinder.

Press the shutter release to lock focus and start the timer. The self-timer lamp will blink and the beeper will sound (unless you've silenced it in the menus) until the final two seconds, when the lamp remains on and the beeper beeps more rapidly.

Taking a Picture

This final section of the chapter guides you through taking your first pictures, reviewing them on the LCD, and transferring your shots to your computer.

Just press the shutter release button halfway to lock in focus at the selected autofocus point for a few seconds. When the shutter button is in the half-depressed position, the exposure, calculated using the shooting mode you've selected, is also locked.

Press the button the rest of the way down to take a picture. At that instant, the mirror flips up out of the light path to the optical viewfinder (assuming you're not using Live View mode, discussed in Chapter 13), the shutter opens, the electronic flash (if attached and enabled) fires, and your 7D Mark II's sensor absorbs a burst of light to capture an exposure. In fractions of a moment, the shutter closes, the mirror flips back down restoring your view, and the image you've taken is escorted off the CMOS sensor chip very quickly into an in-camera store of memory called a buffer, and the EOS 7D Mark II is ready to take another photo. The buffer continues dumping your image onto the memory card as you keep snapping pictures without pause (at least until the buffer fills and you must wait for it to get ahead of your continuous shooting, or your memory card fills completely).

Reviewing the Images You've Taken

The Canon EOS 7D Mark II has a broad range of playback and image review options. Here are the basics, as shown in **Figure 1.6**. I'll explain more choices, such as rotating the image on review, in Chapter 2:

- **Display image.** Press the Playback button (marked with a blue right-pointing triangle at the lower-left edge of the back of the 7D Mark II just above the Trash button) to display the most recent image on the LCD in full-screen single image mode. If you last viewed your images using the thumbnail mode (described later in this list), the Index display appears instead.

- **View additional images**. Rotate the Quick Control Dial to review additional images, one at a time. Turn it counterclockwise to review images from most recent to oldest, or clockwise to start with the first image on the memory card and cycle forward to the newest.

- **Jump ahead or back**. When you're using the single image display (not zoomed or viewing reduced-size thumbnail images), you can zip through your shots more quickly to find a specific image. Just rotate the Main Dial to leap ahead or back

10 or 100 images, depending on the increment you've set using the last entry in the Playback 2 menu. I find the 7D Mark II's use of the Main Dial is faster. You can also jump ahead by screens of images, by date, or by folder, and jump among movies, stills or image "rating." (You can mark favorite images with one to four stars, as I'll explain when I show you how to select all these Playback options in Chapter 13.)

○ **View image information.** Press the INFO. button repeatedly to cycle among overlays of basic image information, detailed shooting information, or no information at all.

○ **Zoom in on an image.** When an image is displayed full-screen on your LCD, press the Magnify/Reduce button (located on the back left of the camera) repeatedly to zoom in or out. When zoomed, you can rotate the Main Dial on the top panel, just aft of the shutter release, to zoom in or out. Press the Playback button to exit magnified display. I'll show you how to specify how much magnification is applied (up to 10X is available) using the Playback 3 menu, in Chapter 13.

○ **Scroll around in a magnified image.** Press the Magnify/Enlarge button, then use the multi-controller (the joystick-like knob to the upper right of the color LCD) to scroll around within a magnified image.

○ **View thumbnail images.** You can also rapidly move among a large number of images using the Index mode described in the section that follows this list.

○ **Compare images.** While reviewing images, you can press the Comparative Photo (Two-Image Display)/Direct Print/Creative Photo button (located at the top of the array located to the left of the back-panel LCD monitor) to split the LCD between two images. The current image is highlighted with a blue frame. Press SET to swap highlighting to the other image, and then rotate the Quick Control Dial to change to another image. The Q button (to the upper left of the QCD) sets both images to the same magnification. Hold down the

Playback button to fill the LCD with the highlighted image.
Press the Two-Image button to return to single image view.

⊙ **Access Functions.** While reviewing pictures in full image
view you can press the Q button to produce a Quick Control
screen that gives you access to many simple functions. You
can protect or rate images, resize them, change the jumping
method, rotate them, perform RAW image processing, enable
or disable highlight alerts, and activate/deactivate AF point
display. When the Quick Control screen is visible, use the
multi-controller joystick to select the function to perform. I'll
show you how to use the Quick Control screen in Chapter 2.

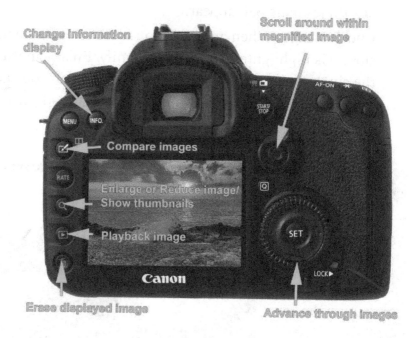

Figure 1.6

Review your images.

Cruising through Index Views

You can navigate quickly among thumbnails representing a series of images using the 7D Mark II's Index mode. Here are your
basic options.

- **Display thumbnails.** Press the Playback button to display an image on the color LCD. If an image pops up full-screen in single-image mode, press the Magnify/Reduce button and rotate the Main Dial counter-clockwise to view 4, 9, or 36 thumbnails. Rotating the Main Dial clockwise enlarges the images, from thumbnails to single-image and then zooming in on the frame.

- **Navigate within a screen of index images.** In Index mode, use the multi-controller joystick to move the orange highlight box around within the current Index display screen.

- **View more Index pages.** To view additional Index pages (if available), rotate the QCD and the next/previous page of index thumbnails will appear.

- **Check image.** When an image you want to examine more closely is highlighted, press the Magnify/Enlarge button until the single-image version appears full-screen on your LCD.

- **Compare images.** Two-image review, described earlier, also works in Index mode.

Figure 1.7
Review thumbnails of 4, 9, or 36 images using Index review.

Transferring Photos to Your Computer

The final step in your picture-taking session will be to transfer the photos you've taken to your computer for printing, further review, or image editing. Your 7D Mark II allows you to print directly to PictBridge-compatible printers and to create print orders right in the camera.

For now, you'll probably want to transfer your images either by using a cable transfer from the camera to the computer or by removing the memory card from the 7D Mark II and transferring the images with a card reader. The latter option is generally the best, because it's usually much faster and doesn't deplete the battery of your camera. However, you can use a cable transfer when you have the cable and a computer, but no card reader (perhaps you're using the computer of a friend or colleague, or at a public library.)

To transfer images from the camera to a Mac or PC computer using the USB cable:

1. Turn off the camera.
2. Pry back the rubber cover that protects the EOS 7D Mark II's USB port, and plug the USB cable furnished with the camera into the digital terminal/USB port. (See **Figure 1.8**.)
3. Connect the other end of the USB cable to a USB port on your computer.
4. Turn on the camera. Your installed software usually detects the camera and offers to transfer the pictures, or the camera appears on your desktop as a mass storage device, enabling you to drag and drop the files to your computer.

To transfer images from a memory card to the computer using a card reader.

1. Turn off the camera.
2. Slide open the memory card door, and press the gray button, which ejects the card.
3. Insert the memory card into your memory card reader. Your installed software detects the files on the card and offers to transfer them. The card can also appear as a mass storage device on your desktop, which you can open and then drag and drop the files to your computer.

Figure 1.8

Images can be transferred to your computer using a USB cable.

Chapter 2

Canon EOS 7D Mark II Roadmap

Most of the Canon EOS 7D Mark II's key functions and settings that are changed frequently can be accessed directly using the array of dials and buttons and knobs that populate the camera's surface. With so many dedicated controls available, you'll find that the bulk of your shooting won't be slowed down by a visit to the vast thicket of text options called Menuland. With the 7D II, you can use specific controls dedicated to white balance, ISO sensitivity, shooting mode, exposure compensation, and playback options, and make further adjustments using the multi controller.

While it might take some time to learn the position and function of each of these controls, once you've mastered them the 7D II camera is remarkably easy to use. That's because dedicated buttons with only one or two functions each are much faster to access than the alternative -- a maze of menus that must be navigated every time you want to use a feature. The advantage of menu systems -- dating back to early computer user interfaces of the 1980s -- is that they are easy to *learn*. The ironic disadvantage of menus is that they are clumsy to *use*.

Imagine that you are familiar with digital SLRs in general, but know virtually nothing about the Canon EOS 7D Mark II. You've decided that you want to format the memory card. A-ha! There's a big 'ol MENU button on the left side of the camera. Press it, and you'll see a series of different menu icons, which, when you scroll through them, have entries for shooting options, playback, camera set-up, and customized functions. In the case of the 7D II, none of the menu screens you see scroll; all the choices available for that screen are shown each time the menu tab appears. So, with a couple clicks of the Main Dial, you spy a Set-up menu with the command Format as its fifth entry. Scroll down to Format using the other dial (the Quick Control Dial), press the SET ("enter") button, and there you are, looking at the Format screen. A couple more button presses, and you've successfully formatted your memory card.

You didn't really need instructions -- the menu system itself led you to the right command. If you don't format another card for weeks and weeks, you can come back to the menus and discover how to perform the task all over again. The main cost to you was the time required to negotiate through all the menus to carry out the function; while menus are easy to learn, the multiple steps they call for (10 or more dial twirls or button presses may be required) can be cumbersome to use.

Direct access command buttons are the exact opposite: you have to teach yourself how to use them, and then remember what you've learned over time, but, once learned, buttons are much faster to use. For example, to change the autofocus mode with the 7D II, all you need to do is press the AF-DRIVE button on top of the camera and rotate the Main Dial until the autofocus mode you want to use is indicated on the top-panel LCD. To switch from single exposure to continuous shooting, self-timer, or other "drive" modes, hold down the same button and rotate the Quick Command Dial. No menus required -- but you have to learn the location of the particular button you need to use.

Or, if you need to change the ISO setting on your 7D II, would you rather press the ISO button and spin the Main Dial until the desired value appears on the LCD -- or would you prefer tapping a menu button, using cursor keys to locate the ISO setting submenu, pressing a button to select the ISO menu, navigating to the ISO value you want, and then pressing an OK button to confirm your choice? Yet, that's the procedure mandated by countless point-and-shoot digital cameras and more than a few digital SLRs. The Canon dedicated button approach is a much better design.

So, if you want to operate your 7D II efficiently, you'll need to learn the location, function, and application of all these controls. What you really need is a street-level roadmap that shows where everything is, and how it's used. But what Canon gives you in the user's manual is akin to a world globe with an overall view and many cross-references to the pages that will tell you what you really need to know. Check out the Nomenclature pages of the Canon 7D II manual (pages 22 to 35), which offer tiny black-and-white line drawings of the camera body that show front, back, two sides, and the top and bottom of the 7D II, plus lenses, screens, and other features. There are more than 10 *dozen* callouts pointing to various buttons, dials, controls, components, and icons. If you can find the control you want in this cramped layout, you'll still need to flip back and forth among multiple pages (individual buttons can have several different cross-references!) to locate the information.

Most other third-party books follow this format, featuring black-and-white photos or line drawings of front, back, and top views, and many labels. I originated the up-close-and-personal full-color, street-level roadmap (rather than a satellite view) that I use in this book and my previous camera guidebooks. I provide you with many different views and lots of explanation accompanying each zone of the camera, so that by the time you finish this chapter, you'll have a basic understanding of every control and what it does. I'm not going to delve into menu functions here -- you'll find a discussion of each of the 7D II's menu options in Chapters 8, 9, 10, and 11. Everything here is devoted to the button pusher and dial twirler in you.

You'll also find this "roadmap" chapter a good guide to the rest of the book, as well. I'll try to provide as much detail here about the use of the main controls as I can, but some topics (such as autofocus and exposure) are too complex to address in depth right away. So, I'll point you to the relevant chapters that discuss things like set-up options, exposure, use of electronic flash, and working with lenses with the occasional cross-reference.

Front View

The front of the 7D II (see **Figure 2.1**) is the face seen by your victims as you snap away. For the photographer, though, the front is the surface your fingers curl around as you hold the camera, and there are really only three buttons to press, all within easy reach of the fingers of your left hand, plus the shutter button and Main Dial, which are on the top/front of the hand grip. There are additional controls on the lens itself. You'll need to look at several different views to see everything.

Figure 2.1 is a view of the front of the EOS 7D Mark II with the lens detached. The other main components you need to know about are as follows:

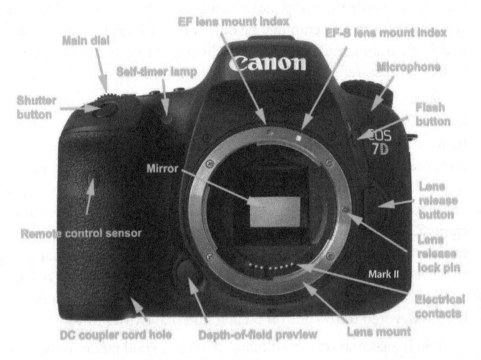

Figure 2.1

Selecting a Shooting Mode

You can choose a shooting method from the Mode Dial located on the top-left edge of the 7D Mark II. The camera has one fully automatic mode called Scene Intelligent Auto, which makes virtually all the decisions for you (except when to press the shutter). There are also five semi-automatic/manual modes (what Canon calls Creative Zone on its entry- and mid-level models), including Program, Shutter-priority, Aperture-priority, Manual, and Bulb, which allow you to provide input over the exposure and settings the camera uses. There are also three camera user settings (Custom shooting modes) that can be used to store specific groups of camera settings, which you can then recall quickly by spinning the Mode Dial to C1,

C2, or C3. You'll find a complete description of fully automatic and semi-automatic/manual modes in Chapter 4, as well as Custom shooting modes in Chapter 14.

Turn your camera on by flipping the power switch to ON. Next, you need to select which shooting mode to use. If you're very new to digital photography, you might want to set the camera to Auto (the green frame on the Mode Dial) or P (Program mode) and start snapping away. These modes will make all the appropriate settings for you for many shooting situations. Your choices are as follows:

- **Shutter button.** Angled on top of the hand grip is the shutter release button. Press this button down halfway to lock exposure and focus (in One-Shot mode and AI Focus with non-moving subjects).

- **Main Dial.** This dial is used to change shooting settings. When settings are available in pairs (such as shutter speed/aperture), this dial will be used to make one type of setting, such as shutter speed, while the Quick Control Dial (on the back of the camera) will be used to make the other, such as aperture setting.

- **Remote control sensor.** This infrared sensor detects the invisible flash of a Canon remote control, like the RC-6.

- **Self-timer lamp.** When using the self-timer, this lamp also flashes to mark the countdown until the photo is taken. (You can turn off the lamp if you don't want it.)

- **DC power cord cover.** This cover, on the inside edge of the hand grip, opens to allow the DC power cable to connect to the 7D II through the battery compartment.

- **Lens release button.** Press and hold this button to unlock the lens so you can rotate the lens to remove it from the camera.

- **Lens release locking pin.** This pin on the lens mount flange retracts when the release button is held down to unlock the lens.

- **Depth-of-field preview button.** This button, adjacent to the lens mount, stops down the lens to the taking aperture so you can see in the viewfinder how much of the image is in focus. The view grows dimmer as the aperture is reduced.

- **EF lens mount index.** Line up this dot with the raised red dot on the barrel of your EF lens to align the lens as you mount it on the camera. If your lens has a raised white square instead, it's an EF-S lens and should be aligned with the white square on the mount.

- **Mirror.** The partially silvered mirror reflects light up to the optical viewfinder, and allows some light to pass downward to the autofocus sensor.

- **Electrical contacts.** These contacts connect to matching points on the lens to allow the camera and lens to communicate electronically.

- **Microphone.** Record monaural sound with this built-in microphone. For stereo sound, you'll need to connect an external mic, as described in Chapter 13.

The main feature on the side of the EOS 7D Mark II are two flexible covers (see **Figure 2.2**) that protect the six connector ports underneath from dust and moisture:

- **Digital terminal/USB port.** Plug the USB cable furnished with your camera into this digital terminal and connect the other end to a USB port in your computer to transfer photos, or to your PictBridge-compatible printer to output hard copies. An optional 15.4 foot IFC-500U cable can be purchased if you need a longer link-up. The terminal can be used with the Wireless File Transmitter WFT-E7 and GPS Receiver GP-E2 (if you don't care to use the 7D II's built-in GPS.) You can also connect your camera to a Stereo AV Cable AVC-DC400ST through this port to output video/audio to a standard definition television or other AV device, such as a VCR. Connect the yellow RCA plug to the matching yellow color-coded video input of your destination device, and the red/white RCA plugs to the left/right audio jacks of the destination. Should your input device have only a single white-coded monaural audio input, purchase a stereo-to-monoaural Y-connector.

- **Audio OUT.** Connect headphones or other audio playback gear here. It accepts a 3.5mm stereo mini-plug.

- **PC/X terminal.** This connector is for a non-dedicated electronic flash unit, including studio flash, using the old-style PC cord. (In this case, *PC* stands for *Prontor-Computer*, two old-time shutter manufacturers, rather than *personal computer*.)

- **Remote control terminal.** You can plug various Canon remote release switches, timers, and wireless controllers into this N3-type connector.

- **HDMI OUT port.** You need to buy an accessory cable to connect your 7D II to an HDTV, as one to fit this port is not provided with the camera. If you have a high-resolution television, it's worth the expenditure to be able to view your camera's output in all its glory. Canon's HDMI cable HTC-100, and other Type C HDMI cables are compatible.

- **External microphone IN.** Connect an external stereo microphone with a 3.5mm stereo mini-plug here to bypass the internal microphone when recording sound.

- **AF/MF switch.** Use this switch on the lens to toggle between autofocus and manual focus.

- **Stabilizer switch.** You can disable image stabilization if you'd rather not use it, say, when the camera is mounted on a tripod.

- **Flash button/Pop-up flash.** The flash button is used to elevate the built-in flash and to gain access to the Built-In Flash menu operations.

Figure 2.2

The Business End

The back panel of the EOS 7D Mark II bristles with more than a dozen different controls, buttons, and knobs. That might seem like a lot of controls to learn, but you'll find, as I noted earlier, that it's a lot easier to press a dedicated button and spin a dial than to jump to a menu every time you want to change a setting.

Viewfinder eyepiece

Speaker (sound)

INFO button

Menu button

Creative Photo/
Two-Image display

Rating button

Magnify/Reduce/
Index button

Playback button

Erase button

Speaker (beeps)

LCD monitor

Canon

Figure 2.3

You can see the controls clustered on the left side of the 7D II in **Figure 2.3**. The key buttons and components and their functions are as follows:

- ◉ **Viewfinder eyepiece.** You can frame your composition by peering into the viewfinder. It's surrounded by a soft rubber eyecup/frame that seals out extraneous light when pressing your eye tightly up to the viewfinder, and it also protects your eyeglass lenses (if worn) from scratching. It can be removed and replaced by the cap attached to your neck strap when you use the camera on a tripod, to ensure that light coming from the back of the camera doesn't venture inside and possibly affect the exposure reading.

- ◉ **Speaker (sound).** Audio from your movie clips play back through this speaker.

- ◉ **INFO. button (Live View/Movie mode).** When pressed repeatedly while using Live View or Movie mode, the INFO. button cycles among a slightly different set of informational screens. I'll show you those screens, and how to use them, in Chapter 13, which shows you how to use Live View mode and shoot video clips with your EOS 7D Mark II.

- ◉ **INFO. button (Shooting mode).** When pressed, cycles among Electronic Level, Camera Settings and Shooting Functions screens, and Off (no information displayed). You can disable any of these (except Off) using the INFO Button Display Options entry in the Setup 3 menu, as described in Chapter 10. Electronic Level allows you to orient the camera; use the Camera Settings screen to review the current settings. When the Shooting Functions screen is visible, you can adjust the values of the settings. Choose Off when you want a blank screen and no distractions or to save power.

  - • **Electronic level.** This readout includes indicators that show the amount of front/back tilt of the camera and horizontal rotation (along the axis passing through the center of the lens). The 7D II has three different modes for this feature. The INFO. button produces the electronic level on the LCD monitor in both still shooting (see **Figure 2.4**) and Live View/Movie shooting modes. You can also view a slightly different leveling display in the optical viewfinder, using the AF points to show orientation. That display is not activated using the INFO. button; you must assign the viewfinder electronic level to a custom control, as described in Chapter 11.

- **Camera settings.** Shows a list of basic settings for the camera, including color space, white balance information, and the actual number of free shots remaining on your memory card. (Up to 9999; the counter on the top-panel LCD can display no more than 1999 shots remaining.) (See **Figure 2.5**.)

- **Shooting functions**. Displays the current shooting settings of the camera, including shutter speed, aperture, ISO sensitivity, battery status, and image quality settings. (See Figure 2.6.) Press the Q button on the back of the camera, and the Quick Control screen appears, as described in the sidebar that follows.

⊙ **INFO. button (Playback mode).** In Playback mode, while reviewing images, pressing the INFO. button cycles among basic display of the image; a detailed display with a thumbnail of the image, shooting parameters, and a brightness histogram; and a display with less detail but with separate histograms for brightness, red, green, and blue channels. I'll show you the screens with the histograms -- and how to use the histograms -- in Chapter 4.

⊙ **INFO. button (other modes).** When setting Picture Styles, the INFO. button is used to select a highlighted Picture Style for modification. When trimming an image, the INFO. button selects the orientation.

⊙ **MENU button.** Summons/exits the menu displayed on the rear LCD monitor of the 7D II. When you're working with submenus, this button also serves to exit a submenu and return to the main menu.

- **Creative Photo/Direct print/Comparative Photo (Two-image display).** In *Shooting mode* (including Live View still mode), this useful button gives you quick access to Picture Style, Multiple Exposure, and HDR (high dynamic range) features. When you press the button, the screen shown in **Figure 2.7** pops up on the LCD monitor so you can select one of these creative effects. In Live View Movie mode, only Picture Styles are available. *In Playback mode*, this button activates the Direct Printing function, as described in Chapter 13 when you're connected to a PictBridge compatible device. Otherwise, in Playback mode, the button produces the Comparative Photo/Two-image display described in Chapter 1.

- **Rating button.** This button can be used to assign a star rating to an image during picture review, or to protect an image from accidental erasure. In Shooting mode, it has no function. Although image "ratings" has long been a feature on amateur cameras, Canon has been especially clever in implementing it for advanced models like the 7D II. See the "Rating Images" section that follows for some ideas for using this feature that you might not have thought of.

- **Playback button.** Displays the last picture taken. Thereafter, you can move back and forth among the available images by rotating the Quick Control Dial, to advance or reverse one image at a time, or the Main Dial, to jump forward or back using the jump method described in the discussion of the Playback menu in Chapter 10. To quit playback, press this button again. The 7D II also exits Playback mode automatically when you press the shutter button (so you'll never be prevented from taking a picture on the spur of the moment because you happened to be viewing an image).

- **Erase button.** Press to erase the image shown on the LCD. A menu will pop up displaying Cancel and Erase choices. Rotate the Main Dial or the Quick Control Dial to select one of these actions, then press the SET button to activate your choice.

○ **Speaker (beeps.)** Beep sounds emitting from your camera, such as the self-timer countdown, emanate from here.

○ **LCD monitor.** This 3-inch full-color liquid crystal presents your menus, review images, and live previews as you make adjustments, shoot, and evaluate your images. Although often referred to as just the *LCD*, the official name is *LCD monitor*, because the monochrome panel on top of the 7D II is called the *LCD panel*.

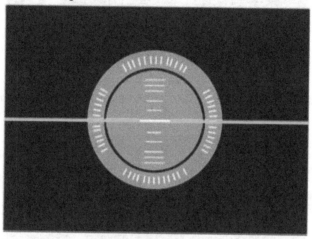

Figure 2.4

The outer ring shows the amount of horizontal rotation; the inner circle shows front/back tilt. When the bar turns from red to green, the camera is level.

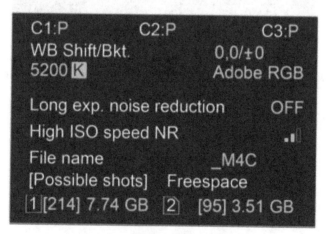

Figure 2.5

The Camera Settings screen.

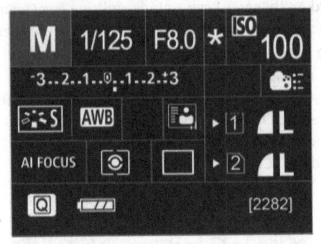

Figure 2.6

The Shooting Functions screen provides basic shooting information.

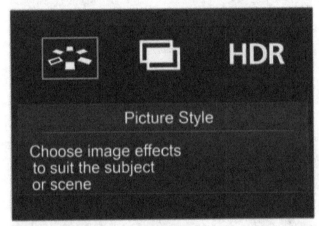

Figure 2.7

Choose from Picture Style, Multiple Exposure, or HDR features.

Using the Quick Control Screen

You can activate the Quick Control screen (shown in **Figure 2.8**) by pressing the Q button located just below the multi controller, to the right of the color LCD monitor. Then, use the multi controller joystick to highlight one of the settings in the screen.

You can't change the exposure mode; instead rotate the Mode Dial to Bulb, Manual, Av (Aperture-priority), Tv (Shutter-priority), or P (Program). The choices you can select change, depend on the position of the Mode Dial. Once you've highlighted a setting, you can change it by rotating either the Main Dial or Quick Control Dial. You can then move the highlighting to a different setting using the multi controller, if you want to make multiple changes. Press the Q button a second time to lock in the settings and exit the Quick Con-

trol screen.

Figure 2.8

Use the Q button to select settings to modify in the Quick Control screen.

Rating Images

Why did Canon assign a button located on prime back panel real estate to the Rating function alone? Isn't this the equivalent of pasting a shiny Gold Star sticker on your images, like amateur snapshooters are wont to do? Think again, because Canon has put a powerful tool at your disposal. There's a lot more you can do with this button than specify, "This shot's nice, but this other one is better!"

- **Think categories.** Instead of equating the one to five stars you can apply to quality, consider them to represent other types of image categories. These categories can be very broad, or very specific. The assignments are up to you. Once you instigate a particular system, you'll find it easy to memorize and recall when you're actually applying ratings.

- **Specify types of images.** You might want to use one star for landscapes; two stars for portraits; three stars for action; four stars for close-ups; and five stars for concerts and performances. Then, you can use the 7D II's Main Dial Jump by Rating capability to quickly move through all your images of a particular type. Canon software that can "read" ratings can be used to group these picture types together.

- **Group by venue/location.** You can access images by date created, but using the Rating system you can also "mark" them by logical locations. If you're on a long trip to Spain, assign one star to pictures taken in Madrid; two stars to photos captured in Toledo; three stars to Granada and Seville; four stars to Barcelona and Valencia; and five stars for everywhere else.

- **Categorize by style or type or subject.** Say you're at a track meet. You can assign different star ratings to running, jumping, or throwing events. Or, you can use ratings for individual and relay events. Differentiate between trials and finals if you like. That gives you the freedom to wander around among simultaneous events, and mark all your shots (or just your best ones) for easy retrieval.

- **Assemble slide shows.** You can select images for display in a slide show based on ratings. You can choose specific star ratings to display in your show, as described in Chapter 10. For example, your presentation can include All, only images marked with five stars (your best ones, if you use a quality rating system), or those marked with either two or four stars (if you used some sort of category system).

⊙ **"Protect" images.** The Rank button can be reassigned to mark images as Protected, instead. And the protection attribute does a lot more than just keep you from accidentally erasing photos. For example, the Eye-Fi wireless card can be set so that it will upload only images you've marked as Protected, rather than every single shot you take.

To rate images during picture review, just follow these steps (you can also rate images in the Playback 2 menu):

1. **Display the image or movie to be rated.** Use the Quick Control Dial (QCD) to advance/rewind among your images (or use one of the other image review tools, such as Jumping or Index thumbnails) to find an image to mark.

2. **Press the Rate button.** Each time the Rate button is pressed, the rating will change, cycling from one star to five stars and then to None. *However,* you can disable a particular star rating, so that you can apply, say, one, three, and five stars (only), or, if you've mentally assigned categories to star ranks, you could use only two, four, and five stars. I'll show you how to do this using the Rate Button Function setting in the Setup 3 menu in Chapter 10.

3. **Protect instead.** If you've reassigned the Rate button to the Protect function, you can mark the displayed image as Protected instead.

4. **Continue marking.** Press the Playback button when you're finished to exit the ranking function.

Right Side Controls

More buttons reside on the right side of the back panel, as shown in **Figure 2.9**. The key controls and their functions are as follows:

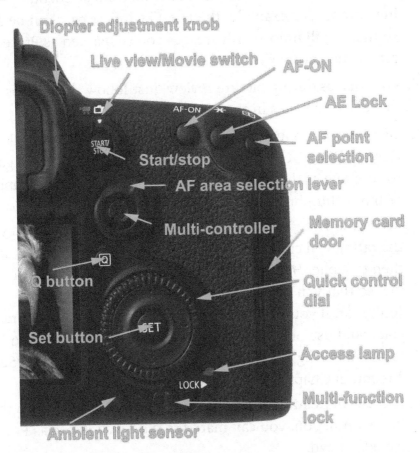

Figure 2.9

- **Diopter adjustment knob.** Rotate this knob to adjust the diopter correction for your eyesight.
- **Live view/movie switch.** Flip to switch between Live View and Movie modes.
- **Start/Stop button.** Press once to begin live view or movie capture, and again to exit.
- **AF-ON.** Press this button to activate the autofocus system without needing to partially depress the shutter release. This control, used with other buttons, allows you to lock exposure

and focus separately. Lock exposure by pressing the shutter release halfway, or by pressing the AE Lock button; autofocus by pressing the shutter release halfway, or by pressing the AF-ON button. Functions of this button will be explained in more detail in Chapter 5.

⊙ **AE/FE (autoexposure/flash exposure) Lock.** In Shooting mode, it locks the exposure or external flash exposure that the camera sets when you partially depress the shutter button. The exposure lock indication (*) appears in the viewfinder. If you want to recalculate exposure with the shutter button still partially depressed, press the * button again. The exposure will be unlocked when you release the shutter button or take the picture. To retain the exposure lock for subsequent photos, keep the * button pressed while shooting. When using external flash, pressing the * button fires an extra pre-flash when you partially depress the shutter button that allows the unit to calculate and lock exposure prior to taking the picture.

⊙ **AF point selection button.** In Shooting mode, this button activates autofocus point selection. (See Chapter 5 for information on setting autofocus/exposure point selection.)

⊙ **Multi-controller.** This joystick-like button can be shifted up, down, side to side, and diagonally for a total of eight directions, or pressed. It can be used for several functions, including AF point selection, scrolling around a magnified image, trimming a photo, or setting white balance correction.

⊙ **AF area selection lever.** Press this convenient lever, which rings the Multi-controller, to switch AF area selection methods.

⊙ **Q (Quick Control) button.** Press this button to produce the Quick Control screen, which gives you access to many features when in Shooting mode. When you're reviewing images in Playback, a different Quick Control screen pops up that allows you to protect or rate images, change jump method, resize, or perform other functions.

- **Quick Control Dial (QCD).** Used to select shooting options, such as f/stop or exposure compensation value, or to navigate through menus. It also serves as an alternate controller for some functions set with other controls, such as AF point.

- **SET button.** Selects a highlighted setting or menu option.

- **Access lamp.** When lit or blinking, this lamp indicates that the memory card is being accessed.

- **Multi-function lock switch.** Set to the right, it prevents the Main Dial, QCD, and multi controller from changing a setting. If you try to use one of these locked controls, an L warning will be displayed in the optical viewfinder and the LCD panel; in the Shooting Settings display, Lock will be shown. You can select which of the three are locked out using the Multi Function Lock entry in the Custom Functions 2 menu. Choose any combination of one, two, or all three controls to freeze with this lock switch.

- **Ambient light sensor.** The 7D II is smart enough to automatically adjust the brightness of the LCD monitor for ambient light levels. The sensor that measures the amount of light is located here. You can fine-tune the brightness levels in the Setup 2 menu, as described in Chapter 10.

Going Topside

The top surface of the Canon EOS 7D Mark II has its own set of frequently accessed controls. The three of them just forward of the status LCD panel have dual functions and are marked with hyphenated labels. Press the relevant button (you don't need to hold it down) and then rotate the Main Dial to choose the left function of the pair, such as metering mode, autofocus, or ISO, and the Quick Control Dial to select the right function, such as white balance, drive mode, or flash exposure compensation. The settings you make will be indicated in the LCD status panel, which is described in the section that follows this one. The key controls, shown in **Figure 2.10**, are as follows:

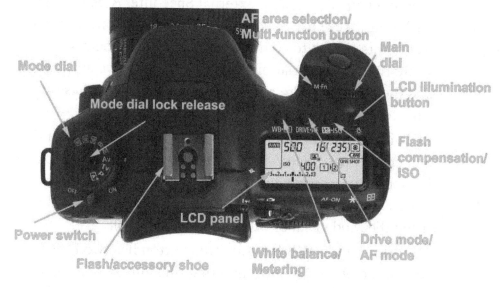

Figure 2.10

- ⊙ **M-Fn button.** This multi-function button can be used to change the autofocus area selection mode (as described in Chapter 5). You can assign an additional function to this control using the Custom Controls feature, as described in Chapter 14. Your choices include Flash Exposure Lock, Autoexposure Lock (both toggle and hold versions), One-touch image quality setting (both toggle and hold versions), and activate viewfinder electronic level.

- ⊙ **Mode Dial Lock Release.** Unlocks the Mode Dial so it can be rotated.

- ⊙ **Mode Dial.** Press the Mode Dial Lock Release and then rotate this dial to switch among exposure modes, and to choose one of the camera user settings (C1, C2, or C3). You'll find these modes and options described in more detail in Chapter 10(where I show you how to register your settings in the C1/C2/C3 "slots").

- ⊙ **Sensor focal plane.** Precision macro and scientific photography sometimes requires knowing exactly where the focal plane of the sensor is. The symbol on the side of the pentaprism marks that plane.

- ⊙ **Flash/accessory shoe.** Slide an electronic flash into this mount when you need an external Speedlite. A dedicated flash unit, like those from Canon, can use the multiple contact points shown to communicate exposure, zoom setting, white balance information, and other data between the flash and the camera. There's more on using electronic flash in Chapter 12.

- ⊙ **LCD illumination button.** Press this button to turn on the amber LCD panel lamp that backlights the LCD status panel for about six seconds, or to turn it off if illuminated. The lamp will remain lit beyond the six-second period if you are using the Mode Dial or other shooting control.

- ⊙ **Metering mode-WB button.** This button has two functions. Rotate the Main Dial after pressing this button to change between Evaluative, Partial, Spot, or Center-weighted metering. Rotate the Quick Control Dial to cycle among AWB (Automatic White Balance), Daylight, Shade, Cloudy/Twilight/Sunset, Tungsten, White Fluorescent, Flash, Custom, and Color Temperature.

- ⊙ **AF-DRIVE button.** Press once and then rotate the Main Dial to change between One-Shot, AI Focus, and AI Servo autofocus modes (you'll find more about those modes in Chapter 5). Drive mode settings include single shooting, continuous (up to 6 fps), and 10- or 2-second self-timer/remote control, selected by holding down the button and rotating the Quick Control Dial.

- ☉ **ISO/Flash exposure compensation button.** Press and rotate the Main Dial to choose an ISO setting; use the Quick Control Dial to change electronic flash exposure compensation. You'll find more about ISO options in Chapter 4, and flash EV settings in Chapter 12.

- ☉ **Monochrome LCD panel.** The LCD panel provides information about the status of your camera and its settings, including exposure mode, number of pictures remaining, battery status, and many other settings. I'll illustrate all these in the next section.

- ☉ **Main Dial.** This dial is used to make many shooting settings. When settings come in pairs (such as shutter speed/aperture in Manual shooting mode), the Main Dial is used for one (for example, shutter speed), while the Quick Control Dial is used for the other (aperture). When an image is on the screen during playback, this dial also specifies the leaps that skip a particular number of images during playback of the shots you've already taken. Jumps can be 1 image, 10 images, 100 images, jump by date, or jump by screen (that is, by screens of thumbnails when using Index mode), date, or folder. (Jump method is selected in the Playback 2 menu, as described in Chapter 10.) This dial is also used to move among tabs when the MENU button has been pressed, and is used within some menus (in conjunction with the Quick Control Dial) to change pairs of settings.

Table 2.1 - Control Button Functions

Button	Main Dial	Quick Control Dial
Meter/WB	Evaluative/Partial/Spot/Center-weighted average metering modes	Auto/Daylight/Shade/Cloudy/Tungsten/White Fluorescent/Flash/Custom/Kelvin color temperatures
AF-DRIVE	One-Shot/AI Focus/AI Servo autofocus modes	Single shooting/Continuous/Self-timer 2 seconds/Self-timer 10 seconds/Remote
ISO-Flash EV	(12800)-H2(102800)	Flash compensation (+ or – up to 2 stops)

LCD Panel Readouts

The top panel of the EOS 7D Mark II contains an amber-colored (when backlit) monochrome LCD readout that displays status information about most of the shooting settings. All of the information segments available are shown in **Figure 2.11**. I've color-coded the display to make it easier to differentiate them; the information does *not* appear in those colors on the actual 7D II. Many of the information items are mutually exclusive (that is, in the white balance area at upper left, only one of the possible settings illustrated will appear).

Some of the items on the status LCD also appear in the viewfinder, such as the shutter speed and aperture (pictured at top in blue in the figure), and the exposure level (in yellow at the bottom). The color-coded readouts include:

- **Magenta:** White balance.
- **Dark Blue:** Shutter speed, Flash Exposure Lock, buSY, Multifunction lock, No Card, Image Sensor Cleaning, GPS Logging.
- **Gray:** Possible Shots, Self-timer Countdown, Bulb Exposure time, Card Error, Remaining Images.
- **Orange:** Metering Mode.

- **Brown:** Auto Exposure Bracketing, GPS, White Balance Correction, Auto Lighting Optimizer, Multiple Exposure.
- **Cyan:** HDR, Interval Timer, Battery Check.
- **White:** ISO Speed, Highlight Tone Priority.
- **Red:** Compact Flash, SD Card Indicators.
- **Dark Green:** Focus Modes, Drive Modes.
- **Yellow:** Exposure Level, Exposure Compensation, Auto Exposure Bracketing Range, Flash Exposure Compensation Amount.
- **Light Green:** Flash Exposure Compensation.
- **Black:** Warning.

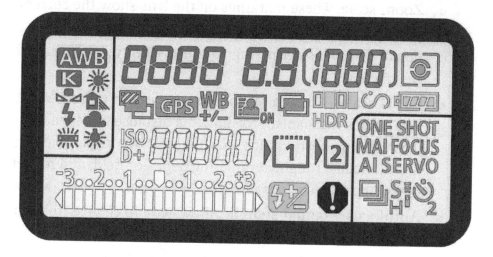

Figure 2.11

Lens Components

The typical lens, like the one shown in **Figure 2.12**, has seven or eight common features:

- **Filter thread.** Lenses have a thread on the front for attaching filters and other add-ons. Some also use this thread for attaching a lens hood (you screw on the filter first, and then attach the hood to the screw thread on the front of the filter).

- **Lens hood bayonet.** This is used to mount the lens hood for lenses that don't use screw-mount hoods (the majority).

- **Zoom ring.** Turn this ring to change the zoom setting.

- **Zoom scale.** These markings on the lens show the current focal length selected.

- **Focus ring.** This is the ring you turn when you manually focus the lens.

- **Focus scale.** This is a readout that rotates in unison with the lens's focus mechanism to show the distance at which the lens has been focused. It's a useful indicator for double-checking autofocus, roughly evaluating depth-of-field, and for setting manual focus guesstimates.

- **Autofocus/Manual switch.** Allows you to change from automatic focus to manual focus.

- **Image stabilization switch.** Lenses with IS include a separate switch for adjusting the stabilization feature.

- **Infrared adjustment indicator.** If you're shooting infrared photos (with a suitable visible light cut-off filter), you should know that IR illumination focuses at a different point from ordinary light. If you want the most accurate focus and you're using a lens with IR indicators, the focus point should be adjusted from the white line on the lens barrel to the red line representing your current zoom setting. With the 24-105mm lens shown, indicators are provided for 24mm, 35mm, and 50mm focal lengths. The focus difference diminishes as focal length increases, from 50-105mm you can "guestimate" the correct adjustment, or ignore it altogether. In many cases, depth-of-field (when using f/stops of f/8 or smaller) may take care of the disparity.

⊙ **Electrical contacts (not shown).** The gold contacts on the rear of the lens mate with the contacts on the camera body, allowing the lens and camera to communicate electronically.

⊙ **Lens mount bayonet (not shown).** This is the component used to mount the lens on the camera.

Figure 2.12

Looking Inside the Viewfinder

Much of the important shooting status information is shown inside the viewfinder of the EOS 7D Mark II. As with the status LCD up on top, not all of this information will be shown at any one time. **Figure 2.13** shows what you can expect to see, color-coded for reference (you will *not* see these colors in the viewfinder!) In the center of the frame, you'll find these readouts:

- **Electronic level (Yellow.)** These boxes are illuminated when the viewfinder level is active to show the amount of side to side or front/back tilt of the camera.

- **Spot metering reference circle (Brown).** Shows the circle that delineates the spot metering area.

- **AF points (Red).** Shows the 65 areas used by the 7D II to focus. The small boxes represent single AF points, and the larger boxes delineate spot AF points. The camera can select the appropriate focus point for you, or you can manually select one or all of the points, as described in Chapter 5.

- **AF area frames (Black.)** These brackets are shown to represent the boundaries of the AF points and AF point zones selected by the camera or you.

- **Grid (Light Green.)** These horizontal and vertical lines can be turned on or off and used to compose your image.

In the bottom area of the frame are indicators that display various bits of information. You can elect whether any or all of these appear using the Viewfinder Display entry of the Setup 2 menu, as described in Chapter 10:

- **Memory slot (Light gray.)** Indicates that one of the three user memory registers (C1, C2, or C3) is in use.

- **Shooting mode (Black.)** Shows whether Bulb, Manual, Av, Tv, or P mode is active.

- **White balance (Magenta.)** Shows the current white balance setting.

- **Drive mode (Dark Green.)** Lets you know whether single shot, continuous, self-timer, or remote drive modes are active

- **Focus mode (Cyan.)** Displays One Shot, AI Focus, AI Servo, or Manual focus modes.

- **Metering mode (Orange.)** Icons display whether Evaluative, Partial, Spot, or Center-weighted metering is active.

- **Image Quality (Blue.)** Let's you know if you're shooting RAW, JPEG, or both.

- **Flicker detection (Pink.)** Shows that the camera is looking for flickering light, such as fluorescents, and corrects to reduce the effect on exposure or color.

- **Warning (Black.)** Provides a warning if you're using the Monochrome Picture Style; have dialed in white blance correction; are using the one-touch image quality function, spot metering, or multi-shot noise reduction. These (all described later in the book) are settings that depart from the everyday norm, and Canon deems them worthy of this warning reminder.

- **Autofocus Status Indicator (Brown.)** Shows that the camera is autofocusing.

In the black frame surrounding the actual picture area, additional indicators appear. I've color coded these as well:

- **Battery check** (White.)
- **Auto Exposure Lock/Bracketing in Progress/High Speed Sync., Flash Exposure Compensation (Cyan.)**
- **Multiple Indicators (Dark Blue.)** Most of the time, these readouts show the current shutter speed and aperture. This pair can also warn you of memory card conditions (full, error, or missing), ISO speed, flash exposure lock, and a buSY indicator when the camera is busy doing other things (including flash recycling). AF point selection status is also shown here.

- **Exposure level indicator (Yellow.)** This scale shows the current exposure level, with the bottom indicator centered when the exposure is correct as metered. The indicator may also move to the left or right to indicate under- or overexposure (respectively). The scale is also used to show the amount of EV and flash EV adjustments, and the number of stops covered by the current automatic exposure bracketing range.

◉ **ISO sensitivity (Dark Green.)** This useful indicator shows the current ISO setting value. Those who have accidentally taken dozens of shots under bright sunlight at ISO 1600 because they forgot to change the setting back after some indoor shooting will treasure this addition. It also shows when Highlight Tone Priority is active.

◉ **Remaining Exposures/Maximum burst available (Dark Green, in brackets.)** Changes to a number to indicate the number of frames that can be taken in continuous mode using the current settings.

◉ **Focus confirmation (Light Green.)** This green dot appears when the subject covered by the active autofocus zone is in sharp focus.

◉ **Exposure level indicator (Magenta.)** This exposure index shows ambient light exposure levels (including under and overexposure) with the left set of blocks, and flash exposure levels (under and over) with the right set of blocks.

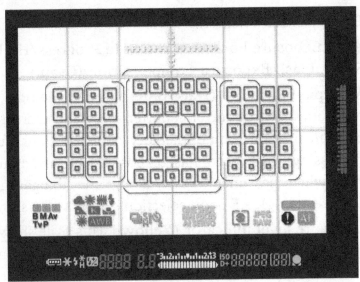

Figure 2.13

Underneath Your EOS 7D Mark II

There's not a lot going on with the bottom panel of your EOS 7D Mark II. You'll find a tripod socket, which secures the camera to a tripod, and is also used to lock on the optional BG-E16 battery grip, which provides more juice to run your camera to take more exposures with a single charge. It also adds a vertically oriented shutter release, Main Dial, AE Lock/FE Lock, and AF point selection controls for easier vertical shooting. To mount the grip, slide the battery door latch to open the door, then push down on the small pin that projects from the hinge. That will let you remove the battery door. Then slide the grip into the battery cavity, aligning the pin on the grip with the small hole on the other side of the tripod socket. Tighten the grip's tripod socket screw to lock the grip onto the bottom of your 7D II. **Figure 2.14** shows the underside view of the

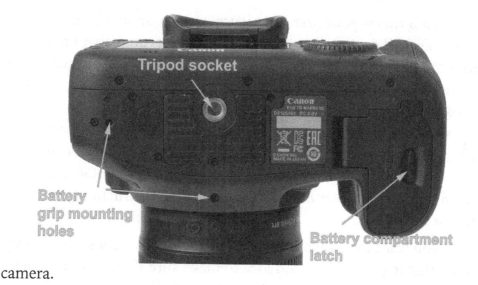

camera.

Figure 2.14

Chapter 3

Some Basic Recommended Settings

This chapter is purely optional, especially for those who are new to an advanced Canon at the 7D II's level, who should skip it entirely for now, and return when they've gained some experience with this full-featured camera. This section is for the benefit of those who want to know *now* some of the most common changes I recommend to the default settings of your 7D II. Canon has excellent reasons for using these settings as a default; I have better reasons for changing them.

Changing Default Settings

Even if this is your first experience with a Canon digital SLR, you can easily make a few changes to the default settings that I'm going to recommend, and then take your time learning *why* I suggest these changes when they're explained in the more detailed chapters of this book. I'm not going to provide step-by-step instructions for changing settings here; I'll give you an overview of how to make any setting adjustment, and leave you to navigate through the fairly intuitive 7D II menu system to make the changes yourself. Or, you can jump ahead to Chapter 8-11 for more detailed instructions on a particular setting.

If you want to change from the factory default values, you might think that it would be a good idea to make sure that the Canon 7D II is set to the factory defaults in the first place. After all, even a brand-new camera might have had its settings changed at the retailer, or during a demo. Most of the time, however, you'll prefer to use the Clear All Camera Settings option in the Set-up 4 menu, which returns most settings (other than Custom Functions) to their default values. The tables that follow show the settings defaults after using the Clear All Camera Settings menu option.

Recommended Default Changes

Although I won't be explaining how to use the Canon 7D II's menu system in detail until Chapter 8-11, you can make some simple changes now. These general instructions will serve you to make any of the setting changes I recommend next.

The 7D II divides its menu entries into "tabbed" sections -- Shooting, Autofocus, Playback, Set-up, Custom Functions, and My Menu -- which, except for My Menu, each have separate pages. The available pages can vary, depending on your shooting mode, as I'll explain in Chapter 8.

To access menus, tap the MENU button. Use the Main Dial to move from menu to menu, and the Quick Control Dial to highlight a particular menu entry. Press the SET button to select a menu item. You can also navigate with the joystick-like multi-controller. When you've highlighted the menu item you want to work with, press the SET button to select it. The current settings for the other menu items in the list will be hidden, and a list of options for the selected menu item (or a submenu screen) will appear. Or, you may be shown a separate settings screen for that entry. Within the menu choices, you can scroll up or down with the Quick Control Dial; press SET to select the choice you've made; and press the MENU button again to exit.

Once you've made changes for a specific type of shooting, you should store each set of parameters in one of the Custom Shooting mode user slots C1, C2, or C3 in the Set-up 4 menu, as explained in Chapter 10. Here are some recommended settings to consider.

Note: These tables don't correspond to entire menus; I'm listing *only* the settings that most often need attention. If a particular parameter is not listed, you can use a setting of your choice, or can learn more about special techniques with that parameter in Chapters 8-11

Stage Performances, Long Exposure, HDR, Portrait

	Default	All Purpose	Sports: Outdoors	Sports: Indoors
SETTINGS				
Exposure Mode	Your choice	Your choice	Tv	Tv
Autofocus Mode	One-Shot	AI Focus	AI Servo	AI Servo
Drive Mode	Single Shooting	Single Shooting	Continuous Shooting	Continuous Shooting
SHOOTING MENUS				
Beep	Enable	Enable	Enable	Enable
Image Review	2 sec.	2 sec.	Off	Off
Metering Mode	Evaluative	Evaluative	Evaluative	Evaluative
Color Space	sRGB	sRGB	sRGB	sRGB
Picture Style	Auto	Auto	Standard	Standard
ISO Speed	Auto	Auto	800-3200	800-3200
ISO Speed Range	100-25600	100-12800	200-3200	200-12800
Auto ISO Range	100-12800	100-6400	200-6400	400-12800
ISO Auto minimum shutter speed	Auto	Auto	1/250	1/250

Stage Performances, Long Exposure, HDR, Portrait

	Default	All Purpose	Sports: Outdoors	Sports: Indoors
Long Exposure NR	Disable	Disable	Disable	Disable
High ISO speed NR	Standard	Standard	Standard	Standard
Highlight Tone priority	Disable	Disable	Disable	Disable
AF MENUS				
Case	Case 1	Case 1	Case 4	Case 2 / Case 4
AF Assist Beam	Enable	Enable	Disable	Disable
Selectable AF point	65 points	65 points	9 points	15 points
Select AF area selection mode	65 point automatic selection AF	65 point automatic selection AF	AF point expansion	AF point expansion
SET-UP MENUS				
Auto Power Off	1 minute	30 sec.	Off	Off
LCD Brightness	Auto	Medium	Medium	Medium

73

Stage Performances, Long Exposure, HDR, Portrait

	Stage Performances	Long Exposure	HDR	Portrait
SETTINGS				
Exposure Mode	Your choice	Manual/Your choice	One-Shot	One-Shot
Autofocus Mode	One-Shot	AI Focus	AI Servo	AI Servo
Drive Mode	Continuous Shooting	Single Shooting	Continuous Shooting	Continuous Shooting
SHOOTING MENUS				
Beep	Disable	Enable	Enable	Enable
Image Review	Off	Off	Off	2 sec.
Metering Mode	Spot	Center-weighted	Evaluative	Center-weighted
Color Space	Adobe RGB	Adobe RGB	Adobe RGB	Adobe RGB
Picture Style	User - Reduce contrast, add sharpening	Neutral	Standard	Portrait
ISO Speed	800-3200	800-3200	Auto	Auto
ISO Speed Range	100-25600	100-12800	200-3200	200-1600
Auto ISO Range	100-12800	100-6400	200-6400	100-3200
ISO Auto minimum shutter speed	Auto	Auto	1/250	1/250
Long Exposure NR	Disable	Disable	Disable	Disable
High ISO speed NR	Standard	Standard	Standard	Standard
Highlight Tone priority	Disable	Disable	Disable	Disable
AF MENUS				
Case	Case 1	Case 1	Case 1	Case 1
AF Assist Beam	Disable	Disable	Disable	Disable
Selectable AF point	65 points	65 points	65 points	15 points

Stage Performances, Long Exposure, HDR, Portrait

	Stage Performances	Long Exposure	HDR	Portrait
Select AF area selection mode	65 point automatic selection AF	65 point automatic selection AF	65 point automatic selection AF	65 point automatic selection AF
SET-UP MENUS				
Auto Power Off	1 minute	Disable	Disable	Disable
LCD Brightness	Dimmer	Dimmer	Medium	Medium

75

Studio Flash, Landscape, Macro, Travel, E-Mail

	Studio Flash	Landscape	Macro	Travel	E-Mail
SETTINGS					
Exposure Mode	Manual	Av	Tv	Tv	Av
Autofocus Mode	One-Shot	One-Shot	Manual	One-Shot	One-Shot
Drive Mode	Single Shooting	Single Shooting	Single Shooting	Single Shooting	Single Shooting
SHOOTING MENUS					
Beep	Disable	Enable	Enable	Enable	Enable
Image Review	2 sec.	2 sec.	2 sec.	2 sec.	2 sec.
Metering Mode	Evaluative	Evaluative	Spot	Evaluative	Evaluative
Color Space	Adobe RGB	Adobe RGB	Adobe RGB	Adobe RGB	Adobe RGB
Picture Style	User - Reduce contrast, add sharpening	Landscape	Auto	Landscape	Auto
ISO Speed	100-400	100-1600	100-1600	Auto	Auto
ISO Speed Range	100-25600	100-12800	200-3200	200-1600	100-3200
Auto ISO Range	100-12800	100-6400	200-6400	100-3200	100-6400
ISO Auto minimum shutter speed	Auto	Auto	1/250	1/250	Auto
Long Exposure NR	Disable	Disable	Disable	Disable	Disable
High ISO speed NR	Standard	Standard	Standard	Standard	Standard
Highlight tone priority	Disable	Enable	Disable	Enable	Enable
AF MENUS					
Case	Case 1	Case 1	Case 1	Case 1	
AF Assist Beam	Disable	Disable	Disable	Disable	
Selectable AF point	65 points	65 points	65 points	15 points	

Studio Flash, Landscape, Macro, Travel, E-Mail

	Studio Flash	Landscape	Macro	Travel	E-Mail
Select AF area selection mode	65 point automatic selection AF	65 point automatic selection AF	65 point automatic selection AF	65 point automatic selection AF	
SET-UP MENUS					
Auto Power Off	1 minute	Disable	Disable	Disable	Disable
LCD Brightness	Dimmer	Dimmer	Medium	Medium	Medium
Set-up Menus					
Auto Power Off	Off	Off	Off	30 sec.	30 sec.
LCD Auto Off	Enable	Enable	Enable	Enable	Enable
LCD Brightness	Medium	Medium	Medium	Medium	Medium

Chapter 4

Nailing the Right Exposure

As you learn to use your 7D II creatively, you're going to find that the right settings -- as determined by the camera's exposure meter and intelligence -- need to be *adjusted* to account for your creative decisions or to fine-tune the image for special situations.

For example, when you shoot with the main light source behind the subject, you end up with *backlighting*, which results in an overexposed background and/or an underexposed subject. The 7D II recognizes backlit situations nicely, and can properly base exposure on the main subject, producing a decent photo. Features like Highlight Tone Priority and the Auto Lighting Optimizer can fine-tune exposure to preserve detail in the highlights and shadows.

But what if you *want* to underexpose the subject, to produce a silhouette effect? Or, perhaps, you might want to use an external electronic flash to fill in the shadows on your subject. The more you know about how to use your 7D II, the more you'll run into situations where you want to creatively tweak the exposure to provide a different look than you'd get with a straight shot.

This chapter shows you the fundamentals of exposure, so you'll be better equipped to override the 7D II's default settings when you want to, or need to. After all, correct exposure is one of the foundations of good photography, along with accurate focus and sharpness, appropriate color balance, freedom from unwanted noise and excessive contrast, as well as pleasing composition.

The 7D II gives you a great deal of control over all of these, although composition is entirely up to you. You must still frame the photograph to create an interesting arrangement of subject matter, but all the other parameters are basic functions of the camera. You can let your 7D II set them for you automatically, you can fine-tune how the camera applies its automatic settings, or you can make them yourself, manually. The amount of control you have over exposure, sensitivity (ISO settings), color balance, focus, and image parameters like sharpness and contrast make the 7D II a versatile tool for creating images.

In the next few pages, I'm going to give you a grounding in one of those foundations, and explain the basics of exposure, either as an introduction or as a refresher course, depending on your current level of expertise. When you finish this chapter, you'll understand most of what you need to know to take well-exposed photographs creatively in a broad range of situations with the EOS 7D Mark II.

Getting a Handle on Exposure

In the most basic sense, exposure is all about light. Exposure can make or break your photo. Correct exposure brings out the detail in the areas you want to picture, providing the range of tones and colors you need to create the desired image. Poor exposure can cloak important details in shadow, or wash them out in glare-filled featureless expanses of white. However, getting the perfect exposure requires some intelligence -- either that built into the camera, or the smarts in your head -- because digital sensors can't capture all the tones we are able to see. If the range of tones in an image is extensive, embracing both inky black shadows and bright highlights, we often must settle for an exposure that renders most of those tones -- but not all -- in a way that best suits the photo we want to produce.

As the owner of a Canon 7D II, you're probably well aware of the traditional "exposure triangle" of aperture (quantity of light, light passed by the lens), shutter speed (the amount of time the shutter is open), and the ISO sensitivity of the sensor -- all working proportionately and reciprocally to produce an exposure. The trio is itself affected by the amount of illumination that is available to work with. So, if you double the amount of light, increase the aperture by one stop, make the shutter speed twice as long, or boost the ISO setting 2X, you'll get twice as much exposure. Similarly, you can increase any of these factors while decreasing one of the others by a similar amount to keep the same exposure.

Working with any of the three controls involves trade-offs. Larger f/stops provide less depth-of-field, while smaller f/stops increase depth-of-field (and potentially at the same time can *decrease* sharpness through a phenomenon called *diffraction*). Shorter shutter speeds do a better job of reducing the effects of camera/subject motion, while longer shutter speeds make that motion blur more likely. Higher ISO settings increase the amount of visual noise and artifacts in your image, while lower ISO settings reduce the effects of noise. (See **Figure 4.1**.)

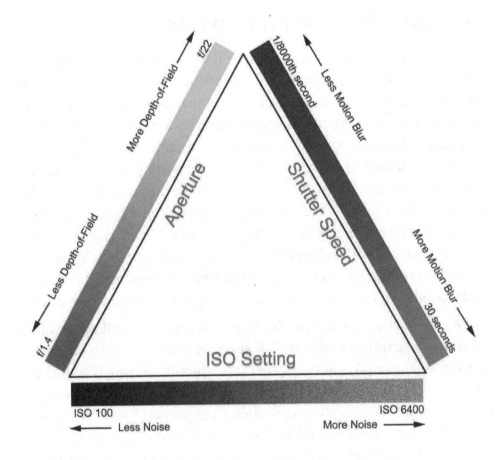

Figure 4.1
The traditional exposure triangle includes aperture, shutter speed, and ISO sensitivity.

Exposure determines the look, feel, and tone of an image, in more ways than one. Incorrect exposure can impair even the best-composed image by cloaking important tones in darkness, or by washing them out so they become featureless to the eye. On the other hand, correct exposure brings out the detail in the areas you want to picture, and provides the range of tones and colors you need to create the desired image. However, getting the perfect exposure can be tricky, because digital sensors can't capture all the tones we are able to see. If the range of tones in an image is extensive, embracing both inky black shadows and bright highlights, the sensor may not be able to capture them all. Sometimes, we must settle for an exposure that renders most of those tones -- but not all -- in a way that best suits the photo we want to produce. You'll often need to make choices about which details are important, and which are not, so that you can grab the tones that truly matter in your image. That's part of the creativity you bring to bear in realizing your photographic vision.

For example, look at two bracketed exposures presented in at top in **Figure 4.2**. For the image at the top, the highlights (chiefly the clouds at upper left and the top left edge of the skyscraper) are well exposed, but everything else in the shot is seriously underexposed. The version at the bottom, taken an instant later with the tripod-mounted camera, shows detail in the shadow areas of the buildings, but the highlights are completely washed out. The camera's sensor simply can't capture detail in both dark areas and bright areas in a single shot.

With digital camera sensors, it's tricky to capture detail in both highlights and shadows in a single image, because the number of tones, the *dynamic range* of the sensor, is limited. The solution, in this particular case, was to resort to a technique called high dynamic range (HDR) photography, in which the two exposures from **Figure 4.2** were combined in an image editor such as Photoshop, or a specialized HDR tool like Photomatix. The resulting shot is shown at bottom **Figure 4.2**. I'll explain more about HDR photography later in this chapter. For now, though, I'm going to concentrate on showing you how to get the best exposures possible without resorting to such tools, using only the features of your Canon 7D II.

Figure 4.2

At top, the image is exposed for the highlights (left) and shadows (right.) At bottom, combining the two exposures produces the best compromise image.

To understand exposure, you need to understand the six aspects of light that combine to produce an image. Start with a light source -- the sun, an interior lamp, or the glow from a campfire -- and trace its path to your camera, through the lens, and finally to the sensor that captures the illumination. Here's a brief review of the things within our control that affect exposure.

- **Light at its source.** Our eyes and our cameras -- film or digital -- are most sensitive to that portion of the electromagnetic spectrum we call *visible light*. That light has several important aspects that are relevant to photography, such as color and harshness (which is determined primarily by the apparent size of the light source as it illuminates a subject). But, in terms of exposure, the important attribute of a light source is its *intensity*. We may have direct control over intensity, which might be the case with an interior light that can be brightened or dimmed. Or, we might have only indirect control over intensity, as with sunlight, which can be made to appear dimmer by introducing translucent light-absorbing or reflective materials in its path.

- ⊙ **Light's duration.** We tend to think of most light sources as continuous. But, as you'll learn in Chapter 12, the duration of light can change quickly enough to modify the exposure, as when the main illumination in a photograph comes from an intermittent source, such as an electronic flash.

- ⊙ **Light reflected, transmitted, or emitted.** Once light is produced by its source, either continuously or in a brief burst, we are able to see and photograph objects by the light that is reflected from our subjects toward the camera lens; transmitted (say, from translucent objects that are lit from behind); or emitted (by a candle or television screen). When more or less light reaches the lens from the subject, we need to adjust the exposure. This part of the equation is under our control to the extent we can increase the amount of light falling on or passing through the subject (by adding extra light sources or using reflectors), or by pumping up the light that's emitted (by increasing the brightness of the glowing object).

- ⊙ **Light passed by the lens.** Not all the illumination that reaches the front of the lens makes it all the way through. Filters can remove some of the light before it enters the lens. Inside the lens barrel is a variable-sized diaphragm that dilates and contracts to vary the size of the aperture and control the amount of light that enters the lens. You, or the 7D II's auto-exposure system, can control exposure by varying the size of the aperture. The relative size of the aperture is called the *f/stop* (see **Figure 4.4**).

- ⊙ **Light passing through the shutter.** Once light passes through the lens, the amount of time the sensor receives it is determined by the 7D II's shutter, which can remain open for as long as 30 seconds (or even longer if you use the Bulb setting) or as briefly as 1/8,000th second.

- **Light captured by the sensor.** Not all the light falling onto the sensor is captured. If the number of photons reaching a particular photosite doesn't pass a set threshold, no information is recorded. Similarly, if too much light illuminates a pixel in the sensor, then the excess isn't recorded or, worse, spills over to contaminate adjacent pixels. We can modify the minimum and maximum number of pixels that contribute to image detail by adjusting the ISO setting. At higher ISOs, the incoming light is amplified to boost the effective sensitivity of the sensor.

These factors -- the quantity of light produced by the light source, the amount reflected or transmitted toward the camera, the light passed by the lens, the amount of time the shutter is open, and the sensitivity of the sensor -- all work proportionately and reciprocally to produce an exposure. That is, if you double the amount of light that's available, increase the aperture by one stop, make the shutter speed twice as long, or boost the ISO setting 2X, you'll get twice as much exposure. Similarly, you can increase any of these factors while decreasing one of the others by a similar amount to keep the same exposure.

F/STOPS AND SHUTTER SPEEDS

If you're really new to more advanced cameras (and I realize that many soon-to-be-ambitious photographers do purchase the 7D II as their first digital SLR), you might need to know that the lens aperture, or f/stop, is a ratio, much like a fraction, which is why f/2 is larger than f/4, just as 1/2 is larger than 1/4. However, f/2 is actually four times as large as f/4. (If you remember your high school geometry, you'll know that to double the area of a circle, you multiply its diameter by the square root of two: 1.4.)

Lenses are usually marked with intermediate f/stops that represent a size that's twice as much/half as much as the previous aperture. So, a lens might be marked f/4, f/5.6, f/8, f/11, f/16, f/22, with each larger number representing an aperture that admits half as much light as the one before, as shown in Figure 4.3.

Shutter speeds are actual fractions (of a second), but the numerator is omitted, so that 60, 125, 250, 500, 1,000, and so forth represent 1/60th, 1/125th, 1/250th, 1/500th, and 1/1,000th second. To avoid confusion, Canon uses quotation marks to signify longer exposures: 2", 2"5, 4", and so forth representing 2.0, 2.5, and 4.0-second exposures, respectively.

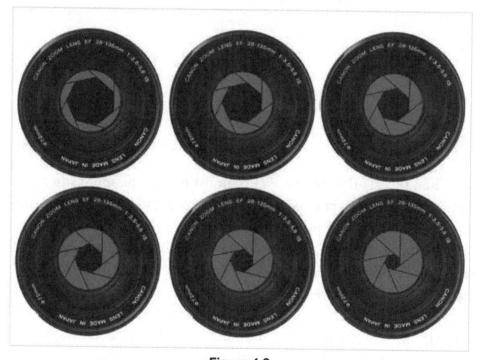

Figure 4.3
Top row (left to right): f/4, f/5.6, f/8; bottom row: f11, f/16, f/22.

Most commonly, exposure settings are made using the aperture and shutter speed, followed by adjusting the ISO sensitivity if it's not possible to get the preferred exposure; that is, the one that uses the "best" f/stop or shutter speed for the depth-of-field (range of sharp focus) or action stopping we want (produced by short shutter speeds, as I'll explain later). **Table 4.1** shows equivalent exposure settings using various shutter speeds and f/stops.

Table 4.1 Equivalent Exposures

Shutter Speed	f/stop
1/30th second	f/22
1/60th second	f/16
1/125th second	f/11
1/250th second	f/8
1/500th second	f/5.6
1/1,000th second	f/4
1/2,000th second	f/2.8
1/4,000th second	f/2
1/8,000th second	f/1.4

When the 7D II is set for P (Program) mode, the metering system selects the correct exposure for you automatically, but you can change quickly to an equivalent exposure by locking the current exposure, and then spinning the Main Dial until the desired *equivalent* exposure combination is displayed. You can use this standard Program Shift feature more easily if you remember that you need to rotate the dial toward the *left* when you want to increase the amount of depth-of-field or use a slower shutter speed; rotate to the *right* when you want to reduce the depth-of-field or use a faster shutter speed. The need for more/less DOF and slower/faster shutter speed are the primary reasons you'd want to use Program Shift. I'll explain Program mode exposure shifting options in more detail later in this chapter.

In Aperture-priority (Av) and Shutter-priority (Tv) modes, you can change to an equivalent exposure using a different combination of shutter speed and aperture, but only by either adjusting the aperture in Aperture-priority mode (the camera then chooses the shutter speed) or shutter speed in Shutter-priority mode (the camera then selects the aperture). I'll cover all these exposure modes and their differences later in the chapter.

How the 7D II Calculates Exposure

Your Canon 7D II calculates exposure by measuring the light that passes through the lens and is bounced up by the mirror to sensors located near the focusing surface, using a pattern you can select (more on that later) and based on the assumption that each area being measured reflects about the same amount of light as a neutral gray card that reflects a "middle" gray of about 12- to 18-percent reflectance. (The photographic "gray cards" you buy at a camera store have an 18-percent gray tone, which does represent middle gray; however, your camera is calibrated to interpret a somewhat darker 12-percent gray; I'll explain more about this later.) That "average" 12- to 18-percent gray assumption is necessary, because different subjects reflect different amounts of light. In a photo containing, say, a white cat and a dark gray cat, the white cat might reflect five times as much light as the gray cat. An exposure based on the white cat will cause the gray cat to appear to be black, while an exposure based only on the gray cat will make the white cat washed out.

This is more easily understood if you look at some photos of subjects that are dark (they reflect little light), those that have predominantly middle tones, and subjects that are highly reflective. The next few figures show some images of actual cats (actually, the *same* cat rendered in black, gray, and white varieties through the magic of Photoshop), with each of the three strips exposed using a different cat for reference.

Correctly Exposed

The three pictures shown in at top in **Figure 4.4** represent how the black, gray, and white cats would appear if the exposure were calculated by measuring the light reflecting from the middle, gray cat, which, for the sake of illustration, we'll assume reflects approximately 12 to 18 percent of the light that strikes it. The exposure meter sees an object that it thinks is a middle gray, calculates an exposure based on that, and the feline in the center of the strip is rendered at its proper tonal value. Best of all, because the resulting exposure is correct, the black cat at left and white cat at right are rendered properly as well.

When you're shooting pictures with your 7D II, and the meter happens to base its exposure on a subject that averages that "ideal" middle gray, then you'll end up with similar (accurate) results. The camera's exposure algorithms are concocted to ensure this kind of result as often as possible, barring any unusual subjects (that is, those that are backlit, or have uneven illumination). The 7D II has four different metering modes (described on the next few pages), each of which is equipped to handle certain types of unusual subjects, as I'll outline.

Overexposed

The strip of three images in the middle of **Figure 4.4** shows what would happen if the exposure were calculated based on metering the leftmost, black cat. The light meter sees less light reflecting from the black cat than it would see from a gray middle-tone subject, and so figures, "Aha! I need to add exposure to brighten this subject up to a middle gray!" That lightens the black cat, so it now appears to be gray.

But now, the cat in the middle that was *originally* middle gray is overexposed and becomes light gray. And the white cat at right is now seriously overexposed, and loses detail in the highlights, which have become a featureless white.

Underexposed

The third possibility in this simplified scenario is that the light meter might measure the illumination bouncing off the white cat, and try to render that feline as a middle gray. A lot of light is reflected by the white kitty, so the exposure is *reduced*, bringing that cat closer to a middle gray tone. The cats that were originally gray and black are now rendered too dark. Clearly, measuring the gray cat -- or a substitute that reflects about the same amount of light, is the only way to ensure that the exposure is precisely correct. (See the bottom strip of images in **Figure 4.4**.)

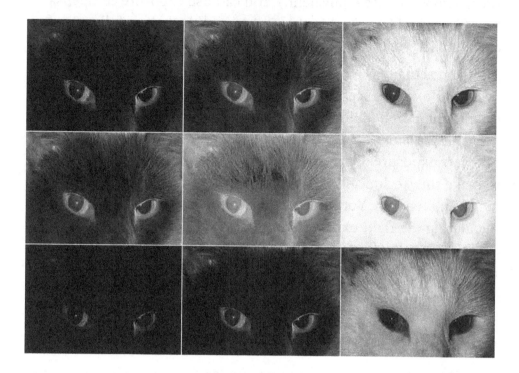

Figure 4.4

Exposure based on the middle-gray cat (top); dark gray cat (middle); and white cat (bottom.)

As you can see, the ideal way to measure exposure is to meter from a subject that reflects 12 to18 percent of the light that reaches it. If you want the most precise exposure calculations, if you don't have a gray cat handy, the solution is to use a stand-in, such as the evenly illuminated gray card I mentioned earlier. But, because the standard Kodak gray card reflects 18 percent of the light that reaches it and, as I said, your camera is calibrated for a somewhat darker 12-percent tone, you would need to add about one-half stop *more* exposure than the value metered from the card.

Another substitute for a gray card is the palm of a human hand (the backside of the hand is too variable). But a human palm, regardless of ethnic group, is even brighter than a standard gray card, so instead of one-half stop more exposure, you need to add one additional stop. That is, if your meter reading is 1/500th of a second at f/11, use 1/500th second at f/8 or 1/250th second at f/11 instead. (Both exposures are equivalent.) You can use exposure compensation (described later in this chapter) to add the half or full stop of exposure in either case.

If you actually wanted to use a gray card, place it in your frame near your main subject, facing the camera, and with the exact same even illumination falling on it that is falling on your subject. Then, use the Spot metering function (described in the next section) to calculate exposure. Of course, in most situations, it's not necessary to make the (technically correct) adjustment from the gray card/human hand reading. Your camera's light meter will do a good job of calculating the right exposure that's close enough for practical purposes, especially if you use the exposure tips in the next section. But, I felt that explaining exactly what is going on during exposure calculation would help you understand how your 7D II's metering system works.

Origin of the 18-Percent "Myth"

Why are so many photographers under the impression that camera light meters are calibrated to the 18-percent "standard," rather than the true value, which may be 12 to 14 percent, depending on the vendor? You'll find this misinformation in an alarming number of places. I've seen the 18-percent "myth" taught in camera classes; I've found it in many other books, and even been given this wrong information from the technical staff of camera vendors. (They should know better[md]the same vendors' engineers who design and calibrate the cameras have the right figure.)

The confusion started many years ago, when Eastman Kodak Company decided to use an 18-percent gray value as a reference for its exposure guidelines, even though light meters of the time were themselves not calibrated to that value. However, the human eye perceives light in a non-linear fashion, detecting darker tones to a different degree than lighter tones, so, as it turns out, a "middle" gray, on a scale of 0 percent (black) to 100 percent (white) falls at the 18-percent marker (not 50 percent, as you might guess). The printing industry was already using 18-percent gray as a printing standard, and 18-percent gray cards were thus inexpensive to produce, so Kodak adopted them for its KODAK Gray Card, Publication R-27Q (which is still available from authorized non-Kodak sources).

Kodak advised measuring from an 18-percent gray card, and *then making an adjustment* to account for the fact that meters were calibrated to a different value. The directions read (with a bit of paraphrasing from me in italics):

1. For subjects of normal reflectance *increase* the indicated exposure by 1/2 stop.

2. For light subjects use the indicated exposure; for very light subjects, *decrease* the exposure by 1/2 stop. *(That is, you're measuring a subject that's lighter than middle gray.)*

3. If the subject is dark to very dark, *increase* the indicated exposure by 1 to 1-1/2 stops. *(You're shooting a dark subject.)***

Note that these adjustments apply when you're measuring from an 18-percent gray card, whereas the adjustments in the previous sections referred to measuring black, gray, and white patches. (I often receive e-mail from readers who forget that and think the earlier examples contradict Kodak's recommendations.)

Kodak's guidelines worked well for many years, and then, after a revision of Kodak's instructions for its gray cards in the 1970s, the advice to make the adjustments in the list was omitted, and a whole generation of shooters grew up thinking that a measurement off a gray card could be used as-is. Many of them have gone on to teach each new crop of photographers the same incorrect information. The proviso returned to the instructions by 1987, it's said, but by then it was too late. My most recent copy of Publication R-27Q is dated 2006, but there are many other sources of 18-percent gray cards designed for photographers.

EXTERNAL METERS CAN BE CALIBRATED

The light meters built into your camera are calibrated at the factory. But if you use a hand-held incident or reflective light meter, you can calibrate it, using the instructions supplied with your meter. Because a hand-held meter can be calibrated to the 18-percent gray standard (or any other value you choose), my rant about the myth of the 18-percent gray card doesn't apply.

Choosing a Metering Method

Your 7D II can calculate exposure quite accurately using its 150,000-pixel RGB+IR exposure meter sensor. As you can guess from its name, the metering sensor is able to interpret the red, green, and blue tones in your image separately, adds in a little infra-red sensitivity. That allows it to not only sense tonal variations within your frame, but differentiate your subject matter by color (such as blue skies or green foliage in landscape images.)

However, even this sophisticated exposure system needs some help from you to do the best job. To arrive at the optimum exposure automatically, you need to tell the 7D II *where* in the frame to meas-ure the light (this is called the *metering method*) and *what controls* should be used (aperture, shutter speed, or both) to set the expo-sure. That's called *exposure mode*, and includes Program (P), Shutter-priority (Tv), Aperture-priority (Av), or Manual (M) options, plus Scene Intelligent Auto. I'll explain all these next.

But first, I'm going to introduce you to the four metering meth-ods. You can select any of the four if you're working with P, Tv, Av, or M exposure modes; if you're using Scene Intelligent Auto, Evalu-ative metering is selected automatically and cannot be changed. In Live View mode, the same metering methods are available, but the camera measures light directly falling on the sensor, and the 150,000-pixel exposure sensor is not used.

Choose a metering mode by pressing the Metering mode/White balance selection button on the top panel, and using the Main Dial until the icon for the mode you want appears in the status LCD. You can also select the metering mode by pressing the Q button and nav-igating to the metering mode icon in the bottom row of the Quick Control screen. Then, choose your mode:

- ⊙ **Evaluative.** The 7D II slices up the frame into 252 different zones, shown as cyan rectangles at left in **Figure 4.5.** (Don't confuse these zones with the 65 *autofocus* zones shown in red;

they are different.) The zones used are linked to the autofocus system such that as the camera evaluates the measurements, it gives extra emphasis to the metering zones that indicate sharp focus. From this data, it makes an educated guess about what kind of picture you're taking, based on examination of thousands of different real-world photos in the camera's database. For example, if the top sections of a picture are much lighter than the bottom portions, the algorithm can assume that the scene is a landscape photo with lots of sky. This mode is the best all-purpose metering method for most pictures. I'll explain how to choose an autofocus/exposure zone in the section on autofocus operation later in this chapter. See the image at right in **Figure 4.5** for an example of a scene that can be easily interpreted by the Evaluative metering mode.

- **Partial.** This is a *faux* spot mode, using roughly 6 percent of the image area to calculate exposure, which, as you can see at left in **Figure 4.6**, is a rather large spot, represented by the larger cyan circle. The status LCD icon is shown in the upper-left corner. Use this mode if the background is much brighter or darker than the subject, as in **Figure 4.6**, right.

- **Spot.** This mode confines the reading to a limited area in the center of the viewfinder, as shown at left in **Figure 4.7**, making up only 1.8 percent of the image. This mode is useful when you want to base exposure on a small area in the frame, especially backlit images like the one shown in **Figure 4.7**, right. If that area is in the center of the frame, so much the better, but for the example photograph, I had to meter a middle-tone area of the structure, and then lock exposure by pressing the shutter release halfway before recomposing the image. I could have also pressed the AE lock (*) button.

- **Center-weighted averaging.** In this mode, the exposure meter emphasizes a zone in the center of the frame to calculate exposure, as shown at left in Figure 4.8, on the theory that, for most pictures, the main subject will be located in the center. Center-weighting works best for portraits, architectural photos, and other pictures in which the most important subject is located in the middle of the frame, as in **Figure 4.8**, right. As the name suggests, the light reading is *weighted* toward the central portion, but information is also used from the rest of the frame. If your main subject is surrounded by very bright or very dark areas, the exposure might not be exactly right. However, this scheme works well in many situations if you don't want to use one of the other modes.

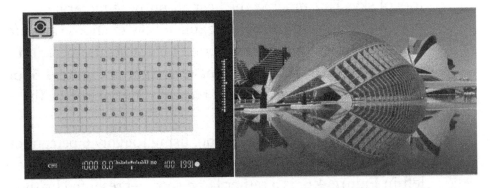

Figure 4.5

Evaluative metering uses 252 zones marked by cyan rectangles, linked to the autofocus points shown as red squares (left.). It's useful for evenly lit scenes (right).

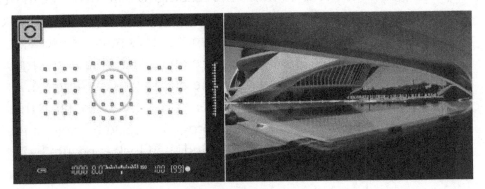

Figure 4.6

Partial metering uses a center spot that's roughly 6 percent of the frame area (left). It allowed measuring exposure from the central area of the image, while giving less emphasis to the darker areas at top and bottom.

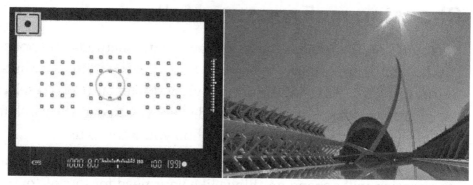

Figure 4.7

Spot metering calculates exposure based on a center spot that's only 1.8 percent of the image area (left). It's useful for calculating exposure with backlit scenes

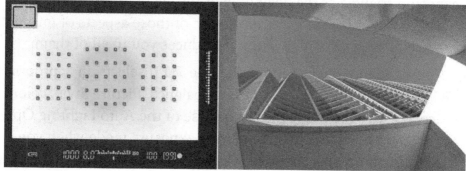

(right) .

Figure 4.8

Center-weighted metering calculates exposure based on the full frame, but emphasizes the center area (left). It the exposure for the shot at right from the large area in the center of the frame.

Choosing an Exposure Method

You'll find four manual and semi-automatic methods for choosing the appropriate shutter speed and aperture: Program (P), Shutter-priority (Tv), Aperture-priority (Av), and Manual (M). To select one of these modes, just spin the Mode Dial (located at the top-left side of the camera) to choose the method you want to use.

Your choice of which exposure method is best for a given shooting situation will depend on things like your need for lots of (or less) depth-of-field, a desire to freeze action or allow motion blur, or how much noise you find acceptable in an image. (Remember that exposure triangle at the beginning of the chapter.) Each of the 7D II's exposure methods emphasizes one of those aspects of image capture or another. This section introduces you to all of them.

In Scene Intelligent Auto mode, the 7D II selects an appropriate ISO sensitivity setting, color (white) balance, Picture Style, color space, noise reduction features, and use of the Auto Lighting Optimizer. Use the Scene Intelligent Auto exposure mode when you hand your camera to a friend to take a picture (say, of you standing in front of the Eiffel Tower), and want to be sure they won't accidentally change any settings.

Aperture-Priority

In Av mode, you specify the lens opening used, and the 7D II selects the shutter speed. Aperture-priority is especially good when you want to use a particular lens opening to achieve a desired effect. Perhaps you'd like to use the smallest f/stop possible to maximize depth-of-field in a close-up picture. Or, you might want to use a large f/stop to throw everything except your main subject out of focus, as in **Figure 4.9**. Maybe you'd just like to "lock in" a particular f/stop smaller than the maximum aperture because it's the sharpest available aperture with that lens. Or, you might prefer to use, say, f/2.8 on a lens with a maximum aperture of f/1.4, because you want the best compromise between speed and sharpness.

Figure 4.9

Use Aperture-priority to "lock in" a large f/stop when you want to blur the background.

Aperture-priority can even be used to specify a *range* of shutter speeds you want to use under varying lighting conditions, which seems almost contradictory. But think about it. You're shooting a soccer game outdoors with a telephoto lens and want a relatively high shutter speed, but you don't care if the speed changes a little should the sun duck behind a cloud. Set your 7D II to Av, and adjust the aperture until a shutter speed of, say, 1/1,000th second is selected at your current ISO setting. (In bright sunlight at ISO 400, that aperture is likely to be around f/11.) Then, go ahead and shoot, knowing that your 7D II will maintain that f/11 aperture (for sufficient DOF as the soccer players move about the field), but will drop down to 1/750th or 1/500th second if necessary should the lighting change a little.

If the shutter speed in the viewfinder or on the Shooting Settings screen is blinking, that indicates that the 7D II is unable to select an appropriate shutter speed at the selected aperture and that overexposure (the 8000 is blinking) or underexposure (the 30 shutter speed is blinking) will occur at the current ISO setting. To correct overexposure, select a smaller aperture (if available) or choose a lower ISO sensitivity. Fix underexposure conditions by choosing a larger aperture (if possible) or a higher ISO setting.

That's the major pitfall of using Av: you might select an f/stop that is too small or too large to allow an optimal exposure with the available shutter speeds. For example, if you choose f/2.8 as your aperture and the illumination is quite bright (say, at the beach or in snow), even your camera's fastest shutter speed might not be able to cut down the amount of light reaching the sensor to provide the right exposure. Or, if you select f/8 in a dimly lit room, you might find yourself shooting with a very slow shutter speed that can cause blurring from subject movement or camera shake. Aperture-priority is best used by those with a bit of experience in choosing settings. Many seasoned photographers leave their 7D II set on Av all the time.

When to use Aperture-priority:

- **General landscape photography.** The 7D II is a great camera for landscape photography, of course, because its 20MP of resolution allows making huge, gorgeous prints, as well as smaller prints that are filled with eye-popping detail. Aperture-priority is a good tool for ensuring that your landscape is sharp from foreground to infinity, if you select an f/stop that provides maximum depth-of-field. If you use Av mode and select an aperture like f/11 or f/16, it's your responsibility to make sure the shutter speed selected is fast enough to avoid losing detail to camera shake, or that the 7D II is mounted on a tripod. One thing that new landscape photographers fail to account for is the movement of distant leaves and tree branches. When seeking the ultimate in sharpness, go ahead and use Aperture-priority, but boost ISO sensitivity a bit, if necessary, to provide a sufficiently fast shutter speed, whether shooting hand-held or with a tripod.

- ⊙ **Specific landscape situations.** Aperture-priority is also useful when you have no objection to using a long shutter speed, or, particularly, *want* the 7D II to select one. Waterfalls are a perfect example. You can use Av mode, set your camera to ISO 100, use a small f/stop, and let the camera select a longer shutter speed that will allow the water to blur as it flows. Indeed, you might need to use a neutral-density filter to get a sufficiently long shutter speed. But Aperture-priority mode is a good start.

- ⊙ **Portrait photography.** Portraits are the most common applications of selective focus. A medium large aperture (say, f/5.6 or f/8) with a longer lens/zoom setting (in the 85mm-135mm range) will allow the background behind your portrait subject to blur. A *very* large aperture (I frequently shoot wide open with my 85mm f/1.2 lens) lets you apply selective focus to your subject's *face*. With a three-quarters view of your subject, as long as their eyes are sharp, it's okay if the far ear or their hair is out of focus.

- ⊙ **When you want to ensure optimal sharpness.** All lenses have an aperture or two at which they perform best, providing the level of sharpness you expect from a camera with the resolution of the 7D II. That's usually about two stops down from wide open, and thus will vary depending on the maximum aperture of the lens. My 85mm f/1.2 is good wide open, but it's even sharper at f/2.8 or f/4; I shoot my 70-200mm f/2.8 wide open at concerts, but, if I can use f/4 instead, I'll get better results. Aperture-priority allows me to use each lens at its very best f/stop.

- ⊙ **Close-up/Macro photography.** Depth-of-field is typically very shallow when shooting macro photos, and you'll want to choose your f/stop carefully. Perhaps you need the smallest aperture you can get away with to maximize DOF. Or, you might want to use a wider stop to emphasize your subject, as I did with the photo of the owl in **Figure 4.9**. A mode comes in very useful when shooting close-up pictures. Because macro work is frequently done with the 7D II mounted on a tripod, and your close-up subjects, if not living creatures, may not be moving much, a longer shutter speed isn't a problem. Aperture-priority (Av mode) can be your preferred choice.

Shutter-Priority

Shutter-priority (Tv) is the inverse of Aperture-priority: you choose the shutter speed you'd like to use, and the camera's metering system selects the appropriate f/stop. Perhaps you're shooting action photos and you want to use the absolute fastest shutter speed available with your camera; in other cases, you might want to use a slow shutter speed to add some blur to a ballet photo that would be mundane if the action were completely frozen. Shutter-priority mode gives you some control over how much action-freezing capability your digital camera brings to bear in a particular situation, as you can see in **Figure 4.10**.

Figure 4.10

Lock the shutter at a slow speed to introduce a little blur into a shot, seen here in the flying fingers of ukelele virtuoso Jake Shimabukuro.

You'll also encounter the same problem as with Aperture-priority when you select a shutter speed that's too long or too short for correct exposure under some conditions. I've shot outdoor soccer games on sunny Fall evenings and used Shutter-priority mode to lock in a 1/1,000th second shutter speed, which triggered the blinking warning, even with the lens wide open.

Like Av mode, it's possible to choose an inappropriate shutter speed. If that's the case, the maximum aperture of your lens (to indicate underexposure) or the minimum aperture (to indicate overexposure) will blink. To fix, select a longer shutter speed or higher ISO setting (for underexposure), or a faster shutter speed/lower ISO setting (for overexposure).

When to use Shutter-priority:

- **To reduce blur from subject motion.** Set the shutter speed of the 7D II to a higher value to reduce the amount of blur from subjects that are moving. The exact speed will vary depending on how fast your subject is moving and how much blur is acceptable. You might want to freeze a basketball player in mid-dunk with a 1/1,000th second shutter speed, or use 1/250th second to allow the spinning wheels of a motocross racer to blur a tiny bit to add the feeling of motion.

- **To add blur from subject motion.** There are times when you want a subject to blur, say, when shooting waterfalls with the camera set for a one- or two-second exposure in Shutter-priority mode.

- **To add blur from camera motion when *you* are moving.** Say you're panning to follow a pair of relay runners. You might want to use Shutter-priority mode and set the 7D II for 1/60th second, so that the background will blur as you pan with the runners. The shutter speed will be fast enough to provide a sharp image of the athletes.

- **To reduce blur from camera motion when *you* are moving.** In other situations, the camera may be in motion, say, because you're shooting from a moving train or auto, and you want to minimize the amount of blur caused by the motion of the camera. Shutter-priority is a good choice here, too.

- **Landscape photography hand-held.** If you can't use a tripod for your landscape shots, you'll still probably want the sharpest image possible. Shutter-priority can allow you to specify a shutter speed that's fast enough to reduce or eliminate the effects of camera shake. Just make sure that your ISO setting is high enough that the 7D II will select an aperture with sufficient depth-of-field, too.

- **Concerts, stage performances.** I shoot a lot of concerts with my 70-200mm f/2.8 lens, and have discovered that, when image stabilization is taken into account, a shutter speed of 1/180th second is fast enough to eliminate blur from hand-holding the 7D II with this lens, and also to avoid blur from the movement of all but the most energetic performers. I use Shutter-priority and set the ISO so the camera will select an aperture in the f/4-5.6 range.

Program AE Mode

Program mode (P) uses the 7D II's built-in smarts to select the correct f/stop and shutter speed using a database of picture information that tells it which combination of shutter speed and aperture will work best for a particular photo. If the correct exposure cannot be achieved at the current ISO setting, the shutter speed or aperture indicator in the viewfinder will blink, indicating under- or overexposure. You can then boost or reduce the ISO to increase or decrease sensitivity.

The 7D II's recommended exposure can be overridden if you want. Use the EV setting feature (described later, because it also applies to Tv and Av modes) to add or subtract exposure from the metered value. And, as I mentioned earlier in this chapter, you can change from the recommended setting to an equivalent setting (as shown in **Table 4.1**) that produces the same exposure, but using a different combination of f/stop and shutter speed. To accomplish this:

- ⊙ Press the shutter release halfway to lock in the current base exposure, or press the AE Lock button (*) on the back of the camera (in which case the * indicator will illuminate in the viewfinder to show that the exposure has been locked).

- ⊙ If the camera cannot select an appropriate exposure, the shutter speed and aperture display will blink:

  - **Underexposure.** The 30 shutter speed indicator will flash, along with the maximum (largest) aperture of the lens. (The exact number will vary, depending on which lens you are using.) To compensate, you must either use a higher ISO setting or provide additional illumination, such as electronic flash.

  - **Overexposure.** The 8000 shutter speed indicator will flash, along with the minimum (smallest available) f/stop, such as f/16, f/22, or f/32, depending on the lens you are using. You can usually compensate for this by reducing the ISO speed to a lower setting. Your scene must be *very* bright indeed to trigger overexposure at a shutter speed of 1/8,000ᵗʰ second and the lowest L (ISO 50 equivalent) sensitivity setting. But if you're photographing, say, a blast furnace, and still have an overexposure situation, you can resort to a neutral density filter or find some way to reduce the amount of illumination.

- ⊙ Once an exposure is set, you can spin the Main Dial to change to a different combination of settings. Rotate left to select a longer shutter speed/smaller aperture, or to the right to choose a faster shutter speed/larger aperture.

Your adjustment remains in force for a single exposure; if you want to change from the recommended settings for the next exposure, you'll need to repeat those steps.

When to use Program mode priority:

⊙ **When you're in a hurry to get a grab shot.** The 7D II will do a pretty good job of calculating an appropriate exposure for you, without any input from you.

⊙ **When you hand your camera to a novice.** Set the 7D II to P, hand the camera to your friend, relative, or trustworthy stranger you meet in front of the Eiffel Tower, point to the shutter release button and viewfinder, and say, "Look through here, and press this button."

⊙ **When no special shutter speed or aperture settings are needed.** If your subject doesn't require special anti- or pro-blur techniques, and depth-of-field or selective focus aren't important, use P as a general-purpose setting. You can still make adjustments to increase/decrease depth-of-field or add/reduce motion blur with a minimum of fuss.

Scene Intelligent Auto

On first consideration, including an exposure mode with no user options might seem counterintuitive on a camera as advanced as the 7D II, because it essentially transforms a sophisticated pro/enthusiast camera into a point-and-click snapshooter. Delve deeper, and you'll discover that there is method in Canon's madness, and that Scene Intelligent Auto is a lot more than a less versatile version of Program mode. The key is the *Intelligent* part of the mode's nomenclature.

With P mode, only the shutter speed and aperture are determined by the camera. You can change the metering mode, autofocus mode, white balance, and virtually all other settings. In Scene Intelligent Auto mode, the 7D II will analyze your scene, even to the extent of evaluating whether or not your subject is static or moving, and then intelligently choose optimum settings without any input from you. Its choices include:

⊙ **ISO speed.** The camera will choose an ISO sensitivity automatically.

- ⊙ **Picture Style.** The A (automatic) Picture Style is active, and the camera will choose appropriate settings. Note that if you have made changes to the Auto Picture Style (I'll show you how to do that in Chapter 8), they will be ignored in Scene Intelligent Auto.

- ⊙ **White balance.** White balance is set automatically and cannot be changed.

- ⊙ **Auto Lighting Optimizer.** Always active in Scene Intelligent Auto mode.

- ⊙ **Color space.** Forced to sRGB.

- ⊙ **Autofocus.** AI Focus AF is always used, and AF Area Selection modes cannot be specified. AF point selection is always automatic, and the AF-assist beam activated.

- ⊙ **Metering mode.** Evaluative metering is always used.

Things that you *can* choose in Scene Intelligent Auto mode include:

- ⊙ **Manual focus.** Manual focus can be chosen by toggling the AF/MF switch on the lens to Manual.

- ⊙ **Drive mode.** You use the Quick Control screen or Drive mode button to choose from single shooting, high/low speed continuous shooting, silent single shooting, silent continuous shooting, and 10 sec/2 sec self-timer modes.

- ⊙ **Memory card options.** The Q button will also give you access to the options for your Card 1 or Card 2 storage.

- ⊙ **Image Quality/Size.** Press the Q button to select among your RAW, JPEG, and other image size options.

- ⊙ **Flash modes.** You can select from Auto Flash, Flash On, or Flash Off.

Some choices are available from the truncated menu system offered in Scene Intelligent Auto mode. I'll explain all menu entries for all exposure modes in Chapters 8 to 11. While some Playback and Set-up menu choices are accessible, those you most commonly might need to access while shooting include:

- Image Quality
- Image Review duration
- Beep enable/disable
- Release Shutter without Card
- Lens Aberration Correction
- Live View enable/disable
- AF mode in Live View
- Live View Grid display

Manual Exposure

Part of being an experienced photographer comes from knowing when to rely on your 7D II's automation (including Scene Intelligent Auto or P mode), when to go semi-automatic (with Tv or Av), and when to set exposure manually (using M). Some photographers actually prefer to set their exposure manually most of the time, as the 7D II will be happy to provide an indication of when its metering system judges your settings provide the proper exposure, using the analog exposure scale at the bottom of the viewfinder and on the status LCD.

Manual exposure can come in handy in some situations. You might be taking a silhouette photo and find that none of the exposure modes or EV correction features give you exactly the effect you want. For example, I was trying to shoot a ballet dancer performing in front of a mostly dark background highlighted by an illuminated curtain off to the right, there was no way any of my 7D II's exposure modes would be able to interpret the scene the way I wanted to shoot it, even with Spot metering, which didn't have a narrow enough field-of-view from my position. So, I took a couple test exposures, and set the exposure manually using the exact shutter speed and f/stop I needed. You might be working in a studio environment using multiple flash units. The additional flash are triggered by slave devices (gadgets that set off the flash when they sense the light from another flash, or, perhaps from a radio or infrared remote control). Your camera's exposure meter doesn't compensate for the extra illumination, and can't interpret the flash exposure at all, so you need to set the aperture manually.

Because, depending on your proclivities, you might not need to set exposure manually very often, you should still make sure you understand how it works. Fortunately, the 7D II makes setting exposure manually very easy. Just set the Mode Dial to M, turn the Main Dial to set the shutter speed, and hold down the Av button while rotating the Main Dial to adjust the aperture. Press the shutter release halfway or press the AE Lock button, and the exposure scale in the viewfinder shows you how far your chosen setting diverges from the metered exposure.

When to use manual exposure:

- ◉ **When working in the studio.** If you're working in a studio environment, you generally have total control over the lighting and can set exposure exactly as you want. The last thing you need is for the 7D II to interpret the scene and make adjustments of its own. Use M and shutter speed, aperture, and (as long as you don't use ISO-Auto) the ISO setting are totally up to you.

- ◉ **When using non-dedicated flash.** External Canon dedicated flash units are cool, but if you're working with a non-compatible flash unit, particularly studio flash plugged into the side-mounted PC/X socket, or into a PC/X sync adapter mounted on the hot shoe, the camera has no clue about the intensity of the flash, so you'll have to dial in the appropriate aperture manually.

- ◉ **If you're using a hand-held light meter.** The appropriate aperture, both for flash exposures and shots taken under continuous lighting, can be determined by a hand-held light meter, flash meter, or combo meter that measures both kinds of illumination. With an external meter, you can measure high-lights, shadows, backgrounds, or additional subjects separately, and use Manual exposure to make your settings.

⊙ **When you want to outsmart the metering system.** Your 7D II's metering system is "trained" to react to unusual lighting situations, such as backlighting, extra bright illumination, or low-key images with murky shadows. In many cases, it can counter these "problems" and produce a well-exposed image. But what if you don't *want* a well-exposed image? Manual exposure allows you to produce silhouettes in backlit situations, wash out all the middle tones to produce a luminous look, or underexpose to create a moody or ominous dark-toned photograph.

Adjusting Exposure with ISO Settings

Another way of adjusting exposures is by changing the ISO sensitivity setting. Sometimes photographers forget about this option, because the common practice is to set the ISO once for a particular shooting session (say, at ISO 100 or 200 for bright sunlight outdoors, or ISO 800 when shooting indoors) and then forget about ISO. ISOs higher than ISO 100 or 200 are seen as "bad" or "necessary evils." However, changing the ISO is a valid way of adjusting exposure settings, particularly with the Canon EOS 7D Mark II, which produces good results at ISO settings that create grainy, unusable pictures with some other camera models.

Indeed, I find myself using ISO adjustment as a convenient alternate way of adding or subtracting EV when shooting in Manual mode, and as a quick way of choosing equivalent exposures when in Auto or semi-automatic modes. For example, I've selected a Manual exposure with both f/stop and shutter speed suitable for my image using, say, ISO 200. I can change the exposure in full-stop increments by pressing the ISO button on top of the camera, and spinning the Main Dial one click at a time. The difference in image quality/noise at the base setting of ISO 200 is negligible if I dial in ISO

100 to reduce exposure a little, or change to ISO 400 to increase exposure. I keep my preferred f/stop and shutter speed, but still adjust the exposure.

Or, perhaps, I am using Tv mode and the metered exposure at ISO 200 is 1/500th second at f/11. If I decide on the spur of the moment I'd rather use 1/500th second at f/8, I can press the ISO button and spin the Main Dial to switch to ISO 100. Of course, it's a good idea to monitor your ISO changes, so you don't end up at ISO 1600 accidentally. ISO settings can, of course, also be used to boost or reduce sensitivity in particular shooting situations. Your available ISO options for the various exposure modes include:

- **Scene Intelligent Auto.** ISO is set automatically in the range ISO 100-6400.

- **P/Tv/Av/M modes.** Auto ISO (ISO 100-16000); Manual settings (ISO 100-16000) with H1 and H2 values (ISO 25600 and ISO 56200 equivalents) available if ISO Expansion has been enabled. H2 not available in Movie mode.

- **B mode.** Auto ISO (ISO 400); Manual settings (ISO 100-16000) with H1 and H2 values (ISO 25600 and ISO 56200 equivalents) available if ISO Expansion has been enabled. H2 not available in Movie mode.

- **Built-in or External Flash (normal).** ISO 400, but may be reduced to as low as ISO 100 to avoid overexposure in P, Av, Tv modes.

- **External Flash (bounce).** ISO 400-1600 when using P mode.

With ISO expansion, mentioned earlier, you can select H1 and H2 (equivalent to ISO 25600 and 51200). If Highlight Tone Priority is set to Enable in the Shooting 3 menu, the "expanded" H1, and H2 settings are not available. To activate ISO expansion, you'll need to use the ISO Speed Range option within the ISO Speed Settings entry in the Shooting 2 menu. You can actually select the minimum and maximum available ISO values there, as I'll explain in Chapter 11.

As noted above, when using flash or the Bulb setting, ISO Auto produces a setting of ISO 400 automatically, except when overexposure would occur (as when shooting subjects very close to the camera or using fill flash), in which case a lower setting (down to ISO 100) will be used. If your external tiltable flash is used in bounce mode, the 7D II can set ISO in the range 400-1600 automatically. That's a lot of exceptions! Remember that if the Auto ISO ranges aren't suitable for you, individual ISO values can also be selected in any mode other than Scene Intelligent Auto.

Dealing with Visual Noise

Visual image noise is that random grainy effect that some like to use as a special effect, but which, most of the time, is objectionable because it robs your image of detail even as it adds that "interesting" texture. Noise is caused by two different phenomena: high ISO settings and long exposures.

High ISO noise commonly first appears when you raise your camera's sensitivity setting above ISO 1600. With Canon cameras, which are renown for their good ISO noise characteristics, noise may become visible at ISO 3200, and is usually fairly noticeable at ISO 6400. At the H1 and H2 settings (ISO 25600 and 51200 equivalents), noise is usually quite bothersome, which is why those lofty sensitivity ratings are disabled by default and must be activated with ISO expansion. This kind of noise appears as a result of the amplification needed to increase the sensitivity of the sensor. While higher ISOs do pull details out of dark areas, they also amplify non-signal information randomly, creating noise.

A similar noisy phenomenon occurs during long time exposures, which allow more photons to reach the sensor, increasing your ability to capture a picture under low-light conditions. However, the longer exposures also increase the likelihood that some pixels will register random phantom photons, often because the longer an imager is "hot," the warmer it gets, and that heat can be mistaken for photons. CMOS imagers contain millions of individual amplifiers and A/D converters, all working in unison. Because all these circuits don't necessarily process in precisely the same way all the time, they can introduce something called fixed-pattern noise into the image data.

Fortunately, Canon's electronics geniuses have done an exceptional job minimizing noise from all causes in the 7D II. Even so, you might still want to apply the optional long exposure noise reduction that can be activated in the Shooting 3 menu. This type of noise reduction involves the 7D II taking a second, blank exposure, and comparing the random pixels in that image with the photograph you just took. Pixels that coincide in the two represent noise and can safely be suppressed. This noise reduction system, called *dark frame subtraction*, effectively doubles the amount of time required to take a picture, and is used only for exposures longer than one second. Noise reduction can reduce the amount of detail in your picture, as some image information may be removed along with the noise. So, you might want to use this feature with moderation. Some types of images don't require noise reduction, because the grainy pattern tends to blend into the overall scene.

To activate your 7D II's long exposure noise reduction features, go to the Shooting 3 menu, as explained further in Chapter 8.

You can also apply noise reduction to a lesser extent using Photoshop, and when converting RAW files to some other format, using your favorite RAW converter, or an industrial-strength product like Noise Ninja (www.picturecode.com) to wipe out noise after you've already taken the picture.

Making EV Changes

Sometimes you'll want more or less exposure than indicated by the 7D II's metering system. Perhaps you want to underexpose to create a silhouette effect, or overexpose to produce a high key look. It's easy to use the 7D II's exposure compensation (EV) system to override the exposure recommendations, available in P, Tv, and Av exposure modes. Keep in mind that when the Auto Lighting Optimizer (described in Chapter 11) is enabled, the viewfinder image may appear bright even when EV adjustments have been made.

There are four ways to make exposure value (EV) changes with the 7D II.

- **Viewfinder/Quick Control Dial.** When looking through the optical viewfinder, you can add/subtract exposure compensation +/- 3 stops. Press the shutter release halfway, enabling EV adjustment for about four seconds. Then rotate the Quick Control Dial. Turn clockwise to add exposure, or counter-clockwise to reduce exposure. You may have to tap the shutter release halfway again to reactivate after four seconds have elapsed. As you rotate the QCD, the exposure scale at the bottom of the screen and in the top-panel monochrome LCD will indicate the amount of exposure compensation you've dialed in. (See **Figure 4.11**, top.)

- **Quick Control Screen/Quick Control Dial.** You can adjust exposure compensation with the Quick Control screen. Press the Q button and use the multi-selector to highlight the EV scale, as shown in **Figure 4.11** at bottom. You can then rotate the QCD clockwise to add exposure, or counter-clockwise to reduce exposure. The exposure scale on the screen will indicate the amount of exposure compensation.to adjust EV. If you want an expanded EV scale (plus or minus 5 stops), when the EV scale is highlighted, press the SET button. The Exposure Comp./AEB Setting screen, shown in **Figure 4.12** appears, and rotating the Quick Control dial produces EV adjustments up to +/-5 stops.

- **Shooting Functions Screen/Quick Control Dial.** You can also adjust exposure compensation when the Shooting Functions screen is displayed on the LCD monitor. Press the Info button (if necessary) to produce the Shooting Functions screen, tap the shutter release button halfway, and rotate the QCD within four seconds to make the adjustment. The Shooting Functions screen is similar to the Quick Control screen shown in the figure, but without the orange highlighting.

⊚ **Shooting 2 menu 2.** Press the MENU button and rotate the Main Dial to select the Shooting 2 menu. Then rotate the QCD or use the multi-selector joystick to highlight the Expo. Comp/AEB entry. Press SET to access the screen shown in **Figure 4.12**. Then rotate the QCD to select the amount of exposure compensation. The screen has helpful labels (Darker on the left and Brighter on the right) to make sure you're adding/subtracting when you really want to. Note that this method has two advantages: you can choose up to five stops of exposure compensation (rather than just three

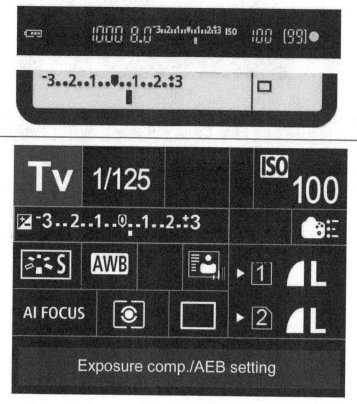

with the first two methods), and you can specify automatic exposure bracketing from this screen just by rotating the Main Dial. I'll explain bracketing in more detail later in this chapter.

Figure 4.11

When you set exposure compensation with the Quick Control Dial, the amount of adjustment is shown in the viewfinder and top-panel monochrome LCD (top). You can also use the Quick Control screen (bottom).

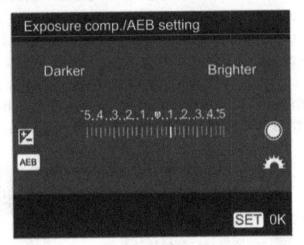

Figure 4.12

A wider range of exposure compensation adjustments (up to five stops) can be made using the Expo. Comp/AEB entry in the Shooting 2 menu.

Bracketing Parameters

Bracketing is a method for shooting several consecutive exposures using different settings, as a way of improving the odds that one will be exactly right. Before digital cameras took over the universe, it was common to bracket exposures, shooting, say, a series of three photos at 1/125th second, but varying the f/stop from f/8 to f/11 to f/16. In practice, smaller than whole-stop increments were used for greater precision. Plus, it was just as common to keep the same aperture and vary the shutter speed, although in the days before electronic shutters, film cameras often had only whole increment shutter speeds available. **Figure 4.13** shows a typical bracketed series.

Figure 4.13

In this bracketed series you can see overexposure (left), metered exposure (center), and underexposure (right).

Today, cameras like the 7D II can bracket exposures much more precisely, and bracket white balance as well (using the WB Shift/Bkt entry found in the Shooting 2 menu and described in Chapter 8).

While WB bracketing is sometimes used when getting color absolutely correct in the camera is important, autoexposure bracketing (AEB) is used much more often. When this feature is activated, the 7D II takes a series of shots, each at a different exposure value, one at the standard exposure, and the others with more or less exposure. In Av mode, the shutter speed will change, whereas in Tv mode, the aperture speed will change. The next sections will explain the parameters you can select.

Number of Exposures

In the Custom Function 1 menu, under the Number of Bracketed Shots entry, you can elect to bracket 2, 3, 5, or 7 shots:

- **2 shots.** The 7D II will capture one image at the *base* or standard exposure (which can be the metered exposure, or one that's more or less than the metered exposure, as I'll explain shortly). It then takes one additional shot that's provides either *more* or *less* exposure relative to that "base" image. Rotate the QCD to the right to specify more exposure for the second shot, or to the left to specify less exposure. The *amount* of additional/less exposure is determined by the increment you select. (Read on! I'll tie all the parameters together in an upcoming section.)
- **3, 5, 7 shots.** The camera captures one image at the base exposure, and then two, four, or six shots bracketed around that exposure, respectively. That translates to one over/one under at the 3-shot setting, two over/two under at the 5-shot setting, and three over/three under when using the 7-shot option.

Bracketing Sequence

Also in the Custom Function 1 menu, you'll find a Bracketing Sequence entry, which allows you to specify the order in which the autoexposure bracketing series are exposed. Your choice will depend both on personal preference, and what you intend to do with the bracketed shots. The options include:

- ⊙ **0 - + :** The exposure sequence is standard exposure, decreased exposure, increased exposure. With this default value, your base exposure will be captured and saved first on your memory card, followed by the progressively reduced exposure images, then the shots with increased exposure. You might prefer this order if you expect your standard exposure will be the preferred image and arranged first in the queue of each bracket set, and want the alternate exposures to follow.

- ⊙ **0 +:** The sequence is decreased exposure, standard exposure, increased exposure. This order is the most logical to use if you're shooting with the intention to combine images using HDR (high dynamic range) techniques in your image editor or HDR utility. The final bracketed array is stored on your memory card starting with the most underexposed shot, and progressing to the best exposed, and then on to the overexposures. That makes it easy to use all of your bracketed shots in the HDR sequence, or to select only some of them to combine.

- ⊙ **+ 0 -:** This sequence is the inverse of the last one, progressing from increased exposure to standard exposure and decreased exposure. You might prefer this order if you expect to see your best exposures on the plus side of the exposure sequence, and want them to be displayed first.

Bracketing Auto Cancel

The final relevant entry in the Custom Function 1 menu is Bracketing Auto Cancel. When you activate bracketing (in the Shooting 2 menu, described shortly), the 7D II continues to shoot bracketed exposures until you manually turn the bracket feature off, assuming you have this setting disabled. That's a good thing. If you're out shooting a series of bracketed exposures (especially for HDR), it's convenient to have your bracket setting be "sticky" and still be active even if you turn your camera off. Some shooters like to bracket virtually *everything* and like to leave bracketing on routinely.

However, much of the time you'll want to turn bracketing off, and may not want to visit the Shooting 2 menu to deactivate it manually. Set Bracketing Auto Cancel to Enable, and bracketing is cancelled when you turn the 7D II off, change lenses, use the flash, or change memory cards. When this setting is set to Disable, bracketing remains in effect until you manually turn it off *or use the flash.* The flash still cancels bracketing, but your settings are retained.

Increment Between Exposures

You can choose the size of the jump between each of the bracketed exposures. To do that, you'll need to visit the Expo. Comp/AEB entry in the Shooting 2 menu. There, you can select from plus/minus 1/3 to 3 full stops in 1/3 stop increments, by rotating the Main Dial. (See **Figure 4.14.**) The next section provides instructions for producing a bracketed set.

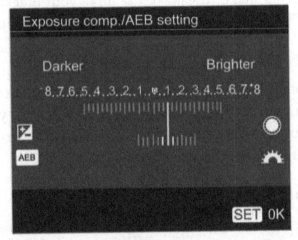

Figure 4.14

The Main Dial can be used to set the bracket increment from 1/3 to 3 full stops.

Creating a Bracketed Set

Using autoexposure bracketing is trickier than it needs to be, but has been made more flexible than with some earlier models. With the 7D II you are not limited to only three exposures (up to seven shots can be taken), and you can choose to bracket only overexposures or underexposures -- a very useful improvement! Just follow these steps:

1. **Specify number of exposures and sequence.** Choose the number of bracketed exposures you want and the sequence in which they will be shot in the Custom Function 1 menu, as described earlier.

2. **Activate the Expo. Comp./AEB screen.** Press the MENU button and navigate to the Shooting 2 menu, where you'll find the Expo. Comp./AEB option. Press SET to select this entry.

3. **Set the bracket range/increment.** Rotate the Main Dial to spread out or contract the three bars to include the desired range and exposure increment you want to use. The wider the spread, the larger the increment and the larger the range of bracketed shots you'll end up with. The Main Dial will allow you to set the bracket range to up to three stops on either side of the standard (middle) exposure. For example, in **Figure 4.15** (top), the red highlighted bars are separated from the center bar by a full f/stop, so the bracketing will produce one image at one stop *less* than the zero point (the large center bar), one at the zero point, and one at one stop more than that. **Figure 4.15** (bottom) shows the bars more widely separated, for a bracketed set two stops under and two stops over the midpoint, or standard/base exposure.

4. **Adjust zero point/standard exposure.** By default, the bracketing is zeroed around the center of the scale, which represents the correct exposure as metered by the 7D II. But you might want to have your three bracketed shots *all* biased toward overexposure or underexposure. Perhaps you feel that the metered exposure will be too dark or too light, and you want the bracketed shots to lean in the other direction. Use the Quick Control Dial to move the bracket spread toward one end of the scale or the other. **Figure 4.15** (top) shows the bracketing biased toward overexposure, while in **Figure 4.15** (bottom), the zero point is clustered around underexposure. (Actually, the exposure bar at left will be four stops under the metered exposure, the center bar two stops under, and the right bar ends up at the metered value.)

NON-BRACKETING IS EXPOSURE COMPENSATION

When the three bracket indicators aren't separated, using the QCD simply, in effect, adds or subtracts exposure compensation. You'll be shooting a "bracketed" set of one picture, with the zero point placed at the portion of the scale you indicated. Until you rotate the Main Dial to separate the three bracket indicators by at least one indicator, this screen just supplies EV adjustment. Also, keep in mind that the increments shown will be either 1/3 stop or 1/2 stop, depending on how you've set Exposure Level Increments in the Custom Function 1 menu.

1. **Confirm your choice.** Press the SET button to enter the settings.
2. **Take your photo sequence.** Press the shutter release to start capturing the bracketed sequence. The drive mode you select will determine when they are taken:
3. **Single shooting/Silent single shooting.** Press the shutter release one time for each exposure in the sequence.
4. **High speed continuous/Low speed continuous/Silent continuous.** You can hold down the shutter release and all the shots in the sequence will be exposed. The 7D II stops shooting when the series is complete.
5. **10 sec./2 sec. self-timer modes.** After the appropriate delay, all the shots in the sequence will be taken.
6. **Monitor your shots.** As the images are captured, three indicators will appear on the exposure scale in the viewfinder, with one of them flashing for each bracketed photo, showing when the base exposure, underexposure, and overexposure are taken.
7. **Turn bracketing off when done.** Bracketing remains in effect when the set is taken so you can continue shooting bracketed exposures until you use the electronic flash, turn off the camera, or return to the menu to cancel bracketing.

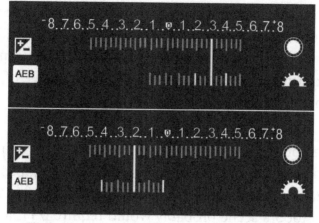

Figure 4.15

Use the Quick Control Dial to bias the bracketing toward more or less exposure, and the Main Dial to set the bracket range.

NOTE: AEB is disabled when you're using flash, Multi Shot Noise Reduction, taking long time exposures with the Bulb setting, or have enabled the Auto Lighting Optimizer in the Shooting 2 menu (in which case the optimizer will probably override and nullify bracketing).

Working with HDR

High dynamic range (HDR) photography is quite the rage these days, and entire books have been written on the subject. It's not really a new technique -- film photographers have been combining multiple exposures for ages to produce a single image of, say, an interior room while maintaining detail in the scene visible through the windows.

Suppose you wanted to photograph a dimly lit room that had a bright window showing an outdoors scene. Proper exposure for the room might be on the order of 1/60th second at f/2.8 at ISO 200, while the outdoors scene probably would require f/11 at 1/400th second. That's almost a 7 EV step difference (approximately 7 f/stops) and well beyond the dynamic range of any digital camera, including the Canon 7D II.

Until camera sensors gain much higher dynamic ranges (which may not be as far into the distant future as we think), special tricks like Active D-Lighting and HDR photography will remain basic tools. With the Canon 7D II, you can create in-camera HDR exposures, or shoot HDR the old-fashioned way -- with separate bracketed exposures that are later combined in a tool like Photomatix or Adobe's Merge to HDR Pro image editing feature. I'm going to show you how to use both.

The 7D II's in-camera HDR feature, is simple, flexible, and surprisingly effective in creating high dynamic range images. It's also remarkably easy to use. Although it combines only three images to create a single HDR photograph, and while it's not always as good as the manual HDR method I'll describe in the section after this one, it's a *lot* faster.

Here is a typical situation in which you might want to use this setting. When the exposure is set for the interior of the cathedral, the beautiful backlit stained glass windows are washed out and have no detail (**Figure 4.16**, top left.) When the exposure is adjusted to produce detail in the glass panes (see **Figure 4.16**, top right), the rest of the cathedral goes dark. The quickie solution is to use the 7D

II's HDR mode, described next. It captures three consecutive images and then merges them as a JPEG image that preserves both highlight and shadow detail, as you can see in **Figure 4.16**, bottom, which has a much fuller range of tones.

Figure 4.16

Exposing for the cathedral interior produces overexposed backlit stained glass windows (top left), while exposing for the windows captures a murky cathedral interior (top right.) The 7D II's HDR mode captures a full range of tones (bottom.)

Using HDR Mode

Here are some tips for using this feature:

- ◉ **Use a tripod if possible.** Because there may be some camera movement between the continuous shots, you'll get better results if you mount the 7D II on a tripod.

- ◉ **Moving objects may produce ghosts.** In this case, there may be some *subject* motion between shots, producing "ghost" effects.

- ◉ **Misalignment.** If you *don't* use a tripod, when Auto Image Align is activated, this mode does a good job of realigning your multiple images when they are merged. However, it can't do a perfect job, particularly with repetitive patterns that are difficult for the camera's "brains" to sort out. Some misalignment is possible.

- **Shutter speeds vary.** The camera brackets by adjusting the shutter speed within the increment range selected, *even if you're using Tv or M modes and have specified a shutter speed.*

- **Unwanted cropping.** Because the processor needs to be able to shift each individual image slightly in any (or all) of four directions in Auto Align mode (described next), it needs to crop the image slightly to trim out any non-image areas that result. Your final image will be slightly smaller than one shot in other modes.

- **Weird colors.** Some types of lighting, including fluorescent and LED illumination, "cycle" many times a second, and colors can vary between shots. You may not even notice this when single shooting, but it becomes more obvious when using any continuous shooting mode, including HDR mode. The combined images may have strange color effects.

- **Can't use any RAW mode, or ISOs higher than 25600.** Your image will be recorded as a Large JPEG only, and HDR is disabled when you're using ISO expansion to enable sensitivity settings higher than 25600. While you can use HDR mode if Auto Lighting Optimizer has been enabled, the camera will disable it while shooting your HDR images, then re-enable it when you turn HDR mode off.

- **The process takes time.** Forget about firing off a large number of HDR shots in a row. After the 7D II captures its three images, it takes a few seconds to process them and save your final image. Be patient.

HDR mode has a "hidden" menu that you can access by pressing the Creative Photo button, located to the upper left of the LCD monitor on the back panel of the 7D II. Rotate the QCD to choose HDR Mode from the screen that pops up (see **Figure 4.17**), press the SET button, and you'll be taken to the menu shown in **Figure 4.18.**

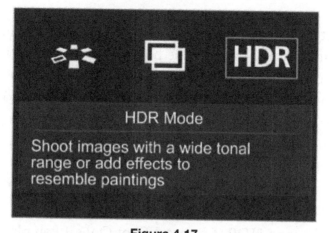

Figure 4.17

Press the Creative Photo button and choose HDR mode.

HDR Mode	
Adjust dyn range	Disable HDR
Effect	Natural
Continous HDR	1 shot only
Auto Image Align	Enable
Save source imgs	All images

Figure 4.18

The HDR Mode menu has five entries.

This menu has five separate entries:

- **Adjust Dynamic Range.** There are five choices in this entry. Select Disable HDR to turn HDR completely off. The others select the number of stops of dynamic range improvement the HDR feature will provide. Choose Auto to allow the 7D II to examine your scene and select an appropriate EV range. As you gain experience you might want to select the range yourself, in order to achieve a particular look. You can choose plus/minus 1, 2, or 3 EV.

- **Effect.** If you've worked with HDR utilities (such as Photomatix) in the past, you know that various parameters can be adjusted while combining HDR images to produce various effects. These include the amount of color saturation (the "richness" of the hues); the boldness of the edge transitions between portions of the image (producing mild to distinct outlines); brightness of the resulting image; and contrast/tone. Various combinations of these settings produce what can only be called special effects. Select from what Canon terms Natural, Art Standard, Art Vivid, Art Bold, or Art Embossed. Note that these effects are *added* to the settings of any Picture Style currently in use.

- **Continuous HDR.** Choose 1 Shot Only if you plan to take just a single HDR exposure and want the feature disabled automatically thereafter, or Every Shot to continue using HDR mode for all subsequent exposures until you turn it off.

- **Auto Image Align.** HDR images are ideally produced with the camera on a tripod, in order to reduce the ghosting effects from a series of pictures that each aren't perfectly aligned with the other. You can choose Enable to have the camera attempt to align all three HDR exposures, or select Disable when using a tripod. The success of the automatic alignment will vary, depending on the shutter speed used (higher is better), and the amount of camera movement (less is better!)

- **Save Source Images.** When the 7D II has finished creating its HDR image from your three shots, you can choose to save all the images on your memory card (so you can manually combine them later or perform other manipulations using your image editor). Or, you can elect to save your final HDR image only. You might prefer that choice to save card space, reduce the number of images you won't be using anyway, or if shooting a lot of HDR and are confident that the camera's results will suit your needs.

SPECIAL HDR EFFECTS

The Effect parameters generate five different special effects (see **Figure 4.19**):

- ⊙ **Natural.** Provides the most useful range of highlight and shadow details.

- ⊙ **Art Standard.** Offers a great deal of highlight and shadow detail, but with lower overall contrast and outlines accentuated, making the image look more like a painting. Saturation, bold outline, and brightness are adjusted to the default levels, and tonal range is lower in contrast.

- ⊙ **Art Vivid.** Similar to Art Standard, but saturation is boosted to produce richer colors, and the bold outlines not as strong, producing a poster-like effect.

- ⊙ **Art Bold.** Even higher saturation than Art Vivid, with emphasized edge transitions, producing what Canon calls an "oil painting" effect.

- ⊙ **Art Embossed.** Reduces saturation, darker tones, and lower contrast, and gives the image a faded, aged look. The edge transitions are brighter or darker to emphasize them.

Figure 4.19

Top row (left to right): Natural, Art Standard, Art Vivid; bottom row: Art Bold, Art Embossed.

Bracketing and Merge to HDR

HDR (high dynamic range) photography is, at the moment, an incredibly popular fad. There are even entire books that do nothing but tell you how to shoot HDR images. If you aren't familiar with the technique, HDR involves shooting two or three or more images at different bracketed exposures, giving you an "underexposed" version with lots of detail in highlights that would otherwise be washed out; an "overexposed" rendition that preserves detail in the shadows; and several intermediate shots. These are combined to produce a single image that has an amazing amount of detail throughout the scene's entire tonal range.

I call this technique a fad because the reason it exists in the first place is due to a (temporary, I hope) defect in current digital camera sensors. It's presently impossible to capture the full range of brightness that we perceive; digital cameras, including the EOS 7D Mark II, can't even grab the full range of brightness that *film* can see.

But as the megapixel race slows down, sensor designers have already begun designing capture electronics that have larger density (dynamic) ranges, and cameras like the 7D II with its HDR Backlight Control feature, will eventually produce images similar to what we're getting now with HDR manipulation in image editors.

When you're using Merge to HDR Pro, a feature found in Adobe Photoshop (similar functions are available in other programs, including the Mac/PC utility Photomatix [www.hdrsoft.com; free to try, $99 to buy]), you'd take several pictures. As I mentioned earlier, one would be exposed for the shadows, one for the highlights, and perhaps one for the midtones. Then, you'd use the Merge to HDR command (or the equivalent in other software) to combine all of the images into one HDR image that integrates the well-exposed sections of each version. You can use the EOS 7D Mark II's bracketing feature to produce those images.

The next steps show you how to combine the separate exposures into one merged high dynamic range image. The sample images in

Figure 4.20, left, show the results you can get from a four-shot (manually) bracketed sequence.

The images should be as identical as possible, except for exposure. So, as with HDR mode, it's a good idea to mount the 7D II on a tripod, use a remote release, and take all the exposures at once. Just follow these steps:

1. **Set up the camera.** Mount the 7D II on a tripod.

2. **Choose an f/stop.** Set the camera for Manual exposure and select an aperture that will provide a correct exposure at your initial settings for the series of manually bracketed shots. *And then leave this adjustment alone!* You don't want the aperture to change for your series, as that would change the depth-of-field. You want the 7D II to adjust exposure *only* using the shutter speed.

3. **Choose manual focus.** You don't want the focus to change between shots, so set the 7D II to manual focus, and carefully focus your shot.

4. **Choose RAW exposures.** Set the camera to take RAW files, which will give you the widest range of tones in your images.

5. **Take your bracketed set.** Press the button on the remote (or carefully press the shutter release or use the self-timer) and take the set of bracketed exposures, adjusting the shutter speed manually. Try spacing your shots one f/stop apart.

6. **Continue with the Merge to HDR Pro steps listed next.** You can also use a different program, such as Photomatix, if you know how to use it.

The next section shows you how to combine the separate exposures into one merged high dynamic range image. Just follow these steps:

1. **Copy your images to your computer.** If you use an application to transfer the files to your computer, make sure it does not make any adjustments to brightness, contrast, or exposure. You want the real raw information for Merge to HDR Pro to work with.

2. **Activate Merge to HDR Pro.** Choose File > Automate > Merge to HDR Pro.

3. **Select the photos to be merged.** Use the Browse feature to locate and select your photos to be merged. You'll note a checkbox that can be used to automatically align the images if they were not taken with the camera mounted on a rock-steadysupport. This will adjust for any slight movement of the camera that might have occurred when you changed exposure settings.

4. **Choose parameters (optional).** The first time you use Merge to HDR Pro, you can let the program work with its default parameters. Once you've played with the feature a few times, you can read the Adobe help files and learn more about the options than I can present in this non-software-oriented camera guide.

5. **Click OK.** The merger begins.

6. **Save.** Once HDR merge has done its thing, save the file to your computer.

If you do everything correctly, you'll end up with a photo like the one shown in **Figure 4.20**, right.

Figure 4.20

Four bracketed photos should look like this (left.) You'll end up with an extended dynamic range photo like this one (right.)

What if you don't have the opportunity, inclination, or skills to create several images at different exposures, as described? If you shoot in RAW format, you can still use Merge to HDR, working with a *single* original image file. What you do is import the image into Photoshop several times, using Adobe Camera Raw to create multiple copies of the file at different exposure levels.

For example, you'd create one copy that's too dark, so the shadows lose detail, but the highlights are preserved. Create another copy with the shadows intact and allow the highlights to wash out. Then, you can use Merge to HDR to combine the two and end up with a finished image that has the extended dynamic range you're looking for. (This concludes the image-editing portion of the chapter. We now return you to our alternate sponsor: photography.)

Fixing Exposures with Histograms

Your 7D II's histograms are a simplified display of the numbers of pixels at each of 256 brightness levels, producing an interesting mountain range effect. When reviewing an image during playback, you can press the INFO button until the display similar to the one shown in **Figure 4.21** appears. There are two different histograms available during playback, either or both can be displayed at one time. The two are both shown at right in **Figure 4.21**. The top histogram in the figure shows the brightness (luminance) values for your image while the bottom histogram shows separate values for the red, green, and blue channels that make up a color image.

In the Histogram Display entry of the Playback 3 menu, you can choose whether the brightness or RGB histogram is displayed at the top of the screen. It will be shown along with other data, such as exposure mode, ISO, white balnce, shutter speed and aperture. You can use the multi-selector to scroll the display down to show the alternate histogram display, as I've done for the figure.

Although separate charts may be provided for brightness and the red, green, and blue channels, when you first start using histograms, you'll want to concentrate on the brightness histogram, so I recommend setting it as the primary histogram display. The 7D II also provides a "live" histogram on the screen when using Live View mode.

Each vertical line in a histogram graph represents the number of pixels in the image for each brightness value, from 0 (black) on the left to 255 (white) on the right. The vertical axis measures that number of pixels at each level.

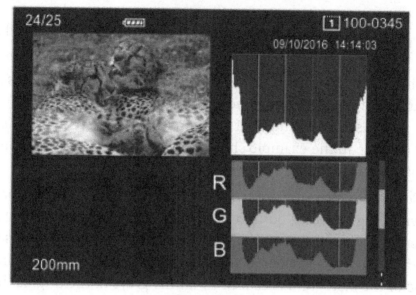

Figure 4.21

Playback display, with luminance histogram (top right);and with red, green, and blue histograms (bottom right.)

Histograms and Contrast

Although histograms are most often used to fine-tune exposure, you can glean other information from them, such as the relative contrast of the image. **Figure 4.22**, top, shows a histogram representing an image having normal contrast. In such an image, most of the pixels are spread across the image, with a healthy distribution of tones throughout the midtone section of the graph. That large peak at the right side of the graph represents all those light tones in the sky. A normal-contrast image you shoot may have less sky area, and less of a peak at the right side, but notice that very few pixels hug the right edge of the histogram, indicating that the lightest tones are not being clipped because they are off the chart.

Increasing the contrast of an image produces a histogram like the one shown in **Figure 4.22**, middle. In this case, the tonal range is now spread over the entire width of the chart, but, except for the bright sky (which you can see peaks at right), there is not much variation in the middle tones; the mountain "peaks" are not very high. When you stretch the grayscale in both directions like this, the darkest tones become darker (that may not be possible) and the lightest tones become lighter (ditto). In fact, shades that might have been gray before can change to black or white as they are moved toward either end of the scale.

The effect of increasing contrast may be to move some tones off either end of the scale altogether, while spreading the remaining grays over a smaller number of locations on the spectrum. That's exactly the case in the example shown. The number of possible tones is smaller and the image appears harsher.

Going the other way, with a lower-contrast image, like the one shown in **Figure 4.22**, bottom, the basic shape of the previous histogram will remain recognizable, but gradually will be compressed together to cover a smaller area of the gray spectrum. The squished shape of the histogram is caused by all the grays in the original image being represented by a limited number of gray tones in a smaller range of the scale.

Instead of the darkest tones of the image reaching into the black end of the spectrum and the whitest tones extending to the lightest end, there is a small gap at either end. Consequently, the blackest areas of the scene are now represented by a light gray, and the whites by a somewhat lighter gray. The overall contrast of the image is reduced. Because all the darker tones are actually a middle gray or lighter, the scene in this version of the photo appears lighter as well.

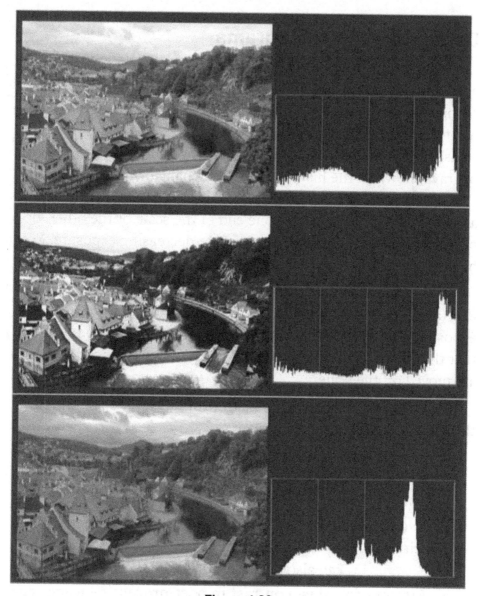

Figure 4.22

Top: The image has fairly normal contrast, even though there is a peak of light tones at the right side representing the sky. Middle: A high-contrast image produces a histogram in which the tones are spread out. Bottom: This low-contrast image has all the tones squished into one section of the grayscale.

Understanding Histograms

The important thing to remember when working with the histogram display in your 7D II is that changing the exposure does *not* change the contrast of an image. The curves illustrated in the previous three examples remain exactly the same shape when you increase or decrease exposure. I repeat: The proportional distribution of grays shown in the histogram doesn't change when exposure changes; it is neither stretched nor compressed. However, the tones as a whole are moved toward one end of the scale or the other, depending on whether you're increasing or decreasing exposure. You'll be able to see that in some illustrations that follow.

So, as you reduce exposure, tones gradually move to the black end (and off the scale), while the reverse is true when you increase exposure. The contrast within the image is changed only to the extent that some of the tones can no longer be represented when they are moved off the scale.

To change the *contrast* of an image, you must do one of three things:

- **Change the 7D II's contrast setting** using the menu system. You'll find these adjustments in your camera's Picture Styles, as explained in Chapter 11.

- **Use your camera's tone "booster."** The Highlight Tone Priority and Auto Lighting Optimizer features, described in Chapter 11, can also adjust contrast.

- **Attempt to adjust contrast in post-processing** using your image editor or RAW file converter. You may use features such as Levels or Curves (in Photoshop, Photoshop Elements, and many other image editors), or work with HDR software to cherry-pick the best values in shadows and highlights from multiple images.

- **Alter the contrast of the scene itself,** for example by using a fill light or reflectors to add illumination to shadows that are too dark.

Of the four of these, the last -- changing the contrast of the scene -- is the most desirable, because attempting to fix contrast by fiddling with the tonal values is unlikely to be a perfect remedy. However, adding a little contrast can be successful because you can discard some tones to make the image more contrasty. However, the opposite is much more difficult. An overly contrasty image rarely can be fixed, because you can't add information that isn't there in the first place.

What you *can* do is adjust the exposure so that the tones *that are already present in the scene* are captured correctly. **Figure 4.23**, top, shows the histogram for an image that is badly underexposed. You can guess from the shape of the histogram that many of the dark tones to the left of the graph have been clipped off. There's plenty of room on the right side for additional pixels to reside without having them become overexposed. So, you can increase the exposure (either by changing the f/stop or shutter speed, or by adding an EV value) to produce the corrected histogram shown in **Figure 4.23**, middle.

Conversely, if your histogram looks like the one shown in **Figure 4.23**, bottom, with bright tones pushed off the right edge of the chart, you have an overexposed image, and you can correct it by reducing exposure. In addition to the histogram, the 7D II has its Highlight Alert option (found in the Playback 3 menu), which, when activated, shows areas that are overexposed with flashing tones (often called "blinkies") in the review screen. Depending on the importance of this "clipped" detail, you can adjust exposure or leave it alone. For example, if all the dark-coded areas in the review are in a background that you care little about, you can forget about them and not change the exposure, but if such areas appear in facial details of your subject, you may want to make some adjustments.

Figure 4.23

Top: A histogram of an underexposed image may look like this. Middle: Adding exposure will produce a histogram like this one. Bottom: A histogram of an overexposed image will show clipping at the right side.

In working with histograms, your goal should be to have all the tones in an image spread out between the edges, with none clipped off at the left and right sides. Underexposing (to preserve highlights) should be done only as a last resort, because retrieving the underexposed shadows in your image editor will frequently increase the noise, even if you're working with RAW files. A better course of action is to expose for the highlights, but, when the subject matter makes it practical, fill in the shadows with additional light, using reflectors, fill flash, or other techniques rather than allowing them to be seriously underexposed.

The more you work with histograms, the more useful they become. One of the first things that histogram veterans notice is that it's possible to overexpose one channel even if the overall exposure appears to be correct. For example, flower photographers soon discover that it's really, really difficult to get a good picture of a rose. The exposure and luminance histogram may look okay -- but there's no detail in the rose's petals. Looking at the RGB histograms can show why: the red channel is probably blown out. If you look at the red histogram, you'll probably see a peak at the right edge that indicates that highlight information has been lost. In fact, the green channel may be blown, too, and so the green parts of the flower also lack detail. Only the blue channel's histogram would typically be entirely contained within the boundaries of the chart, and, on first glance, the white luminance histogram at top of the column of graphs seems fairly normal.

Any of the primary channels, red, green, or blue, can blow out all by themselves, although bright reds seem to be the most common problem area. More difficult to diagnose are overexposed tones in one of the "in-between" hues on the color wheel. Overexposed yellows (which are very common) will be shown by blowouts in *both* the red and green channels. Too-bright cyans will manifest as excessive blue and green highlights, while overexposure in the red and blue channels reduces detail in magenta colors. As you gain experience, you'll be able to see exactly how anomalies in the RGB channels translate into poor highlights and murky shadows.

The only way to correct for color channel blowouts is to reduce exposure. As I mentioned earlier, you might want to consider filling in the shadows with additional light to keep them from becoming too dark when you decrease exposure. In practice, you'll want to monitor the red channel most closely, followed by the blue channel, and slightly decrease exposure to see if that helps. Because of the way our eyes perceive color, we are more sensitive to variations in green, so green channel blowouts are less of a problem, unless your main subject is heavily colored in that hue. If you plan on photographing a frog hopping around on your front lawn, you'll want to be extra careful to preserve detail in the green channel, using bracketing or other exposure techniques outlined in this chapter.

While you can often recover poorly exposed photos in your image editor, your best bet is to arrive at the correct exposure in the camera, minimizing the tweaks that you have to make in post-processing.

Chapter 5

Mastering the Mysteries of Autofocus

Getting the right exposure is one of the foundations of a great photograph, but a lot more goes into a compelling shot than good tonal values. A sharp image, proper white balance, good color, and other factors all can help elevate your image from good to exceptional. One of the most important and, sometimes, the most frustrating aspects of shooting with a highly automated -- yet fully adjustable -- camera like the 7D II is achieving sharp focus. Your camera has lots of AF controls and options and new users or veterans alike can quickly become confused. In this chapter, I'm going to clear up the mysteries of autofocus and show you exactly how to use your 7D II's AF features to their fullest. I'll even tell you when to abandon the autofocus system and turn to the ancient art of manual focus, too.

This chapter concentrates (or focuses, if you will) on the techniques and technology of autofocus, so you'll understand how AF works, and how to choose the best options for particular types of scenes. If you want a greater understanding of individual menu entries and how to use them, you'll find that information in the menu section of this book, specifically Chapter 9, which details each and every entry in the five AF menu screens.

The Canon 7D Mark II's autofocus system is quite complex, and diverging to discuss every single menu entry while simultaneously trying to explain AF techniques would result in a meandering 100-page chapter that might make a confusing topic even more confusing. By separating technique from menu nuts-and-bolts you should be able to master the mysteries of autofocus more quickly.

How Focus Works

This section describes the differences between contrast detection and phase detection autofocus, and details how linear and cross-type AF sensors work in the 7D II's advanced focusing system. Even those who are familiar with these concepts should still read this section carefully, because Canon has made some revolutionary changes in AF with the introduction of its Dual Pixel CMOS AF sensor design in which every single pixel is split into two photodiodes that can be used to provide advanced autofocus features in live view and movie modes. You'll find the nitty-gritty of selecting AF modes and AF areas starting with the section headed "Working with the AF System."

Although Canon added autofocus capabilities in the 1980s, back in the day of film cameras, prior to that focusing was always done manually. Honest. Even though viewfinders were bigger and brighter than they are today, special focusing screens, magnifiers, and other gadgets were often used to help the photographer achieve correct focus. Imagine what it must have been like to focus manually under demanding, fast-moving conditions such as sports photography.

Manual focusing was problematic because our eyes and brains have poor memory for correct focus, which is why your eye doctor must shift back and forth between sets of lenses and ask "Does that look sharper -- or was it sharper before?" in determining your correct prescription. Similarly, manual focusing involves jogging the focus ring back and forth as you go from almost in focus, to sharp focus, to almost focused again. The little clockwise and counterclockwise arcs decrease in size until you've zeroed in on the point of correct focus. What you're looking for is the image with the most contrast between the edges of elements in the image.

The camera also looks for these differences between pixels to determine relative sharpness. There are two ways that sharp focus is determined, *contrast detection* and *phase detection*. To get the most from your camera, you really need to understand both. We'll start with the easier of the two: contrast detection.

Contrast Detection

Contrast detection is a slower mode and was used exclusively by Canon dSLRs in live view and movie modes until very recently, when Canon added a small number of special pixels to the sensor of cameras like the 7D II that allowed a type of phase detection autofocus. The new Dual Pixel CMOS AF used by the Canon 7D Mark II is a great leap forward, as I'll explain later in this chapter. To appreciate the innovation, you need to understand *traditional* contrast detection first.

Contrast detection is a slower mode and used because, to allow live viewing of the sensor image, the camera's mirror has to be flipped up out of the way so that the illumination from the lens can continue through the open shutter to the sensor. Your view through the viewfinder is obstructed, of course, and there is no partially silvered mirror to reflect some light down to the autofocus sensors. So, an alternate means of autofocus must be used, and that method is *contrast detection.* In live view and when shooting movies, focus must be achieved either manually (with the live view on the color LCD monitor as a focusing screen), or, with many earlier cameras, automatically using contrast detection with the image on the sensor.

Contrast detection is easier to understand and is illustrated by **Figure 5.1**, which uses an extreme enlargement of a shot of some wood siding (actually a 19th century outhouse). At top in the figure, the transitions between pixels are soft and blurred. When the image is brought into focus (bottom), the transitions are sharp and clear. Although this example is a bit exaggerated so you can see the results on the printed page, it's easy to understand that when maximum contrast in a subject is achieved, it can be deemed to be in sharp focus.

This type of contrast detection is used in live view and movie modes, even when Dual Pixel CMOS AF is also active. (In effect, you get two AF systems from one sensor.) Contrast detection works best with static subjects, because it is inherently slower and not well suited for tracking moving objects. Contrast detection works less well than phase detection in dim light, because its accuracy is determined by its ability to detect variations in brightness and contrast. You'll find that contrast detection works better with faster lenses, too, because larger lens openings admit more light that can be used by the sensor to measure contrast.

Figure 5.1

Focus in contrast detection mode evaluates the increase in contrast in the edges of subjects, starting with a blurry image (top) and producing a sharp, contrasty image (bottom).

Phase Detection

Like all digital SLRs that use an optical viewfinder and mirror system to preview an image (that is, when not in live view mode), the Canon EOS 7D II calculates focus using what is called a *phase detection* system. The system used in the Mark II is called a *high-density reticular* autofocus system. It's high density because there are now 65 different AF sensors, and reticular just means that the AF pattern forms a network.

Parts of the image from two opposite sides of the lens are directed down to the floor of the camera's mirror box, where an autofocus sensor array resides; the rest of the illumination from the lens bounces upward toward the optical viewfinder system and the autoexposure sensors. **Figure 5.2** is a wildly over-simplified illustration that may help you visualize what is happening.

SIMPLIFICATION MADE OVERLY SIMPLE

To reduce the complexity of the diagram, it doesn't show the actual path of the light passing through the lens, as it converges to the point of focus. That point is either the viewfinder screen when the mirror is down or the sensor plane when the mirror is flipped up and the shutter has opened. Nor does it show the path of the light directed to the autoexposure sensor. Only two of the pairs of autofocus microlenses are shown, and greatly enlarged so you can see their approximate position. All we're concerned about here is how light reaches the autofocus sensor.

As light emerges from the rear element of the lens, most of it is reflected upward toward the focusing screen, where the relative sharp focus (or lack of it) is displayed (and which can be used to evaluate manual focus). It then bounces off two more reflective surfaces in the pentaprism (in the 7D II; other cameras may use a less expensive and less bright *pentamirror* system instead) emerging at the optical viewfinder correctly oriented left/right and up/down. (The image emerges from the lens reversed.) Some of the illumination is directed to the autoexposure sensor at the top of the pentaprism housing.

A small portion of the illumination passes through the partially silvered center of the main mirror, and is directed downward to the autofocus sensor array, which includes 65 separate autofocus "detectors." The illumination arrives from opposite sides of the lens surface and is directed through separate microlenses, producing two half-images. These images are compared with each other, much like (actually, *exactly* like) a two-window rangefinder used in surveying, weaponry, and non-SLR cameras like the venerable Leica M film models.

When the image is out of focus -- or out of phase -- as in **Figure 5.3** (top), the two halves, each representing a slightly different view from opposite sides of the lens, don't line up. Sharp focus is achieved when the images are "in phase," and aligned, as in **Figure 5.3** (bottom).

As with any rangefinder-like function, accuracy is better when the "base length" between the two images is larger. (Think back to your high-school trigonometry; you could calculate a distance more accurately when the separation between the two points where the angles were measured was greater.) For that reason, phase detection autofocus is more accurate with larger (wider) lens openings than with smaller lens openings, and may not work at all when the f/stop is smaller than f/5.6 or f/8. Obviously, the "opposite" edges of the lens opening are farther apart with a lens having an f/2.8 maximum aperture than with one that has a smaller, f/5.6 maximum f/stop, and the base line is much longer. The 7D II is able to perform these comparisons and then move the lens elements directly to the point of correct focus very quickly, in milliseconds.

Unfortunately, while the 7D II's focus system finds it easy to measure degrees of apparent focus at each of the focus points in the viewfinder, it doesn't really know with any certainty *which* object should be in sharpest focus. Is it the closest object? The subject in the center? Something lurking *behind* the closest subject? A person standing over at the side of the picture? Many of the techniques for using autofocus effectively involve telling the EOS 7D II exactly what it should be focusing on, by choosing a focus zone or by allowing the camera to choose a focus zone for you. I'll address that topic shortly.

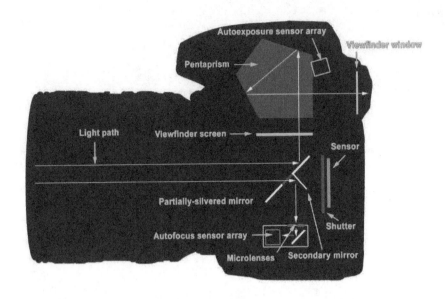

Figure 5.2

Part of the light is bounced downward to the autofocus sensor array, which uses phase detection to calculate sharp focus.

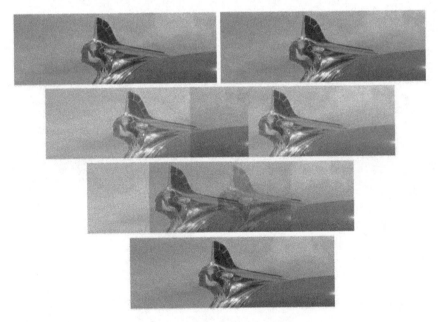

Figure 5.3

In phase detection, parts of an image are split in two and compared. When the image is in focus, the two halves of the image align, as with a rangefinder.

Dual Pixel CMOS AF

Now that you understand contrast and phase detection, you can appreciate the miracle that is Canon's Dual Pixel CMOS AF system. Used in live view mode while shooting stills and movies, it works much more quickly than the camera's more traditional contrast detection system.

However, an array of special pixels, which cover 80 percent of the frame horizontally and vertically, provide the same type of split-image rangefinder phase detection AF that is available when using the optical viewfinder. The most important aspect of the system is that it doesn't rob the camera of any imaging resolution. It would have been possible to place AF sensors *between* the pixels used to capture the image, but that would leave the sensor with less area with which to capture light. Keep in mind that CMOS sensors, unlike earlier CCD sensors, have more on-board circuitry which already consumes some of the light-gathering area. Microlenses are placed above each photosensitive site to focus incoming illumination on the sensor and to correct for the oblique angles from which some photons may approach the imager. (Older lenses, designed for film, are the worst offenders in terms of emitting light at severely oblique angles; newer "digital" lenses do a better job of directing photons onto the sensor plane with a less "slanted" approach.)

With the Dual Pixel CMOS AF system, the *same* photosites capture both image and autofocus information. Each pixel is divided into two photodiodes, facing left and right when the camera is held in horizontal orientation (or above and below each other in vertical orientation; either works fine for autofocus purposes). Each pair functions as a separate AF sensor, allowing a special integrated circuit to process the raw autofocus information before sending it on to the 7D II's digital image processor, which handles both AF and image capture. For the latter, the information grabbed by *both* photodiodes is combined, so that the full photosensitive area of the sensor pixel is used to capture the image.

While traditional contrast detection frequently involves frustrating "hunting" as the camera continually readjusts the focus plane trying to find the position of maximum contrast, adding Dual Pixel CMOS AF phase detection allows the 7D II to focus smoothly, which is important for speed, and essential when shooting movies (where all that hunting is unfortunately captured for posterity). Movie Servo AF tracking is improved, allowing shooting movies of subjects in motion. The system works with (at this writing) more than 100 different lenses, both current and previously available optics, and works especially well with lenses that have speedy USM or STM motors.

Cross-Type Focus Point

I'll explain more about focusing in live view and movie modes in Chapter 13. We're going to explore one special aspect of the optical viewfinder's AF system next. So far, we've only looked at focus sensors that calculate focus in a single direction. **Figure 5.4** (top left and right) illustrates a horizontally oriented linear focus sensor evaluating a subject that is made up, predominantly, of vertical lines. But what does such a sensor do when it encounters a subject that isn't conveniently aligned at right angles to the sensor array? You can see the problem in **Figure 5.4** (bottom left), which pictures the same weathered wood siding rotated 90 degrees. The horizontal grain of the wood isn't divided as neatly by the split image, so focusing using phase detection is more difficult. The lines in the grain don't cross the AF sensor at right angles any more.

You can see the "solution" at bottom right in **Figure 5.4**, in the form of a vertical linear sensor, which does a better job of interpreting horizontal lines. By mixing both types in a focusing system, the vertical sensors could detect differences in horizontal lines, while the horizontal sensors took care of the vertical lines. Both varieties are equally adept at handling *diagonal* lines, which crossed each type of line sensor at a 45-degree angle.

I created **Figure 5.4** to illustrate the "rangefinder" concept behind phase detection AF sensors. In practice, these sensors consist of an *array* of lines and, in the 7D II, none of them are strictly horizontal or vertical in orientation. Instead, the AF points are arranged as shown at left in **Figure 5.5**, using what are called *cross-type* sensors that form a plus-sign shape. All 65 AF points in the 7D II are potentially cross sensors (but may function as horizontal or vertical *line* sensors with some lenses, as described later in this chapter.) In cross sensor mode, such sensors are a merger of vertical and horizontal linear sensors, thus including sensitivity to horizontal, vertical, and lines at any diagonal angle. In lower light levels, with subjects that are moving, or with subjects that have no pattern and less contrast to begin with, the cross-type sensor not only works faster but can focus subjects that a horizontal- or vertical-only sensor can't handle at all.

All of these AF sensors function with lenses that have a maximum aperture of f/5.6 or larger (remember that smaller numbers equal larger apertures; f/4 is larger than f/5.6, for example.) So, if you're using a lens with an f/stop from, say, f/1.2 through f/5.6, all 65 AF points will function as cross-type sensors. If your maximum aperture is even larger – f/2.8 or greater – the *center* AF point will also use a pair of diagonal sensors, represented in red at right in Figure 5.5. Note that the baseline of these diagonal AF points is much larger than that of the green vertically/horizontally oriented sensors. Coupled with the larger baseline of lenses with, say, f/1.2 to f/2.8 maximum apertures, the center AF sensors are significantly more accurate than those at the other 64 locations in the frame.

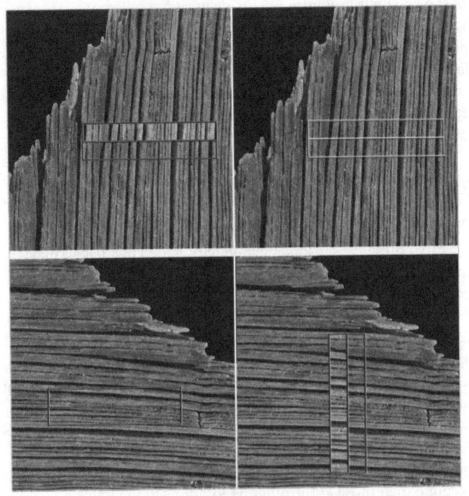

Figure 5.4

A horizontally-oriented sensor handles vertical lines easily (top.) A horizontal sensor has problems with subjects that have parallel horizontal lines (bottom left.) A vertically-oriented sensor is really needed for that type of subject (bottom right.)

Figure 5.5

Cross-type sensors can achieve sharp focus with horizontal, vertical, and diagonal line (left.) The center focus point (right) has additional diagonal sensors (in red) that function with lenses with an f/2.8 or larger maximum aperture.

Usable AF Points and Lens Groups

The 65 AF points in your camera all function as cross-type sensors with the majority of lenses that you are likely to own. However, if you are using certain slower lenses, or use a teleconverter to multiply your lens's focal length, some of the focus points revert to line sensor behavior, or may become totally unavailable for autofocus.

Canon makes sorting out how usable AF points are affected by your choice of lenses and lens+extender combinations easy, by classifying them in groups, labeled A through G. Pages 104-107 of Canon's 7D II manual lists the lenses available *at the time the 7D Mark II was introduced*, and assigns a group to each. If you own lenses introduced in 2014 or later, I urge you to visit the Canon web site for the definitive group for your particular optics.

The lens and lens/teleconverter combinations in the Group A and Group B categories all allow all 65 AF points to function as cross-type sensors, with Group A entries enabling the dual-cross center focus point. With Group C and Group D lenses, some or all of the AF points at the left and right flanks of the center array revert to horizontal line sensitive behavior. With Group E and Group F lenses, the two groups of ten points at the far left and right edges of the array are not available, and Group G lens combinations use only four AF points.

Figure 5.6 provides a quick reference to the function of each AF sensor within a given lens grouping. Dual cross, cross-type, horizontal, and vertical sensors are all represented. If a particular AF point does not appear in the a particular group, that sensor is not used and is not displayed as you shoot. Here's a more detailed listing of the AF point behaviors you can expect:

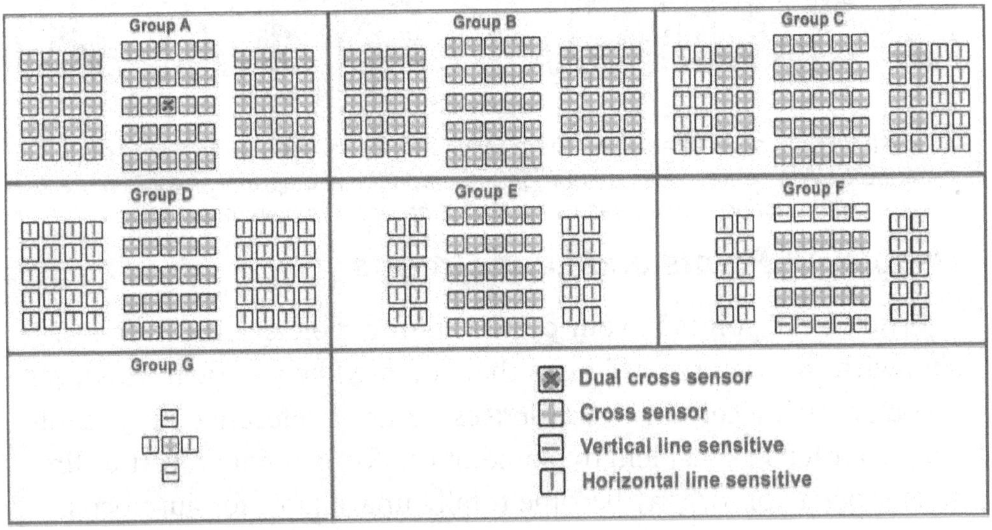

Figure 5.6

Focus point types for each of the seven lens groups defined by Canon.

- **Group A.** Autofocusing with all 65 points is possible, so you can choose any of the AF area selection modes (described later in this chapter). However, with all lenses in this group, the center AF point functions as a high-precision dual cross sensor *if that lens has a maximum aperture of f/2.8 or larger.* The other 64 AF points are cross-type sensors. (See **Figure 5.6** upper left.)

- **Group B.** This group of lens/lens+extender combinations is virtually identical in function to Group A, except that the center AF point serves as a conventional cross-type sensor, rather than a dual cross sensor. Autofocusing with all 65 points is possible, so you can choose any of the AF area selection modes. (See **Figure 5.6** upper center.)

◉ **Group C.** This group of lens/lens+extender combinations uses all 65 AF points, but the outermost 10 sensors on each side are sensitive only to horizontal lines, as you can see represented by orange lines in Figure 5.6 upper right. All AF area selection modes are available.

◉ **Group D.** This fourth group uses all 65 AF points like the previous three, but only the 25 points in the center function as cross-type sensors. The outer sensors all are sensitive only to horizontal lines. (See **Figure 5.6** center left.) All AF area selection modes are available.

◉ **Group E.** Only 45 AF points are used with this group of lens/lens+extender combinations. The center 25 function as cross-type sensors, while the sensors on either side of the center (20 in all) are sensitive only to horizontal lines. (See **Figure 5.6** center.) All AF area selection modes are available.

◉ **Group F.** Just 45 AF points are available with this next group of lens/lens+extender combinations. Only the 15 center sensors are of the cross type. The rows above and below the center function as are sensitive to vertical lines, while the two columns on either side of the center are sensitive to horizontal lines. All AF area selection modes are available.

◉ **Group G.** Only five AF points are available with this group. The center point functions as a cross-type sensor; the adjacent points above and below it are sensitive to vertical lines, while those to either side are sensitive to horizontal lines. The focus point cannot be selected manually, and AF is available only when Expand AF Area (five points) is enabled in the Select AF Area Selection Mode entry of the AF 4 menu (as described in Chapter 9.) It's the third icon from the left on the screen.*

As I'll explain in Chapter 9, you can also choose whether the camera uses all 65 points, 21 points, or just 9 points. Keep in mind that in any autofocus mode, the exact number of sensors and sensor types at work will vary depending on the lens and its maximum aperture.

Adding Circles of Confusion

You know that increased depth-of-field brings more of your subject into focus. But more depth-of-field also makes autofocusing (or manual focusing) more difficult in both phase detect and contrast detect (when focusing manually or in live view) because the contrast is lower between objects at different distances. This is an added factor *beyond* the rangefinder aspects of lens opening size in phase detection. An image that's dimmer is more difficult to focus with any type of focus system, phase detection, contrast detection, or manual focus.

So, focus with a 200mm lens (or zoom setting) may be easier in some respects than at a 28mm focal length (or zoom setting) because the longer lens has less apparent depth-of-field. By the same token, a lens with a maximum aperture of f/1.8 will be easier to autofocus (or manually focus) than one of the same focal length with an f/4 maximum aperture, because the f/4 lens has more depth-of-field *and* a dimmer view. That's yet another reason why lenses with a maximum aperture smaller than f/5.6 can give your 7D II's autofocus system fits -- increased depth-of-field joins forces with a dimmer image that's more difficult to focus using phase detection.

To make things even more complicated, many subjects aren't polite enough to remain still. They move around in the frame, so that even if the 7D II is sharply focused on your main subject, it may change position and require refocusing. An intervening subject may pop into the frame and pass between you and the subject you meant to photograph. You (or the 7D II) have to decide whether to lock focus on this new subject, or remain focused on the original subject. Finally, there are some kinds of subjects that are difficult to bring into sharp focus because they lack enough contrast to allow the 7D II's AF system (or our eyes) to lock in. Blank walls, a clear blue sky, or other subject matter may make focusing difficult.

If you find all these focus factors confusing, you're on the right track. Focus is, in fact, measured using something called a *circle of confusion*. An ideal image consists of zillions of tiny little points, which, like all points, theoretically have no height or width. There is perfect contrast between the point and its surroundings. You can think of each point as a pinpoint of light in a darkened room. When a given point is out of focus, its edges decrease in contrast and it changes from a perfect point to a tiny disc with blurry edges (remember, blur is the lack of contrast between boundaries in an image). (See **Figure 5.7**.)

Figure 5.7

When a pinpoint of light (left) goes out of focus, its blurry edges form a circle of confusion (center and right).

If this blurry disc -- the circle of confusion -- is small enough, our eye still perceives it as a point. It's only when the disc grows large enough that we can see it as a blur rather than a sharp point that a given point is viewed as out of focus. You can see, then, that enlarging an image, either by displaying it larger on your computer monitor or by making a large print, also enlarges the size of each circle of confusion. Moving closer to the image does the same thing. So, parts of an image that may look perfectly sharp in a 5 x 7-inch print viewed at arm's length, might appear blurry when blown up to 11 x 14 and examined at the same distance. Take a few steps back, however, and it may look sharp again.

To a lesser extent, the viewer also affects the apparent size of these circles of confusion. Some people see details better at a given distance and may perceive smaller circles of confusion than someone standing next to them. For the most part, however, such differences are small. Truly blurry images will look blurry to just about everyone under the same conditions.

Technically, there is just one plane within your picture area, parallel to the back of the camera (or sensor, in the case of a digital camera), that is in sharp focus. That's the plane in which the points of the image are rendered as precise points. At every other plane in front of or behind the focus plane, the points show up as discs that range from slightly blurry to extremely blurry until, as you can see in **Figure 5.8**, the out-of-focus areas become one large blur that de-emphasizes an unattractive textured white background.

In practice, the discs in many of these planes will still be so small that we see them as points, and that's where we get depth-of-field. Depth-of-field is just the range of planes that include discs that we perceive as points rather than blurred splotches. The size of this range increases as the aperture is reduced in size and is allocated roughly one-third in front of the plane of sharpest focus, and two-thirds behind it. The range of sharp focus is always greater behind your subject than in front of it.

Figure 5.8

The background is almost totally blurred, thanks to a wide f/stop.

Now that you understand the basics of how the 7D II's autofocus system works, it's time to jump into the actual settings and techniques you have at your disposal. To achieve tack-sharp focus every time, you'll need to master focus modes (*when* to evaluate a scene and lock in focus) and focus area selection (you or the camera decides *what* to focus on). The following sections concentrate on achieving focus when *not* using live view or movie-making modes; in other words, when you're framing a picture using the optical viewfinder window.

Focus Modes: When to Focus

Focus modes tell the camera *when* to evaluate and lock in focus. They don't determine *where* focus should be checked; that's the function of other autofocus features, such as AF area selection. Focus modes tell the camera whether to lock in focus once, say, when you press the shutter release halfway (or use some other control, such as the AF-ON button), or whether, once activated, the camera should continue tracking your subject and, if it's moving, adjust focus to follow it.

When using the optical viewfinder, the 7D II three AF modes: One-Shot AF (also known as single autofocus), AI Servo (continuous autofocus), and AI Focus AF (which switches between the two as appropriate). I'll explain all of these in more detail later in this section. (In live view mode, the AF modes are slightly different, as I'll explain in Chapter 11.) You can also manually focus.

Choosing the right autofocus mode and the way in which focus points are selected is your key to success. Using the wrong mode for a particular type of photography can lead to a series of pictures that are all sharply focused -- on the wrong subject. When I first started shooting sports with an autofocus dSLR, I covered one game alternating between shots of base runners and outfielders with pictures of a promising young pitcher (he will remain nameless, but his initials are CC Sabathia.) I shot the whole game from a position next to the third base dugout. The base runner and outfielder photos were great, because their backgrounds didn't distract the autofocus mechanism. But all my photos of the pitcher had the focus tightly zeroed in on the fans in the stands behind him. Because I was so caught up in the game and didn't review the pictures I had taken, I didn't know about my gaffe until I happened to take some time between innings to check out my images. A simple change, such as locking in focus or focus zone manually, or even manually focusing, would have done the trick.

To save battery power, your 7D II doesn't start to focus the lens until you partially depress the shutter release (or activate focus using the AF-ON button or other defined control.) But, autofocus isn't some mindless beast out there snapping your pictures in and out of focus with no feedback from you after you press that button. There are several settings you can modify that return at least a modicum of control to you. Your first decision should be whether you set the 7D II to One-Shot, AI Servo AF, or AI Focus AF. With the camera set for one of the non-auto modes, press the DRIVE-AF button and spin the Main Dial until the choice you want is displayed on the rear color LCD (if you've set the screen to display Shooting Functions) and LCD status panel (see **Figure 5.9**, left). (The AF/M switch on the lens must be set to AF before you can change autofocus mode.) Remember to press the INFO button, if necessary, to make the screen appear.

Manual Focus

With manual focus activated by sliding the AF/MF switch on the lens, your 7D II lets you set the focus yourself. There are some advantages and disadvantages to this approach. While your batteries will last longer in manual focus mode, it will take you longer to focus the camera for each photo, a process that can be difficult. Modern digital cameras, even dSLRs, depend so much on autofocus that the viewfinders of models that have less than full-frame-sized sensors are no longer designed for optimum manual focus. Pick up any old film camera (if you can find one) and you'll see a bigger, brighter viewfinder with a focusing screen that's a joy to focus on manually.

One-Shot AF

In this mode, also called *single autofocus*, focus is set once and remains at that setting until the button is fully depressed, taking the picture, or until you release the shutter button without taking a shot. This mode is best for subjects that are not moving around a great deal. So, for non-action photography, this setting is usually your best choice, as it minimizes out-of-focus pictures (at the expense of spontaneity). The drawback here is that you might not be able to take a picture at all while the camera is seeking focus; you're locked out until the autofocus mechanism is happy with the current setting. One-Shot AF/single autofocus is sometimes referred to as *focus priority* for that reason, although you can change the priority using the One-Shot AF Release Prior. option in the AF3 menu. Because of the small delay while the camera zeroes in on correct focus during focus priority operation, you might experience slightly more shutter lag. This mode uses less battery power than the other autofocus modes

When sharp focus is achieved, the selected focus point will flash red in the viewfinder (you can adjust whether the point flashes using the VF Display Illumination and AF Point During AI Servo AF options in the AF4 menu, and the focus confirmation icon at the lower right will appear (either within the frame or outside the frame at your option.) (I'll show you how to select these behaviors in Chapter 11.) If you're using Evaluative metering, the exposure will be locked at the same time. By keeping the shutter button depressed halfway, you'll find you can reframe the image while retaining the focus (and exposure) that's been set.

AI Servo AF

This mode, also known as *continuous autofocus* is the mode of choice for sports and other fast-moving subjects, and is often used with continuous shooting modes. With AI Servo AF, once the shutter release is partially depressed, the camera sets the focus on the point that's selected (by the camera or by you manually), but continues to monitor the subject, so that if it moves or you move, the lens will be refocused to suit. Focus and exposure aren't really locked until you press the shutter release down all the way to take the picture. You'll find that AI Servo AF produces the least amount of shutter lag of any autofocus mode: press the button and the camera fires. It also uses the most battery power, because the autofocus system operates as long as the shutter release button is partially depressed.

You'll often see continuous autofocus referred to as *release priority*, because that's the way it has been traditionally used. In that mode, if you press the shutter release down all the way while the system is refining focus, the camera will go ahead and take a picture, even if the image is slightly out of focus. However, you can specify the priority for the first image in a series, and, if you're shooting in continuous mode, for the second shot in a series. Select release priority, focus priority, or give equal weight to each. Use the AF 2 menu, described in Chapter 9.

AI Servo AF uses a technology called *predictive AF*, which allows the 7D II to calculate the correct focus if the subject is moving toward or away from the camera at a constant rate. It uses either the automatically selected AF point or the point you select manually to set focus. AI Servo AF's characteristics can be fine-tuned for particular types of subjects and scenes, called *cases*, as I'll explain later.

While the shutter button is often used to trigger both exposure lock and AF start, you can decouple exposure/focus (for back button focus) so that, say, the shutter release locks exposure, while the AF-ON button activates focus. Back button focus is described at the end of this chapter.

AI Focus AF

This setting is actually a combination of the first two. When selected, the camera focuses using One-Shot AF and locks in the focus setting. But, if the subject begins moving, it will switch automatically to AI Servo AF and change the focus to keep the subject sharp. AI Focus AF is a good choice when you're shooting a mixture of action pictures and less dynamic shots and want to use One-Shot AF when possible. The camera will default to that mode, yet switch automatically to AI Servo AF when it would be useful for subjects that might begin moving unexpectedly.

Setting the AF Area Selection Mode

You or the 7D II can select the AF point(s) to be used. There are six modes in which *you* select the initial point or zone of points (with variations on what additional points will also be used). The camera will start autofocus at that point, but may switch to other AF points as the subject moves. A seventh mode allows the camera to use all the usable points (up to 65 total) to select the initial focus point automatically.

You can quickly switch among any of the AF-area selection modes, and can specify the controls used to make the selection (with the AF Area Selection Method entry in the AF 4 menu, described in Chapter 9.)

If you've selected M-Fn Button as your control in that menu entry, then press the AF selection button on the upper-right corner of the camera's back panel, and then press the M-Fn button (on top of the camera next to the Main dial) *or* swivel the multi controller lever (concentric with the multi controller joystick) repeatedly.

If you've selected Main Dial as your control in the AF Area Selection Method entry, then press the AF selection button, and rotate the Main Dial *or* swivel the multi controller lever to switch among AF area selection modes. (In other words, the multi controller lever switch works with *either* type of control.

In either case, the available modes cycle on the screen for your selection (as shown at right in **Figure 5.9**.) If you generally use only a few of the seven available modes, Canon gives you the ability to "hide" the others that you do not use with the Select AF Area Selec. Mode entry in the AF4 menu. I'll show you how to do that, and describe additional options in the five AF menus in Chapter 9.

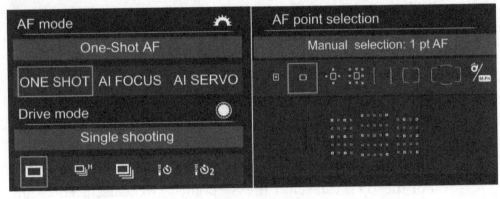

Figure 5.9

Choose an autofocus mode (left), or AF area selection mode (right).

Once you've selected one of the manual selection modes described below, you can change which of the focus points or zones the Canon EOS 7D II uses to calculate correct focus. There are several methods to set the focus point/zone in any of the modes that allow manual selection of the point or zone. Note that the number of individual points that appear will vary, depending on whether you've set the Selectable AF Point entry in the AF 4 menu to 65, 21, or 9 points. I'll show you how to do that, too, in Chapter 9. When you've chosen 21 or 9 points, all 65 points will be shown on the screen, but only 21 or 9 of them will be manually selectable.

Note: You can specify a frequently-used AF point by defining a Custom Control to instantly switch from the current AF point to the point you've registered previously. I'll explain this and other Custom Control options in Chapter 11.

Press the AF point selection button on the back of the camera, look through the viewfinder, and use the multi controller (to the right and below the viewfinder window) to move the focus point to the point or zone you want to use. Pressing the multi controller button inward will move the focus selection to the center AF point or zone.

Press the AF point selection button, look through the viewfinder, and use the Main Dial to move the focus point horizontally throw the available columns, and rotate the Quick Control Dial to move up or down among the available rows. In Zone AF modes, the Main Dial and Quick Control Dial change the zone in a looping sequence instead.

This last method does not work as expected if you've chosen Main Dial as your AF Selection Control. In that case, press the AF point selection button, look through the viewfinder, and use the multi controller to move the focus point/zone.

The next sections provide a description of the available AF Area modes. The first six allow manual selection of the initial focus point or zone, and are illustrated in **Figure 5.10**.

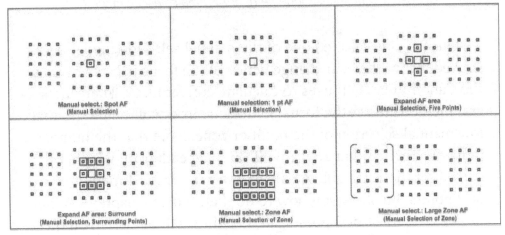

Figure 5.10

Focus area selection modes that allow manual selection of point or zone.

Manual Select.: Spot AF

In this mode, you can zero in and focus on the tiny area covered by a single spot in the 65-point focus array. Use the controls described earlier to move the highlighted spot to a different position within the entire available focus zone. This precision can be too much of a good thing, however; camera movement (as when shooting hand-held, especially with a front-heavy long lens), and subject movement can easily move the focus spot away from your primary subject. **Figure 5.11** shows the focus area in the center of the frame for simplicity; you can actually move it to another location.

This mode may be your best choice when you want to focus precisely on a subject that is surrounded by fine detail, as shown in the figure. The heron was not moving and my camera and 400mm lens were mounted on a sturdy tripod, so it was easy to place the focus spot exactly where I wanted it. Keep in mind that the portion of the sensor used to autofocus is not precisely represented by the rectangle shown in the viewfinder, so if you're focusing on, say, the near eye of a portrait subject turned at a 45-degree angle with a wide aperture, you might end up focusing on the bridge of their noise instead. Single-Point AF (Manual Selection) is not a good choice for moving subjects.

Figure 5.11

Single-Point Spot AF allowed focusing precisely on the heron, despite the surrounding detail.

Manual Selection: 1 pt AF

This mode uses the a slightly larger focus area than Single-Point Spot AF, and is more practical for scenes where you want to focus on a certain point, but your subject may be moving slowly. Position the active focus point with the controls, as described earlier. You can use Single-Point AF (Manual Selection) for everyday shooting where precision is needed, and the subject contains sufficient detail within the area covered by the sensor. If such a small area of your subject is a bit amorphous, you'll want to use one of the selection modes described next, which allow the AF system to take into account surrounding focus points as well as the manually selected point.

Expand AF Area

In this mode, the focus point you select is used, along with the points immediately above, below, and to either side of it (until the manually selected point reaches the edge of the array and one or more of the additional points scroll off). This mode is better for moving objects, like the pelican shown in **Figure 5.12**, because the larger effective zone makes it easier to track subjects that are moving within the frame. As the subject moves outside the area defined by the selected focus point, three to four of the surrounding focus points can pick up and track the movement. In One-Shot AF mode, the manually selected focus point and expanded point used will be displayed in the viewfinder.

Figure 5.12

A larger AF area with AF Point Expansion allows autofocus of moving subjects.

Expand AF Area: Surround

This mode is similar to the one above, except that the four points located diagonally in relation to the manually selected point are included in the focusing array. (See lower left in **Figure 5.10**, shown earlier.) It is slightly better for subjects that don't contain a lot of detail at the manually selected focus point, and the additional points surrounding the initial focus point improve your results. This mode is better for larger moving objects, even though it offers a bit less precision. As always, while the active points are shown in the center of the frame in **Figure 5.10**, you can move the active area around while looking through the viewfinder.

Manual Select.: Zone AF

This is a zone-oriented point selection method, in which the 65 AF points are divided into nine possible zones. When you move the focus "point" using the controls, you are actually simply switching from one entire zone to the next; all the points in a given zone are used to achieve focus. This mode works well when you know the approximate area where your subject will reside, and want to cover a particular zone. For **Figure 5.13**, I was panning to follow the movement of the gondola, and knew I would be keeping it in the lower-left corner of the frame, so that zone worked best for me.

Figure 5.13

The zone near the bottom left of the focus area was used for this shot.

Manual Select.: Large Zone AF

This is a zone-oriented point selection method, in which the 65 AF points are divided into just three possible zones, which are easy to visualize, as they constitute the left-most 20 points (five rows of four points), the right-most 20 points (five rows of four points), and the center 25 points (five rows of five points.)

This mode can be useful when your subject matter is large and in motion, because of all the manual selection modes it makes manually specifying where to focus very easy. There are only three to choose from, and you can switch between them very rapidly, say, as action is unfolding. **Figure 5.14**, a rodeo shot, provides an example of the sort of scene that can be used with these large zones, especially when you don't want to let the camera select the focus area using automatic selection (described next.)

Figure 5.14

It's easy to switch among three large zones rapidly.

Auto Selection: 65 pt AF

If you choose this mode, the camera will be able to use as many as 65 points (depending on how many are usable, as described earlier) to achieve focus. The 7D II will examine the scene and select any of the available points to calculate focus. It's a good choice for general-purpose shooting and action in the center of the scene.

In One-Shot AF focus mode, in most cases, focus will lock on the subject closest to the camera. Then, the AF points used to achieve focus -- from one to all 65 -- will be illuminated. In AI Servo AF mode, you can select the initial focus point manually, but the camera will use any of the others automatically as needed. The point(s) used will be highlighted.

Fine-Tuning Your Autofocus

The options available for the Canon EOS 7D Mark II's autofocus can be overwhelming at times, which is why I'm devoting two full chapters to explaining them – this one, and Chapter 9. If the modes and parameters described so far aren't enough, Canon allows you do some additional fine-tuning, as I'll describe in this section. You can select from six different configuration setups (which Canon calls "Cases"), each tailored for a specific type of shooting when using AI Servo AF. You are able to further tweak how each Case performs if the factory defaults don't suit you. One additional modification, AF Microadjustment (one or more of your lenses consistently focuses in front of or behind your actual subject) is performed very rarely (or never), and will be discussed in Chapter 9. The section that follows is devoted to the AF adjustments available in the AF 1 menu.

AF Configuration Tool

In the AF1 menu tab, you'll find six factory-defined Cases (which are, actually, quite typical autofocus situations) that have been set up to provide good results with a half-dozen different types of scenes when using AI Servo AF (continuous autofocus). Each of the Cases uses different combinations of settings for three different parameters:

- ◎ **Tracking sensitivity.** This determines how quickly the AF system switches to a new subject entering the focus area. Your choices are -2 (Locked On) to +2 (Responsive). Negative numbers allow you to retain focus on the original subject even if it briefly leaves the area covered by the focus points, making tracking easier. The drawback is that if the camera selects the wrong subject, there is a longer delay before the correct subject is captured. Positive numbers cause the AF system to more quickly switch to a new subject. However, such quick response can cause the camera to focus on the wrong subject.

- ◎ **Acceleration/deceleration tracking.** This parameter determines how the AF system responds to sudden acceleration, deceleration, or stopping. Your choices are 0 (for subjects that move at a constant speed) to 2 (for faster reactions to subjects that suddenly change speed). Lower values can cause the camera to be "fooled" if a subject that was moving consistently suddenly stops; focus may change to the position where the subject *would* have been if it'd kept moving. A higher value may cause inconsistent focus with subjects that move at a constant speed.

⊙ **AF point auto switching.** This setting determines how quickly the AF system changes from the current AF point to an adjacent one when the subject moves away from the current point, or an intervening object moves across the frame into the area interpreted by the current point. Your choices are 0 (switch more slowly so focus is stable, with slower tracking response) to 2 (switch to an adjacent point quickly). This parameter operates in 65 Point Auto Selection, Zone AF, and AF Point Expansion area selection modes.

You can adjust any of these three parameters for any Case (with the option of returning the Case to its default values later) by rotating the QCD and pressing SET to select it. I'll show you how to do that later in this section. You should use each Case extensively to get a feeling for how it operates before making any changes. First, check out the default behavior of each of the six Cases (see **Figure 5.15**):

⊙ **Case 1: Versatile multi purpose setting.** Use this as your default setting, as it works well with many moving subjects (and moving subject matter is why you selected AI Servo AF, isn't it?). Use with any type of action that isn't one of the special cases described next. It's good for some motor sports, many track meet events, and action that's moving toward or away from the camera.

⊙ **Case 2: Continue to track subject, ignoring possible obstacles.** This Case could be your mainstay for football games, because you can track a running back, receiver, or another player of interest without having focus disrupted when a referee, coach, or another player passes between you. The camera will delay refocusing on the new object long enough to resume following the original subject.

⊙ **Case 3: Instantly focus on subjects suddenly entering AF points.** This Case is ideal when you're photographing a relatively static scene in anticipation of a moving subject, such as

173

a runner, skier, or bicyclist entering the frame. You could, for example, frame the finish line of a horse race, and the 7D Mark II would instantly lock focus on the winning steed as it crosses the line (or perhaps several horses if one wins "by a nose").

- **Case 4: For subjects that accelerate or decelerate quickly.** Canon earmarks this one for motor sports, but I find that race cars often move predictably at relatively constant speeds. This Case is better for basketball and soccer, because you can have players racing toward you one instant, and crossing your field of view the next.

- **Case 5: For erratic subjects moving quickly in any direction.** This is my choice for hockey games and anything that involves skates -- as well as small children and pets. It's also excellent for that most difficult of subjects: birds in flight (often abbreviated to just BIF because photographers talk about the challenges of photographing pesky avians so frequently).

- **Case 6: For subjects that change speed and move erratically.** This works with 65 Point Auto Selection, Zone AF, and AF Point Expansion area selection modes. (In other words, it doesn't operate with Single-Point Spot AF or Single-Point AF manual selection modes.) I use this one for basketball, too, and you might try it with children and small pets to see if it works better for you than Case 5.

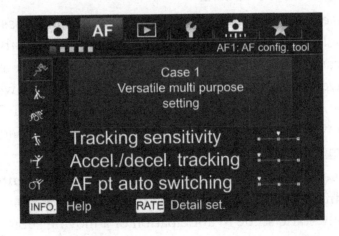

Figure 5.15

The AF 1 menu is used to select and adjust autofocus Cases.

Modifying Cases

To change the values of any of the six AF Cases, just follow these steps:

1. **Access menu.** Navigate to the AF 1 menu and rotate the QCD or use the multi controller joystick to highlight the Case you want to modify.

2. **Choose Detail Set.** Press the Rate button located to the left of the LCD. The Tracking Sensitivity parameter will be high-lighted.

3. **Select parameter to change.** Use the QCD or multi controller joystick to select the parameter you want to modify, and press SET.

4. **Make adjustment.** Use the QCD or multi controller joystick to move the indicator along the scale to the value you want.

5. **Confirm.** Press SET to confirm. Note that the default value for the Case you've modified will be noted with an additional, gray, indicator so you can tell at a glance that you've changed the factory settings.

6. **Exit.** Press MENU to exit, or press the Trash button to re-store that Case's settings to their defaults.

7. **Store in C1-C3** (Optional). It's probably smart to store your modified settings in one of the three User slots. You can, in effect, use the factory default Cases, plus additional sets of Cases you've created for specific shooting situations. You can register settings in the Set-up 4 menu, as described in Chapter 10.

Other AF Options

In addition to the Case adjustments in the AF 1 menu, you'll find additional adjustments available in AF 2, AF 3, AF 4, and AF 5. Most of these aren't used in day-to-day shooting, which is the case with the options explained in this chapter. Instead, the AF 2-AF 5 settings are those that you'll change once, or perhaps modify only once in awhile. Here are some of the most important, which you can explore in Chapter 9.

- ◉ **AF 2:** AI Servo Priority Release/Focus Priority
- ◉ **AF 3:** Use of electronic focus ring with certain lenses; AF-Assist Beam Enable/Disable; One-Shot AF Release Priority
- ◉ **AF 4:** You can tell the Mark II how to behave when AF is impossible; which AF points can be selected; choose an AF area selection mode; whether the M-Fn or Main Dial is used to choose AF area selection method; and whether AF points are linked to the camera's vertical or horizontal orientation.
- ◉ **AF 5:** Whether AF point selection wraps around at boundaries; how AF points are displayed during focus; viewfinder focus point and AF status display; and Autofocus micro adjustment.

Back-button Focus

Once you've been using your camera for a while, you'll invariably encounter the terms *back focus* and *back-button focus*, and wonder if they are good things or bad things. Actually, they are *two different things*, and are often confused with each other. *Back focus* is a bad thing, and occurs when a particular lens consistently autofocuses on a plane that's *behind* your desired subject. This malady may be found in some of your lenses, or all your optics may be free of the defect. The good news is that if the problem lies in a particular lens (rather than a camera misadjustment that applies to *all* your lenses), it can be fixed. I'll show you how to do that using the AF Microadjustment feature in Chapter 7.

Back-button focus, on the other hand, is a tool you can use to separate two functions that are commonly locked together -- exposure and autofocus -- so that you can lock in exposure while allowing focus to be attained at a later point, or vice versa. It's a *good* thing, although using back-button focus effectively may require you to unlearn some habits and acquire new ways of coordinating the action of your fingers.

As you have learned, the default behavior of your Canon 7D Mark II is to set both exposure and focus (when AF is active) when you press the shutter release down halfway. When using One-Shot mode, that's that: both exposure and focus are locked and will not change until you release the shutter button, or press it all the way down to take a picture and then release it for the next shot. In AI Servo mode, exposure is locked and focus is set when you press the shutter release halfway, but the camera will continue to refocus if your subject moves for as long as you hold down the shutter button halfway. Focus isn't locked until you press the button down all the way to take the picture. In AI Focus AF mode, the camera will start out in One-Shot mode, but switch to AI Servo AF if your subject begins moving.

What back-button focus does is *decouple* or separate the two actions. You can retain the exposure lock feature when the shutter is pressed halfway, but assign autofocus *start* and/or autofocus *lock* to a different button. So, in practice, you can press the shutter button halfway, locking exposure, and reframe the image if you like (perhaps you're photographing a backlit subject and want to lock in exposure on the foreground, and then reframe to include a very bright background as well).

But, in this same scenario, you *don't* want autofocus locked at the same time. Indeed, you may not want to start AF until you're good and ready, say, at a sports venue as you wait for a ballplayer to streak into view in your viewfinder. With back-button focus, you can lock exposure on the spot where you expect the athlete to be, and activate AF at the moment your subject appears. The 7D II gives you a great deal of flexibility, both in the choice of which button to use for AF, and the behavior of that button. You can *start* autofocus, *lock* autofocus at a button press, or *lock it while holding the button*. That's where the learning of new habits and mind-finger coordination comes in. You need to learn which back-button focus techniques work for you, and when to use them.

Back-button focus lets you avoid the need to switch from One-Shot to AI Servo AF when your subject begins moving unexpectedly. Nor do you need to use AI Focus AF mode and *hope* the camera switches from One-Shot to AI Servo appropriately. You retain complete control. It's great for sports photography when you want to activate autofocus precisely based on the action in front of you. It also works for static shots. You can press and release your designated focus button, and then take a series of shots using the same focus point. Focus will not change until you once again press your defined back button.

Want to focus on a spot that doesn't reside under one of the camera's 65 focus areas? Use back-button focus to zero in focus on that location, then reframe. Focus will not change. Don't want to miss an important shot at a wedding or a photojournalism assignment? If you're set to *focus priority* your camera may delay taking a picture until the focus is optimum; in *release priority* there may still be a slight delay. With back-button focus you can focus first, and wait until the decisive moment to press the shutter release and take your picture. The 7D II will respond immediately and not bother with focusing at all.

Back-button focus can also save battery power. Ordinarily, your IS lens will begin adjusting for camera shake as soon as you begin focusing. Constantly refocusing can consume a lot of power. With back-button focus, the IS isn't switched on until you actually decide to autofocus on your subject.

Activating Back-button Focus

You'll find the key control for enabling back-button focus at the very bottom of the Custom Function 3 menu, Custom Controls. Just follow these steps:

1. **Access Custom Functions.** Press the MENU button and use the Main Dial to navigate to the Custom Function menus, located between the Setup (wrench icon) and My Menu (star icon) tabs.

2. **Select Custom Controls.** When you reach the Custom Fn. 3 screen, rotate the Quick Control Dial to highlight the Custom Controls enter, and press SET.

3. **Choose Shutter Button function.** Highlight the top entry, "Shutter Butt. Half-Press" and press SET.

4. **Set Shutter Button to metering only.** A screen will appear with three choices (from left to right): Metering and AF Start; Metering Start; and AE lock (white button is pressed.) The default value is Metering and AF Start, which you want to uncouple. Select Metering Start instead, and press SET to confirm.

5. **Set AF-ON button to activate autofocus.** You'll be returned to the Custom Controls menu. Scroll down to the second entry, AF-ON Button and press SET. Select Metering and AF Start (if it's not already selected; it's the default value.) Press Set to confirm.

6. **Exit.** Press the MENU button twice to exit (or just tap the shutter release button.

7. **Use back-button focus.** Henceforth, press the shutter release halfway to meter, and all the way to take a picture, and press the AF-ON button to activate autofocus.

Chapter 6

Advanced Shooting

You can happily spend your entire shooting career using the techniques and features already explained in this book. Great exposures, sharp pictures, and creative compositions are all you really need to produce great shot after great shot. But, those with enough interest in getting the most out of their Canon EOS 7D Mark II who buy this book probably will be interested in going beyond those basics to explore some of the more advanced techniques and capabilities of the camera. Capturing the briefest instant of time, transforming common scenes into the unusual with lengthy time exposures, and working with new tools like Wi-Fi are all tempting avenues for exploration. So, in this chapter, I'm going to offer longer discussions of some of the more advanced techniques and capabilities that I like to put to work.

Continuous Shooting

The Canon EOS 7D Mark II's continuous shooting mode reminds me how far digital photography has brought us. The first accessory I purchased when I worked as a sports photographer some years ago was a motor drive for my film SLR. It enabled me to snap off a series of shots in rapid succession, which came in very handy when a fullback broke through the line and headed for the end zone. Even a seasoned action photographer can miss the decisive instant when a crucial block is made, or a baseball superstar's bat shatters and pieces of cork fly out. Continuous shooting simplifies taking a series of pictures, either to ensure that one has more or less the exact moment you want to capture or to capture a sequence that is interesting as a collection of successive images.

The 7D Mark II's "motor drive" capabilities are, in many ways, much superior to what you get with a film camera. For one thing, a motor-driven film camera can eat up film at an incredible pace, which is why many of them are used with cassettes that hold hundreds of feet of film stock. At three frames per second (typical of film cameras), a short burst of a few seconds can burn up as much as half of an ordinary 36 exposure roll of film. Digital cameras, in contrast, have reusable "film," so if you waste a few dozen shots on non-decisive moments, you can erase them and shoot more. Save only the best shots, like the series shown in **Figure 6.1**.

Figure 6.1

Continuous shooting allows you to capture an entire sequence of exciting moments as they unfold.

To use the 7D Mark II's continuous shooting mode, press the DRIVE-AF button and rotate the Quick Control Dial to select High-speed continuous (10 frames per second, but rates of 2-10 fps can be chosen); Low-speed continuous (4 fps, with rates of 9 to 1 fps optional), or Silent continuous shooting (4 fps, user settable from 4 to 1 fps). Alternatively, you can press the Q button to pop up the Quick Control screen and select the drive mode icon, which is located in the center of the bottom row of icons. You can select the shooting speed you want for High-speed, Low-speed, and Silent (actually, less noisy) continuous shooting in the Shooting 2 menu, as described in Chapter 8. Your camera is able to achieve such high shooting frame rates because it incorporates two miniature high torque motors dedicated to mirror drive and shutter cocking, along with special damping to counter vibration from mirror bounce.

When you partially depress the shutter button, the viewfinder will display a number representing the maximum number of shots you can take at the current quality settings in the lower right corner of the screen. (If your battery is low, this figure will be lower.) Continuous shooting can be affected by the speed with which your 7D Mark II is able to focus. So, in AI Servo AF mode, the frames-per-second rate may be lower, depending on your subject and the lens you are using. Fortunately, this highly flexible camera allows you to tailor how AF functions in AI Servo mode while shooting continuously. In the AF 2 menu, you'll find an entry that lets you select either release priority, focus priority, or equal priority for the *first* image in a series, and another entry that allows you to choose focus priority (which slows down the continuous shooting rate), shooting speed priority (to maintain shooting rate at the potential expense of sharpest focus, and equal priority, which provides a compromise between the two.

Of course, lenses which inherently focus more slowly (see Chapter 7 for information on the various types of autofocus motors built into Canon lenses), and scenes that are poorly lit can also affect the frame rate. As your battery is depleted (especially in low temperatures), your continuous shooting will slow down, too. You'll also see a decrease if lens aberration correction is active, or you have the camera set to do white balance bracketing. (In such cases, the 7D Mark II stores multiple copies of each image snapped, slowing down the burst rate.) While you can use flash in continuous mode, the camera will wait for the flash to recycle between shots, slowing down the continuous shooting rate.

When the 7D Mark II's generous internal buffer fills, the camera will stop capturing images until enough pictures have been written to the memory card to allow shooting to resume. As you might expect, the number of continuous shots you can fire off before that happens varies with the format you choose and the write speed of your card. You can expect a maximum burst of around 130 shots when capturing Large images in JPEG Fine format, but only 24 when shooting RAW, and 18 when shooting RAW+JPEG. If you really *must* shoot continuously, simply dropping down to Large JPEG Standard will allow you to shoot thousands of images, until your memory card is full (depending on the size and speed of your card.)

The reason the size of your bursts is limited by the buffer is that continuous images are first shuttled into the 7D Mark II's internal memory, then doled out to the memory card as quickly as they can be written to the card. Technically, the 7D Mark II takes the RAW data received from the digital image processor and converts it to the output format you've selected -- either JPG or CR2 (RAW) or both -- and deposits it in the buffer ready to store on the card.

This internal "smart" buffer can suck up photos much more quickly than the memory card and, indeed, some memory cards are significantly faster or slower than others. You'll get the best results when using a shutter speed of 1/1000th second, the maximum aperture of the lens, and with anti-flicker shooting and EOS iTR autofocus both disabled. (The latter is the 7D II's face recognition AF point selection mode, discussed in Chapter 9. When active, high speed continuous shooting will max out at roughly 9.5 fps.) When using One-Shot autofocus your continuous shooting speeds will increase if you turn off image stabilization for the EF300mm f/4L IS USM, EF28-135mm f/3.5-5.6 IS USM, EF75-300mm f/4-f5.6 IS USM, and EF100-400mm f4.5-5.6L IS USM lenses.

Bursts Not Only for Action

I often use continuous shooting mode even when I'm not busy shooting action. As I've mentioned before, bursts make sense when you're shooting HDR or bracketing. But here's a technique you might not have thought of -- continuous shooting can give you sharper images!

When I'm photographing concerts, I most frequently use my 70-200mm f/2.8 IS zoom, hand-held, with image stabilization turned on, and using the highest continuous frame rate at my disposal. I enjoy greater mobility by not using a monopod (and a tripod would be even more of a ball-and-chain, even if not forbidden by the venue). I'm generally shooting at around 1/160ᵗʰ second, which is usually fast enough to eliminate blur from the performers' motion. IS has no effect on stopping *their* movement, of course, and it does a fairly good job of eliminating camera/photographer shake. However, I invariably find that if I shoot in continuous, one of the middle frames in a sequence will be sharpest. Even the most seasoned photographer will add a little bump to the camera when they squeeze (not stab) the shutter release.

More Exposure Options

In Chapter 4, you learned techniques for getting the *right* exposure, but I haven't explained all your exposure options just yet. You'll want to know about the *kind* of exposure settings that are available to you with the Canon EOS 7D Mark II. There are options that let you control when the exposure is made, or even how to make an exposure that's out of the ordinary in terms of length (time or bulb exposures). The sections that follow explain your camera's special exposure features, and even discuss a few it does not have (and why it doesn't).

A Tiny Slice of Time

Exposures that seem impossibly brief can reveal a world we didn't know existed. In the 1930s, Dr. Harold Edgerton, a professor of electrical engineering at MIT, pioneered high-speed photography using a repeating electronic flash unit he patented called the *stroboscope*. As the inventor of the electronic flash, he popularized its use to freeze objects in motion, and you've probably seen his photographs of bullets piercing balloons and drops of milk forming a coronet-shaped splash.

Electronic flash freezes action by virtue of its extremely short duration -- as brief as 1/50,000th second or less. You can read more about using electronic flash to stop action in Chapter 12. Of course, the 7D Mark II is fully capable of immobilizing all but the fastest movement using only its shutter speeds, which range all the way up to 1/8,000th second. Indeed, you'll rarely have need for such a brief shutter speed in ordinary shooting. If you wanted to use an aperture of f/2.8 at ISO 100 outdoors in bright sunlight, for some reason, a shutter speed of 1/8,000th second would more than do the job. You'd need a faster shutter speed only if you moved the ISO setting to a higher sensitivity (but why would you do that?). Under less than full sunlight, 1/8,000th second is more than fast enough for any conditions you're likely to encounter.

Most sports action can be frozen at 1/2,000th second or slower, and for many sports a slower shutter speed is actually preferable -- for example, to allow the wheels of a racing automobile or motorcycle, or the propeller on a classic aircraft to blur realistically. But if you want to do some exotic action-freezing photography without resorting to electronic flash, the 7D Mark II's top shutter speed is at your disposal. Here are some things to think about when exploring this type of high-speed photography:

◎ **You'll need a lot of light.** High shutter speeds cut very fine slices of time and sharply reduce the amount of illumination that reaches your sensor. To use 1/4,000th second at an aperture of f/6.3, you'd need an ISO setting of 800 -- even in full daylight. To use an f/stop smaller than f/6.3 or an ISO setting lower than 800, you'd need more light than full daylight provides. (That's why electronic flash units work so well for high-speed photography when used as the sole illumination; they provide both the effect of a brief shutter speed and the high levels of illumination needed.)

◎ **Don't combine high shutter speeds with electronic flash.** You might be tempted to use an electronic flash with a high shutter speed. Perhaps you want to stop some action in daylight with a brief shutter speed and use electronic flash only as supplemental illumination to fill in the shadows. Unfortunately, under most conditions you can't use flash in subdued illumination with your 7D Mark II at any shutter speed faster than 1/200th second. That's the fastest speed at which the camera's focal plane shutter is fully open: at shorter speeds, the "slit" described above comes into play, so that the flash will expose only the small portion of the sensor exposed by the slit during its duration. (Check out "Avoiding Sync Speed Problems" in Chapter 12 if you want to see how you can use shutter speeds shorter than 1/200th second with certain Canon Speedlites, albeit at much-reduced effective power levels.)

Working with Short Exposures

You can have a lot of fun exploring the kinds of pictures you can take using very brief exposure times, whether you decide to take advantage of the action-stopping capabilities of your built-in or external electronic flash or work with the Canon EOS 7D Mark II's faster shutter speeds. Here are a few ideas to get you started:

- **Take revealing images.** Fast shutter speeds can help you reveal the real subject behind the façade, by freezing constant motion to capture an enlightening moment in time. Legendary fashion/portrait photographer Philippe Halsman used leaping photos of famous people, such as the Duke and Duchess of Windsor, Richard Nixon, and Salvador Dali to illuminate their real selves. Halsman said, "*When you ask a person to jump, his attention is mostly directed toward the act of jumping and the mask falls so that the real person appears.*" Try some high-speed portraits of people you know in motion to see how they appear when concentrating on something other than the portrait. (See **Figure 6.2**.)

- **Create unreal images.** High-speed photography can also produce photographs that show your subjects in ways that are quite unreal. A helicopter in mid-air with its rotors frozen makes for an unusual picture. **Figure 6.3** shows a pair of pictures. At top, a shutter speed of 1/1000th second virtually stopped the rotation of the chopper's rotors, while the bottom image, shot at 1/200th second, provides a more realistic view of the blurry blades as they appeared to the eye.

- **Capture unseen perspectives.** Some things are *never* seen in real life, except when viewed in a stop-action photograph.

M.I.T. Professor Harold Edgerton's balloon bursts were only a starting point. Freeze a hummingbird in flight for a view of wings that never seem to stop. Or, capture the splashes as liquid falls into a bowl, as shown in **Figure 6.4.** No electronic flash was required for this image (and wouldn't have illuminated the water in the bowl as evenly). Instead, a clutch of high-intensity lamps and an ISO setting of 1600 allowed the EOS 7D Mark II to capture this image at 1/2,000th second.

- **Vanquish camera shake and gain new angles.** Here's an idea that's so obvious it isn't always explored to its fullest extent. A high enough shutter speed can free you from the tyranny of a tripod, making it easier to capture new angles, or to shoot quickly while moving around, especially with longer lenses. I tend to use a monopod or tripod for almost everything when I'm not using an image-stabilized lens, and I end up missing some shots because of a reluctance to adjust my camera support to get a higher, lower, or different angle. If you have enough light and can use an f/stop wide enough to permit a high shutter speed, you'll find a new freedom to choose your shots. I have a favored 170mm-500mm lens that I use for sports and wildlife photography, almost invariably with a tripod, as I don't find the "reciprocal of the focal length" rule particularly helpful in most cases. (I would *not* hand-hold this hefty lens at its 500mm setting with a 1/500th second shutter speed under most circumstances.) However, at 1/2,000th second or faster, and with a sufficiently high ISO setting (I recommend ISO 800-1600) to allow such a speed, it's entirely possible for a steady hand to use this lens without a tripod or monopod's extra support, and I've found that my whole approach to shooting animals and other elusive subjects changes in high-speed mode. Selective focus allows dramatically isolating my prey wide open at f/6.3, too.

Figure 6.2

When your subjects leap, the real person inside emerges.

Figure 6.3

Top: the chopper's blades are frozen at 1/1,000th second; bottom: a more realistic blurry rendition at 1/200th second shutter speed.

Figure 6.4

A large amount of artificial illumination and an ISO 1600 sensitivity setting allowed capturing this shot at 1/2,000th second without use of an electronic flash.

Long Exposures

Longer exposures are a doorway into another world, showing us how even familiar scenes can look much different when photographed over periods measured in seconds. At night, long exposures produce streaks of light from moving, illuminated subjects like automobiles or amusement park rides. Extra-long exposures of seemingly pitch-dark subjects can reveal interesting views using light levels barely bright enough to see by. At any time of day, including daytime (in which case you'll often need the help of neutral-density filters, which reduce the amount of light passing through the lens, to make the long exposure practical), long exposures can cause moving objects to vanish entirely, because they don't remain stationary long enough to register in a photograph.

Working with Long Exposures

Because the EOS 7D Mark II produces such good images at longer exposures, and there are so many creative things you can do with long-exposure techniques, you'll want to do some experimenting. Get yourself a tripod or another firm support and take some test shots with long exposure noise reduction both enabled and disabled using the entry in the Shooting 3 menu, as explained in Chapter 8 (to see whether you prefer low noise or high detail) and get started. Here are some things to try:

- ⊙ **Make people invisible.** One very cool thing about long exposures is that objects that move rapidly enough won't register at all in a photograph, while the subjects that remain stationary are portrayed in the normal way. That makes it easy to produce people-free landscape photos and architectural photos at night or, even, in full daylight if you use a neutral-density filter (or two or three) to allow an exposure of at least a few seconds. At ISO 100, f/22, and a pair of 8X (three-stop) neutral-density filters, you can use exposures of nearly two seconds; overcast days and/or more neutral-density filtration would work even better if daylight people-vanishing is your goal. They'll have to be walking *very* briskly and across the field of view (rather than directly toward the camera) for this to work. At night, it's much easier to achieve this effect with the 20- to 30-second exposures that are possible.

◉ **Create streaks.** If you aren't shooting for total invisibility, long exposures with the camera on a tripod or monopod can produce some interesting streaky effects. You don't need to limit yourself to indoor photography, however. Even a single 8X ND filter will let you shoot at f/22 and 1/6th second in full daylight at ISO 100.

◉ **Produce light trails.** At night, car headlights and taillights and other moving sources of illumination can generate interesting light trails. Your camera doesn't even need to be mounted on a tripod; hand-holding the 7D Mark II for longer exposures adds movement and patterns to your trails. If you're shooting fireworks (preferably with a tripod), a longer exposure of several seconds may allow you to combine several bursts into one picture.

◉ **Blur waterfalls, etc.** You'll find that waterfalls and other sources of moving liquid produce a special type of long exposure blur, because the water merges into a fantasy-like veil that looks different at different exposure times, and with different waterfalls. Cascades with turbulent flow produce a rougher look at a given longer exposure than falls that flow smoothly. Although blurred waterfalls have become almost a cliché, there are still plenty of variations for a creative photographer to explore, as you can see in **Figure 6.5**.

◉ **Show total darkness in new ways.** Even on the darkest nights, there is enough starlight or glow from distant illumination sources to see by, and, if you use a long exposure, there is enough light to take a picture, too. **Figure 6.6** shows San Juan, Puerto Rico late at night.

Figure 6.5
A 1/4-second exposure blurred the falling water.

Figure 6.6
A 20-second exposure revealed this view of San Juan, Puerto Rico.

Delayed Exposures

Sometimes it's desirable to have a delay of some sort before a picture is actually taken. Perhaps you'd like to get in the picture yourself, and would appreciate it if the camera waited 10 seconds after you press the shutter release to actually take the picture. Maybe you want to give a tripod-mounted camera time to settle down and damp any residual vibration after the release is pressed to improve sharpness for an exposure with a relatively slow shutter speed. It's possible you want to explore the world of time-lapse photography. The next sections present your delayed exposure options.

Time-Lapse/Interval Photography

Who hasn't marveled at a time-lapse photograph of a flower opening, a series of shots of the moon marching across the sky, or one of those extreme time-lapse picture sets showing something that takes a very, very long time, such as a building under construction.

You probably won't be shooting such construction shots, unless you have a spare 7D Mark II you don't need for a few months (or are willing to go through the rigmarole of figuring out how to set up your camera in precisely the same position using the same lens settings to shoot a series of pictures at intervals). However, other kinds of time-lapse photography are entirely within reach.

Although the EOS 7D Mark II can't take time-lapse/interval photographs all by itself, if you're willing to tether the camera to a computer (a laptop will do) using the USB cable, you can take time-lapse photos using EOS Utility software furnished with your camera.

Here are some tips for effective time-lapse photography:

- **Use AC power.** If you're shooting a long sequence, consider connecting your camera to an AC adapter, as leaving the 7D Mark II on for long periods of time will rapidly deplete the battery.

- **Make sure you have enough storage space.** Unless your memory card has enough capacity to hold all the images you'll be taking, you might want to change to a higher compression rate or reduced resolution to maximize the image count.

- **Make a movie.** While time-lapse stills are interesting, you can increase your fun factor by compiling all your shots into a motion picture using your favorite desktop movie-making software.

- **Protect your camera.** If your camera will be set up for an extended period of time (longer than an hour or two), make sure it's protected from weather, earthquakes, animals, young children, innocent bystanders, and theft.

- **Vary intervals.** Experiment with different time intervals. You don't want to take pictures too often or less often than necessary to capture the changes you hope to image.

Working with GPS

You 7D II includes a built-in GPS receiver. It records locational data such as latitude, longitude, and altitude, and saves it to the EXIF metadata in your image files, where it can be retrieved by compatible software to plot to maps or insert into your uploads to Flickr or other sites. You can even track your trajectory of movement with the receiver's logging function.

The Canon EOS 7D Mark II gives you two ways to geotag your photographs, so that you (or your compatible software) can always know exactly where a particular tagged photo was taken. Your options are as follows:

- **Built-in GPS receiver.** The 7D II is one of the first Canon dSLRs with GPS features integrated right into the body, at the top of the camera body, near the accessory shoe. In most cases, its features are all you need for geotagging your photographs. The big advantages of the internal receiver are that you don't need to carry an extra piece of equipment; remember to attach it when geotagging is wanted; or give up use of

195

your camera's hot shoe for other accessories, including a flash. (While geotagging is generally performed outdoors, you still might want to use flash, if only for fill outside, when working with GPS.) Note that the built-in GPS receiver doesn't require separate batteries, and when enabled, drains your camera's internal battery *even when the camera is turned off.*

⊚ **GPS capabilities of a properly configured Eye-Fi memory card.** The 7D II is compatible with Eye-Fi memory cards with built-in Wi-Fi capabilities. Your camera includes options in the Shooting 1 menu for enabling/disabling the features of these cards, which includes geotagging images. (Eye-Fi card GPS features drain your camera's batteries when enabled, just like the 7D II's internal GPS receiver.) You probably won't be using the Eye-Fi card's GPS functions, because your camera's internal feature is superior. I won't be covering use of Eye-Fi cards in this book.

Note that while the Canon GP-E2 external GPS receiver could be used with the previous model 7D Mark I, it is not compatible with the 7D Mark II version.

If your familiarity with GPS is limited to that gadget that sits atop (or within) your dashboard, you'll be pleasantly surprised at the things that a GPS-equipped camera can do with locational information. When active, the GPS system records the latitude and longitude of each location where a picture is snapped, the elevation, Coordinated Universal Time Code (UTC), and the satellite reception status. This information is embedded in the EXIF metadata included in each photo, where it can be read and manipulated by compatible software. There are lots of things you can do with the information:

⊚ **Geotag images.** The exact location, including elevation can accompany your image. The data also includes a digital compass, so you even know which way the camera was pointed when you took the shot. If you've photographed the Grand Canyon, for example, you'll not only know which scenic spot where a photo was captured, but exactly which direction you were shooting the vast chasm.

⊙ **Log your travels.** The 7D II has a GPS logging function that records the camera's location information at intervals you specify. So, the path you took to capture the images of a lifetime can be viewed on a map and used to retrace your steps, or recommend a route to others.

⊙ **Timely time.** Your camera can set its internal clock using GPS information. Indeed, highly accurate time measurements using atomic clocks are necessary for your GPS to function, as the unit calculates your position based on how long it takes for the GPS satellite's signal to arrive – at the speed of light! (The time measurements are so accurate they take into account how much time slows down under stronger gravity fields, and from movement. (And you thought Einstein's General and Special Relativity theories didn't have any impact on your daily life!)

Because the GPS information embedded in the EXIF data has been standardized, many software programs can access and use the data. That includes Canon utilities, such as the Map Utility, Digital Photo Professional, and ImageBrowser EX programs; third-party image-editing software, including iPhoto for the Mac and the Map Module in Lightroom; and many photo sharing sites, such as Flickr, that can display the location where each image was taken when you upload your pictures to an online album. Google Earth can also use your EXIF data.

You can view GPS data on the 7D II's LCD monitor as you review images. Press the INFO. button until the view with the brightness or RGB histogram appears. As you should know, there are several additional data displays available from that screen that can be viewed by pressing the multi controller joystick down. The last screen reveals GPS information for the selected image (if any exists.) The GPS information will be shown at lower left, as you can see in **Figure 6.7**. If you are viewing a movie clip's data, the GPS information at the time *movie capture began* will be shown. First, you'll need to learn how to activate and set up your GPS Receiver.

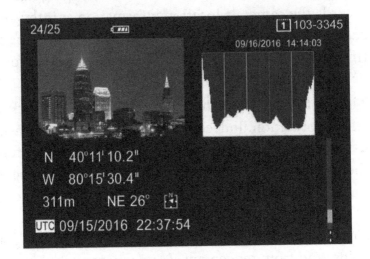

Figure 6.7

GPS data appears within the histogram display.

Using the Internal GPS Receiver

To record GPS information, your 7D II's internal GPS receiver must be able to receive signals from at least three GPS satellites so it can triangulate your exact location; four to calculate your position in 3D (elevation); and five to set the camera's time. To use the internal GPS, just follow these steps:

1. Navigate to the Set-up 2 menu and choose GPS/Digital Compass Settings. Press SET to move to the next screen.

2. **Highlight your GPS and press SET.** Select Enable, and press SET again to activate the GPS. You'll be returned to the top level GPS screen.

3. **Choose Set Up.** In the previous screen, highlight Set Up and press SET once more. A screen showing these six options appears (see **Figure 6.8**).

   - **Auto time setting.** The 7D II can use time data embedded in the GPS signal to set the camera's internal clock accurately. You can choose Auto Update to set the time automatically whenever the camera is powered up and GPS data is available; disable this function, or Set Now to update immediately. As I mentioned earlier, the receiver must be able to link with at least five GPS satellites for the time function to operate; when activated, the time setting in your camera will maintain plus/minus one-second accuracy. (This feature is great for synchronizing several GPS-equipped cameras, especially when shooting and editing videos and still shots contemporaneously.)

- **Position update interval.** Use this to specify the interval the GPS device uses to update position information. Choose from every 1, 5, 10, 15, 30 seconds, or every 1, 2, or 5 minutes. Select a shorter interval when you are moving and/or accuracy is critical, or a longer interval to save power, when GPS reception is not optimal, or you are shooting from one position for a longer period.

- **Digital Compass.** You can enable or disable the digital compass, which records the compass direction the camera is pointed. This compass must be calibrated (it's easy), and I'll show you how to do that shortly.

- **GPS information display.** This entry simply displays a screen of current GPS information, including latitude, longitude, elevation, UTC time (essentially Greenwich Mean Time), and Satellite reception strength/status. (See Figure 6.9.) It's available only when the camera is in range of GPS satellites. The bottom entry in the information display shows current satellite strength. If 2D is displayed next to the satellite icon, elevation information cannot be displayed; when 3D is shown instead, elevation will be shown.

- **GPS logger.** Allows you to enable or disable tracking of GPS position data, transfer log data to your memory card for later manipulation by an appropriate software program, or to delete the camera's current GPS log. Nature and wildlife photographers (now, where did I photograph those rare flowers?), law enforcement personnel, business users, and anyone wandering through a strange city during a vacation will love the ability to track not only individual locations but the routes taken to get from one shooting spot to another.

- **Calibrate Digital Compass**. The digital compass uses geo-magnetism to calculate your camera's direction (just like a real compass.) As such, it can be affected by nearby metal, magnetic objects, high-voltage power lines, and when you're inside masonry/concrete buildings, elevators, underground, or in moving vehicles. If you happen to be in a high latitude (and thus nearer the magnetic north pole), the compass direction may be inaccurate. You may need to recalibrate at intervals (your 7D II may even tell you when it's necessary), especially if you notice that the headings displayed don't seem quite right. Once activated, the digital compass can be displayed as you shoot by pressing the INFO button until it appears on the LCD monitor, or on an overlay on the live view screen.

4. **Set your parameters**. Highlight your choices, select parameters, and press SET to confirm. When finished, press the MENU button twice to back out of the menu system (or just tap the shutter release button).

5. **Begin using GPS**. After a delay of about 30 to 60 seconds while the receiver connects to the optimum number of satellites, GPS functions will be activated, and remain so until you return to the menu to disable GPS features. If you turn the camera off, it will automatically re-acquire the satellites within a few seconds when it's powered up again, assuming that GPS reception is available at that location.

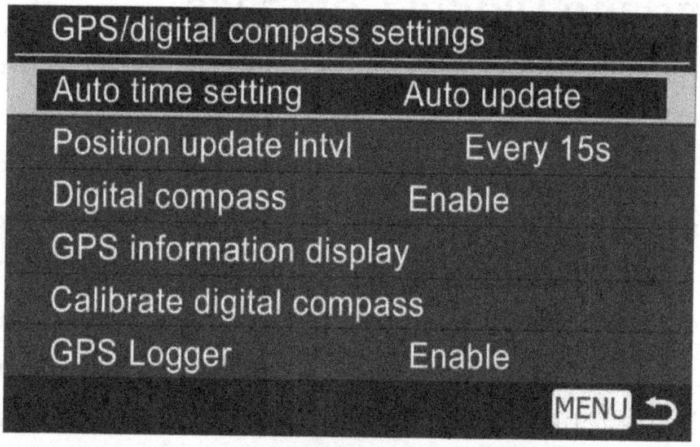

GPS/digital compass settings

Auto time setting	Auto update
Position update intvl	Every 15s
Digital compass	Enable
GPS information display	
Calibrate digital compass	
GPS Logger	Enable

MENU ⤺

Figure 6.8

GPS parameters.

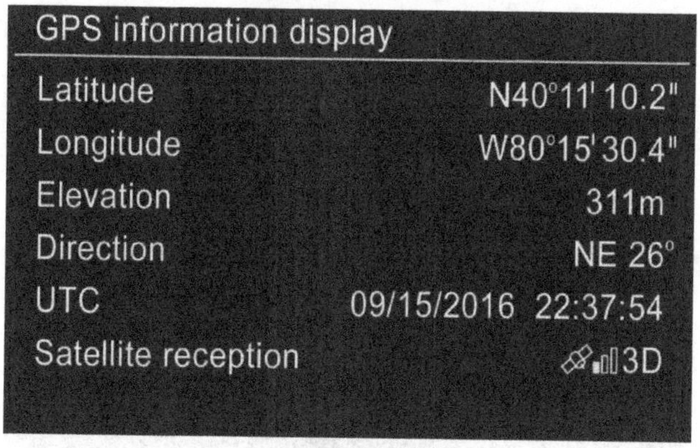

GPS information display

Latitude	N40°11' 10.2"
Longitude	W80°15' 30.4"
Elevation	311m
Direction	NE 26°
UTC	09/15/2016 22:37:54
Satellite reception	📡.ıl3D

Figure 6.9

GPS information display.

When GPS is active, a GPS indicator will be displayed on the 7D II's monochrome LCD top panel – even when the camera is off (so you'll know the receiver is still drawing power until you disable it.) The receiver's antenna is clustered around the hot shoe, but the camera can receive satellite signals whether held in vertical or horizontal orientations. However, if an external Speedlite is attached, sensitivity will be decreased slightly.

Calibrating the Digital Compass

Calibrating the compass is easy. Select Calibrate Digital Compass from the GPS parameters screen shown earlier in **Figure 6.8**. A screen like the one shown in **Figure 6.10** appears. While it's visible rotate the camera at least 180 degrees along the three axes shown in the screen.. I usually calibrate the compass by first rotating the camera along the axis running through the tripod socket. Then I tilt the camera forward and back, and finish by rotating along the axis running through the lens – rotating the camera counter clock wise to a vertical orientation, and then clockwise to horizontal and then on to vertical in the other direction. The camera isn't fussy, and a message appears on the LCD monitor to let you know when calibration is successful.

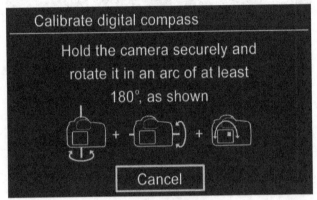

Figure 6.10
GPS Logger

Logging Your Results

To log your position, choose the GPS Logger entry in the Set Up screen. Enable logging, and the message LOG will appear on your monochrome LCD panel when the camera is turned off (again, as a reminder.) The same menu entry allows you to transfer the log data to either memory card in the camera, or to delete it.

Your Canon Map Utility, when connected to the internet through your computer, can easily trace a path for you on a standard road map or satellite view. The logger's NMEA-0813 format log file, which includes all the information for a single day's shooting, can be converted by the utility to a .KMZ file and uploaded to Google Earth, where it can be shared and viewed. Depending on how often the position update timing is recorded (from every second to every five minutes), the 7D II can store from less than a week to as much as 100 days worth of data. However, you'll probably use the Transfer Log Data to Card option more often than that.

Chapter 7

Working with Lenses

If you think that choosing a Canon EOS 7D II was the most important equipment decision you've made recently, think again. Camera bodies come and go – and the 7D II is certainly the best non-full frame camera that Canon has ever produced (to date) – but lenses are *forever*, or, almost. As great as the 7D II is, odds are much greater that you'll be using the same lenses you have now in 10 years than the same camera body. The camera may *capture* a moment in time, but the optics you select for a shot create the image on the sensor, bring it to life through the magic of focus, and, largely, determine how sharp and vivid your picture is.

Indeed, many photographers don't choose the Canon system exclusively because of the features found in the camera itself. The number, variety, and quality of the available lenses is often just as important, especially since once you've made an investment in excellent optics, switching to a different camera platform can be a complicated, expensive procedure.

Fortunately, when it comes to lenses, Canon makes the commitment worthwhile. By mid-decade, Canon had produced in excess of 110 *million* EF and EF-S lenses. The company currently has more than six dozen lenses in its product lineup, and that figure does not include hundreds of other different lenses produced by Canon and third-party vendors since 1987. Every single one of those optics is fully compatible with your 7D II, with many older, excellent quality lenses available used at attractive prices. These lenses can be used to give you a wider view, bring distant subjects closer, let you focus closer, shoot under lower-light conditions, or provide a more detailed, sharper image for critical work. Other than the sensor itself, the lens you choose for your dSLR is the most important component in determining image quality and perspective of your images. This chapter explains how to select the best lenses for the kinds of photography you want to do.

About That Crop Factor...

From time to time you've heard the term *crop factor*, and you've probably also heard the term *lens multiplier factor*. Both are misleading and inaccurate terms used to describe the same phenomenon: the fact that cameras like the 7D II provide a field of view that's smaller and narrower than that produced by certain other (often more expensive) cameras, when fitted with exactly the same lens.

Figure 7.1 quite clearly shows the phenomenon at work. The outer rectangle, marked 1X, shows the field of view you might expect with a 28mm lens mounted on a Canon EOS 5DS, a so-called "full-frame" model. The rectangle marked 1.3X shows the effective field of view from the same vantage point with the exact same lens mounted on the discontinued Canon EOS 1D Mark III camera, while the area marked 1.6X shows the field of view you'd get with that 28mm lens installed on a 7D II. It's easy to see from the illustration that the 1X rendition provides a wider, more expansive view, while the other two are, in comparison, *cropped*.

The cropping effect is produced because the sensors of the latter two cameras are smaller than the sensors of the 5DS. The "full-frame" camera has a sensor that's the size of the standard 35mm film frame, 24mm x 36mm. Your 7D II's sensor does *not* measure 24mm x 36mm; instead, it specs out at 22.3mm x 14.9mm, or about 62.5 percent of the area of a full-frame sensor, as shown by the yellow boxes in the figure. You can calculate the relative field of view by dividing the focal length of the lens by .625. Thus, a 100mm lens mounted on a 7D II has the same field of view as a 160mm lens on the 5DS. We humans tend to perform multiplication operations in our heads more easily than division, so such field of view comparisons are usually calculated using the reciprocal of .625 -- 1.6 -- so we can multiply instead. (100 / .625=160; 100 x 1.6=160)

This translation is generally useful only if you're accustomed to using full-frame cameras (usually of the film variety) and want to know how a familiar lens will perform on a digital camera. I strongly prefer *crop factor* over *lens multiplier*, because nothing is being multiplied; a 100mm lens doesn't "become" a 160mm lens -- the depth-of-field and lens aperture remain the same. (I'll explain more about these later in this chapter.) Only the field of view is cropped. But *crop factor* isn't much better, as it implies that the 24mm x 36mm frame is "full" and anything else is "less." I get e-mails all the time from photographers who point out that their Phase One XF camera is a full frame model, too, with a sensor that measures (roughly) 54 x 40mm. By their reckoning, all lesser sensors are severely "cropped."

Figure 7.1

Canon has offered digital SLRs with full-frame (1X) crops, as well as 1.3X and 1.6X crops.

If you're accustomed to using full-frame film cameras, you might find it helpful to use the crop factor "multiplier" to translate a lens's real focal length into the full-frame equivalent, even though, as I said, nothing is actually being multiplied. Throughout most of this book, I've been using actual focal lengths and not equivalents, except when referring to specific wide-angle or telephoto focal length ranges and their fields of view.

Your First Lens

There are three ways you might have purchased your 7D II. If you already had owned a Canon camera (and thus had that investment in lenses), you might have purchased just the 7D II body. Given that most buyers of the 7D are not novices, virtually every retailer keeps a few body-only configurations in stock. You might also have purchased your camera in a kit that included a basic zoom lens. The 7D II is often packaged as kits that include either a basic Canon EF-S 18-55mm f/3.5-5.6 IS STM lens, or the Canon EF-S 18-135mm f/3.5-5.6 IS STM lens, shown in **Figure 7.2**. When you purchase a kit, the combined price of the camera and kit lens are always somewhat less than if you'd bought them separately. The 18-135mm zoom adds only $350.00 to the price of the 7D II.

Figure 7.2

The Canon EF-S 18-55mm f/3.5-5.6 IS STM or Canon EF-S 18-135 f/3.5-5.6 IS STM autofocus lenses ship as a basic kit lens for entry-level Canon cameras, including the 7D II.

The third way you might have purchased your camera is in a bundle that included a box containing the camera body, and a separate box with a lens. Such bundles are often put together by vendors, and often authorized by Canon, which frequently offers discounts and rebates to bring down the total cost of the two products purchased together. Bundles are a way for the retailer to give you the exact combination of camera body and lens that you want, accompanied by a more attractive price. Perhaps you shoot architecture or landscapes extensively, and wanted to equip your 7D II with Canon's EF-S 10-18mm f/4.5-5.6 IS STM wide-angle lens.

Or, if you're heavily into movie-shooting, you might prefer the newer Canon EF-S 18-135mm f/3.5-5.6 IS USM lens, introduced in 2016, which is compatible with the PZ-E1 Power Zoom Adapter, which fits under the lens and provides a useful power zoom feature. However, that lens alone sells for about $600, so purchasing in a bundle (which often results in a $200-$300 discount or rebate) can save some money.

So, depending on which category you fall into, you'll need to make a decision about what lens to buy (if any), or decide what other kind of lenses you need to fill out your existing complement of Canon optics. This section will cover "first lens" concerns, while later in the chapter we'll look at "add-on lens" considerations. When deciding on a first lens, there are several factors you'll want to consider:

- **Cost.** You might have stretched your budget a bit to purchase your 7D II, so you might want to keep the cost of your first lens fairly low. Fortunately, as I've noted, there are excellent lenses available that will add from $100 to $600 to the price of your camera if purchased at the same time.

- **Zoom range.** If you have only one lens, you'll want a fairly long zoom range to provide as much flexibility as possible. Fortunately, two popular basic lenses for the 7D II have 3X to 5X zoom ranges, extending from moderate wide-angle/normal out to medium telephoto. These are fine for everyday shooting, portraits, and some types of sports.

- **Adequate maximum aperture.** You'll want an f/stop of at least f/3.5 to f/4 for shooting under fairly low-light conditions. The thing to watch for is the maximum aperture when the lens is zoomed to its telephoto end. You may end up with no better than an f/5.6 maximum aperture. That's not great, but you can often live with it.

- ◉ **Image quality.** Your starter lens should have good image quality, befitting a camera with 20.2 MP of resolution, because that's one of the primary factors that will be used to judge your photos. Even at a low price, the several different lenses sold with the 7D II as a kit include extra-low dispersion glass and aspherical elements that minimize distortion and chromatic aberration; they are sharp enough for most applications. If you read the user evaluations in the online photography forums, you know that owners of the kit lenses have been very pleased with their image quality.

- ◉ **Size matters.** A good walking-around lens is compact in size and light in weight.

- ◉ **Fast/close focusing.** Your first lens should have a speedy autofocus system (which is where the ultrasonic motor/USM and STM system found in many moderately priced Canon lenses is an advantage). Close focusing (to 12 inches or closer) will let you use your basic lens for some types of macro photography.

You can find comparisons of the lenses discussed in the next section, as well as third-party lenses from Sigma, Tokina, Tamron, and other vendors, in online groups and websites. I'll provide my recommendations, but obtaining more information from these additional sources is always helpful when making a lens purchase, because, while camera bodies come and go, lenses may be a lifetime addition to your kit.

Your lens arsenal

The 7D II is commonly available with several good, basic lenses that can serve you well as a "walk-around" lens (one you keep on the camera most of the time, especially when you're out and about without your camera bag). The number of options available to you is actually quite amazing, even if your budget is limited to about $100

to $500 for your first lens. Canon's best-bet first lenses are as fol-
lows:

- **Canon EF-S 18-55mm f/3.5-5.6 IS STM autofocus lens.**
  This lens, shown in **Figure 7.2**, replaces the old "II" version,
  and is a bit larger than the older optic. It boasts the new STM
  stepper motor technology that Canon video fans have found
  to be so useful. It has image stabilization that can counter
  camera shake by providing the vibration-stopping capabilities
  of a shutter speed four stops faster than the one you've dialed
  in. That is, with image stabilization activated, you can shoot
  at 1/30th second and eliminate camera shake as if you were
  using a shutter speed of 1/250th second. (At least, that's
  what Canon claims; I usually have slightly less impressive results.) Of course, IS doesn't freeze subject motion -- that basketball player driving for a layup will still be blurry at 1/30th
  second, even though the effects of camera shake will be effectively nullified. But this lens is an all-around good choice if
  your budget is tight.

- **Canon EF-S 18-135mm f/3.5-5.6 IS STM autofocus lens.**
  This one, priced at about $350 when purchased in a kit, is an
  upgrade from a similar earlier lens without the stepper motor
  technology. It's also light, compact (you can see it mounted
  on the 7D II in Figure 7.3), and covers a useful range from
  true wide-angle to intermediate telephoto. As with Canon's
  other affordable zoom lenses, image stabilization partially
  compensates for the slow f/5.6 maximum aperture at the telephoto end, by allowing you to use longer shutter speeds to
  capture an image under poor lighting conditions. I'll explain
  the advantages of the STM autofocus later in this chapter.

- **Canon EF-S 18-200mm f/3.5-5.6 IS autofocus lens.** This
  one, priced at about $700, has been popular as a basic lens
  for the 7D II, because it's light, compact, and covers a full
  range from true wide-angle to long telephoto. Image stabilization keeps your pictures sharp at the long end of the zoom

range, allowing the longer shutter speeds that the f/5.6 maximum aperture demands at 200mm. Automatic panning detection turns the IS feature off when panning in both horizontal and vertical directions. An improved "Super Spectra Coating" minimizes flare and ghosting, while optimizing color rendition.

⊙ **Canon EF-S 17-85mm f/4-5.6 IS USM autofocus lens.** This older lens (introduced in 2004 with the EOS 20D) is a very popular "basic" lens still sold for the 7D II. The allure here with this $600 lens is the longer telephoto range, coupled with the built-in image stabilization, which allows you to shoot rock-solid photos at shutter speeds that are at least two or three notches slower than you'd need normally (say, 1/8th second instead of 1/30th or 1/60th second), as long as your subject isn't moving. It also has a quiet, fast, reliable ultrasonic motor (more on that later, too). This is another lens designed for the 1.6X crop factor; all but one of the remaining lenses in this list can also be used on full-frame cameras. (I'll tell you why later in this chapter.)

⊙ **Canon EF 55-200mm f/4.5-5.6 IS STM autofocus lightweight compact telephoto zoom lens.** If you bought the 18-55mm kit lens, this one picks up where that one leaves off, going from short telephoto to medium long (88mm-320mm full-frame equivalent). It features a desirable ultrasonic motor. Best of all, it's very affordable at less than $300. If you can afford only two lenses, the 18-55mm and this one make a good basic set. (See **Figure 7.3**.)

⊙ **Canon EF 24-85mm f/3.5-4.5 USM autofocus wide-angle telephoto zoom lens.** If you can get by with normal focal length to medium telephoto range, Canon offers four affordable lenses, plus one more expensive killer lens that's worth the extra expenditure. All of them can be used on full-frame or cropped-frame digital Canons, which is why they include "wide angle" in their product names. They're really wide-angle lenses only when mounted on a full-frame camera. This one, priced in the $300 range, offers a useful range of focal lengths, extending from the equivalent of 38mm to 136mm.

◉ **Canon EF 28-105mm f/3.5-4.5 II USM autofocus wide-angle telephoto zoom lens.** If you want to save about $100 and gain a little reach compared to the 24-85mm zoom, this 45mm-168mm (equivalent lens) might be what you are looking for.

◉ **Canon EF 28-200mm f/3.5-5.6 USM autofocus wide-angle telephoto zoom lens.** If you want one lens to do everything except wide-angle photography, this 7X zoom lens costs less than $400 and takes you from the equivalent of 45mm out to a long 320mm.

◉ **Canon EF 24-70mm f/2.8L II USM autofocus zoom wide-angle-telephoto lens.** I couldn't leave this premium lens out of the mix, even though it costs well nearly $2,000. As part of Canon's L-series (Luxury) lens line, it offers the best sharpness over its focal range than any of the other lenses in this list. Best of all, it's fast (for a zoom), with an f/.2.8 maximum aperture that *doesn't change* as you zoom out. Unlike the other lenses, which may offer only an f/5.6 maximum f/stop at their longest zoom setting, this is a constant aperture lens, which retains its maximum f/stop. The added sharpness, constant aperture, and ultra-smooth USM motor are what you're paying for with this lens. Another version with an f/4 maximum aperture with image stabilization can be purchased for less than $1,000.

Figure 7.3

FAST TRACK GUIDE

Some vendors are including the Canon EF-S 55-250mm f/4-5.6 IS STM lens in a bundle with some kits.

Lens Compatibility

The previous section helped you sort out what lens you need to buy with your 7D II (assuming you already didn't own any Canon lenses). Now, you're probably wondering what lenses can be added to your growing collection (trust me, it will grow). You need to know which lenses are suitable and, most importantly, which lenses are fully compatible with your 7D II.

With the Canon 7D II, the compatibility issue is a simple one: It accepts any lens with the EF or EF-S designation, with full availability of all autofocus, autoaperture, autoexposure, and image-stabilization features (if present). It's comforting to know that any EF (for full-frame or cropped sensors) or EF-S (for cropped sensor cameras only) lens will work as designed with your camera. As I noted at the beginning of the chapter, that's more than 110 million lenses!

But wait, there's more. You can also attach Nikon F mount, Leica R, Olympus OM, and M42 ("Pentax screw mount") lenses with a simple adapter, if you don't mind losing automatic focus and aperture control. If you use one of these lenses, you'll need to focus manually (even if the lens operates in Autofocus mode on the camera it was designed for), and adjust the f/stop to the aperture you want to use to take the picture. That means that lenses that don't have an aperture ring (such as Nikon G-series lenses) must be used only at their maximum aperture if you use them with a simple adapter. However, Novoflex makes expensive adapter rings (the Nikon-Lens-on-Canon-Camera version is called EOS/NIK NT) with an integral aperture control that allows adjusting the aperture of lenses that do not have an old-style aperture ring. Expect to pay nearly $300 for an adapter of this type. Should you decide to pick up a new Canon EOS-M mirrorless camera, you'll be able to get double-duty with your EF and EF-S lenses, too, with an adapter that will allow you to use the same lenses on your 7D II and companion EOS-M cameras.

Because of the limitations imposed on using "foreign" lenses on your 7D II, you probably won't want to make extensive use of them, but an adapter can help you when you really, really need to use a particular focal length but don't have a suitable Canon-compatible lens. For example, I occasionally use an older 400mm lens that was originally designed for the Nikon line on my 7D II. The lens needs to be mounted on a tripod for steadiness, anyway, so its slower operation isn't a major pain. Another good match is the 105mm Micro-Nikkor I sometimes use with my Canon 7D II. Macro photos, too, are most often taken with the camera mounted on a tripod, and manual focus makes a lot of sense for fine-tuning focus and depth-of-field. Because of the contemplative nature of close-up photography, it's not much of an inconvenience to stop down to the taking aperture just before exposure.

The restrictions on use of lenses within Canon's own product line (as well as lenses produced for earlier Canon SLRs by third-party vendors) are fairly clear-cut. The 7D II cannot be used with any of Canon's earlier lens mounting schemes for its film cameras, including the immediate predecessor to the EF mount, the FD mount (introduced with the Canon F1 in 1964 and used until the Canon T60 in 1990), FL (1964-1971), or the original Canon R mount (1959-1964). That's really all you need to know. While you'll find FD-to-EF adapters for about $40, you'll lose so many functions that it's rarely worth the bother.

WHY SO MANY LENS MOUNTS?

Four different lens mounts in 40-plus years (five, if you count the EF-M mount for the new EOS-M cameras) might seem like a lot of different mounting systems, especially when compared to the Nikon F mount of 1959, which retained quite a bit of compatibility with that company's film and digital camera bodies during that same span. However, in digital photography terms, the EF mount itself is positively ancient, having remained reasonably stable for more than 25 years. Lenses designed for the EF system work reliably with every EOS film and digital camera ever produced.

However, at the time, yet another lens mount switch, especially a change from the traditional breech system to a more conventional bayonet-type mount, was indeed a daring move by Canon. One of the reasons for staying with a particular lens type is to "lock" current users into a specific camera system. By introducing the EF mount, Canon in effect cut loose every photographer in its existing user base. If they chose to upgrade, they were free to choose another vendor's products and lenses. Only satisfaction with the previous Canon product line and the promise of the new system would keep them in the fold.

In retrospect, the switch to the EF mount seems like a very good idea, as the initial EOS film cameras can now be seen as the beginning of Canon's rise to eventually become the leader in film and (later) digital SLR cameras. By completely revamping its lens mounting system, the company was able to take advantage of the latest advances in technology without compromise.

For example, when the original EF bayonet mount was introduced in 1987, the system incorporated new autofocus technology (EF actually stands for "electro focus") in a more rugged and less complicated form. A tiny motor was built into the lens itself, eliminating the need for mechanical linkages with the camera. Instead, electrical contacts are used to send power and the required focusing information to the motor. That's a much more robust and resilient system that made it easier for Canon to design faster and more accurate autofocus mechanisms just by redesigning the lenses.

EF vs. EF-S

Today, in addition to its EF lenses, Canon offers lenses that use the EF-S (the S stands for "short back focus") mount, with the chief difference being (as you might expect) lens components that extend farther back into the camera body of some of Canon's latest digital cameras (specifically those with smaller than full-frame sensors), such as the 7D II. As I'll explain next, this refinement allows designing more compact, less-expensive lenses especially for those cameras, but not for models that include current cameras like the EOS 5D Mark III, 1D X, or 1D Mark III (even though the latter camera does have a sensor that is slightly smaller than full frame).

Canon's EF-S lens mount variation was born in 2003, when the company virtually invented the consumer-oriented digital SLR category by introducing the original EOS 300D/Digital Rebel, a dSLR that cost less than $1,000 *with lens* at a time when all other interchangeable lens digital cameras (including the 7D II's "grandparent," the original EOS 10D) were priced closer to $2,000 with a basic lens. Like the EOS 10D, the EOS 7D II features a smaller than full-frame sensor with a 1.6X crop factor (Canon calls this format APS-C). But the EOS Digital Rebel accepted lenses that took advantage of the shorter mirror found in APS-C cameras, with elements of shorter focal length lenses (wide angles) that extended *into* the camera, space that was off limits in other models because the mirror passed through that territory as it flipped up to expose the shutter and sensor. (Canon even calls its flip-up reflector a "half mirror.")

In short (so to speak), the EF-S mount made it easier to design less-expensive wide-angle lenses that could be used *only* with 1.6X-crop cameras, and featured a simpler design and reduced coverage area suitable for those non-full-frame models. The new mount made it possible to produce lenses like the ultra-wide EF-S 10-22mm f/3.5-4.5 USM lens, which has the equivalent field of view as a 16mm-35mm zoom on a full-frame camera. (See **Figure 7.4**.)

This lens was more or less replaced by the 10-18mm f/4.5-5.6 version that incorporates image stabilization and, at less than $400, is quite affordable.

Figure 7.4

The EF-S 10-22mm ultra-wide lens was made possible by the shorter back focus difference offered by the original Digital Rebel and subsequent Canon 1.6X "cropped sensor" models.

Suitable cameras for EF-S lenses include all recent non-full-frame models. The EF-S lenses cannot be used on the APS-C-sensor EOS 10D, the 1D Mark II N/Mark III (which have a 28.7mm x 19.1mm APS-H sensor with a 1.3X crop factor), or any of the full-frame digital or film EOS models, such as the EOS 1D X, EOS 1Ds Mark III, or EOS 5D Mark III, or EOS 5DS/5DS R. It's easy to tell an EF lens from an EF-S lens: The latter incorporate EF-S into their name! Plus, EF lenses have a raised red dot on the barrel that is used to align the lens with a matching dot on the camera when attaching the lens. EF-S lenses and compatible bodies use a white square instead. Some EF-S lenses also have a rubber ring at the attachment end that provides a bit of weather/dust sealing and protects the back components of the lens if a user attempts to mount it on a camera that is not EF-S compatible.

Canon Lens Nomenclature

The actual product names of individual Canon lenses are fairly easy to decipher; they'll include either the EF or EF-S designation, the focal length or focal length range of the lens, its maximum aperture, and some other information. Additional data may be engraved or painted on the barrel or ring surrounding the front element of the lens. Here's a decoding of what the individual designations mean:

- **EF/EF-S.** If the lens is marked EF, it can safely be used on any Canon EOS camera, film or digital. If it is an EF-S lens, it should be used only on an EF-S compatible camera.
- **Focal length.** Given in millimeters or a millimeter range, such as 60mm in the case of a popular Canon macro lens, or 17-55mm, used to describe a medium-wide to short-telephoto zoom.
- **Maximum aperture.** The largest f/stop available with a particular lens is given in a string of numbers that might seem confusing at first glance. For example, you might see 1:1.8 for a fixed-focal length (prime) lens, and 1:4.5-5.6 for a zoom. The initial 1: signifies that the f/stop given is actually a ratio or fraction (in regular notation, f/ replaces the 1:), which is

why a 1:2 (or f/2) aperture is larger than an 1:4 (or f/4) aperture -- just as 1/2 is larger than 1/4. With most zoom lenses, the maximum aperture changes as the lens is zoomed to the telephoto position, so a range is given instead: 1:4.5-5.6. (Some zooms, called *constant aperture* lenses, keep the same maximum aperture throughout their range.)

- **Autofocus type.** Most newer Canon lenses that aren't of the bargain-basement type use Canon's *ultrasonic motor* autofocus system (more on that later) and are given the USM designation. Several of the company's newest optics use the Stepper Motor (STM) technology. If USM or STM does not appear on the lens or its model name, the lens uses the less sophisticated AFD (arc-form drive) autofocus system or the micromotor (MM) drive mechanism.

- **Series.** Canon adds a Roman numeral to many of its products to represent an updated model with the same focal length or focal length range, so some lenses will have a II or III added to their name.

- **Pro quality.** Canon's more expensive lenses with more rugged construction and higher optical quality, intended for professional use, include the letter L (for "luxury") in their product name. You can further differentiate these lenses visually by a red ring around the lens barrel and the off-white color of the metal barrel itself in virtually all telephoto L-series lenses. (Some L-series lenses have shiny or textured black plastic exterior barrels.) Internally, every L lens includes at least one lens element that is built of ultra-low dispersion glass, is constructed of expensive fluorite crystal, or uses an expensive ground (not molded) aspheric (non-spherical) lens component.

- **Filter size.** You'll find the front lens filter thread diameter in millimeters included on the lens, preceded by a Ø symbol, as in Ø67 or Ø72.

- **Special-purpose lenses.** Some Canon lenses are designed for specific types of work, and they include appropriate designations in their names. For example, close-focusing lenses such as the Canon EF-S 60mm f/2.8 Macro USM lens incorporate the word *Macro* into their name. Lenses with perspective control features preface the lens name with T-S (for tilt-shift). Lenses with built-in image-stabilization features, such as the nifty EF 28-300mm f/3.5-5.6L IS USM telephoto zoom include *IS* in their product names.

Motor Drive Types

Incorporating the autofocus motor inside the lens was an innovative move by Canon, and this allowed the company to produce better and more sophisticated lenses as technology became available to upgrade the focusing system. As a result, you'll find four different types of motors in Canon-designed lenses, each with cost and practical considerations. Most newer lenses use only the latest USM motor, and incorporate that designation in their names.

- **AFD (Arc-form drive)** and **Micromotor (MM)** drives are built around tiny versions of electromagnetic motors, which generally use gear trains to produce the motion needed to adjust the focus of the lens. Both are slow, noisy, and not particularly effective with larger lenses. Manual focus adjustments are possible only when the motor drive is disengaged.

- **Micromotor ultrasonic motor (USM)** drives use high-frequency vibration to produce the motion used to drive the gear train, resulting in a quieter operating system at a cost that's not much more than that of electromagnetic motor drives. With the exception of a couple lenses that have a slipping clutch mechanism, manual focus with this kind of system is possible only when the motor drive is switched off and the lens is set in manual mode. This is the kind of USM system you'll find in lower-cost lenses.

- **Ring ultrasonic motor (USM)** drives, available in two different types (*electronic focus ring USM* and *ring USM*), also use high-frequency movement, but generate motion using a pair of vibrating metal rings to adjust focus. Both variations allow a feature called Full Time Manual (FTM) focus, which lets you make manual adjustments to the lens's focus even when the autofocus mechanism is engaged. With electronic focus ring USM, manual focus is possible only when the lens is mounted on the camera and the camera is turned on; the focus ring of lenses with ring USM can be turned at any time.

◎ **Stepper motor (STM) drives.** In autofocus mode, the precision motor of STM lenses, along with a new aperture mechanism, allows lenses equipped with this technology to focus quickly, accurately, silently, and with smooth continuous increments. If you think about video capture, you can see how these advantages pay off. Silent operation is a plus, especially when noise from autofocusing can easily be transferred to the camera's built-in microphones through the air or transmitted through the body itself. In addition, because autofocus is often done during capture, it's important that the focus increments are continuous. USM motors are not as smooth, but are better at jumping quickly to the exact focus point. You can adjust focus manually, using a focus-by-wire process. As you rotate the focus ring, that action doesn't move the lens elements; instead, your rotation of the ring sends a signal to the motor to change the focus. **Figure 7.5** shows the Canon EF-S 40mm f/2.8 STM lens, part of a series that also includes the two kit lenses previously mentioned and a 50mm f/1.8 "nifty fifty" that costs just $125.00.

Figure 7.5

Canon's 40mm f/2.8 lens, with an STM motor, is designed for video capture.

What Lenses Can Do for You

A saner approach to expanding your lens collection is to consider what each of your options can do for you and then choosing the type of lens that will really boost your creative opportunities. Here's a general guide to the sort of capabilities you can gain by adding a lens to your repertoire.

- ◎ **Wider perspective.** Your 18-55mm f/3.5-5.6 or 17-85mm f/4-5.6 or 18-200mm lens has served you well for moderate wide-angle shots. Now you find your back is up against a wall and you *can't* take a step backwards to take in more subject matter. Perhaps you're standing on the rim of the Grand Canyon, and you want to take in as much of the breathtaking view as you can. You might find yourself just behind the baseline at a high school basketball game and want an interesting shot with a little perspective distortion tossed in the mix. There's a lens out there that will provide you with what you need, such as the EF-S 10-22mm f/3.5-4.5 USM zoom (about $650). If you want to stay in the sub-$800 price category, you'll need something like the Sigma Super Wide-Angle 10-20mm f/4-5.6 EX DC HSM autofocus lens. The two lenses provide the equivalent of a 16mm to 32/35mm wide-angle view. For a distorted view, there is the Canon Fisheye EF 15mm f/2.8 autofocus, with a similar lens available from Sigma, which offers an extra-wide circular fisheye, and the Sigma Fisheye 8mm f/3.5 EX DG Circular Fisheye. Your extra-wide choices may not be abundant, but they are there. **Figure 7.6** (left) shows the perspective you get from an ultrawide-angle, non-fisheye lens.

- ◎ **Bring objects closer.** A long lens brings distant subjects closer to you, offers better control over depth-of-field, and avoids the perspective distortion that wide-angle lenses provide. They compress the apparent distance between objects in your frame. In the telephoto realm, Canon is second to none, with a dozen or more offerings in the sub-$650 range, including the Canon EF 100-300mm f/4.5-5.6 USM autofocus and

Canon EF 70-300mm f/4-5.6 IS USM autofocus telephoto zoom lenses, and a broad array of zooms and fixed-focal length optics if you're willing to spend up to $1,000 or a bit more. Don't forget that the 7D II's crop factor narrows the field of view of all these lenses, so your 70-300mm lens looks more like a 112mm-480mm zoom through the viewfinder. The images in center and right of **Figure 7.6** were taken from the same position as, but with an 85mm and 500mm lens, respectively.

- **Bring your camera closer.** Macro lenses allow you to focus to within an inch or two of your subject. Canon's best close-up lenses are all fixed focal length optics in the 50mm to 180mm range (including the well-regarded Canon EF-S 60mm f/2.8 compact and Canon EF 100mm f/2.8 USM macro autofocus lenses). But you'll find macro zooms available from Sigma and others. They don't tend to focus quite as close, but they provide a bit of flexibility when you want to vary your subject distance (say, to avoid spooking a skittish creature).

- **Look sharp.** Many lenses, particularly Canon's luxury "L" line, are prized for their sharpness and overall image quality. While your run-of-the-mill lens is likely to be plenty sharp for most applications, the very best optics are even better over their entire field of view (which means no fuzzy corners), are sharper at a wider range of focal lengths (in the case of zooms), and have better correction for various types of distortion.

- **More speed.** Your Canon EF 100-300mm f/4.5-5.6 telephoto zoom lens might have the perfect focal length and sharpness for sports photography, but the maximum aperture won't cut it for night baseball or football games, or, even, any sports shooting in daylight if the weather is cloudy or you need to use some unusually fast shutter speed, such as 1/4,000th second. You might be happier with the Canon EF 100mm f/2 medium telephoto for close-range stuff, or even the pricier Canon EF 135mm f/2L. If money is no object, you can spring for Canon's 400mm f/2.8 and 600mm f/4 L-series lenses (both with image stabilization and priced in the four- and five-figure stratosphere). Or, maybe you just need the speed and can benefit from an f/1.8 or f/1.4 lens in the 20mm-85mm range. They're all available in Canon mounts (there's even an 85mm f/1.2 and 50mm f/1.2 for the real speed demons). With any of these lenses you can continue photographing under the dimmest of lighting conditions without the need for a tripod or flash.

- **Special features.** Accessory lenses give you special features, such as tilt/shift capabilities to correct for perspective distortion in architectural shots. Canon offers four of these TS-E lenses in 17mm, 24mm, 45mm, and 90mm focal lengths, at more than $1,300 to $2,000 (and up) each. You'll also find macro lenses, including the MP-E 65mm f/2.8 1-5x macro photo lens, a manual focus lens which shoots *only* in the 1X to 5X life-size range. If you want diffused images, check out the EF 135mm f/2.8 with two soft-focus settings. The fisheye lenses mentioned earlier and all IS (image-stabilized) lenses also count as special-feature optics. The recent Canon EF 8-15mm f/4L Fisheye USM ultra-wide zoom lens is highly unusual in offering a *zoomable* fisheye range. Tokina's 10-17mm fisheye zoom is its chief competitor; I've owned one and it is not in the same league in terms of sharpness and speed as the Canon optic.

Figure 7.6

Ultra wide, medium, and telephoto shots of Prague Castle in the Czech Republic.

Zoom vs. Prime

Zoom lenses have changed the way serious photographers take pictures. One of the reasons that I own 12 SLR film bodies is that in ancient times it was common to mount a different fixed focal length prime lens on various cameras and take pictures with two or three cameras around your neck (or tucked in a camera case) so you'd be ready to take a long shot or an intimate close-up or wide-angle view on a moment's notice, without the need to switch lenses. It made sense (at the time) to have a half dozen or so bodies (two to use, one in the shop, one in transit, and a couple backups). Zoom lenses of the time had a limited zoom range, were heavy, and not very sharp (especially when you tried to wield one of those monsters handheld).

That's all changed today. Lenses like the razor-sharp Canon EF 28-300mm f/3.5-5.6L IS USM can boast 10X or longer zoom ranges, in a package that's about 7 inches long, and while not petite at 3.7 pounds, it is quite usable handheld (especially with IS switched on). Although such a lens might seem expensive at close to $2,500, it's actually much less costly than the six or so lenses it replaces.

When selecting between zoom and prime lenses, there are several considerations to ponder. Here's a checklist of the most important factors. I already mentioned image quality and maximum aperture earlier, but those aspects take on additional meaning when comparing zooms and primes.

- ◉ **Logistics.** As prime lenses offer just a single focal length, you'll need more of them to encompass the full range offered by a single zoom. More lenses mean additional slots in your camera bag, and extra weight to carry. Just within Canon's line alone you can select from about a dozen general-purpose prime lenses in 28mm, 35mm, 50mm, 85mm, 100mm, 135mm, 200mm, and 300mm focal lengths, all of which are overlapped by the 28-300mm zoom I mentioned earlier. Even so, you might be willing to carry an extra prime lens or two in order to gain the speed or image quality that lens offers.

- **Image quality.** Prime lenses usually produce better image quality at their focal length than even the most sophisticated zoom lenses at the same magnification. Zoom lenses, with their shifting elements and f/stops that can vary from zoom position to zoom position, are in general more complex to design than fixed focal length lenses. That's not to say that the very best prime lenses can't be complicated as well. However, the exotic designs, aspheric elements, low-dispersion glass, and Canon's diffraction optics (DO) technology (a three-layer diffraction grating to better control how light is captured by a lens) can be applied to improving the quality of the lens, rather than wasting a lot of it on compensating for problems caused by the zoom process itself.

- **Maximum aperture.** Because of the same design constraints, zoom lenses usually have smaller maximum apertures than prime lenses, and the most affordable zooms have a lens opening that grows effectively smaller as you zoom in. The difference in lens speed verges on the ridiculous at some focal lengths. For example, the 18mm-55mm basic zoom gives you a 55mm f/5.6 lens when zoomed all the way out, while prime lenses in that focal length commonly have f/1.8 or faster maximum apertures. Indeed, the fastest f/2, f/1.8, f/1.4, and f/1.2 lenses are all primes, and if you require speed, a fixed focal length lens is what you should rely on.

- **Speed.** Using prime lenses takes time and slows you down. It takes a few seconds to remove your current lens and mount a new one, and the more often you need to do that, the more time is wasted. If you choose not to swap lenses, when using a fixed focal length lens you'll still have to move closer or farther away from your subject to get the field of view you want. A zoom lens allows you to change magnifications and focal lengths with the twist of a ring and generally saves a great deal of time.

- **Special features.** Prime lenses often have special features not found in zoom lenses. For example, the new EF 40mm f/2.8

STM lens boasts that smooth, silent autofocus motor described earlier in this chapter. It functions as a wide-angle lens on a full-frame camera like the 5D Mark III, and as a short telephoto, portrait lens on cameras like the 7D II. You'll also find close-focusing capabilities and perspective control features on prime lenses.

Categories of Lenses

Lenses can be categorized by their intended purpose -- general photography, macro photography, and so forth -- or by their focal length. The range of available focal lengths is usually divided into three main groups: wide-angle, normal, and telephoto. Prime lenses fall neatly into one of these classifications. Zooms can overlap designations, with a significant number falling into the catch-all, wide-to-telephoto zoom range. This section provides more information about focal length ranges, and how they are used.

Any lens with an equivalent focal length of 10mm to 20mm is said to be an *ultra-wide-angle lens*; from about 20mm to 40mm (equivalent) is said to be a *wide-angle lens*. *Normal lenses* have a focal length roughly equivalent to the diagonal of the film or sensor, in millimeters, and so fall into the range of about 45mm to 60mm (on a full-frame camera). *Telephoto lenses* usually fall into the 75mm and longer focal lengths, while those from about 300mm to 400mm and longer often are referred to as *super-telephotos*.

Using Wide-Angle and Wide-Zoom Lenses

To use wide-angle prime lenses and wide zooms, you need to understand how they affect your photography. Here's a quick summary of the things you need to know.

- ⊙ **More depth-of-field.** Practically speaking, wide-angle lenses offer more depth-of-field at a particular subject distance and aperture. (But see the sidebar below for an important note.) You'll find that helpful when you want to maximize sharpness of a large zone, but not very useful when you'd rather isolate your subject using selective focus (telephoto lenses are better for that).

- ◎ **Stepping back.** Wide-angle lenses have the effect of making it seem that you are standing farther from your subject than you really are. They're helpful when you don't want to back up, or can't because there are impediments in your way.

- ◎ **Wider field of view.** While making your subject seem farther away, as implied above, a wide-angle lens also provides a larger field of view, including more of the subject in your photos.

- ◎ **More foreground.** As background objects retreat, more of the foreground is brought into view by a wide-angle lens. That gives you extra emphasis on the area that's closest to the camera. Photograph your home with a normal lens/normal zoom setting, and the front yard probably looks fairly conventional in your photo (that's why they're called "normal" lenses). Switch to a wider lens and you'll discover that your lawn now makes up much more of the photo. So, wide-angle lenses are great when you want to emphasize that lake in the foreground, but problematic when your intended subject is located farther in the distance.

- ◎ **Super-sized subjects.** The tendency of a wide-angle lens to emphasize objects in the foreground, while de-emphasizing objects in the background can lead to a kind of size distortion that may be more objectionable for some types of subjects than others. Shoot a bed of flowers up close with a wide angle, and you might like the distorted effect of the larger blossoms nearer the lens. Take a photo of a family member with the same lens from the same distance, and you're likely to get some complaints about that gigantic nose in the foreground.

- ◎ **Perspective distortion.** When you tilt the camera so the plane of the sensor is no longer perpendicular to the vertical plane of your subject, some parts of the subject are now closer to the sensor than they were before, while other parts are farther away. So, buildings, flagpoles, or NBA players appear to be falling backwards, as you can see in **Figure 7.7.** While this kind of apparent distortion (it's not caused by a defect in the lens) can happen with any lens, it's most apparent when a wide angle is used.

○ **Steady cam.** You'll find that you can better handhold a wide-angle lens at slower shutter speeds, without need for image stabilization, than you can with a telephoto lens. The reduced magnification of the wide-lens or wide-zoom setting doesn't emphasize camera shake like a telephoto lens does.

○ **Interesting angles.** Many of the factors already listed combine to produce more interesting angles when shooting with wide-angle lenses. Raising or lowering a telephoto lens a few feet probably will have little effect on the appearance of the distant subjects you're shooting. The same change in elevation can produce a dramatic effect for the much-closer subjects typically captured with a wide-angle lens or wide-zoom setting.

Figure 7.7

Tilting the camera back produces this "falling back" look in architectural photos.

DOF IN DEPTH

The depth-of-field (DOF) advantage of wide-angle lenses is diminished when you enlarge your picture; believe it or not, a wide-angle image enlarged and cropped to provide the same subject size as a telephoto shot would have the *same* depth-of-field. Try it: take a wide-angle photo of a friend from a fair distance, and then zoom in to duplicate the picture in a telephoto image. Then, enlarge the wide shot so your friend is the same size in both. The wide photo will have the same DOF (and will have much less detail, too).

Avoiding Potential Wide-Angle Problems

Wide-angle lenses have a few quirks that you'll want to keep in mind when shooting so you can avoid falling into some common traps. Here's a checklist of tips for avoiding common problems:

- **Symptom: converging lines.** Unless you want to use wildly diverging lines as a creative effect, it's a good idea to keep horizontal and vertical lines in landscapes, architecture, and other subjects carefully aligned with the sides, top, and bottom of the frame. That will help you avoid undesired perspective distortion. Sometimes it helps to shoot from a slightly elevated position so you don't have to tilt the camera up or down.

- **Symptom: color fringes around objects.** Lenses are often plagued with fringes of color around backlit objects, produced by *chromatic aberration*, which comes in two forms: *longitudinal/axial*, in which all the colors of light don't focus in the same plane; and *lateral/transverse*, in which the colors are shifted to one side. Axial chromatic aberration can be reduced by stopping down the lens, but transverse chromatic aberration cannot. Both can be reduced by using lenses with low diffraction index glass (or UD elements, in Canon nomenclature) and by incorporating elements that cancel the chromatic aberration of other glass in the lens. For example, a strong positive lens made of low-dispersion crown glass (made of a soda-lime-silica composite) may be mated with a weaker negative lens made of high-dispersion flint glass, which contains lead.

- **Symptom: lines that bow outward.** Some wide-angle lenses cause straight lines to bow outward, with the strongest effect at the edges. In fisheye (or *curvilinear*) lenses, this defect is a feature, as you can see in **Figure 7.8**. When distortion is not desired, you'll need to use a lens that has corrected barrel distortion. Manufacturers like Canon do their best to minimize or eliminate it (producing a *rectilinear* lens), often using *aspherical* lens elements (which are not cross-sections of a sphere). You can also minimize less severe barrel distortion simply by framing your photo with some extra space all around, so the edges where the defect is most obvious can be cropped out of the picture.

- **Symptom: dark corners and shadows in flash photos.** The Canon EOS 7D II's built-in electronic flash is designed to provide even coverage for lenses as wide as 17mm. If you use a wider lens, you can expect darkening, or *vignetting*, in the corners of the frame. At wider focal lengths, the lens hood of some lenses (my 17mm-85mm lens is a prime offender) can cast a semi-circular shadow in the lower portion of the frame when using the built-in flash. Sometimes removing the lens hood or zooming in a bit can eliminate the shadow. Mounting an external flash unit, such as the mighty Canon 580EX II or 600EX-RT, can solve both problems, as it has zoomable coverage up to 114 degrees with the included adapter, sufficient for a 15mm rectilinear lens. Its higher vantage point eliminates the problem of lens hood shadow, too.

- **Symptom: light and dark areas when using polarizing filter.** If you know that polarizers work best when the camera is pointed 90 degrees away from the sun and have the least effect when the camera is oriented 180 degrees from the sun, you know only half the story. With lenses having a focal length of 10mm to 18mm (the equivalent of 16mm-28mm), the angle of view (107 to 75 degrees diagonally, or 97 to 44 degrees horizontally) is extensive enough to cause problems. Think about it: when a 10mm lens is pointed at the proper 90-degree angle from the sun, objects at the edges of the frame will be oriented at 135 to 41 degrees, with only the center at exactly 90 degrees. Either edge will have much less of a polarized effect. The solution is to avoid using a polarizing filter with lenses having an actual focal length of less than 18mm (or 28mm equivalent).

Figure 7.8

Many wide-angle lenses cause lines to bow outward toward the edges of the image; with a fisheye lens, this tendency is especially useful for creating special effects, as in this shot.

Using Telephoto and Tele-Zoom Lenses

Telephoto lenses also can have a dramatic effect on your photography, and Canon is especially strong in the long-lens arena, with lots of choices in many focal lengths and zoom ranges. You should be able to find an affordable telephoto or tele-zoom to enhance your photography in several different ways. Here are the most important things you need to know. In the next section, I'll concentrate on telephoto considerations that can be problematic -- and how to avoid those problems.

- **Selective focus.** Long lenses have reduced depth-of-field within the frame, allowing you to use selective focus to isolate your subject. You can open the lens up wide to create shallow depth-of-field, or close it down a bit to allow more to be in focus. The flip side of the coin is that when you *want* to make a range of objects sharp, you'll need to use a smaller f/stop to get the depth-of-field you need. Like fire, the depth-of-field of a telephoto lens can be friend or foe.

- **Getting closer.** Telephoto lenses bring you closer to wildlife, sports action, and candid subjects. No one wants to get a reputation as a surreptitious or "sneaky" photographer (except for paparazzi), but when applied to candids in an open and honest way, a long lens can help you capture memorable moments while retaining enough distance to stay out of the way of events as they transpire.

- **Reduced foreground/increased compression.** Telephoto lenses have the opposite effect of wide angles: they reduce the importance of things in the foreground by squeezing everything together. This compression even makes distant objects appear to be closer to subjects in the foreground and middle ranges. You can use this effect as a creative tool.

- **Accentuates camera shakiness.** Telephoto focal lengths hit you with a double-whammy in terms of camera/photographer shake. The lenses themselves are bulkier, more difficult to hold steady, and may even produce a barely perceptible see-saw rocking effect when you support them with one hand halfway down the lens barrel. Telephotos also magnify any camera shake. It's no wonder that image stabilization is popular in longer lenses.

⊚ **Interesting angles require creativity.** Telephoto lenses require more imagination in selecting interesting angles, because the "angle" you do get on your subjects is so narrow. Moving from side to side or a bit higher or lower can make a dramatic difference in a wide-angle shot, but raising or lowering a telephoto lens a few feet probably will have little effect on the appearance of the distant subjects you're shooting.

Avoiding Telephoto Lens Problems

Many of the "problems" that telephoto lenses pose are really just challenges and not that difficult to overcome. Here is a list of the seven most common picture maladies and suggested solutions.

⊚ **Symptom: flat faces in portraits.** Head-and-shoulders portraits of humans tend to be more flattering when a focal length of 50mm to 85mm is used. Longer focal lengths compress the distance between features like noses and ears, making the face look wider and flat. A wide-angle might make noses look huge and ears tiny when you fill the frame with a face. So stick with 50mm to 85mm focal lengths, going longer only when you're forced to shoot from a greater distance, and wider only when shooting three-quarters/full-length portraits, or group shots.

⊚ **Symptom: blur due to camera shake.** Use a higher shutter speed (boosting ISO if necessary), consider an image-stabilized lens, or mount your camera on a tripod, monopod, or brace it with some other support. Of those three solutions, only the first will reduce blur caused by *subject* motion; an IS lens or tripod won't help you freeze a race car in mid-lap.

⊚ **Symptom: color fringes.** Chromatic aberration is the most pernicious optical problem found in telephoto lenses. There are others, including spherical aberration, astigmatism, coma, curvature of field, and similarly scary-sounding phenomena.

The best solution for any of these is to use a better lens that offers the proper degree of correction, or stop down the lens to minimize the problem. But that's not always possible. Your second-best choice may be to correct the fringing in your favorite RAW conversion tool or image editor. Photoshop's Lens Correction filter offers sliders that minimize both red/cyan and blue/yellow fringing.

- **Symptom: lines that curve inward.** Pincushion distortion is found in many telephoto lenses. You might find after a bit of testing that it is worse at certain focal lengths with your particular zoom lens. Like chromatic aberration, it can be partially corrected using tools like Photoshop's Lens Correction filter and Photoshop Elements' Correct Camera Distortion filter.

- **Symptom: low contrast from haze or fog.** When you're photographing distant objects, a long lens shoots through a lot more atmosphere, which generally is muddied up with extra haze and fog. That dirt or moisture in the atmosphere can reduce contrast and mute colors. Some feel that a skylight or UV filter can help, but this practice is mostly a holdover from the film days. Digital sensors are not sensitive enough to UV light for a UV filter to have much effect. So you should be prepared to boost contrast and color saturation in your Picture Styles menu or image editor if necessary.

- **Symptom: low contrast from flare.** Lenses are furnished with lens hoods for a good reason: to reduce flare from bright light sources at the periphery of the picture area, or completely outside it. Because telephoto lenses often create images that are lower in contrast in the first place, you'll want to be especially careful to use a lens hood to prevent further effects on your image (or shade the front of the lens with your hand).

- **Symptom: dark flash photos.** Edge-to-edge flash coverage isn't a problem with telephoto lenses as it is with wide angles. The shooting distance is. A long lens might make a subject that's 50 feet away look as if it's right next to you, but your camera's flash isn't fooled. You'll need extra power for distant flash shots, and probably more power than your 7D II's built-in flash provides. The shoe-mount Canon 580EX II or 600EX-RT Speedlites, for example, can automatically zoom its coverage down to that of a medium telephoto lens, providing a theoretical full-power shooting aperture of about f/8 at 50 feet and ISO 400. (Try *that* with the built-in flash!)

Telephotos and Bokeh

Bokeh describes the aesthetic qualities of the out-of-focus parts of an image and whether out-of-focus points of light -- circles of confusion -- are rendered as distracting fuzzy discs or smoothly fade into the background. *Boke* is a Japanese word for "blur," and the h was added to keep English speakers from rendering it monosyllabically to rhyme with *broke*. Although bokeh is visible in blurry portions of any image, it's of particular concern with telephoto lenses, which, thanks to the magic of reduced depth-of-field, produce more obviously out-of-focus areas.

Bokeh can vary from lens to lens, or even within a given lens depending on the f/stop in use. Bokeh becomes objectionable when the circles of confusion are evenly illuminated, making them stand out as distinct discs, or, worse, when these circles are darker in the center, producing an ugly "doughnut" effect. A lens defect called spherical aberration may produce out-of-focus discs that are brighter on the edges and darker in the center, because the lens doesn't focus light passing through the edges of the lens exactly as it does light going through the center. (Mirror or *catadioptric* lenses also produce this effect.)

Other kinds of spherical aberration generate circles of confusion that are brightest in the center and fade out at the edges, producing a smooth blending effect. Ironically, when no spherical aberration is present at all, the discs are a uniform shade, which, while better than the doughnut effect, is not as pleasing as the bright center/dark edge rendition. The shape of the disc also comes into play, with round smooth circles considered the best, and nonagonal or some other polygon (determined by the shape of the lens diaphragm) considered less desirable.

If you plan to use selective focus a lot, you should investigate the bokeh characteristics of a particular lens before you buy. Canon user groups and forums will usually be full of comments and questions about bokeh, so the research is fairly easy.

Lens Hoods

Lens hoods are an important accessory for all lenses, but they're especially valuable with telephotos. As I mentioned earlier, lens hoods do a good job of preserving image contrast by keeping bright light sources outside the field of view from striking the lens and, potentially, bouncing around inside that long tube to generate flare that, when coupled with atmospheric haze, can rob your image of detail and snap. In addition, lens hoods serve as valuable protection for that large, vulnerable, front lens element. It's easy to forget that you've got that long tube sticking out in front of your camera and accidentally whack the front of your lens into something. It's cheaper to replace a lens hood than it is to have a lens repaired, so you might find that a good hood is valuable protection for your prized optics.

When choosing a lens hood, it's important to have the right hood for the lens, usually the one offered for that lens by Canon or the third-party manufacturer. You want a hood that blocks precisely the right amount of light: neither too much light nor too little. A hood with a front diameter that is too small can show up in your pictures as vignetting. A hood that has a front diameter that's too large isn't stopping all the light it should. Generic lens hoods may not do the job.

When your telephoto is a zoom lens, it's even more important to get the right hood, because you need one that does what it is supposed to at both the wide-angle and telephoto ends of the zoom range. Lens hoods may be cylindrical, rectangular (shaped like the image frame), or petal shaped (that is, cylindrical, but with cut-out areas at the corners which correspond to the actual image area). Lens hoods should be mounted in the correct orientation (a bayonet mount for the hood on the front of the lens usually takes care of this).

Telephoto Extenders

Telephoto extenders (often called teleconverters outside the Canon world), multiply the actual focal length of your lens, giving you a longer telephoto for much less than the price of a lens with that actual focal length. These extenders fit between the lens and your camera and contain optical elements that magnify the image produced by the lens. Available in 1.4X and 2.0X configurations from Canon, an extender transforms, say, a 200mm lens into a 280mm or 400mm optic, respectively. Given the 7D II's crop factor, your 200mm lens now has the same field of view as a 448mm or 640mm lens on a full-frame camera. At a little more than $400 each, they're quite a bargain, aren't they?

Actually, there are some downsides. While extenders retain the closest focusing distance of your original lens, autofocus is maintained only if the lens's original maximum aperture is f/4 or larger (for the 1.4X extender) or f/2.8 or larger (for the 2X extender). The components reduce the effective aperture of any lens they are used with, by one f/stop with the 1.4X extender, and 2 f/stops with the 2X extender. So, your EF 200mm f/2.8L II USM becomes a 280mm f/4 or 400mm f/5.6 lens. Although Canon extenders are precision optical devices, they do cost you a little sharpness, but that improves when you reduce the aperture by a stop or two. Each of the extenders is compatible only with a particular set of lenses of 135mm focal length or greater, so you'll want to check Canon's compatibility chart to see if the component can be used with the lens you want to attach to it.

If your lenses are compatible and you're shooting under bright lighting conditions, the Canon Extender EF 1.4x III, and Canon Extender EF 2x III make handy accessories.

Macro Focusing

Some telephotos and telephoto zooms available for the 7D II have particularly close focusing capabilities, making them *macro* lenses. Of course, the object is not necessarily to get close (get too close and you'll find it difficult to light your subject). What you're really looking for in a macro lens is to magnify the apparent size of the subject in the final image. Camera-to-subject distance is most important when you want to back up farther from your subject (say, to avoid spooking skittish insects or small animals). In that case, you'll want a macro lens with a longer focal length to allow that distance while retaining the desired magnification.

Canon makes 50mm, 60mm, 65mm, 100mm, and 180mm lenses with official macro designations. You'll also find macro lenses, macro zooms, and other close-focusing lenses available from Sigma, Tamron, and Tokina. If you want to focus closer with a macro lens, or any other lens, you can add an accessory called an *extension tube*. These add-ons move the lens farther from the focal plane, allowing it to focus more closely. Canon also sells add-on close-up lenses, which look like filters, and allow lenses to focus more closely.

Image Stabilization

Canon has a burgeoning line of lenses with built-in image stabilization (IS) capabilities. This feature uses lens elements that are shifted internally in response to the motion of the lens during handheld photography, countering the shakiness the camera and photographer produce and which telephoto lenses magnify. However, IS is not limited to long lenses; the feature works like a champ at the 17mm zoom position of Canon's EF-S 17-85mm f/4-5.6 IS USM and EF-S 17-55mm f/2.8 IS USM lenses. Other Canon IS lenses provide stabilization with zooms that are as wide as 10-18mm.

Image stabilization provides you with camera steadiness that's the equivalent of at least two or three shutter speed increments. (Canon claims four, which I feel may be optimistic.) This extra margin can be invaluable when you're shooting under dim lighting conditions or handholding a long lens for, say, wildlife photography. Perhaps that shot of a foraging deer calls for a shutter speed of 1/1,000th second at f/5.6 with your EF 100-400mm f/4.5-5.6L IS USM lens. Relax. You can shoot at 1/250th second at f/11 and get virtually the same results, as long as the deer doesn't decide to bound off.

Or, maybe you're shooting a high school play without a tripod or monopod, and you'd really, really like to use 1/15th second at f/4. Assuming the actors aren't flitting around the stage at high speed, your 17-85mm IS lens can grab the shot for you at its wide-angle position. However, keep these facts in mind:

- **IS doesn't stop action.** Unfortunately, no IS lens is a panacea to replace the action-stopping capabilities of a higher shutter speed. Image stabilization applies only to camera shake. You still need a fast shutter speed to freeze action. IS works great in low light, when you're using long lenses, and for macro photography. It's not always the best choice for action photography (unless you're willing to let subject motion become part of your image). In other situations, you may need enough light to allow a sufficiently high shutter speed. But in that case, IS can make your shot even sharper.

- **IS slows you down.** The process of adjusting the lens elements takes time, just as autofocus does, so you might find that IS adds to the lag between when you press the shutter and when the picture is actually taken. That's another reason why image stabilization might not be a good choice for sports.

- **Use when appropriate.** Some IS lenses produce worse results if you use them while you're panning, although newer Canon IS lenses have a mode that works fine when the camera is deliberately moved from side to side (or up and down) during exposure. Older lenses can confuse the motion with camera shake and overcompensate. You might want to switch off IS when panning or when your camera is mounted on a tripod.

⊙ **Do you need IS at all?** Remember that an inexpensive monopod might be able to provide the same additional steadiness as an IS lens, at a much lower cost. If you're out in the field shooting wild animals or flowers and think a tripod isn't practical, try a monopod first.

Chapter 8

Customizing with the Shooting Menu

This chapter and the next three will help you sort out the settings you can make to customize how your Canon EOS 7D Mark II uses its features, shoots photos, displays images, and processes the pictures after they've been taken. I'm not going to waste a lot of space on some of the more obvious menu choices. For example, you can probably figure out that the Beep option in Shooting 1 menu deals with the solid-state beeper in your camera that sounds off during various activities (such as the self-timer countdown). You can certainly decipher the import of the two options available for the Beep entry (Enable and Disable). In this chapter, I'll devote no more than a sentence or two to the blatantly obvious settings and concentrate on the more confusing aspects of 7D Mark II set-up, such as Automatic Exposure Bracketing.

The Shooting menus discussed in this chapter are those available in still shooting mode. If you rotate the Live View switch to the Movie position, the Movie Shooting 4 and 5 menus are activated. I'll explain those in Chapter 13, where I've collected all the basic video capture information for the 7D Mark II. For now, let's start off with an overview of the 7D Mark II's menus themselves.

Anatomy of the 7D Mark II's Menus

Canon's current lineup of cameras, like the 7D Mark II, have divided the entries into six major .sections -- Shooting, Autofocus, Playback, Set-up, Custom Functions, and My Menu -- each of which (except for the last) is further subdivided into three to five separate pages. Each page's listings are shown as a separate screen with no scrolling. The menus are cleaner and easy to use, too. Just press the MENU button, spin the Main Dial to highlight the menu tab and page you want to access, and then scroll up and down within a menu with the Quick Control Dial. What could be easier?

Tapping the MENU button brings up a typical menu like the one shown in **Figure 8.1**. (If the camera goes to "sleep" while you're reviewing a menu, you may need to wake it up again by tapping the shutter release button.) Different menu tabs are provided, depending on the shooting mode. In Bulb (B), Manual (M), Shutter-priority (Tv), Aperture-priority (Av), and Program Auto (P) modes, you can access Shooting 1-6, Autofocus 1-5, Playback 1-3, Set-up 1-4, Custom Functions 1-5, and My Menu. If you've selected Scene Intelligent Auto (the green-accented A+ icon), the available menus are limited to Shooting 1, 2, and 3, Playback 1, 2, and 3, and Set-up 1, 2, and 3.

The 7D Mark II's tabs are color-coded: red for Shooting, magenta for Autofocus, blue for Playback, amber for Set-up, brown for Custom Functions, and Green for My Menu. The currently selected menu tab's icon is white within a background corresponding to its color code. A set of three to five square dots appears underneath the icon representing the total number of screens available in that tab, with the current screen's number highlighted. All the inactive menus are gray and dimmed.

HYPER MENU NAVIGATION

As I mentioned, you can use the Main Dial to move from menu to menu, and the Quick Control Dial to highlight a particular menu entry. Press the SET button to select a menu item. That procedure is probably the best way to start out, because those controls are used to make so many settings with the EOS 7D Mark II that they quickly become almost intuitive. The 7D Mark II manual uses the Main Dial/Quick Control Dial method in its Menu Setting description. But, there's a better way.

If you have an agile thumb, you can do all your menu navigation with the joystick-like multi-controller:

- Shift the multi-controller left/right to jump from tab to tab.

- Press the multi-controller up/down to move within the menu choices of a given tab.

- Press the multi-controller in to select a menu item, and press it again to return to the menu choices. (Note that, for your protection, you must press the SET button to activate the Format Card screen in the Set-up 1 menu.

It gets even better. You can jump from tab to tab even if you've highlighted a particular menu setting on another tab -- and the 7D Mark II will remember which menu entry you've highlighted when you return to that menu. The memorization works even if you leave the menu system or turn off your camera. The 7D Mark II always remembers the last menu entry you used with a particular tab. So, if you generally use the Format command each time you access the Set-up 1 menu, that's the entry that will be highlighted when you choose that tab. The camera remembers which tab was last used, too, so, potentially, formatting your memory card might take just a couple presses (the MENU button, the SET button to select the highlighted Format command, then a click of the Quick Control Dial to choose OK, and another press of SET to start the format process).

Here are the things to watch for as you navigate the menus:

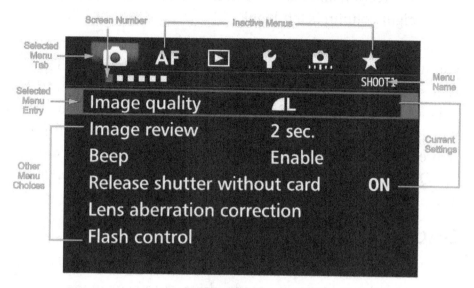

Figure 8.1

The 7D Mark II's menus are arranged in a series of tabs.

- **Menu tabs.** In the top row of the menu screen, the menu that is currently active will be highlighted as described earlier. The dots in the tab let you know if you are in, say Set-up 1, Set-up 2, Set-up 3, or Set-up 4. Just remember that the red camera icons stand for still, live view, and movie shooting options; the two blue right-pointing triangles represent playback options; the yellow wrench icons stand for Set-up options; the brown camera icons represent Custom Functions, and the green star stands for personalized menus defined for the star of the show -- you.

- **Selected menu item.** The currently selected menu entry within a given tab will have a black background and will be surrounded by a box the same hue as its color code.

- **Other menu choices.** The other menu items visible on the screen will have a dark gray background.

- **Current setting.** The current settings for visible menu items are shown in the right-hand column, until one menu entry is selected (by pressing the SET key). Current settings aren't appropriate for some menu entries (often because the main entry has several sub menus; for example the Lens Aberration

Correction and Flash Control entries in the figure), so the right column is left blank.

When you've moved the menu highlighting to the menu item you want to work with, press the SET button to select it. The current settings for the other menu items in the list will be hidden, and a list of options for the selected menu item (or a submenu screen) will appear. Or, you may be shown a separate settings screen for that entry. Within the menu choices, you can scroll up or down with the Quick Control Dial; press SET to select the choice you've made; and press the MENU button again to exit.

Shooting Menu Options

The various direct setting buttons on the top panel of the camera for white balance/metering mode, drive/autofocus mode, flash exposure compensation/ISO are likely to be the most common settings changes you make, with changes during a particular session fairly common. You'll find that the Shooting menu options are those that you access second most frequently when you're using your 7D Mark II. You might make such adjustments as you begin a shooting session, or when you move from one type of subject to another. Canon makes accessing these changes very easy.

This section explains the options of the six Shooting menus for still photography and how to use them.

Note: When the Live View Switch is rotated to the Movie position, the first three still photography shooting menus are more or less as discussed next. However, the Shooting 4, 5, and 6 menus are replaced with the Movie Shooting 4 and 5 menus. I'll save explanations of the Movie Shooting menus for Chapter 13.

Image Quality	Live View Shooting	Multiple Exposure
WB Shift/Bkt	Lens Aberration Correction	Aspect Ratio
Bulb Timer	High ISO Speed Noise Reduction	Auto Lighting Optimizer
Image Review	AF Method	HDR Mode
Color Space	Flash Control	Exposure Simulation
Anti-Flicker Shooting	Highlight Tone Priority	White Balance
Beep	Continuous AF	Red-eye Reduction
Picture Style	Exposure Compensation/AEB (Automatic Exposure Bracketing)	Silent Live View Shooting
Mirror Lockup	Dust Delete Data	Custom White Balance
Release Shutter without Card	Grid Display	Interval Timer
Long Exposure Noise Reduction	ISO Speed Settings	Metering Timer

Image Quality Settings

You can choose the image quality settings used by the 7D Mark II to store its files. You have four choices to make when selecting a quality setting:

- ◎ **Resolution**. The number of pixels captured determines the absolute resolution of the photos you shoot with your 7D II. Your choices range from 20 megapixels (Large or L), measuring 5472 x 3648; 8.9 megapixels (Medium or M), measuring 3648 x 2432 pixels; 5 megapixels (Small 1 or S1), 2736 x 1824 pixels; 2.5 megapixels (Small 2 or S2), 1920 x 1280; and 350,000 pixels (Small 3 or S3), 720 x 480. You can also choose RAW-only sizes of RAW (5472 x 3648 pixels; 20MP); M-RAW (4104 x 2736; 11 MP); or S-RAW (2736 x 1824; 5 MP).

- ◎ **JPEG compression**. To reduce the size of your image files and allow more photos to be stored on a given memory card, the 7D Mark II uses JPEG compression to squeeze the images down to a smaller size. This compacting reduces the image quality a little, so you're offered your choice of Fine compression and Normal compression. The symbols help you remember that Fine compression (represented by a quarter-circle) provides the smoothest results, while Normal compression (signified by a stair-step icon) provides "jaggier" images.

○ **JPEG, RAW, or both.** You can elect to store only JPEG versions of the images you shoot (6.4MB each at the Large Fine resolution setting) or you can save your photos as uncompressed, loss-free RAW files, which consume about four times as much space on your memory card (up to 20MB per file). Or, you can store both at once as you shoot. Many photographers elect to save both a JPEG and a RAW file, so they'll have a JPEG version that might be usable as-is, as well as the original "digital negative" RAW file in case they want to do some processing of the image later. You'll end up with two different versions of the same file: one with a JPG extension, and one with the CR2 extension that signifies a Canon RAW file.

To choose the combination you want, access the menus, scroll to Image Quality, and press the SET button. A screen similar to the one shown in **Figure 8.2** will appear with two rows of choices. Spin the Main Dial to choose from: -- (no RAW), RAW, M RAW, or S RAW. Rotate the QCD to select one of the JPEG choices: -- (no JPEG), Large, Medium, or Small in Fine or Normal compression (represented by smooth and stepped icons, respectively), plus Small 2 or Small 3 JPEG, at the resolutions listed above. A red box appears around the currently selected choice. If you choose -- for both RAW and JPEG, then JPEG Fine will be used.

Why so many choices? There are some limited advantages to using the Medium and Small resolution settings, Normal JPEG compression setting, and the two lower resolution RAW formats. They all allow stretching the capacity of your memory card so you can shoehorn quite a few more pictures onto a single memory card. That can come in useful when on vacation and you're running out of storage, or when you're shooting non-critical work that doesn't require full resolution. The Small 2 and Small 3 settings can be useful for photos taken for real estate listings, web page display, photo ID cards, or similar non-critical applications.

For most work, using lower resolution and extra compression is often false economy. You never know when you might actually need that extra bit of picture detail. Your best bet is to have enough memory cards to handle all the shooting you want to do until you have the chance to transfer your photos to your computer or a personal storage device.

However, reduced image quality can sometimes be beneficial if you're shooting sequences of photos rapidly, as the 7D Mark II is able to hold more of them in its internal memory buffer before transferring to the memory card. Still, for most sports and other applications, you'd probably rather have better, sharper pictures than longer periods of continuous shooting.

Note that the screen shown in the figure may vary slightly, depending on how you've set the Record Function+Card/Folder Selection entry in the Set-up 1 menu (also described in Chapter 10). That entry determines *which* memory card(s) are used to store the RAW and JPEG file formats you select here. The Record Function feature, which is active when you have more than one memory card inserted in the 7D Mark II, can be set to:

- **Standard**. All images will be recorded only to the memory card specified by the Record/Play setting of the Record Function+Card/Folder Selection entry in the Set-up 1 menu, using the settings established in the Image Quality screen.

- **Auto Switch Card**. All images will be recorded only to the memory card specified by the Record/Play setting using the Image Quality specifications you apply, but when that card is full, the camera switches automatically to the other card.

- ◎ **Rec. separately.** When this option is active, all images will be stored on both cards, but you can specify the image recording quality separately for each memory card in the Image Quality screen.
- ◎ **Rec. to Multiple.** All images are stored on both cards, using the quality settings you specify in the Image Quality screen.

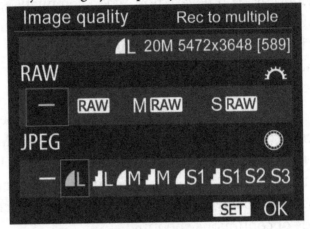

Figure 8.2

Choose your resolution, JPEG compression, and file format from this screen.

JPEG vs. RAW

You'll sometimes be told that RAW files are the "unprocessed" image information your camera produces, before it's been modified. That's nonsense. RAW files are no more unprocessed than your camera film is after it's been through the chemicals to produce a negative or transparency. A lot can happen in the developer that can affect the quality of a film image -- positively and negatively -- and, similarly, your digital image undergoes a significant amount of processing before it is saved as a RAW file. Canon even applies a name (DIGIC 6) to the digital image processing (DIP) chips used to perform this magic. chips. Your 7D II actually has *two* of them, for extra processing speed -- which makes the camera's blazing 10 fps continuous shooting (and some other features) possible.

A RAW file is more similar to a film camera's processed negative. It contains all the information, captured in 14-bit channels per color (and stored in a 16-bit space), with no compression, no sharpening, no application of any special filters or other settings you might have specified when you took the picture. Those settings are *stored* with the RAW file so they can be applied when the image is converted to a form compatible with your favorite image editor. However, using RAW conversion software such as Adobe Camera Raw or Canon's Digital Photo Professional, you can override those settings and apply settings of your own. You can select essentially the same changes there that you might have specified in your camera's picture-taking options.

RAW exists because sometimes we want to have access to all the information captured by the camera, before the camera's internal logic has processed it and converted the image to a standard file format. RAW doesn't save as much space as JPEG. What it does do is preserve all the information captured by your camera after it's been converted from analog to digital form. Of course, the 7D Mark II's RAW format preserves the *settings* information.

So, why don't we always use RAW? Although some photographers do save only in RAW format, it's more common to use either RAW plus one of the JPEG options or just shoot JPEG and avoid RAW altogether. That's because having only RAW files to work with can significantly slow down your workflow. While RAW is overwhelmingly helpful when an image needs to be fine-tuned, in other situations working with a RAW file, when all you really need is a good-quality, un-tweaked JPEG image, consumes time that you may not want to waste. For example, RAW images take longer to store on the memory card, and require more post-processing effort, whether you elect to go with the default settings in force when the picture was taken, or just make minor adjustments.

As a result, those who depend on speedy access to images or who shoot large numbers of photos at once may prefer JPEG over RAW. Wedding photographers, for example, might expose several thousand photos during a bridal affair and offer hundreds to clients as electronic proofs for possible inclusion in an album or transfer to a CD or DVD. These wedding shooters, who want JPEG images as their final product, take the time to make sure that their in-camera settings are correct, minimizing the need to post-process photos after the event. Given that their JPEGs are so good (in most cases thanks, in large part, to the pro photographer's extensive experience), there is little need to get bogged down shooting RAW.

Sports photographers also eschew RAW files. I visited a local Division III college one sunny September afternoon and managed to cover a football game, trot down a hill to shoot a women's soccer match later that afternoon, and ended up in the adjacent field house shooting a volleyball invitational tournament an hour later. I managed to shoot 1,920 photos, most of them at a 6 fps clip, in about four hours. I certainly didn't have any plans to do post-processing on very many of those shots, and firing the 7D Mark II at its maximum frame rate didn't allow RAW shooting, so carefully exposed and precisely focused JPEG images were my file format of choice that day.

JPEG was invented as a more compact file format that can store most of the information in a digital image, but in a much smaller size. JPEG predates most digital SLRs, and was initially used to squeeze down files for transmission over slow dialup connections. Even if you were using an early dSLR with 1.3 megapixel files for news photography, you didn't want to send them back to the office over a modem (Google it) at 1,200 bps.

But, as I noted, JPEG provides smaller files by compressing the information in a way that loses some image data. JPEG remains a viable alternative because it offers several different quality levels. At the highest quality Fine level, you might not be able to tell the difference between the original RAW file and the JPEG version. You've squeezed the image significantly without losing much visual information at all.

In my case, I shoot virtually everything at RAW+JPEG Fine. Most of the time, I'm not concerned about filling up my memory cards, as I usually have a minimum of five fast 64GB or 128GB memory cards with me. As I mentioned earlier, when shooting sports I'll shift to JPEG Fine (with no RAW file) to squeeze a little extra speed out of my 7D Mark II's continuous shooting mode, and to reduce the need to wade through eight-photo bursts taken in RAW format. On the other hand, on my last trip to Europe, I took only RAW (instead of my customary RAW+JPEG) photos, as I planned on doing at least some post-processing on many of the images for a travel book I was working on.

Image Review

You can adjust the amount of time an image is displayed for review on the LCD after each shot is taken. You can elect to disable this review entirely (Off), or choose display times of 2, 4, or 8 seconds. You can also select Hold, an indefinite display, which will keep your image on the screen until you use one of the other controls, such as the shutter button, Main Dial, or Quick Control Dial. Turning the review display off or choosing a brief duration can help preserve battery power. However, the 7D Mark II will always override the review display when the shutter button is partially or fully depressed, so you'll never miss a shot because a previous image was on the screen. Choose Review Time from the Shooting 1 menu, and select Off, 2 sec., 4 sec., 8 sec., or Hold. If you want to retain an image on the screen for a longer period, but don't want to use Hold as your default, press the Erase button under the Playback button monitor. The image will display until you choose Cancel or Erase from the menu that pops up at the bottom of the screen. A longer review time gives you an opportunity to delete a non-keeper quickly without a visit to the menu system.

Beep

The 7D Mark II's internal beeper provides a helpful chirp to signify various functions, such as the countdown of your camera's self-timer. You can switch it off if you want to avoid the beep because it's annoying, impolite, or distracting (at a concert or museum), or undesired for any other reason. It's one of the few ways to make the 7D Mark II a bit quieter, other than Live View's "silent shoot" mode. (I've actually had new dSLR owners ask me how to turn off the "shutter sound" the camera makes; such an option was available in the point-and-shoot camera they'd used previously.) Select Beep from the menu, press SET, and use the Quick Control Dial to choose Enable or Disable. Press SET again to activate your choice.

Release Shutter without Card

This entry in the Set-up 1 menu gives you the ability to snap off "pictures" without a memory card installed -- or to lock the camera shutter release if that is the case. It is sometimes called Play mode, because you can experiment with your camera's features or even hand your 7D Mark II to a friend to let him fool around, without any danger of pictures actually being taken. Back in our film days, we'd sometimes finish a roll, rewind the film back into its cassette surreptitiously, and then hand the camera to a child to take a few pictures -- without actually wasting any film. It's hard to waste digital film, but Release Shutter without Card mode is still appreciated by some, especially camera vendors who want to be able to demo a camera at a store or trade show, but don't want to have to equip each and every demonstrator model with a memory card. Choose this menu item, press SET, select Enable or Disable, and press SET again to turn this capability on or off.

Lens Aberration Correction

With certain lenses, under certain conditions, your images might suffer from one of three aberrations, each of which can be partially corrected by activating the correction items offered in this menu entry. Canon has compiled a database of corrections needed for many lenses *in Canon's own product line* (third-party lenses are not included), and you can enable or disable each of the three types of aberrations, depending on how much of a problem they are for you.

When you select this menu option from the Shooting 1 menu, the screen shown in **Figure 8.3** appears. The lens currently attached to the camera is shown, along with a notation whether correction data needed to brighten the corners is already registered in the camera. (Information about 30 of the most popular lenses is included in the 7D II's firmware.) If so, you can choose Enable to activate the feature, or Disable to turn it off. Select SET to confirm your choice. By default, Peripheral Illumination and Chromatic Aberration are set to Enable, and Distortion correction is set to Disable. All three types of corrections are discussed next.

Figure 8.3

The Lens Aberration Correction entry can help eliminate three kinds of lens de-

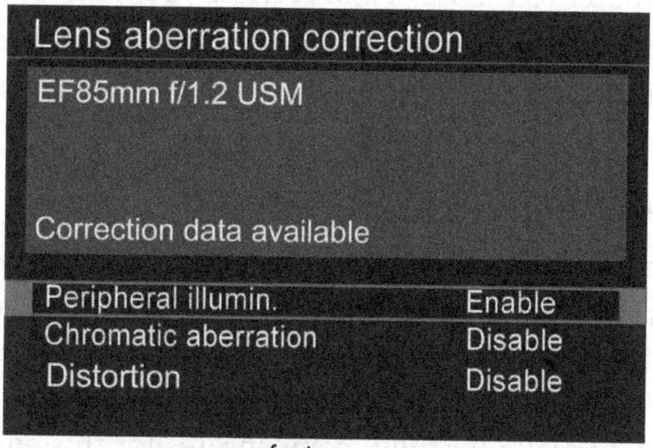

Lens aberration correction	
EF85mm f/1.2 USM	
Correction data available	
Peripheral illumin.	Enable
Chromatic aberration	Disable
Distortion	Disable

fects.

Note that in-camera correction must be specified *before* you take the photo, so that the magical DIGIC 6 processing engines can improve the photo before it is saved to the memory card. If you see the message "Cannot Correct -- No Data," the lens you have mounted is not included in the 7D II's built-in database. You can use the EOS Utility software to check which lenses are included, and can transfer information about unregistered lenses to your camera. Just follow these steps:

1. **Link up your camera.** Connect your 7D II to your computer using the USB cable supplied with the camera.

2. **Launch the EOS Utility.** Load the utility and click on Camera Settings/Remote Shooting from the splash screen that appears.

3. **Select the Shooting menu.** It's located on the menu bar about midway in the control panel that appears on your computer display. The Shooting menu icon is the white camera on a red background.

4. **Click on the Lens Aberration Correction choice**. The selection screen will appear.

5. **Choose your lens.** Select the category containing the lens you want to register from the panels at the top of the new

screen; then place a check mark next to all the lenses you'd like to register in the camera.

6. **Confirm your choice.** Click OK to send the data from your computer to the 7D II and register your lenses.

7. **Activate correction.** When a newly registered lens is mounted on the camera, you will be able to activate the correction feature for that lens from the Shooting 1 menu.

Peripheral Illumination Correction

One key defect is caused by a phenomenon called *vignetting*, which is a darkening of the four corners of the frame because of a slight amount of fall-off in illumination at those nether regions. This menu option allows you to activate Peripheral Illumination Correction, which partially (or fully) compensates for this effect. Depending on the f/stop you use, the lens mounted on the camera, and the focal length setting, vignetting can be non-existent, slight, or may be so strong that it appears you've used a too-small hood on your camera. (Indeed, the wrong lens hood can produce a vignette effect of its own.) Vignetting can be affected by the use of a telephoto converter (more on those in Chapter 7).

Peripheral illumination drop-off, even if pronounced, may not be much of a problem for you. I actually *add* vignetting, sometimes, in my image editor when shooting portraits and some other subjects. Slightly dark corners tend to focus attention on a subject in the middle of the frame. On the other hand, vignetting with subjects that are supposed to be evenly illuminated, such as landscapes, is seldom a benefit.

To minimize the effects of corner light fall-off, you can process RAW files using Digital Photo Professional (DPP), or, if you prefer to have your JPEG files fixed as you shoot them, use this menu option. **Figure 8.4** shows an image without peripheral illumination correction at top, and a corrected image at the bottom. I've exaggerated the vignetting a little to make it more evident on the printed page. Keep in mind that the amount of correction available with Digital Photo Pro can be a little more intense than that applied in the camera. In addition, the higher the ISO speed, the less correction is applied. If you see severe vignetting with a particular lens, focal length, or ISO setting, you might want to turn off this feature, shoot RAW, and apply correction using DPP instead.

Figure 8.4

Vignetting (top) is undesirable in a landscape photo. Peripheral illumination correction can fix these dark corners.

Chromatic Aberration

The second defect involves fringes of color around backlit objects, produced by *chromatic aberration*, which comes in two forms: *longitudinal/axial*, in which all the colors of light don't focus in the same plane; and *lateral/transverse*, in which the colors are shifted in one direction. (See **Figure 8.5**, top.) Your 7D II has a database of information about certain lenses, similar to the one provided for peripheral illumination correction. When this feature is enabled, the 7D II will automatically correct images taken with one of the supported lenses to reduce or eliminate the amount of color fringing seen in the final photograph. (See **Figure 8.5**, bottom.)

Figure 8.5

Lateral chromatic aberration, which shows as color fringes (top), can be corrected using the lens aberration correction feature (bottom).

Distortion

Distortion is the tendency of some lenses to bow outward (most often wide-angle lenses) or curve inward (found in some telephoto lenses). **Figure 8.6** (left) shows an exaggerated version of the outward curving variety, called *barrel distortion*, exhibited by many wide-angle lenses -- especially in fisheye optics, where the distortion is magically transformed into a feature.

In **Figure 8.6** (right), you can see inward bowing, or *pincushion distortion,* as found in many telephoto lenses. Both types can be partially fixed using Photoshop's Lens Correction or Photoshop Elements' Correct Camera Distortion filters. Or, you can apply this in-camera feature to fix mild distortion, taking advantage of the 7D II's database of EF and EF-S lens characteristics. You should realize that correcting lens distortion involves warping pixels, mostly at the edges of the frame, providing a little less sharpness in those areas. The image area of your final picture will be slightly smaller than the frame you composed, and, during playback the active focus point is not shown in the review image.

In addition, applying distortion correction involves extra processing, which can reduce the number of consecutive shots possible. Because the correction is applied *after* you take the picture, the effect is not displayed when shooting in Live View mode.

Figure 8.6

Left: Barrel distortion in wide-angle lenses becomes a useful feature with fisheye lenses. Right: Pincushion distortion causes straight lines at the edges of the frame to curve inward.

Flash Control

This multi-level menu entry includes six settings for controlling the 7D II's built-in, pop-up electronic flash unit, as well as accessory flash units you can attach to the camera (see **Figure 8.7**). I'll provide in-depth coverage of how you can use these options in Chapter 12, but will list the main options here for reference.

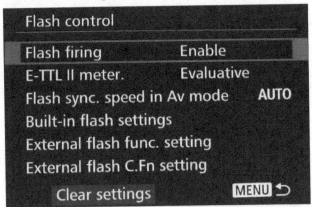

Figure 8.7

The Flash Control menu entry has six setting submenus.

Flash Firing

Use this option to enable or disable the built-in electronic flash. You might want to totally disable the camera's flash (both built-in and accessory flash) when shooting in sensitive environments, such as concerts, in museums, or during religious ceremonies. When disabled, the flash cannot fire even if you accidentally elevate it, or have an accessory flash attached and turned on. If you turn off the flash here, it is disabled in any exposure mode.

Note: To elevate your flash, press the Flash button on the left-hand side of the pentaprism housing. If it doesn't flip up, tap the shutter release button to wake it up.

E-TTL II Metering

You can choose Evaluative (Matrix) or Average metering modes for the electronic flash exposure meter. Evaluative looks at selected areas in the scene to calculate exposure, and is the best choice for most images because it attempts to interpret the type of scene being shot; Average calculates flash exposure by reading the entire scene, and it is possibly a good option if you want exposure to be calculated for the overall scene.

Flash Sync in AV mode

You can select the flash synchronization speed that will be used when working in Aperture-priority mode; choose from Auto (the camera selects the shutter speed from 30 seconds to 1/250th second), to a range embracing only the speeds from 1/250th to 1/60th second, or fixed at 1/250th second.

Normally, in Aperture-priority mode when using flash, you specify the f/stop to be locked in. The exposure is then adjusted by varying the output of the electronic flash. Because the primary exposure comes from the flash, the main effect of the shutter speed selected is on the secondary exposure from the ambient light on the scene.

As I'll explain in Chapter 12, Auto is your best choice under most conditions. The 7D II will choose a shutter speed that balances the flash exposure and available, ambient light. The 1/250th to 1/60th second setting locks out slower shutter speeds, preventing blur from camera/subject movement in the secondary ("ghost") exposure. However, the background may be rendered dark, if the flash is not strong enough to illuminate it. The 1/250th second (fixed) setting further reduces the chance of getting those blurry ghosts, but there is more of a chance the background will be dark. You'll find a more detailed explanation of these options in Chapter 12.

Built-in Flash Settings

The options that appear on this screen may vary, depending on your selected Flash Mode, which is the first entry on the Built-in Flash Settings screen. Select a Flash Mode first, choosing from E-TTL (automatic, through-the-lens flash metering, Manual (you set the exposure), or MULTI (repeating flash.) All these are discussed in more detail in Chapter 12.

In E-TTL mode:

⊙ **Shutter sync.** Available only when Wireless Functions are disabled.)in Normal Firing mode, you can choose 1st curtain sync, which fires the pre-flash used to calculate the exposure before the shutter opens, followed by the main flash as soon as the shutter is completely open. This is the default mode, and you'll generally perceive the pre-flash and main flash as a single burst. Alternatively, you can select 2nd curtain sync, which fires the pre-flash as soon as the shutter opens, and then triggers the main flash in a second burst at the end of the exposure, just before the shutter starts to close. (If the shutter speed is slow enough, you may clearly see both the pre-flash and main flash as separate bursts of light.) This action allows photographing a blurred trail of light of moving objects with sharp flash exposures at the beginning and the end of the exposure. This type of flash exposure is slightly different from what some other cameras produce using 2nd curtain sync. I'll explain how it works in Chapter 12. If you have an external compatible Speedlite attached, you can also choose Hi-speed sync, which allows you to use shutter speeds faster than 1/250th second, using the External Flash Function Setting menu, described next and explained in Chapter 12.

⊚ **Flash exposure compensation.** If you'd rather adjust flash exposure using a menu than with the ISO/Flash exposure compensation button, you can do that here. Select this option with the SET button, then dial in the amount of flash EV compensation you want using the directional buttons. The EV that was in place before you started to make your adjustment is shown as a blue indicator, so you can return to that value quickly. Use SET again to confirm your change, then tap MENU or press the MENU button twice to exit.

⊚ **Wireless functions.** Four options are listed, from top to bottom: Disable, External:Built-in flash ratio (you can set the proportional balance between your built-in and external flash), External Flash (only), and External+ Built-in. I'm going to leave the explanation of these options for Chapter 12, which includes a section on using the 7D II's wireless shooting capabilities.

In Manual Flash mode:

Shutter Sync and Wireless Functions appear, as described above. The Flash Exposure Compensation entry is replaced by a Flash Output option, which allows you to dial in a power level from 1/1 (full power) to 1/128 power.

In MULTI Flash mode:

This repeating strobe effect mode includes the same Flash Output option as Manual mode, but allows you to choose Frequency from 1 to 199 flashes per elapsed second, and Flash Count for up to 30 repeating bursts. In other words, if you selected 30 Hz (cycles per second) and 30 bursts, you'd get 30 bursts within a one-second interval. Select 60 Hz instead, and the 30 bursts would take place in one-half second. You'll find more on MULTI flash in Chapter 12.

External Flash Function Setting

You can access this menu only when you have a compatible electronic flash attached and switched on. If you press the INFO. button while adjusting flash settings, both the changes made to the settings of an attached external flash and to the built-in flash will be cleared. These options are quite complex, so I'm going to save the description of them for Chapter 12.

External Flash Custom Function Setting

Many external Speedlites from Canon include their own list of Custom Functions, which can be used to specify things like flash metering mode and flash bracketing sequences, as well as more sophisticated features, such as modeling light/flash (if available), use of external power sources (if attached), and functions of any slave unit attached to the external flash. This menu entry allows you to set an external flash unit's Custom Functions from your 7DII's menu.

Clear Settings

This entry allows you to zero-out any changes to your built-in flash's settings, your external flashes settings, and your external flash's Custom Functions, returning them all to their factory default settings.

Exposure Compensation/Automatic Exposure Bracketing

The first entry on the Shooting 2 menu is Expo. Comp./AEB, or exposure compensation and automatic exposure bracketing. (See **Figure 8.8**.) As you learned in Chapter 4, exposure compensation (added/subtracted by pressing the directional buttons while this menu screen is visible) increases or decreases exposure from the metered value.

Exposure bracketing using the 7D II's AEB feature is a way to shoot several consecutive exposures using different settings, to improve the odds that one will be exactly right. Automatic exposure bracketing is also an excellent way of creating the base exposures you'll need when you want to combine several shots to create a high dynamic range (HDR) image. (You'll find a discussion of HDR photography -- one of the latest rages -- in Chapter 4, too.)

To activate automatic exposure bracketing, select this menu choice, then rotate the Main Dial to spread or contract the three dots beneath the scale until you've defined the range you want the bracket to cover, shown as full-stop jumps in **Figure 8.14**. Then, use the touch screen or directional buttons to move the brackets right or left, biasing the bracketing toward underexposure (move left) or overexposure (move right).

When AEB is activated, the three bracketed shots will be exposed in this sequence: metered exposure, decreased exposure, increased exposure. You'll find more information about exposure bracketing in Chapter 4.

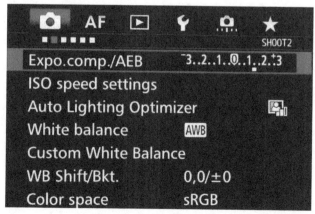

Figure 8.8

Exposure Compensation/AEB is the first entry in the Shooting 2 menu.

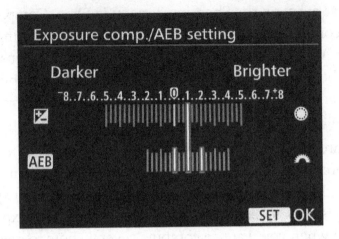

Figure 8.9

Set the range of the bracketed exposures.

ISO Speed Settings

Use this entry to select a specific ISO speed using a menu instead of the top-panel ISO button/menus, or to limit the range of ISO settings and shutter speeds that the camera selects automatically. The four subentries include:

- **ISO Speed.** You can choose Auto (the 7D Mark II will choose an ISO sensitivity appropriate for the light levels/exposure settings you've specified) or a fixed sensitivity from ISO 100 to ISO 16000, in one-third stop increments (for example, ISO 100, 125, or 160). If ISO expansion has been enabled using the ISO Speed Range choice (next), you can also choose, H1, or H2 (ISO 25600 and ISO 51200 equivalents, respectively).

- **ISO Speed Range.** This option lets you specify both a minimum and maximum ISO sensitivity that can be selected manually using the ISO Speed option (above). The minimum value you can select is in the range ISO 100-12800, while the maximum value you can specify for your range is ISO 200 to ISO 16000, plus H1 and H2 (ISO 25600 and 51200 equivalents, respectively.) Perhaps you have a preferred range and don't want to accidentally use any ISO setting below ISO 100 or higher than ISO 3200. You can specify those limits here.

- **Auto ISO Range.** Ordinarily, the 7D Mark II will select only ISO sensitivities between ISO 100 and ISO 6400. You can use the QCD to set the minimum to a range of ISO 100 to ISO 16000 and the maximum up to ISO 16000 using whole stop limits in either case. (You cannot select H1 or H2 even if you have expanded the ISO range using the ISO Speed Range setting above.) Note that you can't set a minimum that's higher than the maximum, or vice versa. This option allows advanced shooters to enable automated ISO selection within limits they can tightly control. If you were shooting indoor sports in Shutter-priority (Tv) mode, you might want to specify a 1/500th second shutter speed, and allow the camera to adjust the ISO between, say, ISO 400 and ISO 3200. Limits you set here will also be applied to the ISO Speed Safety Shift feature.

⊙ **Minimum Shutter Speed.** Use this when working with Program (P) or Aperture-priority (Av) modes to specify the slowest shutter speed that will be used when Auto ISO is enabled. (In Shutter-priority [Tv] mode, you always choose the shutter speed.) This option ensures that the Auto ISO changes will kick in before the camera reduces the shutter speed below a value you select. You can manually specify a speed from 1 second to 1/8000th second. (The latter setting would effectively mean that Auto ISO is enabled whenever the shutter speed is slower than 1/8000th second!) Or, you can let the camera select a kick-in speed, based on the focal length of the lens (that is, longer lenses activate Auto ISO at higher speeds to avoid camera-shake problems.) Use the main dial to specify slower or faster speeds. For example, perhaps you are shooting indoor sports and elect to choose Aperture-priority instead of Shutter-priority (say, your lens works better at f/4 than its maximum aperture of f/2.8, and you want to work with f/4 all the time). Set 1/250th second as a minimum shutter speed, and if a correct exposure calls for a shutter speed slower than that at f/4, Auto ISO will be used to boost the sensitivity instead. However, if you've handicapped the 7D Mark II by selecting an Auto ISO range that doesn't include a sensitivity high enough, the camera will *override this setting* and use a shutter speed lower than the minimum you specify anyway. The camera assumes (rightly or wrongly) that your upper ISO boundary is more important than your lower shutter speed limit. The lesson here is that if you really, really want to enforce a minimum shutter speed when using Auto ISO, make sure your upper limit is high enough. Note that the Minimum Shutter Speed setting is ignored when using flash or shooting movies.

Auto Lighting Optimizer

The Auto Lighting Optimizer provides a partial fix for images that are too dark or flat. Such photos typically have low contrast, and the Auto Lighting Optimizer improves them -- as you shoot -- by increasing both the brightness and contrast as required. The feature can be activated in Program, Aperture-priority, and Shutter-priority modes. You can select from four settings: Standard (the default value, which is always selected when using Scene Intelligent Auto mode), plus Low, Strong, and Disable. Press the INFO. button to add/remove a check mark icon that indicates the Auto Lighting Optimizer is disabled during manual exposure. Since you're likely to be specifying a particular exposure in Manual mode, you probably don't want the optimizer to interfere with your settings, so disabling the feature is the default.

White Balance

If automatic white balance or one of the seven preset settings available (Auto, Daylight, Shade, Cloudy/Twilight/Sunset, Tungsten, White Fluorescent, or Flash) aren't suitable, you can set a custom white balance using this menu option or a specific color temperature value. The screen shown in **Figure 8.10** is identical to the one that pops up when you select White Balance from the Quick Control screen. You can also select White Balance using the Metering Mode/WB button on top of the camera, which produces a slightly different screen that allows you to choose metering mode with the Main Dial, and White Balance with the Quick Control Dial. If you choose the "K" entry, you can select an exact color temperature from 2,500K to 10,000K using the Main Dial.

Of course, unless you own a specialized tool called a color temperature meter, you probably won't know the exact color temperature of your scene. However, knowing the color temperatures of the ten preset options can help you if you decide to tweak them by choosing a different color temperature setting. The values used by the 7D Mark II are as follows:

- **Auto (AWB).** 3000-7000K
- **Daylight.** 5200K
- **Shade.** 7000K
- **Cloudy.** 6000K
- **Twilight/Sunset.** 4000K
- **Tungsten.** 3200K
- **White fluorescent.** 4000K
- **Flash.** 6000K
- **Custom.** 2000-10000K
- **Color temperature.** 2500-10000K (Settable in 100K increments)

Choosing the right white balance can have a dramatic effect on the colors of your image, as you can see in **Figure 8.11**.

Figure 8.10

White balance presets can be chosen here.

Figure 8.11

Adjusting color temperature can provide different results of the same subject at 3,400K (left), 5,000K (center), and 2,800K (right).

The problem with the available presets (Daylight, Shade, etc.) is that you have only six of them, and in any given situation, all of them are likely to be wrong -- strictly speaking. The good news is that they are likely to be only a *little bit* wrong. The human eye is very adaptable, so in most cases you'll be perfectly happy with the results you get if you use Auto, or choose a preset that's in the white balance ballpark.

But if you absolutely must have the correct color balance, or are frequently dissatisfied with the color balance the 7D Mark II produces when using Auto or one of the presets, you can always shoot RAW, and adjust the final color balance in your image editor when converting the .cr2 file. Or, you can use a custom white balance procedure, described next.

If automatic white balance or one of the six preset settings available (Auto, Daylight, Shade, Cloudy/Twilight/Sunset, Tungsten, White Fluorescent, or Flash) aren't suitable, you can set a custom white balance using this menu option. The custom setting you establish will then be applied whenever you select Custom using the White Balance menu entry described earlier.

271

To set the white balance to an appropriate color temperature under the current ambient lighting conditions, focus manually (with the lens set on MF) on a plain white or gray object, such as a card or wall, making sure the object fills the spot metering circle in the center of the viewfinder. Then, take a photo. Next press the MENU button and select Custom WB from the Shooting 2 menu. Use the Quick Control Dial until the reference image you just took appears and press the SET button to store the white balance of the image as your Custom setting.

Using an ExpoDisk

Many photographers prefer to use a gadget called an ExpoDisk, from ExpoImaging, Inc. (www.expoimaging.com), which fits over (or attaches to) the front of your lens and provides a diffuse neutral (or semi-neutral) subject to measure with your camera's custom white balance feature. ExpoDisks cost $75 to $100 or so, depending on the filter size of your lens, but many just buy the 77mm version and hold it in front of their lens or use an adapter. (There's a strap attached, so you won't lose it.) Others have had mixed success using less expensive alternatives (such as the lid of a Pringles can). ExpoImaging also makes ExpoCap lens caps with similar diffusing features, and you can leave one of them on your lens at all times (at least, when you're not shooting).

There are two models, the standard ExpoDisk Neutral, and a Portrait model that produces a slightly warmer color balance suitable for portraits. The product produces the best results when you use it to measure the *incident light*; that is, the light falling onto your subject. In other words, instead of aiming your camera at your subject from the shooting position, take the time (if it's possible) to position yourself at the subject position and point your ExpoDisk-equipped lens toward the light source that will illuminate the scene. (However, don't point your camera directly at the Sun! Aim at the sky instead.)

I like to use the ExpoDisk in two situations:

- ⊚ **Outdoors under mixed lighting.** When you're shooting outdoors, you'll often find that your scene is illuminated by direct sunlight as well as by open shade, full shade, or a mixture of these. A custom white balance reading can help you zero in on the correct color balance in a situation that's hard to judge visually.

- ⊚ **When using studio flash.** It's a nasty secret that many studio flash units change color temperature when you adjust the power slider to scale down the output. Perhaps your 1600ws (watt second) flash puts out too much light to allow you to use a larger f/stop for selective focus. So, you dial it down to 1/4 power. That will likely change the color temperature of the unit slightly, particularly when compared to your 800ws fill light, which you've reduced to *half* power. You can use the ExpoDisk to measure the color temperature of your main light at its new setting, or aim it between two lights to obtain an average reading. The result will probably be close enough to the correct color temperature to satisfy most studio shooters.

White Balance Shift and Bracketing

White balance shift allows you to dial in a white balance color bias along the blue-yellow/amber dimensions, and/or magenta/green scale. In other words, you can set your color balance so that it is a little bluer or yellower (only), a little more magenta or green (only), or a combination of the two bias dimensions. You can also bracket exposures, taking several consecutive pictures each with a slightly different color balance biased in the directions you specify.

The process is a little easier to visualize if you look at **Figure 8.12**. The center intersection of lines BA and GM (remember high school geometry!) is the point of zero bias. Move the point at that intersection using the Quick Control Dial to locate it at any point on the graph using the blue-yellow/amber and green-magenta coordinates. The amount of shift will be displayed in the SHIFT box to the right of the graph.

White balance bracketing is like white balance shifting, only the bracketed changes occur along the bias axis you specify. The three center squares in **Figure 8.12** show that the white balance bracketing will occur in three-stop steps along the blue-yellow/amber axis. The amount of the bracketing is shown in the lower box to the right of the graph.

This form of bracketing is similar to exposure bracketing, but with the added dimension of hue. Bias bracketing can be performed in any JPEG-only mode. You can't use any RAW format or RAW+JPEG format because the RAW files already contain the information needed to fine-tune the white balance and white balance bias.

When you select WB SHIFT/BKT, the adjustment screen appears. First, you press the Quick Control Dial to set the range of the shift in either the green/magenta dimension (move to the left to change the vertical separation of the three dots representing the separate exposures) or in the blue-yellow/amber dimension by pressing the right cross key. Use the joystick-like multi-controller to move the bracket set around within the color space, and outside the green-magenta or blue-yellow/amber axes.

In most cases, it's fairly easy to determine if you want your image to be more green, more magenta, more blue, or more yellow, although judging your current shots on the LCD screen can be tricky unless you view the screen in a darkened location so it will be bright and easy to see. Bracketing is covered in Chapter 4.

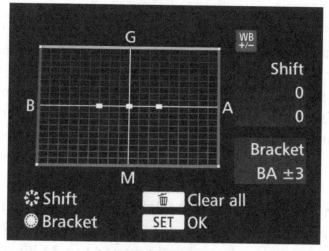

Figure 8.12

Use the Quick Control Dial and multi-controller to specify color balance bracketing using green-magenta bias or to specify blue-yellow/amber bias.

Color Space

When you are using one of the Creative Zone modes, you can select one of two different color spaces (also called *color gamuts*) using this menu entry, shown previously among the other menu choices in **Figure 8.7**. One color space is named *Adobe RGB* (because it was developed by Adobe Systems in 1998), while the other is called *sRGB* (supposedly because it is the *standard* RGB color space). These two color gamuts define a specific set of colors that can be applied to the images your 7D Mark II captures.

The Color Space menu choice applies directly to JPEG images shot using P, Tv, Av, and M exposure modes. When you're using Scene Intelligent Auto mode, the 7D Mark II uses the sRGB color space for all the JPEG images you take. RAW images are a special case. They have the information for *both* sRGB and Adobe RGB, but when you load such photos into your image editor, it will default to sRGB (with Scene Intelligent Auto or Creative Auto shots) or the color space specified here, unless you change that setting while importing the photos.

You may be surprised to learn that the 7D Mark II doesn't automatically capture *all* the colors we see. Unfortunately, that's impossible because of the limitations of the sensor and the filters used to capture the fundamental red, green, and blue colors, as well as that of the elements used to display those colors on your camera and computer monitors. Nor is it possible to *print* every color our eyes detect, because the inks or pigments used don't absorb and reflect colors perfectly. In short, your sensor doesn't capture all the colors that we can see, your monitor can't display all the colors that the sensor captures, and your printer outputs yet another version.

On the other hand, the 7D Mark II does capture quite a few more colors than we need. The original 14-bit RAW image contains a possible 4.4 *trillion* different hues, which are condensed down to a mere 16.8 million possible colors when converted to a 24-bit (eight bits per channel) image. While 16.8 million colors may seem like a lot, it's a small subset of 4.4 trillion captured, and an even smaller subset of all the possible colors we can see. The set of colors, or gamut, that can be reproduced or captured by a given device (scanner, digital camera, monitor, printer, or some other piece of equipment) is represented as a color space that exists within the larger full range of colors.

Adobe RGB is what is often called an *expanded* color space, because it can reproduce a range of colors that is spread over a wider range of the visual spectrum. Adobe RGB is useful for commercial and professional printing. You don't need this range of colors if your images will be displayed primarily on your computer screen or output by your personal printer.

The other color space, sRGB, is recommended for images that will be output locally on the user's own printer, as this color space matches that of the typical inkjet printer fairly closely. While both Adobe RGB and sRGB can reproduce the exact same 16.8 million absolute colors, Adobe RGB spreads those colors over a larger portion of the visible spectrum, as you can see in the figure. Think of a box of crayons (the jumbo 16.8 million crayon variety). Some of the basic crayons from the original sRGB set have been removed and replaced with new hues not contained in the original box. Your "new" box contains colors that can't be reproduced by your computer monitor, but which work just fine with a commercial printing press.

Best of Both Worlds

As I mentioned, if you're using a Basic Zone mode, the 7D Mark II selects the sRGB color space automatically. In addition, you may choose to set the sRGB color space with this menu entry to apply that gamut to all your other photos as well. But, in either case, you can still easily obtain Adobe RGB versions of your photos if you need them. Just shoot using RAW+JPEG. You'll end up with sRGB JPEGs suitable for output on your own printer, but you can still extract an Adobe RGB version from the RAW file at any time. It's like capturing two different color spaces at once -- sRGB and Adobe RGB -- and getting the best of both worlds.

Of course, choosing the right color space doesn't solve the problems that result from having each device in the image chain manipulating or producing a slightly different set of colors. To that end, you'll need to investigate the wonderful world of *color management,* which uses hardware and software tools to match or *calibrate* all your devices, as closely as possible, so that what you see more closely resembles what you capture, what you see on your computer display, and what ends up on a printed hardcopy. Entire books have been devoted to color management, and most of what you need to know doesn't directly involve your Canon 7D Mark II, so I won't detail the nuts and bolts here.

To manage your color, you'll need, at the bare minimum, some sort of calibration system for your computer display, so that your monitor can be adjusted to show a standardized set of colors that is repeatable over time. (What you see on the screen can vary as the monitor ages, or even when the room light changes.) I use a Datacolor (www.datacolor.com) Spyder 4 monitor color correction system for my computer's dual 26-inch wide screen LCD displays. It checks room light levels every five minutes, and reminds me to recalibrate every week or two using a small sensor device that attaches temporarily to the front of the screen and interprets test patches that the software displays during calibration. The rest of the time, the sensor sits in the stand shown, measuring the room illumination, and adjusting my monitors for higher or lower ambient light levels.

Picture Style

Jump to the Shooting 3 menu, and the entry you'll find at the top of the listings is Picture Styles (see **Figure 8.13**). This feature is one of the most important tools for customizing the way your Canon 7D Mark II renders its photos. Picture Styles are a type of fine-tuning you can apply to your photos to change certain characteristics of each image taken using a particular Picture Style setting. The parameters you can specify for full-color images include the amount of sharpness, degree of contrast, the richness of the color, and the hue of skin tones. For black-and-white images, you can tweak the sharpness and contrast, but the two color adjustments (meaningless in a monochrome image) are replaced by controls for filter effects (which I'll explain shortly), and sepia, blue, purple, or green tone overlays.

The Canon 7D Mark II has five preset color Picture Styles, for Standard, Portrait, Landscape, Neutral, and Faithful pictures, plus Auto, and three user-definable settings called User Def. 1, User Def. 2, and User Def. 3, which you can define to apply to any sort of shooting situation you want, such as sports, architecture, or baby pictures. There is also a sixth, Monochrome, Picture Style that allows you to adjust filter effects or add color toning to your black-and-white images. See **Figure 8.14** for the main Picture Style menu.

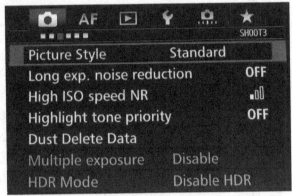

Figure 8.13

FAST TRACK GUIDE

Picture Styles is the first entry in the Shooting 3 menu.

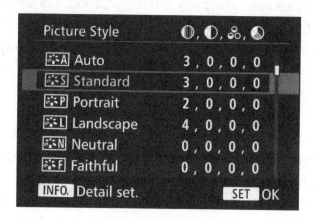

Figure 8.14

Ten different Picture Styles are available from this scrolling menu; these six plus Monochrome and three User Def. styles not shown.

Picture Styles are extremely flexible. Canon has set the parameters for the five predefined color Picture Styles and the single monochrome Picture Style to suit the needs of most photographers. But you can adjust any of those "canned" Picture Styles to settings you prefer. Better yet, you can use those three User Definition files to create brand-new styles that are all your own. If you want rich, bright colors to emulate Velvia film or the work of legendary photographer Pete Turner, you can build your own color-soaked style. If you want soft, muted colors and less sharpness to create a romantic look, you can do that, too. Perhaps you'd like a setting with extra contrast for shooting outdoors on hazy or cloudy days. The parameters applied when using Picture Styles follow and are shown in **Figure 8.15.**

- ◉ **Sharpness.** This parameter determines the apparent contrast between the outlines or edges in an image, which we perceive as image sharpness. You can adjust the sharpness of the image between values of 0 (no sharpening added) to 7 (dramatic additional sharpness). When adjusting sharpness, remember that more is not always a good thing. A little softness is necessary (and is introduced by a blurring "anti-alias" filter in front of the sensor) to reduce or eliminate the moiré effects that can result when details in your image form a pattern that is too close to the pattern, or frequency, of the sensor itself. The default levels of sharpening (which are, for most Picture Styles, not 0) were chosen by Canon to allow most moiré interference to be safely blurred to invisibility, at the cost of a little sharpness. As you boost sharpness (either using a Picture Style or in your image editor), moiré can become a problem, plus, you may end up with those noxious "halos" that appear around the edges of images that have been over sharpened. Use this adjustment with care.

- ◉ **Contrast.** Use this control, with values from -4 (low contrast) to +4 (higher contrast), to change the number of middle tones between the deepest blacks and brightest whites. Low-contrast settings produce a flatter-looking photo, while high-contrast adjustments may improve the tonal rendition while possibly losing detail in the shadows or highlights.

⊙ **Saturation.** This parameter, adjustable from -4 (low saturation) to +4 (high saturation) controls the richness of the color, making, say, a red tone appear to be deeper and fuller when you increase saturation, and tend more toward lighter, pinkish hues when you decrease saturation of the reds. Boosting the saturation too much can mean that detail may be lost in one or more of the color channels, producing what is called "clipping." You can detect this phenomenon when using the RGB histograms, as described in Chapter 4.

⊙ **Color tone.** This adjustment has the most effect on skin tones, making them either redder (0 to -4) or yellower (0 to +4).

⊙ **Filter effect (Monochrome only).** Filter effects do not add any color to a black-and-white image. Instead, they change the rendition of gray tones as if the picture were taken through a color filter. I'll explain this distinction more completely in the sidebar "Filters vs. Toning" later in this section.

⊙ **Toning effect (Monochrome only).** Using toning effects preserves the monochrome tonal values in your image, but adds a color overlay that gives the photo a sepia, blue, purple, or green cast.

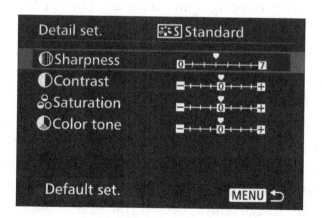

Figure 8.15

The Picture Styles parameters for styles other than Monochrome include Sharpness, Contrast, Saturation, and Color Tone.

The predefined Picture Styles are as follows:

◉ **Auto.** Adjusts the color to make outdoor scenes look more vivid, with richer colors.

◉ **Standard.** This Picture Style applies a set of parameters, including boosted sharpness, that are useful for most picture taking, and which are applied automatically when using Basic Zone modes other than Portrait or Landscape.

◉ **Portrait.** This style boosts saturation for richer colors when shooting portraits, which is particularly beneficial for women and children, while reducing sharpness slightly to provide more flattering skin texture. The Basic Mode Portrait setting uses this Picture Style. You might prefer the Faithful style for portraits of men when you want a more rugged or masculine look, or when you want to emphasize character lines in the faces of older subjects of either gender.

◉ **Landscape.** This style increases the saturation of blues and greens, and increases both color saturation and sharpness for more vivid landscape images. The Basic Zone Landscape mode uses this setting.

◉ **Neutral.** This Picture Style is a less-saturated and lower-contrast version of the Standard style. Use it when you want a more muted look to your images, or when the photos you are taking seem too bright and contrasty (say, at the beach on a sunny day).

◉ **Faithful.** The goal of this style is to render the colors of your image as accurately as possible, roughly in the same relationships as seen by the eye.

◉ **Monochrome.** Use this Picture Style to create black-and-white photos in the camera. If you're shooting JPEG only, the colors are gone forever. But if you're shooting JPEG+RAW you can convert the RAW files to color as you import them into your image editor, even if you've shot using the Monochrome Picture Style. Your 7D Mark II displays the images in black-and-white on the screen during playback, but the colors are there in the RAW file for later retrieval. You can use the

Monochrome Picture Style even if you are using one of the RAW formats alone, without a JPEG version. The 7D Mark II displays your images on the screen in black-and-white, and marks the RAW image as monochrome so it will default to that style when you import it into your image editor. However, the color information is still present in the RAW file and can be retrieved, at your option, when importing the image.

Selecting Picture Styles

Canon makes selecting a Picture Style for use very easy, and, to prevent you from accidentally changing an existing style when you don't mean to, divides *selection* and *modification* functions into two separate tasks. There are actually several different ways to choose from among your existing Picture Styles:

- **Picture Styles menu.** Use this menu entry and scroll down the list shown in **Figure 8.14** with the Quick Control Dial or multi-selector until the style you want to use is highlighted. Then press SET.

- **Quick Control screen.** Press the Q button and navigate to the Picture Styles icon at left of the Quick Control screen with the multi-selector. Press SET, then highlight the Style you want to use and press SET again.

- **Creative Photo button.** The top button in the row of five to the left of the LCD monitor produces a screen allowing you to choose from Picture Style, Multiple Exposure, or HDR. Select Picture Style and press SET and a screen similar to the one shown in **Figure 8.16** appears. (This screen is similar to the one produced by the Quick Control screen.)

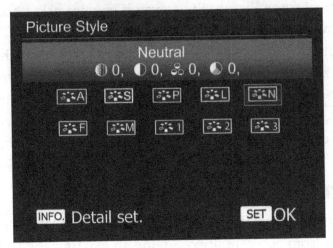

Figure 8.16

*Choose Picture Style from the screen produced by the Creative Photo button (a
similar screen is summoned from the Quick Control menu).*

Defining Picture Styles

Canon makes interpreting current Picture Style settings and applying changes very easy. The current settings of the visible Picture
Style options are shown as numeric values on the menu screen.
Some camera vendors use word descriptions, like Sharp, Extra
Sharp, or Vivid, More Vivid that are difficult to relate to. The 7D
Mark II's settings, on the other hand, are values on uniform scales,
with seven steps (from 1 to 7) for sharpness, and plus/minus four
steps clustered around a zero (no change) value for contrast and saturation (so you can change from low contrast/low saturation, -4, to
high contrast/high saturation, +4), as well as color tone (-4/reddish
to +4/yellowish). The individual icons near the top of **Figure 8.16**
represent (left to right) Sharpness, Contrast, Saturation, and Color
Tone.

You can change one of the existing Picture Styles or define your
own whenever the Picture Styles menu is visible. Just press the
INFO. button and follow these steps:

1. **Choose a style to modify.** Use the Quick Control Dial to
   highlight the style you'd like to adjust.
2. **Activate adjustment mode.** Press the INFO. button to
   choose Detail Set. If you're coming from the Shooting 2

menu, the screen that appears next will look like the one shown in **Figure 8.18** for the five color styles or three User Def. styles. If you've accessed the adjustment screen by pressing the Creative Photo/Picture Styles button or Quick Control screen first, the screen looks much the same, but has blue highlighting instead of red.

3. **Choose a parameter to change.** Use the Quick Control Dial to scroll among the four parameters, plus Default Set. at the bottom of the screen, which restores the values to the preset numbers.

4. **Activate changes.** Press SET to change the values of one of the four parameters.

5. **Adjust values.** Use the Quick Control Dial to move the triangle to the value you want to use. Note that the previous value remains on the scale, represented by a gray triangle. This makes it easy to return to the original setting if you want.

6. **Confirm changes.** Press the SET button to lock in that value, then press the MENU button three times to back out of the menu system.

Any Picture Style that has been changed from its defaults will be shown in the Picture Style menu with blue highlighting the altered parameter. You don't have to worry about changing a Picture Style and then forgetting that you've modified it. A quick glance at the Picture Style menu will show you which styles and parameters have been changed.

Making changes in the Monochrome Picture Style is slightly different, as the Saturation and Color Tone parameters are replaced with Filter Effect and Toning Effect options. (Keep in mind that once you've taken a JPEG photo using a Monochrome Picture Style, you can't convert the image back to full color.) You can choose from Yellow, Orange, Red, Green filters, or None, and specify Sepia, Blue, Purple, or Green toning, or None. You can still set the Sharpness and Contrast parameters that are available with the other Picture Styles. **Figure 8.20** shows filter effects being applied to the Monochrome Picture Style.

Adjusting Styles with the Picture Style Editor

If you'd rather edit Picture Styles in your computer, the Picture Style Editor supplied for your camera in versions for both Windows and Macs, allows you to create your own custom Picture Styles, or edit existing styles, including the Standard, Landscape, Faithful, and other predefined settings already present in your 7D Mark II. You can change sharpness, contrast, color saturation, and color tone -- and a lot more -- and then save the modifications as a PF2 file that can be uploaded to the camera, or used by Digital Photo Professional to modify a RAW image as it is imported.

To create and load your own Picture Style, just follow these steps:

1. **Load the editor.** Launch the Picture Style Editor (PSE, not to be confused with the *other* PSE, Photoshop Elements).

2. **Access a RAW file.** Load a RAW CR2 image you'd like to use as a reference into PSE. You can drag a file from a folder into the editor's main window, or use the Open command in the File menu.

3. **Choose an existing style to base your new style on.** Select any of the base styles except for Standard. Your new style will begin with all the attributes of the base style you choose, so start with one that already is fairly close to the look you want to achieve ("tweaking" is easier than building a style from the ground up).

4. **Split the screen.** You can compare the appearance of your new style with the base style you are working from. Near the lower-left edge of the display pane are three buttons you can click to split the old/new styles vertically, horizontally, or return to a single image.

5. **Dial in basic changes.** Click the Advanced button in the Tool palette to pop up the Advanced Picture Style Settings dialog box that appears at left in the figure. These are the same parameters you can change in the camera. Click OK when you're finished.

6. **Make advanced changes.** The Tool palette has additional functions for adjusting hue, tonal range, and curves. Use of these tools is beyond the scope of a single chapter, let alone a notation in a list, but if you're familiar with the advanced tools in Photoshop, Photoshop Elements, Digital Photo Pro, or another image editor, you can experiment to your heart's content. Note that these modifications go way beyond what you can do with Picture Styles in the camera itself, so learning how to work with them is worth the effort.

7. **Save your Picture Style.** When you're finished, choose Save Picture Style File from the File menu to store your new style as a PF2 file on your hard disk. Add a caption and copyright information to your style in the boxes provided. If you click Disable Subsequent Editing, your style will be "locked" and protected from further changes, and the modifications you did make will be hidden from view (just in case you dream up your own personal, "secret" style). But you'll be unable to edit that style later on. If you think you might want to change your custom Picture Style, save a second copy without marking the Disable Subsequent Editing box.

Uploading a Picture Style to the Camera

Now it's time to upload your new style to your Canon 7D Mark II into one of your three User Def. slots in the Picture Style array. Just follow these steps:

1. **Link your camera for upload.** Connect your camera to your computer using the USB cable, turn the 7D Mark II on, launch the EOS Utility, and click the Camera Settings/Remote Shooting choice in the splash screen.

2. **Choose the Shooting menu.** It's marked with an icon of a white camera on a red background, from the menu bar located about midway in the control panel that appears on your computer display.

3. **Select Register User Defined Style.** Click on the box, outlined in red in the figure, to produce the Register Picture Style dialog box.

4. **Choose a User Def. tab.** Click on one of the three tabs, labeled User Def. 1, User Def. 2, or User Def. 3. Each tab will include the name of the current Picture Style active in that tab.

5. **Click the Open File button and choose the Picture Style file to load.** The Picture Styles you've saved (or downloaded from another source) will appear with a PF2 extension. Click on the one you want to use, and then click the Open button in the Open dialog box.

6. **Upload Picture Style to the camera.** The Register Picture Style File dialog box will return. Click OK and the Picture Style will be uploaded to the camera in the User Def. "slot" represented by the tab you've chosen. The name of the Picture Style will appear in the 7D Mark II's menu in place of User Def. 1 (or User Def. 2/User Def. 3).

Changing a Picture Style's Settings from the EOS Utility

You can modify the settings of a Picture Style that's already loaded into your camera from the EOS Utility when your camera is linked to your computer. Just follow these steps:

1. **Link your camera to the computer.** Connect your camera to your computer using the USB cable, turn the 7D Mark II on, launch the EOS Utility, and click the Camera Settings/Remote Shooting choice in the splash screen.

2. **Choose the Shooting menu.** It's marked with an icon of a white camera on a red background, from the menu bar located about midway in the control panel that appears on your computer display.

3. **Access the Picture Style.** Click on the Picture Style choice. The currently active Picture Style in the camera will be shown, along with its detail settings.

4. **Choose a Picture Style to modify.** Click the Picture Style box to produce a listing of all the available Picture Styles.

5. **Click Detail Set**. At lower left, Landscape is now highlighted. When you click on Detail Set., a dialog box appears. You can move the sliders to change the settings, as described earlier. You can also click the Default Set. button to return the settings to their original values.

6. **Confirm choice.** Click Return when you've finished making changes, and the Picture Style you've modified will be changed in the camera.

7. **Exit EOS Utility.** Disconnect your camera from your computer, and your modified style is ready to use.

Long Exposure Noise Reduction

This entry allows you to enable or disable long exposure noise reduction, or allow the 7D Mark II to evaluate your scene and decide whether to use this noise-canceling adjustment. Visual noise is that graininess that shows up as multicolored specks in images, and this setting helps you manage it. In some ways, noise is like the excessive grain found in some high-speed photographic films. However, while photographic grain is sometimes used as a special effect, it's rarely desirable in a digital photograph.

The visual noise-producing process is something like listening to a CD in your car, and then rolling down all the windows. You're adding sonic noise to the audio signal, and while increasing the CD player's volume may help a bit, you're still contending with an unfavorable signal to noise ratio that probably mutes tones (especially higher treble notes) that you really want to hear.

The same thing happens when the analog signal is amplified: You're increasing the image information in the signal, but boosting the background fuzziness at the same time. Tune in a very faint or distant AM radio station on your car stereo. Then turn up the volume. After a certain point, turning up the volume further no longer helps you hear better. There's a similar point of diminishing returns for digital sensor ISO increases and signal amplification as well.

These processes create several different kinds of noise. Noise can be produced from high ISO settings. As the captured information is amplified to produce higher ISO sensitivities, some random noise in the signal is amplified along with the photon information. Increasing the ISO setting of your camera raises the threshold of sensitivity so that fewer and fewer photons are needed to register as an exposed pixel. Yet, that also increases the chances of one of those phantom photons being counted among the real-life light particles, too.

Fortunately, the 7D Mark II's sensor and its digital processing chip are optimized to produce the low noise levels, so ratings as high as ISO 800 or ISO 3200 can be used routinely (although there will be some noise, of course), and even ISO 6400 can generate good results.

A second way noise is created is through longer exposures. Extended exposure times allow more photons to reach the sensor, but increase the likelihood that some photosites will react randomly even though not struck by a particle of light. Moreover, as the sensor remains switched on for the longer exposure, it heats, and this heat can be mistakenly recorded as if it were a barrage of photons. This entry can be used to tailor the amount of noise-canceling performed by the digital signal processor.

- **Off.** Disables long exposure noise reduction. Use this setting when you want the maximum amount of detail present in your photograph, even though higher noise levels will result. This setting also eliminates the extra time needed to take a picture caused by the noise reduction process. If you plan to use only lower ISO settings (thereby reducing the noise caused by ISO amplification), the noise levels produced by longer exposures may be acceptable. For example, you might be shooting a river spilling over rocks at ISO 100 with the camera mounted on a tripod, using a neutral-density filter and long exposure to cause the pounding water to blur slightly. To maximize detail in the non-moving portions of your photos, you can switch off long exposure noise reduction. Because the noise-reduction process used with Auto and On can effectively double the time required to take a picture,

Off is a good setting to use when you want to avoid this delay when possible.

- **Auto.** The 7D Mark II examines your photo taken with an exposure of one second or longer, and if long exposure noise is detected, a second, blank exposure is made and compared to the first image. Noise found in the "dark frame" image is subtracted from your original picture, and only the noise-corrected image is saved to your memory card.

- **Enable.** When this setting is activated, the 7D Mark II applies dark frame subtraction to all exposures longer than one second. You might want to use this option when you're working with high ISO settings (which will already have noise boosted a bit) and want to make sure that any additional noise from long exposures is eliminated, too. Noise reduction will be applied to some exposures that would not have caused it to kick in using the Auto setting. While the "dark frame" is being exposed, the LCD screen will be blank during Live View mode, and the number of shots you can take in continuous shooting mode will be reduced. White balance bracketing is disabled during this process.

High ISO Speed Noise Reduction

The other type of noise results from using higher ISO settings. This entry allows you to specify just how much or how little of this noise reduction to apply, which can be a valuable option because noise reduction does eliminate detail while blurring the amount of noise. The default is Standard noise reduction, but you can specify Low or High noise reduction, or disable noise reduction entirely. At lower ISO values, noise reduction improves the appearance of shadow areas without affecting highlights; at higher ISO settings, noise reduction is applied to the entire photo. Note that when the High option is selected, the maximum number of continuous shots that can be taken will decrease significantly, because of the additional processing time for the images.

- **Disable.** No additional noise reduction will be applied.

- ⊙ **Low.** A smaller amount of noise reduction is used. This will increase the grainy appearance, but preserve more fine image detail.

- ⊙ **Standard.** At lower ISO values, noise reduction is applied primarily to shadow areas; at higher ISO settings, noise reduction affects the entire image.

- ⊙ **High.** More aggressive noise reduction is used, at the cost of some image detail, adding a "mushy" appearance that may be noticeable and objectionable. Because of the image processing applied by this setting, your continuous shooting maximum burst will decrease significantly.

- ⊙ **Multi Shot Noise Reduction.** The 7D II takes four shots continuously, merges and aligns them into a single image, and applies high intensity noise reduction. This setting is available only if you're shooting JPEG (only.) If you've selected RAW or RAW+JPEG, then Standard noise reduction is applied instead.

Highlight Tone Priority

This setting concentrates the available tones in an image from the middle grays up to the brightest highlights, in effect expanding the dynamic range of the image at the expense of shadow detail. You'd want to activate this option when shooting subjects in which there is lots of important detail in the highlights, and less detail in shadow areas. Highlight tones will be preserved, while shadows will be allowed to go dark more readily (and may exhibit an increase in noise levels). Bright beach or snow scenes, especially those with few shadows (think high noon, when the shadows are smaller) can benefit from using Highlight Tone Priority. Your choices:

- ⊙ **Disable/OFF.** The 7D Mark II's normal dynamic range is applied. Note that when Highlight Tone Priority is switched off, the related Auto Lighting Optimizer setting (discussed earlier in this chapter) functions normally.

- ⊙ **Enable/D+.** Highlight areas are given expanded tonal values, while the tones available for shadow areas are reduced. The

ISO 100 sensitivity setting is disabled and only ISO 200 to ISO 25600 (or ISO 200-12800 for movies) are available. You can tell that this restriction is in effect by viewing the D+ icon shown in the viewfinder, on the ISO Selection screen, and in the shooting information display for a particular image. Image noise may slightly increase as the camera manipulates the image. Note that this setting disables the Auto Lighting Optimizer.

Dust Delete Data

This menu choice lets you "take a picture" of any dust or other particles that may be adhering to your sensor. The 7D Mark II will then append information about the location of this dust to your photos, so that the Digital Photo Professional software can use this reference information to identify dust in your images and remove it automatically. You should capture a Dust Delete Data photo from time to time as your final line of defense against sensor dust.

To use this feature, select Dust Delete Data, select OK and press the SET button. The camera will first perform a self-cleaning operation by applying ultrasonic vibration to the low-pass filter that resides on top of the sensor. Then, a screen will appear asking you to press the shutter button. Point the 7D Mark II at a solid-white card with the lens set on manual focus and rotate the focus ring to infinity. When you press the shutter release, the camera takes a photo of the card using Aperture-priority and f/22 (which provides enough depth-of-field [actually, in this case, *depth-of-focus*] to image the dust sharply). The "picture" is not saved to your memory card but, rather, is stored in a special memory area in the camera. Finally, a "Data obtained" screen appears.

The Dust Delete Data information is retained in the camera until you update it by taking a new "picture." The 7D Mark II adds the information to each image file automatically.

Multiple Exposure

This option, shown in **Figure 8.17**, lets you combine two to nine separate images into one photo without the need for an image editor like Photoshop and can be an entertaining way to return to those thrilling days of yesteryear, when complex photos were created in the camera itself. In truth, prior to the digital age, multiple exposures were a cool, groovy, far-out, hep/hip, phat, sick, fabulous way of producing composite images. Today, it's more common to take the lazy way out, snap two or more pictures, and then assemble them in an image editor like Photoshop.

However, if you're willing to spend the time planning a multiple exposure (or are open to some happy accidents), there is a lot to recommend the multiple exposure capability that Canon has bestowed on the 7D Mark II. For one thing, the camera is able to combine two or more images using the RAW data from the sensor, producing photos that are blended together more smoothly than is likely for anyone who's not a Photoshop guru. In addition, Canon has eliminated one annoying aspect of the feature found in some cameras: it's not necessary to return to the menu to activate multiple exposure for each and every set. If you want to take a series of pictures, you can set it once, and forget it. (But don't forget to turn it off when you're done!)

Multiple exposures cannot be captured if white balance bracketing, HDR shooting, or movie-making modes are in use. Before you begin snapping your own multi-exposures, you'll need to set your parameters using the following options discussed below.

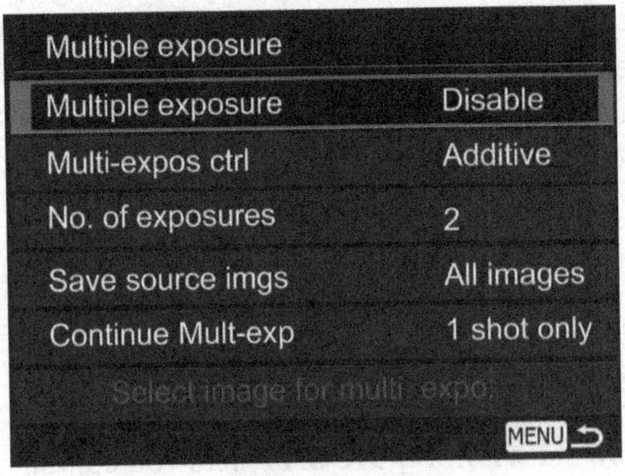

Figure 8.17

Multiple exposure using Additive exposure, and no exposure compensation (left.)
Multiple exposure using Average exposure. (Right.)

Multiple Exposure

The Disable option deactivates the multiexposure feature, but you can quickly choose either of the two On variations. This is the "master control" that allows you to turn multiple exposure on and off (leaving the other parameters you've set unchanged) and to select from two different multiexposure modes.

- ⊚ **Disable.** Deactivates multiple exposure.
- ⊚ **On: Func/Ctrl.** In the Function and Control Priority mode, the camera snaps off each series, but returns control of the 7D Mark II to you between each set so you can review your results or make any adjustments in exposure settings or other parameters. I tend to experiment a lot when firing off multiple exposures and prefer this mode for shooting subjects that aren't moving around a lot, and when I want to carefully arrange objects in the frame between shots. Its main disadvantage is that continuous shooting speed is reduced, so it's not the best choice for action.
- ⊚ **On: ContShtng.** In Continuous Shooting Priority mode, the 7D Mark II is able to operate in continuous mode at whatever speed you specify, up to 6 frames per second. I use this when shooting multiple exposures at dance and ballet performances, as shown in **Figure 8.24**. I can't plan each individual image, anyway, and want to be able to grab separate shots of each movement as they unfold. In this mode, image review, playback, menus, and live view are all disabled while you're shooting. In addition, because of the speed at which images are captured, only the final, combined image is saved on your memory card; the Save Source Imgs option, described below, is disabled. While you can initiate a multiple exposure in this mode while live view is active, the 7D Mark II flips the mirror back down after the first shot and subsequent images as they are taken can be monitored only through the optical viewfinder.

Multi-Expos Ctrl

This essential parameter can determine how successful your multiple exposure is, by controlling how each individual exposure is merged with the overlapping portions of the other images in the series. Picture an image like the one shown in **Figure 8.24**. The dancer was photographed against a plain, dark background. He happened to be moving, too, so none of the three images overlapped with each other, or with any details of the featureless background. But in **Figure 8.25**, the dancer remained in place, so that each subsequent image overlapped the others slightly. The Multi-Exposure Control feature allows you to specify how the images are combined with these choices:

⊙ **Additive.** Each individual shot in the series is by default given the full exposure, which is what I used for **Figure 8.18** (left.) Because the background was totally black and the subject was moving and did not overlap, the effect was to combine three separate images into one image.

However, you can manually adjust the amount of exposure each shot is given by dialing in exposure compensation, making this mode useful for overlapping images as well. The customary procedure is to specify -1 stop exposure compensation for two shots, -1.5 EV for three-shot multiple exposures, and -2 EV for four-shot multis. Manually calculating the amount of negative exposure compensation allows you to fine-tune the look of overlapping images.

⊙ **Average.** Choose this option and the 7D Mark II will apply appropriate negative exposure compensation for you, based on the number of exposures you're combining into a single image. If your multiple exposures happen to be of the same scene (rather than separate subjects), the camera will attempt to ensure that the background receives the equivalent of a full exposure. I used this option for **Figure 8.18** (right.)

⊙ **Bright.** This mode uses special algorithms to compare the first shot in a series with subsequent images that will be added to that base shot, and then give preference to the brighter parts of the image where pixels overlap. Conceptually, this is similar to the "lighten" layer merging routines in Photoshop (and other image editors).

◉ **Dark.** Similar to the Bright option, only preference is given to darker pixels. You may need to use both the Bright and Dark parameters for a while to visualize how they affect your images. I can't really provide hard and fast examples of when to use one or the other; it's a creative process.

Figure 8.18

No. of Exposures

You can choose from 2 to 9 exposures in each multiple exposure set. There is no selection screen for this option; highlight it and spin the QCD to choose the number of exposures. I recommend starting out with three multiple exposures when you begin exploring this tool; you'll quickly discover picture opportunities that call for more combined shots in a single image.

Save Source Imgs

As you might guess, in producing multiple exposures, the 7D Mark II takes each individual shot separately, and then combines them in the camera before saving the combination shot. (In other words, the process is *not* like film multiple exposures, in which the same photosensitive frame collects all the images, adding each subsequent shot to the images that are already there.) Doing it this way keeps the sensor from becoming "overloaded" and losing detail, plus the camera can intelligently combine the images, using exposure compensation and other pixel tricks to produce the final image.

You can elect to save Result Only (just the merged image), or All Images to store each individual image for later use. There are two advantages to the latter approach. You may be able to create a merger of your own manually that is superior to the one generated in the camera . In addition, if one individual shot happens to be a "keeper" on its own, you'll have it available without the distraction of the other merged images. The disadvantage is that saving All Images requires some extra time and memory card space.

Continue Mult-exp

Choose 1 Shot Only or Continuously. Choose the former if you want to take a single multiple exposure series and then return to normal shooting with Multiple Exposure then disabled. Select Continuously if you plan to shoot a batch of different multiple exposures and don't want to return to the menu system to reactivate the feature after each shot.

Multi Notes

Some special conditions are required for your 7D Mark II to shoot multiple exposures. Some features are disabled, and others are locked in at particular values.

- Auto Lighting Optimizer, Highlight Tone Priority, and Peripheral Illumination/Chromatic Aberration Correction are disabled, and the Standard Picture Style will be used if you've chosen the Auto Picture Style setting. Multiple exposures are disabled if your camera is connected to a computer or printer via the USB cable.

- Most settings used for the first shot in a series are locked in for all subsequent images in that series, including image recording quality, ISO sensitivity, Picture Style, high ISO noise reduction, and color space.

- Other functions that cannot be changed while shooting multiple exposures will be dimmed in the camera menu.

HDR Mode

I described using the 7D Mark II's HDR Mode in Chapter 4. To recap, this menu entry has five subentries you can adjust:

○ **Adjust Dynamic Range.** Select Disable HDR, allow the camera to select a dynamic range automatically, or select the range yourself to achieve a particular look. You can choose plus/minus 1, 2, or 3 EV.

○ **Effect.** You can add special effects on top of any Picture Style you are using to produce an even more dramatic HDR image. Your choices are as follows:

  • **Natural.** Provides the most useful range of highlight and shadow details.

  • **Art Standard.** Offers a great deal of highlight and shadow detail, but with lower overall contrast and outlines accentuated, making the image look more like a painting. Saturation, bold outline, and brightness are adjusted to the default levels, and tonal range is lower in contrast.

  • **Art Vivid.** Similar to Art Standard, but saturation is boosted to produce richer colors, and the bold outlines not as strong, producing a poster-like effect.

  • **Art Bold.** Even higher saturation than Art Vivid, with emphasized edge transitions, producing what Canon calls an "oil painting" effect.

  • **Art Embossed.** Reduce saturation, darker tones, and lower contrast give the image a faded, aged look. The edge transitions are brighter or darker to emphasize them.

○ **Continuous HDR.** Choose 1 Shot Only if you plan to take just a single HDR exposure and want the feature disabled automatically thereafter, or Every Shot to continue using HDR mode for all subsequent exposures until you turn it off. This is similar to the multiple exposure option described earlier.

○ **Auto Image Align.** You can choose Enable to have the camera attempt to align all three HDR exposures when shooting hand-held, or select Disable when using a tripod. The success of the automatic alignment will vary, depending on the shutter speed used (higher is better), and the amount of camera movement (less is better!).

◉ **Save Source Images.** When the 7D Mark II has finished creating its HDR image from your three shots, you can choose to save all the images on your memory card (so you can manually combine them later or perform other manipulations using your image editor). Or, you can elect to save your final HDR image only. You might prefer that choice to save card space, reduce the number of images you won't be using anyway, or if shooting a lot of HDR and are confident that the camera's results will suit your needs.

Red-Eye Reduction

This is the first entry in the Shooting Menu 4 menu (see **Figure 8.19.**)

Your 7D II Rebel T6s/T6i has a slightly effective Red-Eye Reduction flash mode. Unfortunately, your camera is unable, on its own, to *eliminate* the red-eye effects that occur when an electronic flash (or, rarely, illumination from other sources) bounces off the retinas of the eye and into the camera lens. Animals seem to suffer from yellow or green glowing pupils, instead; the effect is equally undesirable. The effect is worst under low-light conditions (exactly when you might be using a flash) as the pupils expand to allow more light to reach the retinas. The most you can hope for is to *reduce* or minimize the red-eye effect.

The best way to truly eliminate red-eye is to raise the flash up off the camera so its illumination approaches the eye from an angle that won't reflect directly back to the retina and into the lens. The extra height of the built-in flash may not be sufficient, however. That alone is a good reason for using an external flash. If you're working with your 7D II's built-in flash, your only recourse may be to switch on the Red-Eye Reduction feature with the menu choice. It causes a lamp on the front of the camera to illuminate with a half-press of the shutter release button, which may cause your subjects' pupils to contract, decreasing the amount of the red-eye effect. (You may have to ask your subject to look at the lamp to gain maximum effect.)

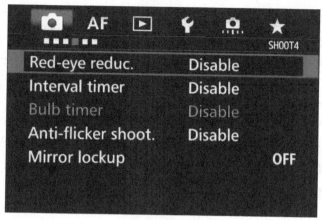

Figure 8.19
The Shooting 4 menu.

Interval Timer

If you want to shoot continuous time lapse stills over a period of time, select this entry and choose Enable and press the INFO. button. A screen will appear that lets you enter an interval between shots (from one second to 99 hours, 59 minutes, and 59 seconds), and the total number of shots to be taken (from 1 to 99.) When you press the shutter release all the way, the sequence starts. Once the sequence has finished, the feature is automatically turned off. The quickest way of quickly canceling your interval shooting is to just power down the 7D II.

You can use this feature for everything from time-lapse photography to a super-long self timer. For example you could set the camera to take just two pictures (it makes little sense to specify only one) with an interval of one hour. Press the shutter release and the first picture is taken immediately, and the second an hour later. Or, you might want to use an interval of 30 seconds to give you plenty of time to get into a family portrait. Using a tripod with this feature (and with Bulb Timer, described next) is a smart idea.

Bulb Timer

While your 7D II can take exposures as long as 30 seconds just by specifying a shutter speed, you can actually use exposures that are much longer – up to 99:59:59 using this menu entry. It's only available when the Mode dial is in the Bulb position. Access Bulb Timer, enable it, press the INFO. button, and you can enter an exposure time from one second to a tick short of 100 hours. Are you thinking star trails, like I am? Are you wondering whether your 7D II's battery would last that long, or whether the camera sensor would overhead, like I am? It's certainly worth a try. Again, cancel the long exposure by turning the camera off.

Anti-Flicker Shooting

Novice sports photographers often ask me why shots they take in certain gymnasiums or arenas have inconsistent exposure, wildly varying color, or banding. The answer is that certain types of artificial lighting actually have a blinking cycle that is imperceptible to the eye, but which the camera can capture. This setting, when enabled, detects the frequency (it's optimized for 100 to 120 Hz illumination) of the light source that is blinking, and takes the picture at the moment when the flicker has the least effect on the final image. It cannot be used in live view or movie shooting.

You may experience a slight shutter release time lag as the camera "waits" for the proper instant, and your continuous shooting speed may be reduced, which makes this setting a necessary evil for sports and other activities involving action. Your results may vary when using P or Av modes, because the shutter speed can change between shots as proper exposure requires. You're better off using Tv or M mode, so the shutter speed remains constant.

A handy Flicker! warning will appear in the viewfinder, alerting you that the feature is enabled, as long as you've set Viewfinder Display in the Set-up 2 menu to include that alert. Anti-Flicker is disabled when using Mirror Lockup, and may not work as well with dark backgrounds, a bright light within the image area, when using wireless flash, and under other shooting conditions. Canon recommends taking test shots to see how effective the feature is under the light source you are working with.

Mirror Lockup

This option allows you to flip up the 7D II's mirror prior to exposure. Note that the camera has a second mirror lockup option available under Sensor Cleaning in the Set-up 4 menu. You should be extra careful not to confuse the two. Here is the difference:

- ◎ **Mirror Lockup.** This option is used while shooting. When enabled from this menu entry, the camera flips the mirror up out of the way when you press the shutter button down all the way. At that point, the viewfinder image will vanish (the mirror is no longer reflecting the image toward the focus screen), and a blinking mirror-up icon appears on the LCD panel. Shooting function settings and menu adjustments are disabled at this point. You must press the shutter release fully a *second* time to actually take the photo. The net result is that the (minor) vibration caused by the action of the mirror is eliminated, which can be important when shooting with a very long telephoto lens, or taking close-ups.

- ◎ **Sensor Cleaning.** Select Clean Manually from the Sensor Cleaning entry in the Set-up 3 menu. The mirror will flip up immediately and the shutter will open, exposing the sensor. You can then safely clean your sensor using your favorite method (as described in Chapter 14). The shutter won't close and the mirror won't flip down until you power off the camera. The function can't be activated unless your battery or external source has enough power to maintain this configuration.

In general, only advanced dSLRs like the 7D II offer the Mirror Lockup option in Shooting mode, so you might not even be familiar with its advantages. In recent years, only the cleaning mode mirror flip-up feature has been common. When using Mirror Lockup, keep the following in mind:

- **Avoid excessive lockup times.** Unlike cleaning mode, the shutter remains closed while the mirror is locked up, and, in virtually all cases, a lens will be attached to the camera and focusing light on the sensor plane (or shutter curtains, before exposure). This bright light can actually damage the shutter, particularly if the camera is accidentally pointed toward the sun. So, a good rule of thumb is to lock up the mirror only just before you want to take the picture (the mirror's vibration will be damped within about one second), and never shoot directly toward the sun. Fortunately, if you lock the mirror up and *don't* take a picture, the mirror will flip back down after 30 seconds automatically.

- **Use a tripod.** Obviously, if you're using mirror lockup to avoid vibration, you're almost certainly working with the camera on a tripod, too. Even with image stabilization, a handheld camera will produce more vibration than any mirror action.

- **Self-timer or remote release recommended.** Even though you've delayed the exposure until mirror vibration has damped, pressing the shutter release (even gently) can introduce a bit of motion to a camera mounted on the sturdiest tripod. The 7D II's self-timer can be used, but that option doesn't allow you to select the precise moment of exposure. Instead, use a remote release. Perhaps you've framed a shot of some distant wildlife with a super-telephoto. Your first press flips the mirror up to ready the camera for the shot; then, a second or two later your quarry looks toward the camera and you press again to take the picture. With a self-timer, you don't have that flexibility.

- **Self-timer with Bulb exposures.** This combination can be problematic. You'll need to hold the shutter button down during the self-timer countdown when using a Bulb exposure. Releasing the button before the countdown has elapsed eliminates the actual exposure. You'll hear a shutter click, but no picture will be taken. You're better off using a remote release for mirror-up Bulb exposures.

- ⊙ **No continuous shooting.** Sorry, but you can't lock up the mirror and take a series of shots. Continuous shooting is disabled when Mirror Lockup is active.

Live View Shooting

This menu entry is the first in the Shooting 5 menu (see Figure 8.20). It enables/disables live view shooting and the Live View button. Disabling live view does not affect movie shooting, which is activated by rotating the On/Off/Movie switch to the Movie position.

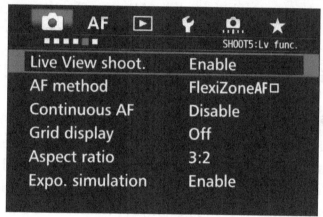

Figure 8.20

The Shooting 5 menu.

AF Method

Here you can select the autofocus mode for live view and movie shooting: Face Detection+Tracking, FlexiZone – Single and Flexi-Zone – Multi. all explained in Chapters 4 and 13. This menu entry enables and disables the Continuous AF feature, which is the live view equivalent of the AI Servo mode explained in Chapter 5. When activated, the 7D Mark II will refocus on objects as their distance from the camera changes.

Continuous AF

This menu entry enables and disables the Continuous AF feature, which is the live view equivalent of the AI Servo mode explained in Chapter 5. When activated, the 7D II will refocus on objects as their distance from the camera changes.

Grid Display

When enabled, this setting overlays Grid 1 on the screen to help you compose your image and align vertical and horizontal lines, or Grid 2, which consists of four rows of six boxes, which allows finer control over placement of images in your frame. Grid 3 adds diagonal lines. (See **Figure 8.22.**)

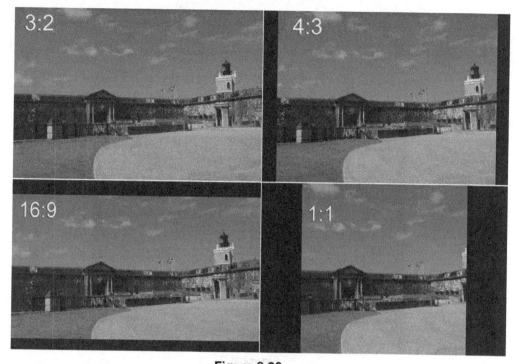

Figure 8.22

Three grids are available when shooting movies to help you align horizontal and vertical subjects.

Aspect Ratio

Allows you to choose an aspect ratio, or proportions of your image, from 3:2, 4:3, 16:9, or 1:1. JPEG images will be stored using the selected ratio; RAW images will be saved using the default 3:2 proportions, but the desired cropping can be restored in your image-editing software. In Custom Function 3 menu, you can choose either Masked or Outlined for LV Shooting Area Display. The former completely obscures with a black mask the area outside your selected aspect ratio; the latter marks the aspect ratio with lines, but allows you to see the area you are cropping out (this is useful for sports when moving subjects may be entering or leaving the masked area). Note that choosing Off for Custom Function 4 menu's Add Cropping Information entry disables this feature entirely.

Selecting proportions other than the 3:2 default results in a cropped image, and the live view display provides a black border on the LCD to show the limits of the image area (see **Figure 8.28**). At the Large or RAW size setting, you end up with images that measure 5760 x 3840/22MP (3:2 ratio); 5120 x 3840 /19.7MP (4:3 ratio); 5760 x 3240 pixels/18.7MP (16:9 ratio); and 3840 x 2840 pixels/14.7MP (1:1 ratio). At Medium (M), Small 1 (S1), Small 2 (S2), and Small 3 (S3), the images are proportionately smaller.

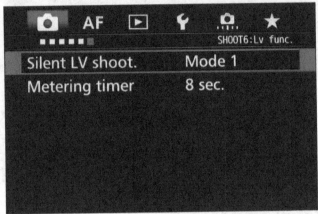

Figure 8.23

You can choose the proportions of your image.

Exposure Simulation

This option allows you to choose whether the live view image mimics the exposure level of the final image, or whether the screen displays a bright image (dependent on the LCD Brightness setting you've specified in the Setup 2 menu) that may be easier to view under high ambient lighting conditions. Your choices are as follows:

- ◉ **Enable.** The live view image on the screen corresponds to the brightness level of the actual image based on the current exposure settings, including any exposure compensation you've specified. Use this option when you want to be able to roughly (but not precisely) monitor the effects of your exposure settings in live view.

- ◉ **During DOF Preview.** The live view image is displayed at standard brightness, but will be adjusted to simulate your exposure settings when you press the depth-of-field preview button. This is your best option when you might want to check exposure from time to time during a shooting session.

◉ **Disable.** The 7D Mark II ignores any exposure settings and compensation, and shows the live view image at standard brightness. This setting is useful outdoors in full sunlight, because any exposure simulation (dimmed LCD) will be diffi-cult to interpret under high ambient lighting anyway.

Silent LV Shooting

This is the first entry in the Shooting 6 menu, which provides additional Live View functions. (See **Figure 8.23.**) Although it's not possible to completely silence the 7D Mark II's shutter noise, Canon gives you two options for making the *ker-clunk* a bit less intrusive. Because Live View mode eliminates the noisy mirror-flap action, si-lent live view shooting *is* actually fairly quiet. Silent shooting is not available when using an electronic flash, and you'll end up with in-consistent exposures if you use either Mode 1 or Mode 2 with a lens mounted on an extension tube, or if you are working with a Canon tilt-shift (TS-E) lens other than the TS-E17mm f/4L or TSE-E24mm f/3.5L II lenses. Your options are as follows:

◉ **Mode 1.** This mode produces a quieter shooting sound level in Live View mode, and enables continuous shooting at up to 6 fps.

◉ **Mode 2.** This mode, technically, isn't any quieter, but it sepa-rates the *ker* from the *clunk* sounds. Press the shutter release all the way, and the camera emits a small click as the picture is taken, and then camera operation is suspended as long as you hold the shutter button down. If you like, you can wait a moment or two before releasing the button to the halfway po-sition or completely, which produces a second quiet click. It's a tiny bit less intrusive than Mode 1, and with enough ambi-ent sound around you, is the closest you'll get to silent shoot-ing with a digital SLR. Continuous shooting can be specified, but is disabled in this mode. Only a single picture will be ex-posed. The camera ignores this setting if you're using a re-mote control, and defaults to Mode 1.

◉ **Disable.** Turns off the silent shooting feature, although the resulting noises are roughly the same as Mode 1.

Metering Timer

This option allows you to specify how long the EOS 7D Mark II's metering system will remain active before switching off. Tap the shutter release to start the timer again after it switches off. You can select 4, 16, or 30 seconds, plus 1, 10, or 30 minutes.

Chapter 9

Fine Tuning with the Autofocus Menu

This chapter contains descriptions of some of the more esoteric options available for the Canon EOS 7D II's complex autofocus system. Except for the Case options in the AF 1 menu, these are the settings that you'll probably set once and forget for a while, or, at least, until you decide to make a significant change in your camera's autofocus behavior.

As much as I would have liked to present one huge, 100-page chapter on autofocus, it made more sense to describe the basic functions and settings in-depth in Chapter 5, and retain the lesser-used AF menu descriptions here with the camera's other menus. I think the need to jump back and forth will be minimal, although, as with any camera manual, you may need a review of other chapters from time to time as a refresher.

AF 1 Menu

This is the menu used to select from among six different factory preset "Cases" with autofocus settings suitable for various types of action scenes. You can also modify those presets to adjust the sensitivity of the camera during tracking of moving objects, its response to acceleration and deceleration, and how quickly it switches between autofocus points as subjects move through the frame.

The icons in the left edge (see **Figure 9.1**) provide reminders of which Case is suitable for which type of action. Highlight the Case you want to use and press SET to confirm. To change any of the three parameters, press the RATE button and use the QCD or multi-controller joystick to adjust the sliding indicator. The 7D II provides helpful information about each Case at the press of the INFO. button, and you can read my own detailed recommendations for this menu in Chapter 5. To recap, the parameters you can change include:

- **Tracking sensitivity.** Determines how swiftly the AF system refocuses on a new subject that enters the focus area. Your choices are -2 (Locked On) to +2 (Responsive). Negative numbers allow you to retain focus on the original subject even if it briefly leaves the area covered by the focus points, making tracking easier. Positive numbers switch more quickly to a new subject.

- **Acceleration/deceleration tracking.** Determines how the AF system responds to sudden acceleration, deceleration, or stopping. Your choices are 0 (constant speed) to 2 (sudden changes).

- **AF point auto switching.** Determines how quickly the AF system changes from the current AF point to an adjacent one when the subject moves away from the current point, or an intervening object moves across the frame into the area interpreted by the current point. Your choices are 0 (slower tracking response) to 2 (faster response). This parameter operates in 65 Point Auto Selection, Zone AF, and AF Point Expansion area selection modes.

While you can adjust these parameters for any case, you may find their default values useful:

- **Case 1: Versatile multi purpose setting.** All purpose setting that works well with many moving subjects including motor sports and track, especially with subjects moving toward or away from your.

- **Case 2: Continue to track subject, ignoring possible obstacles.** Excellent for football and other sports where an intervening subject may pass in front of your primary subject. The camera will delay refocusing on the new object long enough to resume following the original subject.

- **Case 3: Instantly focus on subjects suddenly entering AF points.** Ideal when you're photographing a static scene, waiting for a moving subject, such as the winner of a race, a skier, or bicyclist.

- **Case 4: For subjects that accelerate or decelerate quickly.** I prefer this Case for basketball and soccer, because you can have players racing toward you one instant, and crossing your field of view the next.

- **Case 5: For erratic subjects moving quickly in any direction.** This is my choice for hockey games and anything that involves skates -- as well as small children and pets. It's also excellent for that most difficult of subjects: birds in flight.

- **Case 6: For subjects that change speed and move erratically.** This works with 65 Point Auto Selection, Zone AF, and AF Point Expansion area selection modes. (In other words, it doesn't operate with Single-Point Spot AF or Single-Point AF manual selection modes.) An alternative case for basketball, small children, and pets.

See Chapter 5 for step-by-step instructions for adjusting the values of any of the six AF Cases.

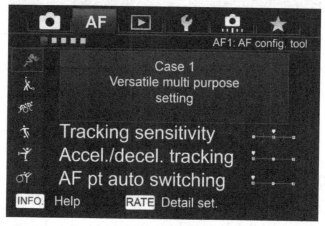

Figure 9.1

The AF 1 menu.

AF 2 Menu

This menu has only two options, both of which deal with how the 7D II autofocuses for the first and second shots in a continuous series when you're working with the AI Servo autofocus mode. The individual options determine whether the camera gives priority to focus (delaying taking a picture until the AF process is complete), or priority to a press of the shutter button (taking the picture when the release is pressed down all the way). Your preference will depend on what type of picture you're taking, as I'll describe next. (See **Figure 9.2**.)

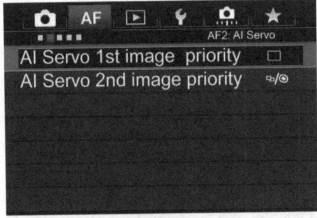

Figure 9.2

The AF 2 menu.

AI Servo 1st Image Priority

This setting determines the point at which the 7D II locks in focus when you push the shutter button all the way down when taking a series of photographs. Remember that if you're using a small f/stop with extended depth-of-field, your chances of getting a shot with acceptable depth-of-field are improved at any of these settings. Also keep in mind that you can further tweak autofocus responsiveness using the AF 1 Case options described in Chapter 5.

Use the Quick Control Dial or multi-controller joystick to move the indicator to any of three positions (see **Figure 9.3**):

- ◉ **Release priority.** The shutter will fire immediately, even if sharp focus has not yet been achieved. Use this setting when getting the shot -- any shot -- is crucial, and a slightly out-of-focus image would be preferable to none at all. Whether you're a photojournalist or a proud parent snapping Baby's first steps, you'd probably prefer not to miss the shot because the camera is still fine-tuning focus. The 7D II focuses so quickly that, unless your subject is low in contrast or otherwise problematic, release priority will probably give you a good shot nearly all the time. Remember that if you're using a small f/stop with extended depth-of-field, your chances of getting a shot with acceptable depth-of-field are improved even though you're using release priority.

- **Equal priority.** If focus is important to you, try out this balanced setting that will give the camera a little extra time -- but not too much -- and improve your chances of getting a precisely focused image without inordinate delay.

- **Focus priority.** Sometimes, accurate focus is all-important, and with a leisurely shooting pace you might not mind waiting an extra fraction of a second while the AF system "hunts" to achieve precise autofocus when faced with the occasional more difficult subject. I tend to use this setting for everything except action shots and birds-in-flight, because my speedy 7D II usually doesn't introduce much of a delay as it autofocuses.

AI Servo 2nd Image Priority

Most of us have an itchy trigger finger, so the first photograph in a series may not capture the decisive moment. When shooting bursts, the 7D II can continue to fine-tune focus for the second and subsequent images in the series, using the priority you set here. The parameters are similar to those of the previous setting (see **Figure 9.4**):

- **Speed priority.** Since this is the second (or ongoing) shot, the shutter has already fired at least once, so this setting tells the camera to keep the same focus setting and continue capturing images. Note that you can select this option regardless of what parameter you've specified for the *first* shot. So, if you've chosen focus priority for the initial image, selecting this setting is a safe bet *if your subject is not moving* quickly enough to require additional focus fine-tuning. But if you selected release priority for the first image, using this setting may mean that the first and all subsequent images may be a little (or a lot) out of focus.

◉ **Equal priority.** This balanced setting allows you to express your trust that the 7D II will provide a reasonable compromise between speed and focus for all images captured after the first.

◉ **Focus priority.** Selecting this option can slow down the continuous shooting speed of your camera, but will almost ensure getting a series of shots that are in optimum focus.

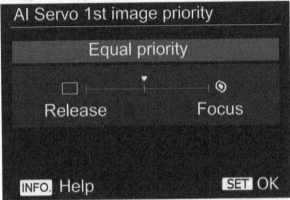

Figure 9.3

Set first image priority.

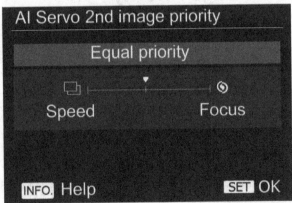

Figure 9.4

Set priority for second and subsequent images.

AF 3 Menu

The AF 3 menu (see **Figure 9.5**) has three entries, all of them fairly easy to understand.

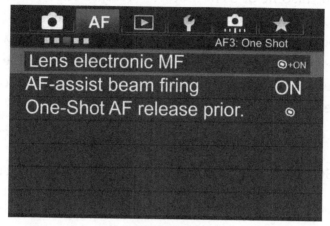

Figure 9.5

The AF 3 menu has just three entries.

Lens Electronic MF

A limited number of Canon prime lenses and zooms -- all of them with ultrasonic or STM motors -- feature super-sensitive electronic focusing rings you can use to fine-tune focus manually after focus has been locked in using One-Shot AF. You might want to disable the use of this ring when using one of the compatible lenses, because even a casual bump against the ring can change focus significantly. The lenses in question are:

EF50mm f/1.0L USM	EF200mm f/1.8L USM
EF300mm f/2.8L USM	EF500mm f/4.5L USM
EF600mm f/4L USM	EF28-80mm f/2.8-4L USM
EF85mm f/1.2L USM	EF40mm f/2.8
EF400 f/2.8L USM	EFS-18-55mm f/3.5-5.6 IS STM
EF1200 f/5.6L USM	EF-S55-250mm f/4-5.6 IS STM
EF85mm f/1.2L II USM	EF-S10-18mm f/4.5-6.3 IS STM
EF400mm f/2.8L II USM	EF-S18-135mm f/3.5-5.6 IS STM

You have two choices:

- **Enable after One-Shot AF.** When active, you can continue to hold the shutter release halfway, while adjusting focus manually. I use this when shooting portraits with my 85mm f/1.2 lens at a large aperture, allowing me to zero focus in on the near eye of a subject seated on a diagonal angle.
- **Disable after One-Shot AF.** Manual focus is disabled. Use this when you are satisfied with the focus set by the camera's autofocus system and don't want to manually tweak it. Remember that if you truly want to use manual focus and bypass the AF system entirely, just slide the AF/MF switch on the lens to the MF position.

AF-Assist Beam Firing

This setting determines when bursts from an electronic flash are used to emit a pulse of light that helps provide enough contrast for the EOS 7D II to focus on a subject. You can select Enable to use an attached Canon Speedlite to produce a focus assist beam. Use Disable to turn this feature off if you find it distracting. Keep in mind that if you select Enable and the Speedlite's own AF-Assist Beam Firing is set to Disable, the AF-assist beam will not be emitted (the flash's setting takes precedence).

- **Enable.** The AF-assist light is emitted by the camera's external flash whenever light levels are too low for accurate focusing using the ambient light.

- **Disable.** The AF-assist illumination is disabled. You might want to use this setting when shooting at concerts, weddings, or darkened locations where the light might prove distracting or discourteous.

- **IR AF Assist beam only.** Some Canon flash units, such as the Speedlite 600EX-RT, have a near-infrared pattern assist beam. Select this option to disable visible light flashes and activate only the less-obtrusive IR beam.

One-Shot AF Release Priority

This setting can be used to specify whether One-Shot AF uses Focus Priority (the default) or Release Priority. Both modes were described earlier in the AF 2 menu discussion.

AF 4 Menu

The AF 4 menu has seven options, shown in **Figure 9.6**, many of them dealing with the selection of AF points and zones.

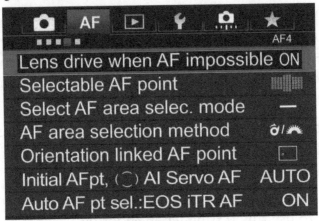

Figure 9.6

The AF 4 menu has seven options.

Lens Drive When AF Impossible

When a scene has little inherent contrast (say, a blank wall or the sky) or if there isn't enough illumination to allow determining contrast accurately (in low light levels, or with lenses having maximum apertures of less than f/5.6), a lens may be unable to achieve autofocus. Very long telephoto lenses suffer from this syndrome because their depth-of-field is so shallow that the correct point of focus may zip past during the AF process before the AF system has a chance to register it.

Use this setting to tell the 7D II either to keep trying to focus if AF seems to be impossible or to stop seeking focus. Your choices are as follows:

- **Continue Focus Search.** The 7D II will keep trying to focus, even if the effort causes the lens to become grossly out of focus. Use this default setting if you'd prefer that the lens keep trying. Sometimes you can point the lens at an object with sufficient contrast at approximately the same distance to let the AF system lock on, then reframe your original subject with the hope that accurate focus will now be achieved.

320

⊙ **Stop Focus Search.** When this option is selected, the camera will stop trying to focus uselessly, allowing you to attempt to manually bring the subject into focus. This setting is best for very long telephoto lenses (around 400mm and up), because they encounter AF difficulties more than most lenses, and are less likely to benefit from extended "hunting."

Selectable AF Point

While the 7D II always uses all 65 AF points (if available with your lens/aperture) when selecting a point automatically, if you're using one of the focus modes that allow specifying the initial focus point or zone, you can select which points will be available. The un-available points will not be displayed when you press the Point Selection button in the upper-right corner of the back panel.

Note: The number of manually selectable points may be fewer when using lenses from Groups E to G. Your options include:

⊙ **65 points.** Any of the available 65 focus points can be se-lected manually.

⊙ **21 points.** Some 21 points are available for manual selection. I use this a lot for sports like football and track, where I know the action is going to be centered around the middle of the frame.

⊙ **9 points.** Nine points in the center of the viewfinder can be selected. This is my favorite setting for basketball; virtually all the action will be in the center of the frame and involving one or two players, so I won't need to select a focus point from a wider range.

Select AF Area Selection Mode

Here you can choose which of the seven AF area selection modes are available when you use the M-Fn button (or Main Dial, depending on the AF Area Selection method, described next) to cycle among them. In effect, you can enable the modes you use most often, and disable those that you rarely or never work with.

When you access this entry, a screen with all seven modes is displayed (see **Figure 9.7**). Use the Quick Control Dial or multi-controller joystick to highlight a mode you want to activate/deactivate and press SET. A check mark above the icon indicates that the mode will be available. Select OK to confirm your choices. To cycle among the modes you've checked, press the AF Point Selection button on the upper-right corner of the back of the 7D II and press the M-Fn button (or Main Dial if you've chosen that as your control) until the mode you want to use is selected. The seven modes (described in detail in Chapter 5) that you can enable/disable are:

- ⊚ Manual Select.: Spot AF
- ⊚ Manual Selection: 1 pt AF
- ⊚ Expand AF Area
- ⊚ Expand AF Area: Surround
- ⊚ Manual Select.: Zone AF
- ⊚ Manual Select.: Large Zone AF
- ⊚ Auto Selection: 65 pt AF

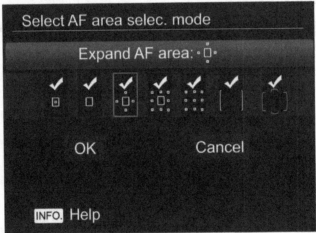

Figure 9.7

Enable or disable any of the six AF Area Selection modes.

AF Area Selection Method

With this setting, you can customize the controls used to choose an autofocus point manually, perhaps making the selection easier or more intuitive for you, or (as is the default) making this process require the use of two controls so that it can't be done accidentally. Your choices are as follows:

- **M-Fn button.** To change the AF point that is active, you must press the AF point selection button (to the immediate right of the * button), then press the M-Fn button multiple times to select the mode you want.

- **Main Dial.** When this option is chosen, you must press the AF point selection button and rotate the Main Dial (or M-Fn button) to select your selection mode. You can also use the Multi controller to move the AF point horizontally in this mode.

Orientation Linked AF Point

If you have a preference for particular AF area selection modes and a manually selected AF point when composing vertical or horizontal pictures, you can specify that preference using this menu entry. Your choices are:

- **Same for both vertical/horizontal orientations.** The specific AF selection mode you've chosen, and your preferred manually-selected AF point or zone is used whether the camera is in the vertical or horizontal shooting position.

- **Separate AF pts: Area+pt.** You can choose an AF selection mode *and* AF point or zone for *each* of three different camera orientations (described next.)

- **Separate AF pts: Pt. Only.** The AF point (only) can be specified separately for each of the three different camera positions, but the same AF area selection mode is used in any orientation.

The three different orientations are:

- **Camera held horizontally.** This orientation assumes that the camera is positioned so the viewfinder/shutter release are on top.

- ☉ **Camera held vertically** with the grip/shutter release above the Mode Dial.
- ☉ **Camera held vertically** with the Mode Dial above the grip/shutter release.

You might want to use this feature when you want to keep the same initial focus point when photographing certain subjects even if you happen to rotate the camera for certain shots. Perhaps you're shooting candid portraits or fashion, and you'd like the focus point to remain at the "top" of the frame at all times. Just follow these steps:

- ▸ Manual Select.: Spot AF
- ▸ Manual Selection: 1 pt AF
- ▸ Expand AF Area
- ▸ Expand AF Area: Surround

1. Choose Select Separate AF Points. Press SET to confirm.
2. **Select AF Area Selection mode.** Choose any of these modes (both Zone AF and 65-Point Auto Selection modes are invalid):
   - ▸ Manual Select.: Spot AF
   - ▸ Manual Selection: 1 pt AF
   - ▸ Expand AF Area
   - ▸ Expand AF Area: Surround

1. Switch to the orientation you want to define. You'll need to define all three separately.
2. **Set desired focus point.** Press the Focus Point Select button and then rotate the Main Dial to choose the AF point for that orientation.
3. **Confirm.** Press the Focus Point Select button again and press the LCD Panel Illumination button (the rightmost button on the top panel between the LCD and the Main Dial). A beep will indicate that your setting has been stored.
4. **Define other orientations.** Repeat steps 2-5 for each of the other orientations.

Initial AF Point, Auto Selection, AI Servo AF

Do you feel that Auto Selection: 65 Pt. AF is *too* automated for you? If you'd like to regain a little control over this automated feature, this is the over-ride for you. You can manually specify the starting point that will be used in AI Servo (continuous autofocus) mode, or mandate that a point you had previously chosen in another AF area selection mode be used when you switch to 65 Pt. AF. If you're confused, this description of your options should clear things up:

- ◎ **Initial Auto Area AF pt Selected.** You can use the AF point selection controls to specify any one of the 65 AF points available. When AI Servo AF starts to focus in Auto Selection: 65 pt AF mode, it will first use the point you have chosen before seeking other points as the 7D II evaluates your scene. You could use this option when you know that your main subject will *probably* be located in a particular area of the frame (say, a racing car approaching from the left), but still want the camera to refocus as the subject moves. This helps reduce AF confusion from movement elsewhere in the frame that is not your main subject.

- ◎ **Manual Spot, Manual 1 pt., Expand AF Area, Expand AF Area: Surround.** If you switch to Auto Selection: 65 pt. AF mode from Manual Select: Spot AF, Manual Selection: 1 pt. AF, Expand AF Area, or Expand Area: Surround, AI Servo will begin operation using the AF point you manually selected in any of those previous modes. This can be a convenient mode to use, because you can define a button to switch from another mode to Auto Selection, using a defined Custom Control under Metering and AF Start. I'll explain the use of Custom Controls in Chapter 11.

- ◎ **Auto.** This default value restores the fully automatic operation of the Auto Selection: 65 pt. AF mode. Use this when you trust your 7D to make the right selection. For the types of action photography I do, I end up with this setting most of the time. Specifying a start point for auto AF selection can prove distracting when trying to capture moving subjects.

Auto AF Point Selection: EOS iTR AF

Your 7D includes a feature called EOS iTR, which is capable of using color and facial recognition to identify and track subjects while autofocusing. The feature is processing-intensive, so autofocus takes a bit longer and maximum speed under continuous – high is limited to about 9.5 frames per second. It can operate when the AF Area Selection mode is Zone AF, Large Zone AF, or 65 Point Automatic AF. Your choices are:

- **On: Enable.** The autofocus point is based on faces, color information, and AF phase detection. This mode is most useful when working in AI Servo AF mode (continuous autofocus), because the 7D II "remembers" the color at the first focus position, and then continues to refocus while tracking your subject using AF points that detect that same color. In One-Shot AF mode, the camera focuses just once, but is able to identify people more easily.

- **Off. Disable.** Only the phase detect AF information is used to select a focus point.

AF 5 Menu

You'll find options for selecting AF points here. See **Figure 9.8**.

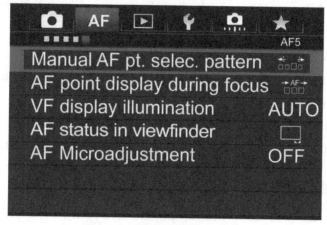

Figure 9.8

The AF 5 menu has four entries.

Manual AF Point Selection Pattern

This entry simply specifies whether manual focus point selection will stop at the edges of the AF point array, or whether it will wrap around, Pac-Man style to continue at the opposite edge (left/right, or top/bottom). The edge stop option is best if you use the points at the edges often and don't want to continue to the opposite side. If you want to move quickly around in the array and aren't worrying about overshooting, then Continuous is speedier than Stops at AF Area Edges.

AF Point Display During Focus

Your 7D II can show you the AF points during shooting, and this entry provides four different options that control the conditions under which the points are displayed. The configuration is largely a matter of personal preference, reflecting when you like to see your focus points or if you find them distracting. The options are as follows:

- **Selected (constant).** The selected AF point(s) (only) are always highlighted.

- **All (constant).** All 65 possible AF points are always shown.

- **Selected (pre-AF, Focused).** Focus points are shown when selecting AF point(s); when the camera is ready to shoot, before AF operation; and when focus is achieved (except when using AI Servo AF).
- **Selected (Focused).** Focus points are shown only when selecting AF point(s) or when focus is achieved (except when using AI Servo AF).
- **Disable display.** The selected AF point(s) will *not* be displayed, except if you've chosen Selected (constant).

VF Display Illumination

You can elect to have the AF points and grid in the viewfinder highlighted in red when focus is achieved. You can select:

- **Auto.** Points and grid illuminate when focus is achieved under low light only. Press the Q button and then choose Off: Non illuminated or On: Illuminated to specify whether the AF points will blink red when using AI Servo AF.
- **Enable.** Points and grid are illuminated when focus is achieved at all times. Press the Q button and then choose Off: Non illuminated or On: Illuminated to specify whether the AF points will blink red when using AI Servo AF.
- **Disable.** Points and grid are never illuminated.

Note that regardless of this setting, the AF points always blink red when the AF Area Selection button is pressed. In addition, when Auto or Enable are selected, the electronic level and viewfinder grid as well as the information specified in Show/Hide in Viewfinder will also illuminate in red.

AF Status in Viewfinder

An AF status icon appears in the viewfinder when you press the shutter button down halfway as soon as focus is achieved, *or* while you are holding down the AF-ON button. This setting lets you specify where you want that icon to appear.

- ◉ **Show in Field of View.** An **AF** indicator is superimposed on the frame in the lower right-hand corner.
- ◉ **Show outside view.** The focus indicator icons are displayed at the lower right edge of the viewfinder, outside the frame.

AF Microadjustment

Caution! Use this control, which allows you to tweak the point of focus of individual lenses, with care. Well-intentioned, but inaccurate adjustments can turn slight focus problems into major ones. I'll cover this drastic correctional step in detail next.

Fine-Tuning the Autofocus of Your Lenses

The Canon EOS 7D II has a feature called AF Microadjustment, which I hope you never need to use, because it is applied only when you find that a particular lens is not focusing properly. If the lens happens to focus a bit ahead or a bit behind the actual point of sharp focus, and it does that consistently, you can use the microadjustment feature to "calibrate" the lens's focus.

Why is the focus "off" for some lenses in the first place? There are lots of factors, including the age of the lens (an older lens may focus slightly differently), temperature effects on certain types of glass, humidity, and tolerances built into a lens's design that all add up to a slight misadjustment, even though the components themselves are, strictly speaking, within specs. A very slight variation in your lens's mount can cause focus to vary slightly. With any luck (if you can call it that), a lens that doesn't focus exactly right will at least be consistent. If a lens always focuses a bit behind the subject, the symptom is *back focus*. If it focuses in front of the subject, it's called *front focus*.

You're almost always better off sending such a lens in to Canon to have them make it right. But that's not always possible. Perhaps you need your lens recalibrated right now, or you purchased a used lens that is long out of warranty. If you want to do it yourself, the first thing to do is determine whether your lens has a back focus or front focus problem.

For a quick-and-dirty diagnosis (*not* a calibration; you'll use a different target for that), lay down a piece of graph paper on a flat surface, and place an object on the line at the middle, which will represent the point of focus (we hope). Then, shoot the target at an angle using your lens's widest aperture and the autofocus mode you want to test. Mount the camera on a tripod so you can get accurate, repeatable results.

If your camera/lens combination doesn't suffer from front or back focus, the point of sharpest focus will be the center line of the chart, as you can see in **Figure 9.9**. If you do have a problem, one of the other lines will be sharply focused instead. Should you discover that your lens consistently front or back focuses, it needs to be re-calibrated. Unfortunately, it's only possible to calibrate a lens for a single focusing distance. So, if you use a particular lens (such as a macro lens) for close focusing, calibrate for that. If you use a lens primarily for middle distances, calibrate for that. Close-to-middle distances are most likely to cause focus problems, anyway, because as you get closer to infinity, small changes in focus are less likely to have an effect.

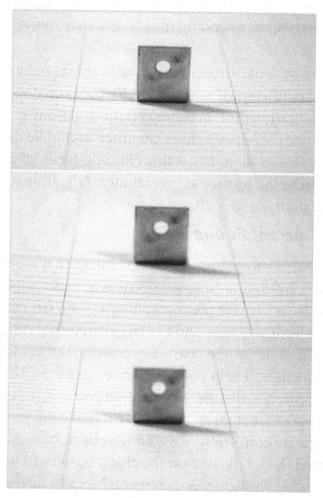

Figure 9.9

Correct focus (top), front focus (middle), and back focus (bottom).

Lens Tune-Up

The key tool you can use to fine-tune your lens is the AF Micro-adjustment entry. You'll find the process easier to understand if you first run through this quick overview of the menu options:

- **Disable.** Deactivates autofocus micro adjustment.
- **Adjust all by same amount.** The same adjustment is applied to all your lenses. You'd use this if your camera, rather than just a lens or two, requires calibration. (In this case, I particularly recommend sending the camera back to Canon for repair.)
- **Adjust by lens.** You can set an adjustment individually for up to 20 different lenses. If you discover you don't care for the calibrations you make in certain situations (say, it works better for the lens you have mounted at middle distances, but is less successful at correcting close-up focus errors), you can deactivate the feature as you require. Adjustment values range from -20 to +20.

Evaluate Current Focus

The first step is to capture a baseline image that represents how the lens you want to fine-tune autofocuses at a particular distance. You'll often see advice for photographing a test chart with millimeter markings from an angle, and the suggestion that you autofocus on a particular point on the chart. Supposedly, the markings that actually *are* in focus will help you recalibrate your lens. The problem with this approach is that the information you get from photographing a test chart at an angle doesn't actually tell you what to do to make a precise correction. So, your lens back focuses three millimeters behind the target area on the chart. So what? Does that mean you change the value -3 increments? Or -15 increments? Angled targets are a "shortcut" that don't save you time.

Instead, you'll want to photograph a target that represents what you're actually trying to achieve: a plane of focus locked in by your lens that represents the actual plane of focus of your subject. For that, you'll need a flat target, mounted precisely perpendicular to the sensor plane of the camera. Then, you can take a photo, see if the plane of focus is correct, and if not, dial in a bit of fine-tuning in the AF Microadjustment menu, and shoot again. Lather, rinse, and repeat until the target is sharply focused.

You can use the focus target shown in **Figure 9.10**, or you can use a chart of your own, as long as it has contrasty areas that will be easily seen by the autofocus system, and without very small details that are likely to confuse the AF. Download your own copy of my chart from www.dslrguides.com/FocusChart.pdf. (The URL is case sensitive.) Then print out a copy on the largest paper your printer can handle. (I don't recommend just displaying the file on your monitor and focusing on that; it's unlikely you'll have the monitor screen lined up perfectly perpendicular to the camera sensor.) Then, follow these steps:

1. **Position the camera.** Place your camera on a sturdy tripod with a remote release attached, positioned at roughly eye-level at a distance from a wall that represents the distance you want to test for. Keep in mind that autofocus problems can be different at varying distances and lens focal lengths, and that you can enter only *one* correction value for a particular lens. So, choose a distance (close-up or mid range) and zoom setting with your shooting habits in mind.

2. **Set the autofocus mode.** Choose the autofocus mode (One-Shot AF or AI Servo AF) you want to test. (Because AI Auto mode just alternates between the two, you don't need to test that mode.)

3. **Level the camera (in an ideal world).** If the wall happens to be perfectly perpendicular, you can use a bubble level, plumb bob, or other device of your choice to ensure that the camera is level to match. Many tripods and tripod heads have bubble levels built in. Avoid using the center column, if you can. When the camera is properly oriented, lock the legs and tripod head tightly.

4. **Level the camera (in the real world).** If your wall is not perfectly perpendicular, use this old trick. Tape a mirror to the wall, and then adjust the camera on the tripod so that when

you look through the viewfinder at the mirror, you see directly into the reflection of the lens. Then, lock the tripod and remove the mirror.

5. **Mount the test chart.** Tape the test chart on the wall so it is centered in your camera's viewfinder.

6. **Photograph the test chart using AF.** Allow the camera to autofocus, and take a test photo, using the remote release to avoid shaking or moving the camera.

7. **Make an adjustment and rephotograph.** Make a fine-tuning adjustment (described next) and photograph the target again.

8. **Evaluate the image.** If you have the camera connected to your computer with a USB cable or through a Wi-Fi connection, so much the better. You can view the image after it's transferred to your computer. Otherwise, *carefully* open the camera card door and slip the memory card out and copy the images to your computer.

9. **Evaluate focus.** Which image is sharpest? That's the setting you need to use for this lens. If your initial range doesn't provide the correction you need, repeat the steps between -20 and +20 until you find the best fine-tuning.

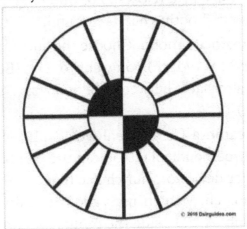

Figure 9.10

Use this focus test chart, or create one of your own.

Make Adjustments

Making the adjustments is simple. From the AF 5 menu, selective Microadjustment, and choose from Adjust All By Same Amount, Adjust By Lens, or Disable.

- ◉ **Adjust All By Same Amount.** Highlight the entry and press the SET button. Then, press the INFO. button to produce a screen with a scale from -20 to +20. Use the Quick Control Dial to choose a value, and press SET to confirm.

- ◉ **Adjust By Lens.** Follow these steps:

  1. Highlight Adjust By Lens and press the INFO. (Register) button. A screen similar to the one shown in **Figure 9.11** will appear. For a prime lens, there will be only a single adjustment scale; for a zoom lens, there will be one scale for W (wide angle) and one for T (telephoto) focal lengths.

  2. Press the INFO. button again. The Review/Edit lens information screen appears. It shows the name of the currently mounted lens and a 10-digit serial number (or 0000000000 if the number cannot be obtained).

  3. If the serial number is obtained, you can select OK to move on to the next step. If you need to edit the serial number, you can use the QCD to highlight any digit, then press SET to edit that digit. Rotate the QCD to increase or decrease the value of the digit. Select OK when finished.

  4. Select the scale and then rotate the QCD to adjust between -20 and +20 (no letters required). Moving the indicator to the right moves the focus point to the rear of the standard point of focus. Adjusting to the left moves the focus point to a position in front of the default focus point.

  5. Press SET to confirm your changes. The 7D II has enough memory to store values for 40 different lenses or lens+tele extender combinations (handy!). If you want to register more than 40 lenses, select a lens with an adjustment that can be deleted, mount it on the camera, and reset its adjustment to 0. That will free up a slot for a different lens.

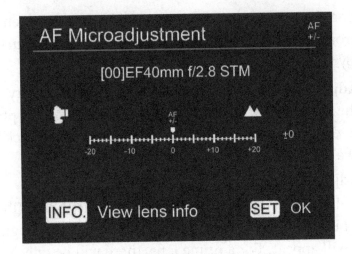

Figure 9.11

Adjustments toward the left move the focus plane closer to the camera; adjustments to the right move it farther away.

Chapter 10

Working with the Playback and Set-Up Menus

In the last two chapters, I introduced you to the layout and general functions of the Canon EOS 7D II's menu system, with specifics on how to customize your camera with the Shooting and Autofocus menus. In this chapter, you'll learn how to work with the two Playback and four Setup menus. If you're jumping directly to this chapter and need some guidance in how to navigate the 7D II's menu system, review the first few pages of Chapter 8. Otherwise, you're welcome to dive right in.

Playback Menu Options

The two blue-coded Playback menus are where you select options related to the display, review, transfer, and printing of the photos you've taken. The choices you'll find include:

Protect Images	Image Copy
Image Transfer	Histogram Disp.
Rotate Images	RAW Image Processing
Image Jump with Main Dial	Movie Play Count
Erase Images	Resize
Highlight Alert	Magnification (apx)
Print Order	Rating
AF Point Disp.	Ctrl over HDMI
Photobook Set-up	Slideshow
Playback Grid	

This is the first of six entries in the Playback 1 menu (see **Figure 10.1**). If you want to keep an image from being accidentally erased (either with the Erase button or by using the Erase menu), you can mark that image for protection. There are several ways to protect one or more images.

- **Q button.** While viewing an image in playback mode, press the Q button. A Quick Control screen appears with a column of playback function choices in the left column. Protect is at the top, and when highlighted allows you to choose from Disable and Enable to mark an image as protected.

- **Playback menu.** Choose Protect Images and a screen appears with five options:

  - Select Images
  - All Images in Folder
  - Unprotect All Images in Folder
  - All Images on Card
  - Unprotect All Images on Card

If you choose Select Images, you can view and select individual images by pressing the SET button when they are displayed on the screen. A key icon will appear at the upper edge of the information display while still in the protection screen, and when reviewing that image later. To remove protection, repeat the process. You can scroll among the other images on your memory card using the QCD and protect/unprotect them in the same way. Image protection will not save your images from removal when the card is reformatted.

As always, if you have images stored on both your Compact Flash and SD cards, you can switch the Record/Play function from one card to the other using the Record Func+Card/Folder Sel. entry in the Set-up 1 menu, as described later in this chapter.

- **Rate Button.** You can also use the Rate button as a shortcut for protecting images. In the Set-up 3 menu, select Protect as the Rate Btn Function (as described later in this chapter). Then, you can simply press the Rate button during image playback to protect that image.

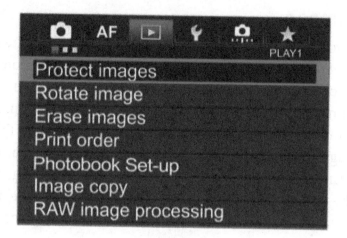

Figure 10.1
The Playback 1 menu.

Rotate Image

While you can set the EOS 7D II to automatically rotate images taken in a vertical orientation using the Auto Rotate option in the Set-up 1 menu (as described later in this chapter), you can manually rotate an image during playback using this menu selection. Select Rotate from the Playback 1 menu, use the Quick Control Dial to page through the available images on your memory card until the one you want to rotate appears, then press SET. The image will appear on the screen rotated 90 degrees, as shown in **Figure 10.2**. Press SET again, and the image will be rotated 270 degrees.

Figure 10.2

A vertically oriented image that isn't rotated appears larger on the LCD, but rotation allows viewing the photo without turning the camera.

Erase Images

Choose this menu entry and you'll be given three choices: Select and Erase Images, All Images in Folder, and All images on card. The first option displays the most recent image. Press SET to mark that image for deletion, and then rotate the Quick Control Dial to view other images, using the SET button to mark those you want to delete. When finished marking pictures, press the Trash button, and you'll see a screen that says Erase Selected Images with two options, Cancel and OK. Use the Quick Control Dial to choose OK, then press the SET button to erase the images, or select Cancel and press the SET button to return to the selection screen. Press the MENU button to unmark your selections and return to the menu.

The All Images on Card choice removes all the pictures on the card, except for those you've marked with the Protect command, and does not reformat the memory card. And, as mentioned earlier, if you have images stored on both memory cards, you can switch between them using the Record Func+Card/Folder Sel. entry in the Set-up 1 menu.

Print Order

The EOS 7D II supports the DPOF (Digital Print Order Format) that is now almost universally used by digital cameras to specify which images on your memory card should be printed, and the number of prints desired of each image. This information is recorded on the memory card, and can be interpreted by a compatible printer when the camera is linked to the printer using the USB cable, or when the memory card is inserted into a card reader slot on the printer itself. Photo labs are also equipped to read this data and make prints when you supply your memory card to them.

If you don't want to print directly from the camera using Pict-Bridge, you can set some of the same options from the Playback 1 menu's Print Order entry, and designate single or multiple images on your memory card for printing. Once marked for DPOF printing, you can print the selected images, or take your memory card to a digital lab or kiosk, which is equipped to read the print order and make the copies you've specified. (You can't "order" prints of RAW images or movies.)

To create a DPOF print order, just follow these steps:

1. **Access Print Order screen.** In the Playback 1 menu, navigate to Print Order. Press SET.

2. **Access Set up.** The Print Order screen will appear. (See **Figure 10.3**.) Use the Quick Control Dial to highlight Set Up. Press SET.

3. **Select Print type.** Choose Print Type (Standard, Index/Thumbnails print, or Both), and specify whether Date or File Number imprinting should be turned on or off. (You can turn one or the other on, but not both Date and File Number imprinting.) Press MENU to return to the Print Order screen.

4. **Choose selection method.** Highlight Sel. Image (choose individual images), By Folder (to select/deselect all images in a folder), or All Image (to mark/unmark all the images on your memory card). Press SET.

5. **Select individual images.** With Sel. Image, use the QCD or Main Dial to view the images, and press SET to mark or unmark an image for printing.

6. **Choose number of prints.** Once an image is selected, rotate the QCD to specify 1 to 99 prints for that image. (For Index prints, you can only specify whether the selected image is included in the index print, not the number of copies.) Press SET to confirm. You can then use the QCD to select additional images. Press MENU when finished selecting to return to the Print Order screen.

7. **Output your hardcopies.** If the camera is linked to a PictBridge-compatible printer, an additional option appears on the Print Order screen -- Print. You can select that; optionally, adjust Paper Settings as described in the previous section, and start the printing process. Alternately, you can exit the Print Order screen by tapping the shutter release button. Then turn

off the camera and printer, remove the memory card, and insert it in the memory card slot of a compatible printer, retailer kiosk, or digital minilab.

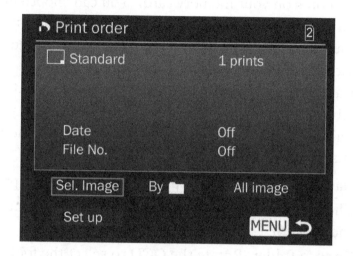

Figure 10.3

Select the images to be printed individually, by folder, or all the images on your memory card.

Photobook Set-up

You can select up to 998 images on your memory card, and then use the EOS Utility to copy them all to a specific folder on your computer. This is a handy way to transfer only specific images to a particular folder, and is especially useful when you're collecting photos to assemble in a photobook. Your choices include:

- ⊙ **Select images.** You can mark individual images from any folder on your memory card.
- ⊙ **All images in folder.** Mark all the images in a particular folder for transfer.
- ⊙ **Clear all in folder.** Unmark all the images in a folder.
- ⊙ **All images on card.** Mark all the images on the memory card for transfer to the specific folder.
- ⊙ **Clear all on card.** Unmark all the images on the card.

Once you marked the images you want to transfer to the specified folder, use the EOS Utility to copy them.

Image Copy

Image Copy allows you to make backup or duplicate images of selected photos on your memory card. You can choose individual images, a folder of images, or all images on the default memory card. You can swap the main and secondary cards in the Set-up menu with the Record/Play function in the Record Func+Card/Folder Sel. entry in the Set-up 1 menu, as described later in this chapter. The Image Copy screen will show you the free space available on the target card before the copy function takes place. Just follow these steps:

1. Navigate to the Image Copy entry. Press SET to proceed.
2. **Choose Sel. Image.** Rotate the QCD to highlight Sel. Image and press SET.
3. **Choose folder.** Rotate the QCD to select the folder with the image(s) to be copied, and press SET. A thumbnail of the images to be copied is displayed on the right.
4. **View individual images.** Rotate the QCD to view images. You can press the Magnify button and rotate the Main Dial counterclockwise to switch from a single image to three-image display. (Rotate the Main Dial clockwise to return to the single image display.)
5. **Mark images.** Press the Rate button to mark an image for copying. A checkmark icon will appear at the upper left of the screen.
6. **Choose Target card/folder.** Choose OK when you're ready to select the folder on the target card. You can choose an existing folder or select Create Folder to set up a new folder as the destination.
7. **Begin copying.** Choose OK to copy files. You'll be warned about duplicate file names and offered the choice of skipping the copy, replacing the existing file, or canceling the copy function entirely.

RAW Image Processing

You can produce JPEG versions of your full-size RAW images (but not M RAW or S RAW files) right in the camera. The original RAW shot is not modified. When you select this menu entry, only compatible RAW images are offered for your selection. Just follow these steps:

1. **View RAW images.** Rotate the QCD to scroll through compatible images. Press the Magnify button and rotate the Main Dial counterclockwise to view a selection of index images instead.

2. **Select image to process.** Press SET to select an image for processing.

3. **Specify parameters.** A screen appears with a selection of parameters you can adjust. Navigate to the parameter you want to manipulate using the joystick-like multi selector. Your choices include:

    - Brightness
    - White Balance
    - Picture Style
    - Auto Lighting Optimizer
    - High ISO Noise Reduction
    - Image Quality
    - Color Space
    - Peripheral Illumination Correction
    - Distortion Correction
    - Chromatic Aberration Correction

4. **Make adjustments.** When a parameter is highlighted you can rotate the QCD or press SET to change the settings; press INFO. to reset the settings to the original values of the RAW image; press the Magnify button to zoom in on the image.

5. **Save JPEG.** Navigate to the Save icon at the bottom left of the screen and press SET. Choose OK to save as a new file, or Cancel to abort the process. If the original was shot using

live view and an aspect ratio other than 3:2, the image will be displayed in those proportions, and the JPEG will be saved in that aspect ratio.

Resize

This entry is the first on the Playback 2 menu. (See **Figure 10.4**.) If you've already taken an image and would like to create a smaller version (say, to send by e-mail), you can create one from this menu entry. Just follow these steps:

1. **Choose Resize.** Select this menu entry from the Playback 1 menu.
2. **View images to resize.** You can scroll through the available images with the touch screen or cross keys, or press the Thumbnail/Reduce Image button to view thumbnails and select from those. Only images that can be resized are shown. They include JPEG Large, Medium, Small 1, and Small 2 images. Small 3 and RAW images of any type cannot be resized.
3. **Select an image.** Choose SET to select an image to resize. A pop-up menu will appear on the screen offering the choice of reduced-size images. These include M (Medium): 10.6MP, 3984 x 2656 pixels); S1 (Small 1: 5.9MP, 2976 x 1984 pixels); S2 (Small 2: 2.5MP, 1920 x 1280 pixels); or S3 (Small 3, .3MP, 720 x 480 pixels). You cannot resize an image to a size that is larger than its current size; that is, you cannot save a JPEG Medium image as JPEG Large.
4. **Resize and save.** Choose SET to save as a new file, and confirm your choice by selecting OK from the screen that pops up, or cancel to exit without saving a new version. The old version of the image is untouched.

Rating

If you want to apply a quality rating to images or movies you've shot (or use the rating system to represent some other criteria), you can simply press the Rating button during playback multiple times to apply a rating. Or, alternatively, use this entry to give particular images one, two, three, four, or five stars, or turn the rating system off. The Image Jump function can display only images with a given rating. Suppose you were photographing a track meet with multiple events. You could apply a one-star rating to jumping events, two-stars to relays, three-stars to throwing events, four-stars to hurdles, and five-stars to dashes. Then, using the Image Jump feature, you could review only images of one particular type. As mentioned earlier, you can also redefine the Rating button to apply the Protect attribute to an image in the Set-up 3 menu.

With a little imagination you can apply the rating system to all sorts of categories. At a wedding, you could classify pictures of the bride, the groom, guests, attendants, and parents of the couple. If you were shooting school portraits, one rating could apply to First Grade, another to Second Grade, and so on. Given a little thought, this feature has many more applications than you might think. Ratings can be used to specify images for a Slide Show, too, or to select images in Digital Photo Professional.

To use the Ratings menu entry, just follow these steps:

1. Choose the Rating menu item.
2. Use the QCD to select an image or movie. When an image or movie is you want to rate is visible, press SET.
3. Now rotate the QCD to apply a one- to five-star rating, or turn a rating off. You can rate up to 999 images.
4. When finished rating, choose MENU to exit.

Slide Show

Slide Show is a convenient way to review images one after another, without the need to manually switch between them. To activate, just choose Slide Show from the Playback 2 menu. During playback, you can press the SET button to pause the "slide show" (in case you want to examine an image more closely), or the INFO. button to change the amount of information displayed on the screen with each image. For example, you might want to review a set of images and their histograms to judge the exposure of the group of pictures. To set up your slide show, follow these steps:

1. **Begin setup.** Choose Slide show from the Playback 2 menu, pressing SET to display the screen shown in **Figure 10.5**.

2. **Choose image selection method.** Rotate the Quick Command Dial to All Images, and press SET. Then rotate the QCD to choose from All Images, Date, Folder, Movies, Stills, or Rating. Press SET to activate that selection mode. If you selected All Images, Stills, or Movies, skip to Step 4.

3. **Choose images.** If you've selected Folder, Date, or Rating, press the INFO. button to produce a screen that allows you to select from the available folders, or the available image creation dates or ratings on your memory card. When you've chosen a folder, date, or rating, press SET to confirm your choice.

4. **Choose Play time and Repeat options.** Rotate the Quick Command Dial to highlight Setup and press SET to produce a screen with playing time (1, 2, 3, 5, 10, or 20 seconds per image), and repeating options (Enable or Disable). When you've specified either value, press the MENU button to confirm your choice, and then MENU once more to go back to the main Slide Show screen.

5. **Start the show.** Rotate the QCD to highlight Start and press SET to begin your show. (If you'd rather cancel the show you've just set up, press MENU instead.)

6. **Use show options during display.** Press SET to pause/re-start; Info to cycle among the four information displays de-scribed in the section before this one; MENU to stop the show.

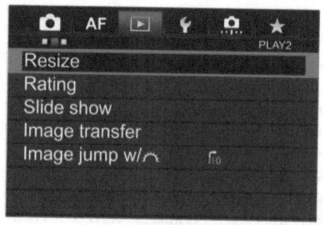

Figure 10.4

The Playback 2 menu.

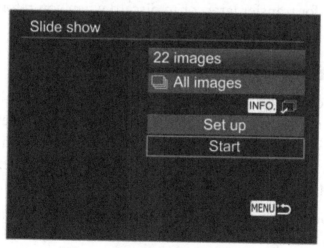

Figure 10.5

Set up your slide show using this screen.

Image Transfer

You can specify which images are to be transferred to your personal computer when the 7D II is linked to the computer with a USB cable. Individual images are "marked" using a review and selection system similar to the one used to specify print orders. Your options include:

- **Image sel./transfer.** You can choose to select individual images (Sel. Image), a folder (Sel. Folder), or All Images. During transfer, the display shows the total number of images to be transferred, the number of images that failed to transfer properly, and the total actually transferred.

- **RAW+JPEG transfer.** You can elect to transfer all selected RAW+JPEG images, or, alternatively, tell the camera to transfer either the JPEG images (only) or RAW image (only). For example, if you plan on working with the RAW versions of each shot, you can leave the JPEG files on the memory card, for transfer later, or to discard when you reformat the card.

Image Jump with Main Dial

As first described in Chapter 2, you can leap ahead or back during picture review by rotating the Main Dial, using a variety of increments that you can select using this menu entry. The Jump method is shown briefly on the screen as you leap ahead to the next image displayed, as shown in **Figure 10.6**. Your options are as follows:

- **1 image.** Rotating the Main Dial one click jumps forward or back 1 image.

- **10 images.** Rotating the Main Dial one click jumps forward or back 10 images.

- **100 images.** Rotating the Main Dial one click jumps forward or back 100 images.

- **Date.** Rotating the Main Dial one click jumps forward or back to the first image taken on the next or previous calendar date.

- ⊚ **Folder.** Rotating the Main Dial one click jumps forward or back to the first image in the next folder available on your memory card (if one exists).

- ⊚ **Movies Only.** Jumps among movies only using the Main Dial.

- ⊚ **Stills Only.** Jumps among still photos only using the Main Dial.

- ⊚ **Protected Images Only.** Shows only images marked as Protected.

- ⊚ **Image Rating.** When this option is visible, rotate the Main Dial to select the rating you want to use. Then, during picture review, spinning the Main Dial will jump among photos with the rating you selected.

Figure 10.6

The Jump method is shown on the LCD briefly when you leap forward or back using the Main Dial.

Highlight Alert

Choose Enable, and overexposed highlight areas will blink on the LCD screen during picture review. Set to Disable if you find this alert distracting. Many 7D II users use the histogram displays during playback as a more precise indicator of over (and under) exposure. This is the first entry in the Playback 3 menu. (See **Figure 10.7.**)

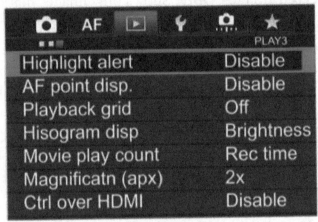

Figure 10.7
The Playback 3 menu.

AF Point Disp.

Select Enable, and the exact AF point(s) used to determine focus will be highlighted in red during playback. If automatic AF point selection was used, you may find multiple points highlighted.

Playback Grid

You can superimpose a 3 x 3, 6 x 4, or 3 x 3 plus diagonal lines grid over your image during playback, or disable the grid display entirely. You can review the layout of the grids, which can also be shown during shooting, in Chapter 8.

Histogram Disp.

Select from Brightness (luminance) or RGB histogram display during playback. I described use of histograms in Chapter 4.

Movie Play Count

Determines whether the movie recording and playback time (Rec Time) is shown on the screen, or whether the Time Code (an absolute positional marker/index) is displayed instead. If you change the Movie Play Count setting in the Shooting 5 (Movie) menu, as described in Chapter 13, or here, the other will be changed automatically. You'll find additional Time Code options in the Shooting 5 (Movie) menu.

Magnification (apx)

This setting allows you to specify the initial magnification for magnified view during playback, as well as the starting position on the screen. Your options are as follows:

- **1x (no magnification).** When you press the Magnify button, the initial view will be the single image display with no magnification. Continue pressing Magnify to zoom in.

- **2x, 4x, 8x, 10x (from the center of the frame).** The initial magnified view will be 2, 4, 8, or 10x (your choice), centered around the middle of the frame.

- **Actual Size (from selected point).** Magnified view starts at 100 percent, centered around the autofocus point used to achieve focus; if manual focus was used, the image will be centered around the middle of the frame.

- **Same as Last Magnification (from the center point).** The 7D II uses the same magnification value you last used, centered around the middle of the frame.

Ctrl over HDMI

When enabled, you can control playback operations over the HDMI cable and a television set's remote control when displaying your camera's output on an HDMI CEC-compatible television with a remote control. This option will allow you to access menus, choose a 9-image index, play movies and slide shows, change the amount of information displayed (similarly to the INFO. button), or rotate the image. Set to Disable if you do not have the correct TV hardware, or

353

when testing has shown that your particular HDMI CEC television does not operate correctly in this mode.

Set-up Menu Options

There are four amber-coded Set-up menus where you make adjustments on how your camera *behaves* during your shooting session, as differentiated from the Shooting menu, which adjusts how the pictures are actually taken. Your choices include:

Record Func+Card/Folder Sel.	Date/Time/Zone	RATE Button Display Options
File Numbering	Language	HDMI Frame Rate
File Name	Viewfinder Grid Display	Custom Shooting Mode (C1-C3)
Auto Rotate	GPS/Digital Compass Settings	Clear All Camera Settings
Format Card	Video System	Copyright Information
Eye-Fi Settings	Battery Info.	Certification Logo Display
Auto Power Off	Sensor Cleaning	Camera Firmware Ver.
LCD Brightness	INFO. Button Display Options	

Phantom Menu Entries

If you have attached the WFT-E4/E4a wireless transmitters, two additional menu entries will appear in the Set-up 1 menu, immediately following Select Folder. Those entries are WFT Settings and Recording Function+Media Select, which lead to a maze of more than a dozen submenus and options, including a Connection Wizard, image selection/transfer options, as well as FTP and USB choices. I won't be covering those options in this chapter, on the theory that only a few readers will own either of the wireless transmitters, and in any case will prefer the explanations in the 50-odd pages in the WFT-E4/E4a manuals to a couple paragraphs of summary here.

Record Funct+Card/Folder Select

That entry, the first in the Set-up 1 menu (see **Figure 10.8**), determines how the 7D II specifies the memory card(s) -- either the Compact Flash or SD card -- and folders where your images are stored. There are three parameters: Record Functions (functions of each slot), which of the two slots is used as the default, and the name of the folder used.

Record Func.

This option is active when you have more than one memory card inserted in the 7D II. You can select any of four different behaviors:

- **Standard (storage on primary card only).** All images will be recorded only to the memory card specified by the Record/Play setting (described next), either Slot 1 (the CF card) or Slot 2 (the SD card). The file format of the images (any of the RAW, JPEG, or RAW+JPEG options) are set in the Image Quality screen, as detailed in Chapter 8. When that memory card fills up, you must replace it with another card, or switch to the card in the other slot manually. I often use this setting when shooting movies to ensure that my clips are stored on the CF card, because, in the 7D II, the SD card is typically much slower, even if a (potentially) fast memory card is installed. (See the sidebar that follows.) I can keep an SD card installed for emergencies, but must manually switch to it.

- **Auto Switch Card (overflow mode).** As with Standard, all images will be recorded only to the memory card specified by the Record/Play setting using the Image Quality specifications you apply, but when that card is full, the camera switches automatically to the other card. I use this setting when I don't want to have to change cards, say, at a wedding or a performance, *and* don't mind having my overflow images diverted to a relatively slow memory card.

- **Rec. separately (flexible backup).** When this option is active, all images will be stored on *both* cards, but you can specify the image recording quality separately for each memory card in the Image Quality screen. After choosing this option, you'll need to navigate to the Shooting 1 menu and select Image Quality. You'll discover that Slot 1 and Slot 2 are now listed separately. Highlight each one individually and choose one (and only one) of the JPEG or RAW options. (You cannot select RAW+JPEG for a particular slot.)

- This is a very cool feature and is a versatile backup method. For example, you could choose to store a RAW format on a fast Compact Flash card, and your JPEG files (which are smaller) on an SD card. Because JPEG files are more compact, using the slower SD card slot wouldn't bog down your camera as much. You'd still end up with two copies of all your images. If something happened to your CF card (loss, damage, or failure), you'd still have the JPEG copies. Should a mishap befall your SD card instead, you'd not only have the RAW version on the CF card, but could regenerate JPEG copies using an image editor.

- I often use this option for very important shoots, particularly overseas. I carry around plenty of memory cards, so I can keep the backup card, plus copy all the files to my iPad or MacBook Air and have multiple copies. I'd recommend *not* using this setting if you're bracketing, because, even with a modest three-shot bracket you'd be writing *six* images to your memory cards every time you captured a bracketed set.

- **Rec. to Multiple (total backup).** All images are stored on both cards, using the quality settings you specify in the Image Quality screen. So, if you've selected a RAW+JPEG combination, both images will be written to both memory cards. The process can be fairly slow, so I don't recommend it for fast-moving sports (especially RAW+JPEG; shoot JPEG only for sports) and like the Record Separately option, it's not the best for bracketing. But it does give you total backup of every image you take.

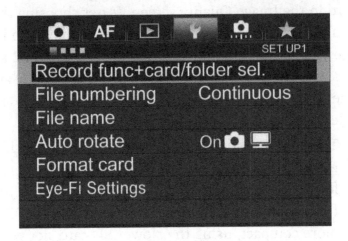

Figure 10.8

The Set-up 1 menu.

Record/Play or Playback

This option allows you to specify which slot is to be considered the primary for recording or playback, or both (depending on the Record Func. you've selected). Confused? The configurations are fairly simple:

- **For Standard or Auto Switch Card.** In either Standard or Auto Switch Card modes, the camera writes images to only one card, either the default card or the alternate when the default card is full. In that case, the entry reads Record/Play, and you can choose whether all images are written to slot 1 (the CF card) or slot 2 (the SD card). The 7D II will use that card for both functions, until (if Auto Switch is selected) the card fills and the alternate slot becomes active.

- **For Rec. Separately or Rec. to Multiple.** In either case, the camera *always* writes to both cards, so you can select only which card is to be used for playback. In general, you'll want to select your fastest memory card to be used for playback, and that will most frequently be the CF card slot.

Folder

This option allows you to select which of the folders currently on your memory card should be used to store the images that you capture. The 7D II will always create folders for you automatically, and will create a new one when the maximum number of images that can be stored in a specific folder have been deposited. However, you might want to create a new folder on your own. I tend to do that when I am traveling. I can create a new folder each day, making it simple to copy that day's shots to my computer when I return to my hotel room. There's no need to copy the previous files, and since they each have their own folders, the process is simple. You might want to create a new folder for each city you visit, or one for each band or group at the next music festival you attend.

File Numbering

The EOS 7D II will automatically apply a file number to each picture you take, using consecutive numbering for all your photos over a long period of time, spanning many different memory cards, starting over from scratch when you insert a new card, or when you manually reset the numbers. Numbers are applied from 0001 to 9999, at which time the camera creates a new folder on the card (100, 101, 102, and so forth), so you can have 0001 to 9999 in folder 100, then numbering will start over in folder 101.

The camera keeps track of the last number used in its internal memory. That can lead to a few quirks you should be aware of. For example, if you insert a memory card that had been used with a different camera, the 7D II may start numbering with the next number after the highest number used by the previous camera. (I once had a brand new 7D II start numbering files in the 8,000 range.) I'll explain how this can happen next.

On the surface, the numbering system seems simple enough: In the menu, you can choose Continuous, Automatic reset, or Manual reset. Here is how each works:

- ◎ **Continuous.** If you're using a blank/reformatted memory card, the 7D II will apply a number that is one greater than the number stored in the camera's internal memory. If the card is not blank and contains images, then the next number will be one greater than the highest number on the card *or* in internal memory. (In other words, if you want to use continuous file numbering consistently, you must always use a card that is blank or freshly formatted.) Here are some examples.

- You've taken 4,235 shots with the camera, and you insert a blank/reformatted memory card. The next number assigned will be 4,236, based on the value stored in internal memory.

- You've taken 4,235 shots with the camera, and you insert a memory card with a picture numbered 2,728. The next picture will be numbered 4,236.

- You've taken 4,235 shots with the camera, and you insert a memory card with a picture numbered 8,281. The next picture will be numbered 8,282, and that value will be stored in the camera's menu as the "high" shot number (and will be applied when you next insert a blank card).

- **Automatic reset.** If you're using a blank/reformatted memory card, the next photo taken will be numbered 0001. If you use a card that is not blank, the next number will be one greater than the highest number found on the memory card. Each time you insert a memory card, the next number will either be 0001 or one higher than the highest already on the card.

- **Manual reset.** The 7D II creates a new folder numbered one higher than the last folder created, and restarts the file numbers at 0001. Then, the camera uses the numbering scheme that was previously set, either Continuous or Automatic reset, each time you subsequently insert a blank or non-blank memory card.

File Name

The 7D II, like other cameras in the Canon product line, automatically applies a name like BB5C0001.jpg or BB5C 0001.cr2 to your image files as they are created. You can use this menu option to change the names applied to your photos -- but only within certain strict limitations. In practice, you can change only four of the eight characters, the *BB5C* (or your camera's counterpart) portion of the file name, using rules and industry conventions, such as those set by the Design Rule for Camera File System (DCF) specification.

DCF limits file names created by conforming digital cameras to a maximum of eight characters, plus a three-character extension (such as .jpg, or cr2) that represents the format of the file. The eight-plus-three (usually called 8.3) length limitation dates back to an evil and frustrating computer operating system that we older photographers would like to forget (its initials are D.O.S), but which, unhappily, lives on as the wraith of a file naming convention.

Of the eight available characters, four are used to represent, in a general sense, the type of camera used to create the image. Canon defaults to 5M4C for these initial four characters. The remaining four are used for numbers from 0000 to 9999, which is why your 7D II "rolls over" to 5DM40000 again when the 9999 number limitation is reached. When the 7D II rolls off the factory assembly line, it is configured to provide a choice of three different file naming schemes:

◉ **Factory Preset Code.** This is unique to your particular camera. By some weird chance, my own 7D II's factory preset code was 5MC4, and I thought this was some sort of programming error (maybe it should have been 5DM3, instead) until I learned that every Mark III has a different preset code, and that mine just happened to resemble the camera's name. When active, your images will be given names like (in my case) 5M4C0001.jpg when using the sRGB color space. If you switch to Adobe RGB, by industry convention the first character is replaced with an underline, yielding _M4C0001.jpg or _M4C001.cr2 file or similar names. You cannot change the factory preset code, but you can switch to one of the alternate naming schemes, as I'll show you next. This is a pretty cool feature, making it easy to tell which of your many Mark III cameras was used to take a given image.

⊙ **User Setting 1.** This is one of two user-definable alternative naming schemes. As the camera comes from the factory, it is set to IMG_0001.jpg/cr2/mov (for video) if you're using the sRGB color space, or _IMG0001.jpg (etc.) for Adobe RGB. You can specify all four initial characters for this setting, but, as always, underscores will replace the first or last characters in the file name when you're using Adobe RGB or sRGB (re-spectively). So, if you choose *OHIO*, you'll never actually see OHIO0001.jpg; you'll get either _HIO0001.jpg or OHI_0001.jpg.

⊙ **User Setting 2.** This second user-definable setting allows you to specify only the first three of the four initial charac-ters. The default is IMG for those characters. The camera uses the fourth position for a code representing the image re-cording quality. So, if your initial three letters are *ABC*, you might end up with file names like _BCL0001.jpg or AB_L001.jpg. The codes are as follows:

- **L.** Large Fine JPEG, Large Standard JPEG, or RAW.
- **M.** Medium Fine JPEG, Medium Standard JPEG, or M RAW.
- **S.** Small 1 Fine JPEG, Small 1 Standard JPEG, or S RAW.
- **T.** Small 2 JPEG.
- **U.** Small 3 JPEG.
- **_ (underscore).** The file is a movie, and quality setting is not indicated.

Redefining User Settings 1 and 2

To change the two User Settings from their defaults, navigate to the File Name screen, as shown in **Figure 10.9**. Then, follow these steps:

1. **Access menu entry.** Highlight the User Setting you want to modify and press SET. The screen shown in Figure 10.10 ap-pears.

2. **Remove old entry.** Press the Trash button at the lower-left corner of the camera repeatedly until the previous entry

(probably the factory default) is removed. A vertical line will be shown at the current cursor position.

3. **Switch to text characters.** The Q button toggles between the text screen at the top and the text characters at the bottom. Press it to jump down to the lower text box.

4. **Select characters.** Use the joystick-like multi-selector to navigate to the first character you want to choose. Only uppercase letters, an underscore, and numerals are available. You can also navigate with the QCD and Mail Dial, but that is slower. Press SET to enter the highlighted character.

5. **Choose remaining characters.** The cursor will advance to the next position, and you can repeat Step 4 to enter the remaining characters (a total of four for Setting 1 and three for Setting 2). You can always press the Q button and use the Trash button to remove one or more characters you've entered in error.

6. **Finish.** Press MENU to confirm your text entry, or INFO. to cancel.

7. **Review.** The updated definitions are shown at the bottom of the screen, as in **Figure 10.10**.

Selecting a Naming Scheme.

Once you've defined your naming alternatives to your satisfaction, you can switch among them at any time during a shooting session. Just access the File Name screen from the Set-up 1 menu, highlight File Name at the top of the screen, and press SET. You can then choose the factory preset code, User Setting 1, or User Setting 2. Renaming a User setting is so easy that I sometimes do it on the fly during a shoot. If you don't need to differentiate between different cameras or models, you can change the characters to anything else that suits your purposes, including your initials (DDB_ or JFK_ for example) or even customize for particular shooting sessions (EUR, GER, FRA, and JAP when taking vacation trips). You can also use the file name flexibility to partially overcome the 9999 numbering limitation. You could, for example, use the template 5D1 to represent the first 10,000 pictures you take with your 7D II, and then 5D2 for the next 10,000, and 5D3 for the 10,000 after that.

That's assuming that you don't rename your image files in your computer. In a way, file naming verges on a moot consideration, because, they apply *only* to the images as they exist in your camera. After (or during) transfer to your computer you can change the names to anything you want, completely disregarding the 8.3 limitations (although it's a good idea to retain the default extensions). If you shot an image file named IMG_4832.jpg in your camera, you could change it to Paris_EiffelTower_32.jpg later on. Indeed, virtually all photo transfer programs, including Photoshop Elements Transfer, allow you to specify a template and rename your photos as they are moved or copied to your computer from your camera or memory card.

I usually don't go to that bother (I generally don't use transfer software; I just drag and drop images from my memory card to folders I have set up), but renaming can be useful for those willing to take the time to do it.

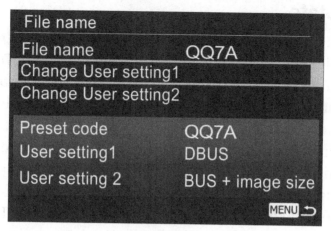

Figure 10.9

Customize and choose your file naming scheme.

Figure 10.10

Enter text here.

Auto Rotate

You can turn this feature On or Off. When activated, the EOS 7D II rotates pictures taken in vertical orientation on the LCD screen so you don't have to turn the camera to view them comfortably. However, this orientation also means that the longest dimension of the image is shown using the shortest dimension of the LCD, so the picture is reduced in size. You have three options. The image can be autorotated when viewing in the camera *and* on your computer screen using your image editing/viewing software (this choice is represented by a pair of camera/computer screen icons). The image can be marked to autorotate *only* when reviewing your image in your image editor or viewing software (just a computer screen icon is used). This option allows you to have rotation applied when using your computer, while retaining the ability to maximize the image on your LCD in the camera. The third choice is Off. The image will not be rotated when displayed in the camera or with your computer. Note that if you switch Auto Rotate off, any pictures shot while the feature is disabled will not be automatically rotated when you turn Auto Rotate back on; information embedded in the image file when the photo *is taken* is used to determine whether autorotation is applied.

Format Card

Use this item to erase everything on your memory card and set up a fresh file system ready for use. When you select Format, you'll be given a choice of selecting Slot 1 (CF card) or Slot 2 (SD card). Highlight your preference and press SET. A display pops up showing the capacity of the card, how much of that space is currently in use, and two choices at the bottom of the screen to Cancel or OK (proceed with the format). A bar appears on the screen to show the progress of the formatting step.

Eye-Fi Settings

This menu item appears when you have an Eye-Fi card inserted in the camera. You can enable and disable Eye-Fi wireless functions, and view connection information. The pair of entries allow you to Enable or Disable the card, and view current connection information. Because the Eye-Fi card draws power from the camera even when it's switched off, you might want to Disable the card (or remove it from the camera) when you don't need to use its features.

Auto Power Off

This setting, the first in Set-up 2 menu (see **Figure 10.11**), allows you to determine how long the EOS 7D II remains active before shutting itself off. You can select 1, 2, 4, 8, 15, or 30 minutes or Off, which leaves the camera turned on indefinitely. However, even if the camera has shut itself off, if the power switch remains in the ON position, you can bring the camera back to life by pressing the shutter button.

There are three settings and several techniques you can use to help stretch the longevity of your 7D II's battery. The first setting is the Image Review time option described in Chapter 11 under the Shooting 1 menu. That big 3.2-inch LCD uses a lot of juice, so reducing the amount of time it is used (either for automatic review or for manually playing back your images) can boost the effectiveness of your battery. Auto Power Off turns off most functions (metering and autofocus shut off by themselves about six seconds after you release the shutter button or take a picture) based on the delay you specify. The third setting is the LCD Brightness adjustment described below. If you're willing to shade the LCD with your hand, you can often get away with lower brightness settings outdoors, which will further increase the useful life of your battery. The techniques? Turn off image stabilization if your lens has that feature and you feel you don't need it. When transferring pictures from your 7D II to your computer, use a card reader instead of the USB cable. Linking your camera to your computer and transferring images using the cable takes longer and uses a lot more power.

Figure 10.11

The Set-up 2 menu has six options.

LCD Brightness

Choose this menu option, and a thumbnail image with a gray-scale strip appears on the LCD, as shown in **Figure 10.12**. You can select both automatic brightness and manually set brightness.

- **Automatic brightness.** Use the Main Dial to toggle between Auto and Manual brightness settings. You may see the LCD dim when switching to Auto, as the camera adjusts for the light level. If you've chosen this option, you can spin the QCD to change from a default mid-level setting to a lower or brighter setting, and the camera will adjust the brightness from that point automatically.

- **Manual brightness.** If you select Manual, you can use the Quick Control Dial or the multi-controller to adjust the brightness to a comfortable viewing level. Use the gray bars as a guide; you want to be able to see both the lightest and darkest steps at top and bottom, and not lose any of the steps in the middle. Brighter settings use more battery power, but can allow you to view an image on the LCD outdoors in bright sunlight. When you have the brightness you want, press the SET button to lock it in and return to the menu.

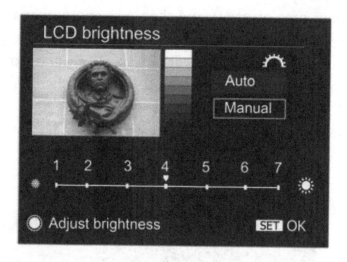

Figure 10.12

Adjust LCD brightness for easier viewing under varying ambient lighting conditions.

Date/Time/Zone

Use this option to set the date and time, which will be embedded in the image file along with exposure information and other data. As first outlined in Chapter 1, you can set the date and time by following these steps:

1. Access this menu entry from the Set-up 2 menu.
2. Rotate the QCD to move the highlighting down to the Date/Time/Zone entry.
3. Press the SET button in the center of the QCD to access the Date/Time/Zone setting screen, shown in **Figure 10.13**.
4. Rotate the QCD to select the value you want to change. When the gold box highlights the month, day, year, hour, minute, or second format you want to adjust, press the SET button to activate that value. A pair of up/down pointing triangles appears above the value.
5. Rotate the QCD to adjust the value up or down. Press the SET button to confirm the value you've entered.
6. Repeat steps 4 and 5 for each of the other values you want to change. The date format can be switched from the default

mm/dd/yy to yy/mm/dd or dd/mm/yy; you can turn Daylight Savings time on or off, and choose an appropriate time zone.

7. When finished, rotate the QCD to select either OK (if you're satisfied with your changes) or Cancel (if you'd like to return to the Set-up 2 menu without making any changes). Press SET to confirm your choice.

8. When finished setting the date and time, press the MENU button to exit, or just tap the shutter release.

Figure 10.13

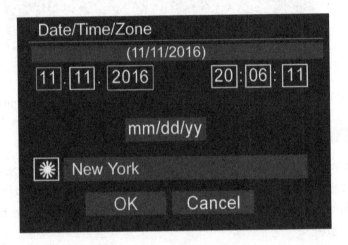

Set the date, time, and time zone here.

Language

Choose from 25 languages for menu display, rotating the Quick Control Dial or using the multi-controller joystick until the language you want to select is highlighted. Press the SET button to activate. Your choices include English, German, French, Dutch, Danish, Portuguese, Finnish, Italian, Ukrainian, Norwegian, Swedish, Spanish, Greek, Russian, Polish, Czech, Magyar, Romanian, Turkish, Arabic, Thai, Simplified Chinese, Traditional Chinese, Korean, and Japanese.

If you accidentally set a language you don't read and find yourself with incomprehensible menus, don't panic. Just choose the fourth option from the top of the Set-up 2 menu, marked with a "speech" icon, and select the idioma, sprache, langue, or kieli of your choice. English is the first selection in the list.

Viewfinder Display

You can enable or disable the display of the viewfinder level or grid on the optical viewfinder, as well as other indictors using this setting. Choose Viewfinder Level, VF Grid, or Show, and then make your selections from the following:

- ⊚ **Viewfinder Level.** You can Show or Hide the level display in the viewfinder. This does not affect the level shown on the LCD monitor when the INFO. button is pressed. You can show/hide that element using the Set-up 3 menu, as explained later in the chapter. I'm not sure why Canon elected to locate the two options in different menu tabs, but at least they're consistent in their inconsistency, as you'll discover next.

- ⊚ **VF Grid.** Here's where you Enable/Disable (not Show/Hide) the viewfinder grid display you selected in the Shooting 5 menu, as explained in Chapter 8.

- ⊚ **Show/hide In Viewfinder.** Here you can elect to display or hide seven different viewfinder elements, thus uncluttering your screen and showing only the information you really care about. Your options include Shooting Mode, White Balance, Drive Mode, Autofocus operation, Metering mode, Image Quality, and Flicker detection. Use the QCD to highlight any of these to remove or add a checkmark and hide/show that indicator.

GPS/Digital Compass Settings

This menu entry is used to enable/disable your 7D II's internal GPS receiver, and to make all its crucial settings for the GPS and your digital compass. I explained how to use the features in this menu in detail in Chapter 6. To recap, your choices are:

- ◉ **GPS.** You can enable or disable the GPS receiver. If you don't use this feature, disabling it is advised, because the receiver drains your battery quite effectively.

- ◉ **Auto time setting.** The 7D II can GPS data set the camera's internal clock accurately. You can choose Auto Update to set the time automatically whenever the camera is powered up and GPS data is available; disable this function, or Set Now to update immediately.

- ◉ **Position update interval.** Use this to specify the interval the GPS device uses to update position information. Choose from every 1, 5, 10, 15, 30 seconds, or every 1, 2, or 5 minutes. Select a shorter interval when you are moving and/or accuracy is critical, or a longer interval to save power, when GPS reception is not optimal, or you are shooting from one position for a longer period.

- ◉ **Digital Compass.** You can enable or disable the digital compass, which records the compass direction the camera is pointed. Calibrate the compass as described in Chapter 6.

- ◉ **GPS information display.** This entry simply displays a screen of current GPS information, including latitude, longitude, elevation, UTC time (essentially Greenwich Mean Time), and Satellite reception strength/status.

- ◉ **GPS logger.** Allows you to enable or disable tracking of GPS position data, transfer log data to your memory card for later manipulation by an appropriate software program, or to delete the camera's current GPS log.

- ◉ **Calibrate Digital Compass.** The digital compass uses geo-magnetism to calculate your camera's direction. Once activated, the digital compass can be displayed as you shoot by pressing the INFO button until it appears on the LCD monitor, or on an overlay on the live view screen.

Video System

This setting, the first on the Set-up 3 screen (see Figure **10.14**), controls the output of the 7D II through the AV cable when you're displaying images on an external monitor. You can select either NTSC, used in the United States, Canada, Mexico, many Central, South American, and Caribbean countries, much of Asia, and other countries, or PAL, which is used in the UK, much of Europe, Africa, India, China, and parts of the Middle East.

Canon makes it quite easy to view your images on a standard television screen, and not much more difficult on a high-definition television (HDTV). (You have to buy a separate cable for HDTV.) For regular TV, just open the right port cover that protects the USB port on the left side of the camera, plug in the Stereo AV Cable AVC-DC400ST supplied with the camera into the socket labeled A/V/Digital, and connect the other end to the yellow VIDEO RCA composite jack on your television or monitor. The red/white plugs connect to the stereo audio inputs of your TV/monitor.

For HDTV display, purchase the optional HDMI Cable HTC-100 and connect it to the HDMI OUT terminal just below the USB/digital port on the left side of the camera.

Connect the other end to an HDMI input port on your television or monitor (my 42-inch HDTV has three of them; my 26-inch monitor has just two). Then turn on the camera and press the Playback button. The image will appear on the external TV/HDTV/monitor and will not be displayed on the camera's LCD. HDTV systems automatically show your images at the appropriate resolution for that set.

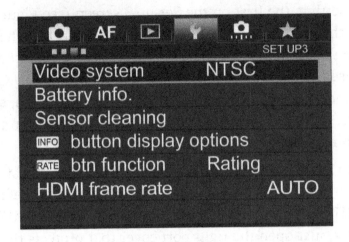

Figure 10.14

The Set-up 3 menu.

Battery Info.

This entry is an exceptionally useful feature that allows you to view battery condition information and performance, and track the data among several different batteries. Your EOS 7D II can keep track of multiple LP-E6 or LP-6N batteries because each of them is given a unique serial number (which is printed on an included sticker you can affix to the battery). The camera reads this serial number and stores information about each of the batteries that you use and have "registered" separately. I always recommend owning at least two and, preferably three or more batteries. That's especially true if you use the Battery Grip BG-E16, which holds two battery packs itself. I also own the EOS 6D, which uses the same battery, so I'm able to justify four batteries to shuttle between my two cameras.

This feature makes it possible to see exactly how each battery you own is performing, allows you to rotate them to even out the usage, and helps you know when it's time to replace a battery. When you select this menu choice, a Battery info screen like the one shown in **Figure 10.15** appears, with a wealth of information (if you use two LP-E6 packs in a BG-E11 grip, information about both packs will appear):

- ◎ **Battery position.** The second line of the screen includes an icon that shows where the battery currently being evaluated is installed (usually the hand grip if you're not using the BG-E6).

- ◎ **Power type.** Next to the position icon is an indicator that shows the model number of the battery installed, or shows that the DC power adapter is being used instead.

- ◎ **Remaining capacity.** The Battery check icon appears showing the remaining capacity visually, along with a percentage number that reads out in 1% increments. You can use this as a rough gauge of how much power you have remaining. If you're in the middle of an important shooting session, you might want to switch to a fully charged battery at the 25-33% level to avoid interruptions at the worst probable time. (If you're using six AA batteries in the BG-E16 grip instead of LP-E6 packs, only this battery capacity notice will appear; the other indicators are not shown.)

- ◎ **Shutter count.** Displays how many times the shutter has been actuated with the current charged battery. This info can help you learn just how much certain features cost you in terms of power. For example if a battery has only 50 percent of its power remaining, but you've taken only a few dozen photos, you know that your power is being sapped by picture review, lots of autofocus, frequent image stabilization because of lower shutter speeds, or (a major culprit) that flip-up flash you've been using. While in most cases knowledge is power, in this instance knowledge can help you *save* power, with a tip-off to use fewer juice-sapping features if the current battery pack must be stretched as far as possible.

- ◎ **Recharge performance.** This indicator shows how well your battery pack is accepting and holding a charge. Three green bars mean that the pack's performance is fine; two bars show that recharge performance is degraded a little. A red bar indicates that your pack is on its last legs and should be replaced soon. To lengthen the service time of your batteries, you might want to rotate usage among several different packs, so they all "age" at roughly the same rate.

Registering Your Battery Packs

The EOS 7D II can "remember" information about up to six LP-E6 battery packs, and provide readouts of their status individually. To register the battery currently in your camera, follow these steps:

1. Access the Battery Info. screen (shown in **Figure 10.15**) from the Set-up 3 menu.
2. Press the INFO. button, located to the left of the LCD screen.
3. Information about the current battery, including its serial number and the current date will be shown on a new screen.
4. Choose Register to log the battery; if the pack has already been registered, you can choose Delete Info. to remove the battery from the list. (You'd want to do this if you already had registered the limit of six batteries and want to add another one.)
5. Press SET to add the battery to the registry.
6. If you're deleting a battery, the 7D II shows you a Battery Info. delete screen instead. (You can delete a battery pack without having that battery installed in the camera -- which could come in handy if you lose one.) Just select the battery (by serial number) and delete.
7. Press MENU to back out of any of the Battery Info. screens.

Once a battery has been registered, you can check on its remaining capacity at any time (even if it isn't currently installed in the 7D II) from the Battery info page. The camera remembers and updates the status of each registered battery whenever it is inserted in the 7D II. The date the battery was last used is also shown.

Use this info with caution, however, as a given battery may have self-discharged slightly during storage and, of course, you may have fully recharged it since the last time it was inserted in the camera. However, this data can be useful in tracking the remaining capacity of several different battery packs during a single shooting session, or over the course of several days when you're not recharging the packs at the conclusion of each session.

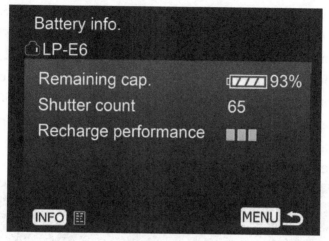

Figure 10.15

View the battery type and position, remaining capacity, number of pictures taken with the current charge, and the performance of your pack.

Sensor Cleaning

One of the Canon EOS 7D II's most useful features is the automatic sensor cleaning system that reduces or eliminates the need to clean your camera's sensor manually using brushes, swabs, or bulb blowers. Canon has applied anti-static coatings to the sensor and other portions of the camera body interior to counter charge build-ups that attract dust. A separate filter over the sensor vibrates ultrasonically each time the 7D II is powered on or off, shaking loose any dust, which is captured by a sticky strip beneath the sensor.

Use this menu entry to enable or disable automatic sensor cleaning on power up (select Auto Cleaning to choose) to activate automatic cleaning during a shooting session (select Clean Now). You can also choose the Clean Manually option to flip up the mirror and clean the sensor yourself with a blower, brush, or swab. If the battery level is too low to safely carry out the cleaning operation, the 7D II will let you know and refuse to proceed, unless you use the optional AC Adapter Kit ACK-E6 with the DC Coupler DR-E6.

INFO. Button Display Options

The INFO. button on the back panel of the Canon EOS 7D II by default alternates between the Camera Settings, Shooting Functions, and Electronic Level information displays (see **Figure 10.16**). If one is shown, press the INFO. button to see the other. If you'd rather have only one or two of those screens shown, choose INFO. button from the Set-up 3 menu and change from the default Normal Disp. to either Camera Set. or Shoot. Func. After that, only the display you specified will be shown. Follow these steps:

Figure 10.16

The INFO. button toggles between the Camera Settings (left), Shooting Functions (center), and Electronic Level screen (right).

1. When you select the menu entry, the INFO. button display options screen appears with three choices (described next). Use the Quick Control Dial or multi-controller to highlight any of the three and press SET to mark or unmark that option.

2. Always mark at least one of the three. The 7D II won't allow you to disable all of the display options.

3. When finished, press the SET button to confirm your changes.

4. Press SET to OK or Cancel and exit the screen. (If you exit in any other way, your changes will not be entered.) Once you've left this options screen, you can press MENU or tap the shutter release to return to shooting mode.

5. Thereafter, the 7D II will cycle among the choices you've activated, plus a blank screen, each time you press the INFO. button.

RATE Button Display Options

Select whether a press of the Rate button during playback will change the rating of the displayed image, or whether the button will apply the Protect attribute instead. If you elect to retain the Rating function, press the Q button to select which of the one- to five-star ratings can be applied. Highlight a particular star rating and then press SET to check or uncheck that rating. Highlight the OK or Cancel options at the bottom of the screen to finish.

You might, for example, want to label only the stellar images and turkeys, and so would select only the One Star and Five Star ratings, disabling the others. Multiple presses of the Rate button while you are rating images jumps from the starting star rating to the next highest, and then wraps around to the lowest activated rating again. If you never use ratings at all, or apply then from the Playback menu only, you might want to go for the Protect option instead.

HDMI Frame Rate

Select Auto to allow the camera to choose the appropriate HDMI display protocol when it is connected to a suitable display. Or, you can choose 24 fps progressive scan or 60 fps interlaced scan. I'll explain more about scan rates in Chapter 13.

Custom Shooting Mode (C1-C3)

This entry, the first on the Set-up 4 menu, allows you to register your EOS 7D II's current camera shooting settings and file them away in the C1, C2, or C3 positions on the Mode Dial. Doing this overwrites any settings previously stored at that Camera user position. You can also clear the settings for any of the three Mode Dial positions individually, returning them to their factory default values.

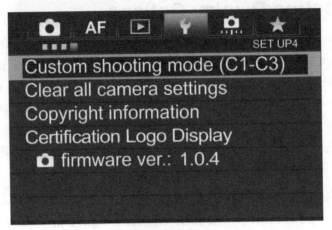

Figure 10.17
Set-up 4 menu.

Table 10.1 shows the settings you can store: Stored Camera User Settings

Mode/Menu	Settings
Shooting functions	Shutter speed, aperture, ISO, AF operation, AF area, AF point, Drive mode, Meter mode, Exposure compensation, flash exposure compensation.
Shooting menu	Shooting 1: Image quality; Image Review; Beep; Release shutter without card; Lens aberration correction; Flash firing, E-TTL II metering, Flash sync speed in Av mode.
	Shooting 2: Exposure compensation/AEB; ISO speed settings; Auto Lighting Optimizer; All white balance settings; Color space
	Shooting 3: Picture Style; Long exposure noise reduction; High ISO speed noise reduction; Highlight tone priority; Multiple exposure, HDR mode
	Shooting 4 (Live View): Live view shooting; AF mode; Grid display; Aspect ratio, Exposure simulation
	Shooting 5 (Live View): Silent live view shooting, Metering timer
	Shooting 4 (Movie): Movie Servo AF' AF method, Grid display, Movie recording quality, sound recording, AF speed during Movie Servo AF, Movie Servo AF tracking sensitivity
	Shooting 5 (Movie): Silent LV shooting, Metering timer, Movie recording count; Movie play count; Silent Control; Movie shooting button function, HDMI output+LCD.
AF menu	AF1: Case 1; Case 2; Case 3; Case 4; Case 5; Case 6
	AF2: AI Servo 1 image priority; AI Servo 2 Image Priority
	AF3: Lens electronic MF; AF-assist beam firing; One-Shot AF release priority
	AF4: Lens drive when AF impossible; Selectable AF point; Select AF area select. mode; AF area selection method; Orientation linked AF point, Initial AF point, Auto AF point selection, EOS iTR AF
	AF5: Manual AF point selection pattern; AF point display during focus; VF display illumination,AF status in viewfinder, AF Micro-adjustment.
Playback menu	Playback 2: Slide show; Image Jump with Main Dial

Mode/Menu	Settings
	Playback 3: Highlight alert; AF point display; Playback grid; Histogram display; Movie play count; Magnification (approximate)
Setup menu	Set-up 1: File numbering; Auto rotate; Eye-Fi Settings
	Set-up 2: Auto power off; LCD brightness; Viewfinder display, Log GPS position.
	Set-up 3: Auto cleaning, INFO. button display options; RATE button function, HDMI frame rate
Custom Functions	Custom 1: Exposure level increments; ISO speed setting increments; Bracketing auto cancel; Bracketing sequence; Number of bracketed shots; Safety shift, Same exposure for new aperture
	Custom 2: Set shutter speed range. Set aperture range. Continuous shooting speed.
	Custom 3: Live view shooting area display; Dial direction during Tv/Av; Multi function lock; Custom controls
	Custom 4: Add cropping information; Default erase option

Register your favorite settings for use in particular situations. I have one for sports, one for portraits, and another for landscapes. If you switch to C1, C2, or C3 and forget what settings you've made for that slot, just press the INFO. button to view the current settings. Keep in mind that My Menu settings are not stored individually. You can have only one roster of My Menu entries available for all of the Mode Dial's positions.

This menu choice has only two options: Register (which stores your current settings in your choice of C1, C2, or C3) and Clear settings (which erases the settings in C1, C2, or C3). Note that you must use this menu entry to clear your settings; when using C1, C2, or C3, the Clear Settings option in the Set-up 4 menu is disabled. The Clear all Custom Func. (C.Fn) option in the Custom Functions menu is disabled as well.

To perform either of these tasks, just follow these steps:

1. **Make your settings.** Set the EOS 7D II to an exposure mode other than Scene Intelligent Auto

2. **Access Camera user settings.** Navigate to the Custom Shooting Mode entry option in Set-up 4 menu, and press SET.

3. **Choose function.** Rotate the Quick Control Dial to choose Register if you want to store your 7D II's current settings in C1, C2, or C3; or select Clear Settings if you want to erase the settings stored in either location. Press SET to access the settings screen for your choice.

4. **Store/Clear settings.** The individual screens for storing/clearing are virtually identical. Use the QCD to highlight Mode Dial: C1, Mode Dial: C2, or Mode Dial: C3, and press SET to store or clear the settings for that position. (You'll be given a choice to proceed or cancel first.)

5. **Auto update.** Keep in mind that if you change a setting while using one of the custom shooting modes and want to retain the new settings, your stored settings can be automatically updated to reflect the modifications. Select Auto Update Set. and choose Enable to activate this option. If you'd rather retain your custom settings until you manually decide to update, select Disable instead.

6. **Exit.** When you confirm, you'll be returned to the Setting 4 menu. Press the MENU button or tap the shutter release button to exit the menu system entirely.

Clear All Camera Settings

This menu choice resets all the settings to their default values. Regardless of how you've set up your EOS 7D II, it will be adjusted for One-Shot AF mode, Automatic AF point selection, Evaluative metering, JPEG Fine Large image quality, automatic ISO, sRGB color mode, automatic white balance, and Standard Picture Style. Any changes you've made to exposure compensation, flash exposure compensation, and white balance will be canceled, and any bracketing for exposure or white balance nullified. Custom white balances and Dust Delete Data will be erased.

Remember, Custom Functions and Camera User Settings will *not* be cleared. If you want to cancel those, as well, you'll need to use the Camera User Setting option (described previously) and the Custom Functions clearing option, which I'll describe in Appendix C. The tables that follow show the settings defaults after using this menu option.

Copyright Information

Here's where you can give yourself credit for the great photos you're shooting with your 7D II:

- **Display Copyright Info.** Enable or disable embedding copyright information in your image files. If you're a double-naught secret agent who wants to submit spy photos anonymously, you'll definitely want to disable copyright information.

- **Enter Author's Name.** You can add your own name (up to 63 characters) to each image file, using a screen like the one shown earlier in **Figure 10.10**, except with a larger array of alphanumeric characters, using the procedure described earlier in this chapter.

- **Enter Copyright Details.** You can add more information using the expanded character set. Up to 63 characters can be entered. Note that no copyright symbol is available. While some use a lowercase *c* within parentheses, technically the correct notification would be (Copyright) or (Copr.)

- **Delete Copyright Information.** This removes all the data you've entered and gives you a clean slate, so to speak.

Certification Logo Display

This cryptic entry is used by Canon to display the logos of some of the certification organizations that have approved the 7D II's specifications. You'll find others on the bottom of the camera itself. As a camera user, you don't really care about certifications, but Canon added this entry as a way of updating any new credentials through a firmware update, thus avoiding the need to change the labels/engravings on the camera body itself. So now you know.

Firmware Version

You can see the current firmware release in use in the menu listing. If you want to update to a new firmware version, insert a memory card containing the binary file, and press the SET button to begin the process.

Chapter 11

Custom Function and My Menus

Custom Functions let you tailor the behavior of your camera in a variety of different ways, such as the function carried out when the SET button is pressed. If you don't like the default way the camera carries out a particular task, you just may be able to do something about it. You can find the Custom Functions in their own menu, color-coded orange-brown, and visible whenever you are using P, Tv, Av, M, and B exposure modes.

If you're a long-time Canon user, you probably know that some Canon EOS cameras (chiefly earlier models and current entry-level cameras) crowded all the Custom Functions on a single screen, with cryptic rows of settings, each with a series of numbers beneath the settings row that represented the current value of that Custom Function. Fortunately, more recent advanced Canon models like the 7D II have divided all the Custom Functions into four separate screens that each have multiple options. There are 18 C.Fn entries in all, plus Clear All Custom Func.

Custom Menu Options:

Exposure Level Increments

ISO Speed Setting Increments

Bracketing Auto Cancel

Bracketing Sequence

Number of Bracketed Shots

Safety Shift

Same Exposure for New Aperture

Set Shutter Speed Range

Set Aperture Range

Focusing Screen

Warnings in Viewfinder

LV Shooting Area Display

Dial Direction During Tv/Av

Multi Function Lock

Custom Controls

Add Cropping Information

Default Erase Option

Clear All Custom Func. (C.Fn)

Continuous Shooting Speed

Custom Function 1 (C.Fn I): Exposure

This is the Custom Function category you can use to set the increments for exposure and ISO, define bracketing parameters, and other settings. See **Figure 11.1**.

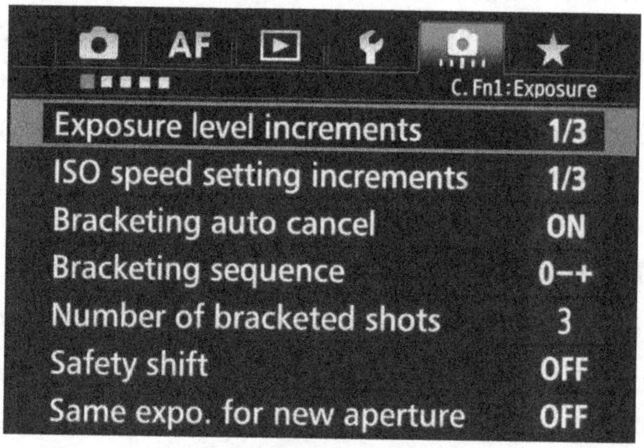

Figure 11.1

The Custom Function 1 menu.

Exposure Level Increments

This setting tells the EOS 7D II the size of the "jumps" it should use when making exposure adjustments -- either one-third or one-half stop. The increment you specify here applies to f/stops, shutter speeds, EV changes, and autoexposure bracketing.

- **1/3 stop.** Choose this setting when you want the finest increments between shutter speeds and/or f/stops. For example, the 7D II will use shutter speeds such as 1/60th, 1/80th, 1/100th, and 1/125th second, and f/stops such as f/5.6, f/6.3, f/7.1, and f/8, giving you (and the autoexposure system) maximum control.

- **1/2 stop.** Use this setting when you want larger and more noticeable changes between increments. The 7D II will apply shutter speeds such as 1/60th, 1/125th, 1/250th, and 1/500th second, and f/stops including f/5.6, f/6.7, f/8, f/9.5, and f/11. These coarser adjustments are useful when you want more dramatic changes between different exposures.

ISO Speed Setting Increments

This setting determines the size of the "jumps" made when adjusting ISO -- either one-third or one full stop. At the one-third stop setting, typical ISO values would be 100, 125, 160, 200, and so forth. Switch to the one-stop setting, and ISO values would be 100, 200, 400, 800, and so forth. The larger increment can help you leap from one ISO setting to one that's twice (or half) as sensitive with one click.

Bracketing Auto Cancel

When Auto Cancel is activated (the default), AEB (Auto Exposure Bracketing) and WB-BKT (White Balance Bracketing) are cancelled when you turn the 7D II off, change lenses, use the flash, or change memory cards; when Auto Cancel is deactivated, bracketing remains in effect until you manually turn it off or use the flash. When Auto Cancel is switched off, the AEB and WB-BKT settings will be kept even when the power switch is turned to the OFF position. The flash still cancels autoexposure bracketing, but your settings are retained.

Bracketing Sequence

You can define the sequence in which AEB and WB-BKT series are exposed. For exposure bracketing, you can determine whether the order is metered exposure, decreased exposure, increased exposure or decreased exposure, metered exposure, increased exposure. Or with white balance bracketing, if your bias preference is set to Blue/Amber in the WB SHIFT/BKT adjustments in the Shooting 2 menu, the white balance sequence when option 0 is selected will be current WB, more blue, more amber. If your bias preference is set to Magenta/Green, then the sequence for option 0 will be current WB, more magenta, more green.

- ⊙ [lb] 0 - +. Exposure sequence is metered exposure, decreased exposure, increased exposure (0, -, +). White balance sequence is current WB, more blue/more magenta (depending on how your bias is set), more amber/more green (ditto).

- ⊚ **[lb] - 0 +.** The sequence is decreased exposure, metered exposure, increased exposure (-, 0, +). White balance sequence is more blue/more magenta, current WB, more amber/more green.

- ⊚ **[lb] + 0 -.** The sequence is increased exposure, metered exposure, decreased exposure (-, 0, +). White balance sequence is more amber/more green, current WB, more blue/more magenta.

Number of Bracketed Shots

Your choices are 2, 3, 5, or 7 shots in a bracket sequence.

Safety Shift

Ordinarily, both Aperture-priority and Shutter-priority modes work fine, because you'll select an f/stop or shutter speed that allows the 7D II to produce a correct exposure using the other type of setting (shutter speed for Av; aperture for Tv). However, when lighting conditions change, it may not be possible to select an appropriate setting with the available exposure options, and the camera will be unable to take a picture at all.

For example, you might be at a concert shooting the performers and, to increase your chances of getting a sharp image, you've selected Tv mode and a shutter speed of 1/250th second. Under bright lights and with an appropriate ISO setting, the 7D II might select f/5.6, f/4, or even f/2.8. Then, in a dramatic moment, the stage lights are dimmed significantly. An exposure of 1/250th second at f/2 is called for, but your lens has an f/2.8 maximum aperture. If you've used this Custom Function to allow the 7D II to override your selection, the camera will automatically switch to 1/125th second to allow the picture to be taken at f/2.8.

Safety Shift will make similar adjustments if your scene suddenly becomes too bright; although, in practice, you'll find that the override will be needed most often when using Tv mode. It's easier to "run out of" f/stops, which generally range no smaller than f/22 or f/32, than to deplete the available supply of shutter speeds, which can be as brief as 1/8,000th second. For example, if you're shooting at ISO 400 in Tv mode at 1/1,000th second, an extra-bright beach scene could easily call for an f/stop smaller than f/22, causing over-exposure. However, Safety Shift would bump your shutter speed up to 1/2,000th second with no problem.

On the other hand, if you were shooting under the same illumination in Av mode with the preferred aperture set to f/16, the EOS 7D II could use 1/1,000th, 1/2,000th, 1/4,000th, or 1/8,000th second shutter speeds to retain that f/16 aperture under conditions that are 2X, 4X, 8X, or 16X as bright as normal daylight. No Safety Shift would be needed, even if the ISO were (for some unknown reason) set much higher than the ISO 400 used in this example. These are your options:

- **Disable.** Turn off Safety Shift. Your specified shutter speed or f/stop remains locked in, even if conditions are too bright or too dim for an appropriate exposure. Use this option if you'd prefer to have the shot taken at the shutter speed, aperture, or ISO you've selected under all circumstances, even if it means an improperly exposed photo. You might be able to salvage the photo in your image editor.

- **Shutter speed/Aperture.** Safety Shift is activated for Tv and Av modes. The 7D II will adjust the preferred shutter speed or f/stop to allow a correct exposure. If you don't mind having your camera countermand your orders, this option can save images that otherwise might be incorrectly exposed. Use when working with a shutter speed or aperture that are *preferable,* but aren't critical.

- **ISO speed.** This option operates in Program AE (P) mode as well as Tv and Av modes. Think of it as an "emergency" Auto ISO option. You can manually select your preferred ISO setting, and the 7D II will generally stick with that, but can adjust the ISO setting if required to produce an acceptable exposure. If you've selected a minimum and maximum allowable ISO range in the ISO Speed Settings entry of the Shooting 2 menu (as explained in Chapter 11), this setting will honor those limits *unless* your current manually selected ISO is out-side those boundaries.

For example, if you've chosen a minimum and maximum auto ISO range of ISO 200-800, this setting will stay within that range when adjusting ISO (even though you have Auto ISO off), but if your camera is currently manually set to ISO 100 or a value higher than ISO 800, it will go ahead and use the extra values, too.

Same Exposure for New Aperture

This is a cryptic feature that's not really difficult to understand. Under certain circumstances, the maximum aperture available from your lens may change, which can affect a user-specified exposure when using Manual exposure mode, and Auto ISO is not in effect. This Custom Function tells the 7D II what to do when that happens.

When is an f/stop not an f/stop? The most common explanation is that you changed lenses. Perhaps you exchanged a lens with an f/2.8 maximum aperture for one that opens up no larger than f/4. Or, you might be using a lens that does not have a constant maximum aperture – it's an f/3.5 lens at the wide angle setting, but is actually has a largest f/stop of f/5.6 at the telephoto position. Your effective maximum aperture changes when you use a tele extender, too. It costs you 1 stop for a 1.4x extender, 1.5 stops for a 1.7x extender, and 2 full stops with a 2x extender.

Ordinarily, using Auto ISO or shutter priority (Tv) mode will compensate for those effects automatically. But that's not the case when shooting in Manual mode using manually selected ISO values. This Custom Function allows you to compensate for those changes. (It also adjusts for changes in the *minimum* f/stop, too, say, if you change from a lens with an f/32 minimum aperture to one that stops down only to f/22.) Unfortunately, the feature does not work with macro lenses, which change their effective aperture as the distance between the center of the lens and the focal plane changes as you shoot close-ups. Nor does it work when shooting movies.

Here are your choices:

- **Off: Disable.** The camera will not make an exposure change to compensate for the new maximum aperture if Auto ISO is not active. You'll need to make adjustments yourself to the ISO value or shutter speed if you want to keep the same aperture.

- **ISO: ISO speed.** With this choice, the camera effectively overrides your ISO setting, and automatically adjusts sensitivity to compensate, giving you the same exposure at the new aperture value. However, the new ISO setting must be within the range allowed by the Set ISO Speed Range Custom Function (described later in this chapter.) If an expanded ISO speed (H1 or H2) is required, the 7D II may adjust shutter speed instead to avoid using those potentially noisy ISO settings.

- **Tv: Shutter speed.** In this case, the shutter speed is adjusted to compensate, as long as the new shutter speed is within the range specified by the Set Shutter Speed Range Custom Function (described later in this chapter.)Custom Function 2 (C.Fn II): Exposure/Drive

This is the Custom Function category, shown in **Figure 11.2**, that you can use to set shutter speed and aperture range, and continuous shooting speed.

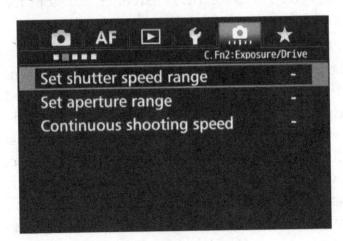

Figure 11.2

The Custom Function 2 menu.

Set Shutter Speed Range

You can customize the range of available shutter speeds, setting both a highest possible speed (from 15 seconds to 1/8000th second and a slowest speed from 30 seconds to 1/4000th second. Highlight the shutter speed parameter you want to change and rotate the Quick Control Dial to make your setting.

Tailoring your shutter speed settings can help you make adjustments more quickly. For example, I've never ever used 1/8000th second during a shoot, and almost never have needed 1/4000th second. Since most sports action can be stopped using a shutter speed of 1/2000th second, the most likely need for a ridiculously high shutter speed might be if I wanted to use f/2.8 for selective focus in bright daylight, and even then 1/4000th second would do the job at ISO 100. So, I set my top shutter speed at 1/2000th second, and don't have to worry about spinning a dial too far in Tv and M mode. If I *do* want a higher shutter speed, I have the default range stored in my C1 user setting (described later in this chapter.)

Similarly, you can use the Lowest Speed setting, say, when shooting sports, to avoid accidentally using a speed below, perhaps, 1/125th second.

Set Aperture Range

This setting is the counterpart to the shutter speed range option. You can specify a minimum aperture of f/1.4 to f/91 (good luck with finding the latter outside the realm of pinhole cameras), and a maximum aperture of f/1.0 (such lenses exist) to f/64. Use this option when you want to limit the largest aperture that will be used (say, because you want to maintain a certain amount of depth-of-field or avoid large apertures when using lenses that aren't particularly sharp at those f/stops.) You might also want to prevent the smallest f/stops from coming into play, primarily because that while smaller f/stops produce greater depth-of-field, the tiniest apertures sacrifice sharpness due to diffraction effects.

Continuous Shooting Speed

You'll often want to maintain control over your continuous shooting speeds. Sometimes extra-high speeds are wasted because changes between frames are small. You won't gain many subtle facial expression differences shooting portraits at 10 fps, and will have to spend more time evaluating all your different shots. This setting allows you to calibrate your continuous shooting speeds with great precision. High Speed can be set within a range of 7-10 frames per second; Low Speed can be set in a range from 1 to 6 fps. (I find that especially useful, as there are some subjects, especially children, that can be captured perfectly while continuously shooting at 1 frame per second.) Silent continuous shooting can be adjusted between 1 and 4 frames per second.

Custom Function 3 (C.Fn III): Display/Operation

This is the Custom Function category, shown in **Figure 11.3**, that fine-tunes display options and various control operations.

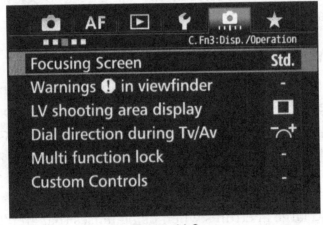

Figure 11.3

Focusing Screen

If you don't like the focusing screen installed in your 7D II at the factory, you can carefully remove it with tweezers and insert a replacement. Once you've done so, you must inform the camera about the upgrade. This is one setting that is "sticky" and isn't cleared by the Clear all Custom Functions option in the Custom Function 5 menu (described later.)

The standard screen is the L- Eh-A, a Precision Matte focusing screen. The optional screen is the P-Eh-S Super Precision Matte focusing screen designed for manual focusing, especially with lenses having a maximum aperture of f/2.8 or larger. (With other lenses, the screen image may actually look darker than with the standard screen.)

Note: You may also find additional screens available from third parties that will fit your 7D II.

Warnings in Viewfinder

This useful function lets you individually enable or disable five different viewfinder warnings, allowing you to reduce the amount of clutter in your field of view as you frame an image, while retaining the warnings that you really, really want to remain in effect. Mark any or all with a check mark by highlighting the option and pressing SET. Your choices include warnings for the following:

- **Monochrome Picture Style.** If you shoot JPEG most of the time, you might want a tip-off that you've set the camera in black-and-white mode, because color information cannot be added in post-processing. If you generally shoot RAW or RAW+JPEG, you won't care, because the RAW image retains the color information.

- **WB Correction.** It's easy to dial in some white balance correction, and easier to forget that you've done so. This warning will let you know -- again, very important when shooting JPEG only.

- ☉ **One-Touch Image Quality.** Later in this chapter you'll learn how to quickly change image quality using a custom control. You can warn yourself when this capability is available.

- ☉ **ISO Expansion.** The 7D II makes you manually enable the highest high and low ISO settings through ISO expansion, as discussed in Chapter 11. While the availability of these extreme settings isn't normally a problem, if you feel you're likely to need a tip-off, you can activate this warning.

- ☉ **Spot metering.** Most users rely on the intelligence of Evaluative metering, and use Spot metering only occasionally. Because exposure results can vary so much when Spot metering is in effect, this warning can be helpful.

LV Shooting Area Display

When you're using an aspect ratio other than the default 3:2 in Live View, the 7D II will always alert you that the full viewable frame is not the active capture area. If you choose Masked, then the extra area will be darkened, which can be very useful in helping you compose your images within the actual proportions of the frame that will be captured. However, you can also choose Outlined, in which case the entire frame can be seen, with lines marking the image area. I like to use this mode when shooting sports in a non-traditional aspect ratio (say, I want the 16:9 wide screen look in my images), because I can follow moving subjects slightly outside the image area and capture them when framed properly.

Dial Direction During Tv/Av

Dial direction during Tv/Av. This setting reverses the result when rotating the Quick Control Dial and Main Dial when using Shutter-priority or Aperture-priority (Tv and Av). That is, rotating the Main Dial to the right will decrease the shutter speed rather than increase it; f/stops will become larger rather than smaller. Use this if you find the default rotation scheme in Tv and Av modes are not to your liking. Activating this option also reverses the dial direction in Manual exposure mode. In other shooting modes, only the Main Dial's direction will be reversed.

- ⊙ **Normal.** The Main Dial and Quick Control Dial change shutter speed and aperture normally.
- ⊙ **Reverse direction.** The dials adjust shutter speed and aperture in the reverse direction when rotated.

Multi Function Lock

Your 7D II includes a Lock switch at the 7 o'clock position of the Quick Control Dial. Slide it to the right when you want to prevent the use of the QCD, Main Dial, or multi-controller from accidentally changing a setting. You can select any or all three of the controls (shown in **Figure 11.4**) to lock, while freeing the other (or none) to act normally. I use this sometimes when I am using manual exposure, especially when I'm fumbling around in a darkened environment, and don't want to unintentionally manipulate my settings. The Multi Function Lock screen has one option for each control; highlight the control and press SET to lock or unlock it. A check mark appears next to the control's name when it's locked, and an L/Lock indicator appears in the viewfinder, top-panel LCD, and shooting settings display. Even if you've locked the QCD, its touch pad functions can still be used during movie shooting even if Silent Control has been activated in the Shooting 5 (Movie) menu.

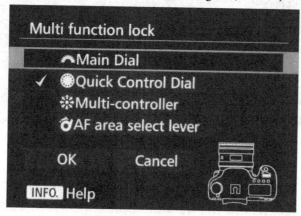

Figure 11.4

Choose which controls to lock.

Custom Controls

If you're eager to totally confuse any poor soul who is not equipped to deal with a custom-configured 7D II (or, perhaps, even yourself), Canon allows you to redefine the behavior of no less than ten different controls in interesting, and potentially hilarious ways. Just highlight any of the ten options, press SET to view the functions you can assign, and make your choice. If you see the INFO. icon at bottom left, there are even more decisions to make. You can truly manipulate your camera to work in a way that's fastest and most efficient for you. There are dozens of combinations of control possibilities (some buttons have as many as 12 different options, plus Off), spelled out in a huge matrix+legend description on pages 445-449 of your factory manual. The options are mind-boggling, with some toggling, others active only while a button is held, and you can even assign multiple functions to a button. You can set the Multi-Function button, for example, so that each time you press it, it cycles among four available features: flash exposure compensation, ISO/Drive settings, AF/WB settings, and Metering mode. (See Figure 11.5.)

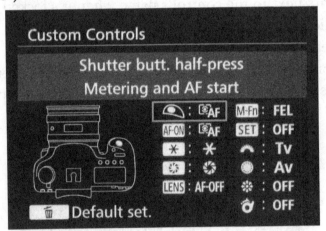

Figure 11.5

Custom Controls.

Press the Trash button from the Custom Controls screen to return all your settings to the default values shown in **Table 11.1.** Custom Controls can be used to set up special features, like Back Button focus, discussed in Chapter 5.

Table 11.1 Assignable Controls

Control	Default	Other Options
Shutter button half-press	Metering and AF start	Metering Start, AE lock (hold)
AF-On button	Metering and AF start	AE lock, AF stop, FE lock, One-Shot/AI Servo toggle, Register/Recall shooting function, AE lock (hold), AE lock/AF stop
AE Lock button	AE Lock	AE lock, Metering/AF start, AF stop, FE lock, One-Shot/AI Servo toggle, Register/Recall shooting function, AE lock (hold), AE lock/AF stop, Off
DOF Preview button	Depth-of-field preview	AF stop, AE lock, One-Shot/AI Servo toggle, IS start, Switch to registered AF function, One Touch Image Quality, One Touch Image Quality (hold), FE lock, Switch to registered AF point, AE Lock (hold), Unlock (hold),Off
Lens AF stop button (if available on lens)	AF stop	Metering and AF start, AE Lock, One-Shot/AI Servo toggle, IS start, Switch to registered AF function, AE lock (hold), Switch to registered AF point.
M-Fn (Multi Function) button	FE lock	FE lock, AE lock, One-Touch Image Quality, One-Touch Image Quality (hold), AE lock (hold), Cycle: FE comp, ISO/Drive, AF/WB, Metering
SET button	No additional function	Off, Image Quality, Picture Style, Menu, Playback, Magnify/Reduce, ISO Speed, Exposure compensation, Flash functions.
Main Dial	Shutter speed setting in Tv and Manual Mode	Aperture setting in Manual mode, Off

Control	Default	Other Options
Quick Control Dial	Aperture setting in Av and Manual Mode	Shutter speed setting in Manual mode, Direct AF point selection, ISO speed, Direct AF point select (vertical), Off
Multi-controller	No additional function	Direct AF point selection
AF-Area Selection Lever	No additional function	Direct AF area selection, AE lock, AE lock (hold), Selected AF pt/Center-Registered toggle, ISO setting, Exposure compensation.

Custom Function 4 (C.Fn IV): Others

This is the Custom Function "miscellaneous" category that you can use to set the specifications for cropping and erase functions. See **Figure 11.6**.

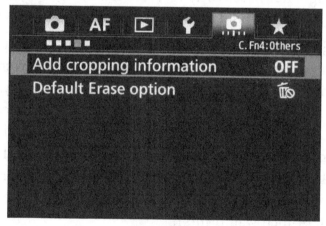

Figure 11.6

The Custom Function 4 menu.

Add Cropping Information

If you want to use image crops other than the default 3:2 aspect ratio in live view, but don't want to lock the settings down in stone, this Custom Function, the first on the third page of the Custom Function menu, may help you. It allows you to specify one of the optional available crops, such that vertical lines will appear on the live view image to delineate that cropping -- but the image you take will be saved in its full-frame form, *without* the actual crop being applied. However, the cropping information *is* embedded in the image file and can be retrieved by compatible software (including Canon's Digital Photo Pro) and used to apply the crop in post processing.

If you're saying, "Wha?" about now, I can clarify. One of the coolest things about live view is that it mimics the ground glass screen of the medium format (say, 120/220 roll film models) or large format (4 x 5, 5 x 7 or larger sheet film cameras) that many of us grew up with. That is, as with a medium format or large format film camera, the actual film/sensor plane image is there for you to view (although, not necessarily reversed left to right or reversed and inverted as in the good old days).

Canon gives you a variety of optional cropping proportions so you can compose and expose your image just as if you were using a camera from those thrilling days of yesteryear -- or simply want to use an alternate aspect ratio for creative effect. Your choices include the 6:6 and 6:7 proportions used to create 6cm x 6cm and 6cm x 7cm film images (think Hasselblad or Pentax 67); 4:5 and 5:7 ratios used with 4 x 5-inch, 8 x 10-inch, and 5 x 7-inch sheet film cameras, plus other formats as well. These include 3:4 and 5:6 (the latter perfect for 20 x 24-inch wall prints).

Of course, these days cameras like the 7D II have enough resolution that you can easily crop the full-frame image to any proportions you like, but many photographers still enjoy composing within a given aspect ratio.

Default Erase Option

Specify what happens during image review and playback when you press the Trash button and the Erase Image screen appears. Choose Cancel, and pressing the Trash button a second time backs you out of the screen with no harm done. You'd choose this if you find you accidentally press Trash from time to time. Or, select Erase, and that second press will delete the image, probably forever. Your choice.

Custom Function 4 (C.Fn IV): Clear

This is the Custom Function category you can use to clear other functions. See **Figure 11.7**.

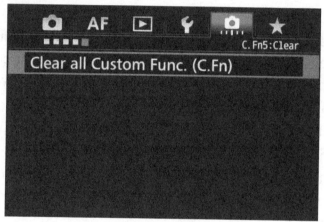

Figure 11.7
The Custom Function 4 menu.

Clear All Custom Func. (C.Fn)

Select this entry and choose Cancel (if you chicken out) or OK to return all your Custom Functions to their default values. But don't panic -- your matrix of Custom Controls is retained. If you want to zero out those settings, you'll need to access the Custom Controls screen in the Custom Functions 3 menu, and press the Trash button.

My Menu

The Canon EOS 7D II has a great feature that allows you to define your own menu, with just the items listed that you want. Remember that the 7D II always returns to the last menu and menu entry accessed when you press the MENU button. So you can set up My Menu to include just the items you want, and jump to those items instantly by pressing the MENU button. Or, you can set your camera so that My Menu appears when the MENU button has been pressed, regardless of what other menu entry you accessed last.

To create your own My Menu, you have to *register* the menu items you want to include. (See **Figure 11.8**) Just follow these steps:

1. Press the MENU button and use the Main Dial or multi-controller to select the My Menu tab. When you first begin, the personalized menu will be empty except for the My Menu Settings entry. Press the SET button to select it.
2. Rotate the Quick Control Dial to select Register, then press the SET button.
3. Use the Quick Control Dial to scroll down through the continuous list of menu entries to find one you would like to add. Press SET.
4. Confirm your choice by selecting OK in the next screen and pressing SET again.
5. Continue to select up to six menu entries for My Menu.
6. When you're finished, press the MENU button twice to return to the My Menu screen to see your customized menu.

In addition to registering menu items, you can perform other functions at the My Menu Settings screen:

- ⊙ **Changing the Order.** Choose Sort to reorder the items in My Menu. Select the menu item and press the SET button. Rotate the Quick Control Dial to move the item up and down within the menu list. When you've placed it where you'd like it, press the MENU button to lock in your selection and return to the previous screen.

- **Delete/Delete All Items.** Use these to remove an individual menu item or all menu items you've registered in My Menu.

- **Display from My Menu.** As I mentioned earlier, the 7D II (almost) always shows the last menu item accessed. That's convenient if you used My Menu last, but if you happen to use another menu, then pressing the MENU button will return to that item instead. If you enable the Display from My Menu option, pressing the MENU button will *always* display My Menu first. You are free to switch to another menu tab if you like, but the next time you press the MENU button, My Menu will come up again. Use this option if you work with My Menu a great deal and make settings with other menu items less frequently.

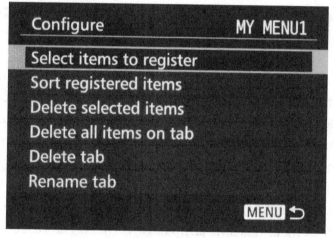

Figure 11.8

You can add one to six menu entries to My Menu.

Chapter 12

Working with Light

Great lighting doesn't happen by accident. Whether you're working with continuous lighting or electronic flash, it's important to understand how to apply light to your creative vision. This chapter provides an introduction to using the two main types of illumination: *continuous* lighting (such as daylight, incandescent, or fluorescent sources) and the brief, but brilliant snippets of light we call *electronic flash*.

Continuous Illumination versus Electronic Flash

Continuous lighting is exactly what you might think: uninterrupted illumination that is available all the time during a shooting session. Daylight, moonlight, and the artificial lighting encountered both indoors and outdoors count as continuous light sources (although all of them can be "interrupted" by passing clouds, solar eclipses, a blown fuse, or simply by switching off a lamp). Indoor continuous illumination includes both the lights that are there already (such as incandescent lamps or overhead fluorescent lights indoors) and fixtures you supply yourself, including photoflood lamps or reflectors used to bounce existing light onto your subject.

Electronic flash is notable because it can be much more intense than continuous lighting, lasts only a brief moment, and can be much more portable than supplementary incandescent sources. It's a light source you can carry with you and use anywhere. Indeed, your 7D II has a flip-up electronic flash unit built in.

But you can also use an external flash, either mounted on the 7D II's accessory shoe or used off-camera and linked with a cable or triggered wirelessly. Studio flash units are electronic flash, too, and aren't limited to "professional" shooters, as there are economical "monolight" (one-piece flash/power supply) units available in the

$200 price range. You can buy a couple to store in a closet and use to set up a home studio, or use as supplementary lighting when traveling away from home.

There are advantages and disadvantages to each type of illumination. Here's a quick checklist of pros and cons:

- **Lighting preview.** With continuous lighting, you always know exactly what kind of lighting effect you're going to get and, if multiple light sources are used, how they will interact with each other. With electronic flash, the general effect you're going to see may be a mystery until you've built some experience, and you may need to review a shot on the LCD, make some adjustments, and then reshoot to get the look you want. (In this sense, a digital camera's review capabilities replace the Polaroid test shots pro photographers relied on in decades past.)

- **Exposure calculation.** Your 7D II has no problem calculating exposure for continuous lighting, because the illumination remains constant and can be measured through a sensor that interprets the light reaching the viewfinder. The camera's Spot metering mode can be used to measure and compare the proportions of light in the highlights and shadows, so you can make an adjustment (such as using more or less fill light) if necessary. In contrast, electronic flash illumination doesn't exist until the flash fires. The light must be measured metering the intensity of a pre-flash triggered an instant before the main flash, as it is reflected back to the camera and through the lens.

- **Freezing Action.** When it comes to the ability to freeze moving objects in their tracks, the advantage goes to electronic flash. The brief duration of electronic flash serves as a very high "shutter speed" when the flash is the main or only source of illumination for the photo. Your 's shutter speed may be set for 1/250th second during a flash exposure, but if the flash illumination predominates, the *effective* exposure time will be the 1/1,000th to 1/50,000th second or less duration of the flash. Action stopping with continuous light sources is completely dependent on the shutter speed you've dialed in on the camera. And the speeds available are dependent on the amount of light available and your ISO sensitivity setting.

◉ **Price tag.** Incandescent or fluorescent lamps are generally much less expensive than electronic flash units, which can easily cost several hundred dollars. I've used everything from desktop high-intensity lamps to reflector flood lights for continuous illumination at very little cost. There are lamps made especially for photographic purposes, too, priced up to $50 or so. Maintenance is economical, too: many incandescent or fluorescents use bulbs that cost only a few dollars. The lowest-cost dedicated flash designed specifically for the Canon dSLRs is about $150. Such units are limited in features, however, and intended for those with entry-level cameras. Plan on spending some money to get the features that a sophisticated electronic flash offers.

◉ **Flexibility.** Electronic flash's action-freezing power allows you to work without a tripod in the studio (and elsewhere), adding flexibility and speed when choosing angles and positions. Flash units can be easily filtered, and, because the filtration is placed over the light source rather than the lens, you don't need to use high-quality filter material. Because incandescent and fluorescent lamps are not as bright as electronic flash, the slower shutter speeds required mean that you may have to use a tripod more often. Incandescent lighting gets hot and heat also makes it more difficult to add filtration to incandescent sources.

Continuous Lighting Basics

While continuous lighting and its effects are generally much easier to visualize and use than electronic flash, there are some factors you need to take into account, particularly the color temperature of the light. (Color temperature concerns aren't exclusive to continuous light sources, of course, but the variations tend to be more extreme and less predictable than those of electronic flash.)

Living with Color Temperature

Canon and vendors with equipment compatible with the 7D II have been valiant in their efforts to help us tame the color balance monster. One popular color balancing technology lives on in the form of ExpoDisc filter/caps and their ilk (www.expoimaging.com), which allow the camera's built-in custom white balance measuring feature to evaluate the illumination that passes through the disc/cap/filter/Pringle's can lid, or whatever neutral-color substitute you employ. (A white or gray card also works.)

Color temperature, in practical terms, is how "bluish" or how "reddish" the light appears to be to the digital camera's sensor. Indoor illumination is quite warm, comparatively, and appears reddish to the sensor. Daylight, in contrast, seems much bluer to the sensor. Our eyes (our brains, actually) are quite adaptable to these variations, so white objects don't appear to have an orange tinge when viewed indoors, nor do they seem excessively blue outdoors in full daylight. Yet, these color temperature variations are real and the sensor is not fooled. To capture the most accurate colors, we need to take the color temperature into account in setting the color balance (or *white balance*) of the 7D II -- either automatically using the camera's smarts or manually, using our own knowledge and experience.

Color temperature can be confusing, because of a seeming contradiction in how color temperatures are named: warmer (more reddish) color temperatures (measured in degrees Kelvin) are the *lower* numbers, while cooler (bluer) color temperatures are *higher* numbers. It might not make sense to say that 3,400K is warmer than 6,000K, but that's the way it is. If it helps, think of a glowing red ember contrasted with a white-hot welder's torch, rather than fire and ice.

The confusion comes from physics. Scientists calculate color temperature from the light emitted by a mythical object called a black body radiator, which absorbs all the radiant energy that strikes it, and reflects none at all. Such a black body not only *absorbs* light perfectly, but it *emits* it perfectly when heated (and since nothing in the universe is perfect, that makes it mythical).

At a particular physical temperature, this imaginary object always emits light of the same wavelength or color. That makes it possible to define color temperature in terms of actual temperature in degrees on the Kelvin scale that scientists use. Incandescent light, for example, typically has a color temperature of 3,200K to 3,400K. Daylight might range from 5,500K to 6,000K. Each type of illumination we use for photography has its own color temperature range -- with some cautions. The next sections will summarize everything you need to know about the qualities of these light sources.

Daylight

Daylight is produced by the sun, and so is moonlight (which is just reflected sunlight). Daylight is present, of course, even when you can't see the sun. When sunlight is direct, it can be bright and harsh. If daylight is diffused by clouds, softened by bouncing off objects such as walls or your photo reflectors, or filtered by shade, it can be much dimmer and less contrasty.

Daylight's color temperature can vary quite widely. It is highest (most blue) at noon when the sun is directly overhead, because the light is traveling through a minimum amount of the filtering layer we call the atmosphere. The color temperature at high noon may be 6,000K. At other times of day, the sun is lower in the sky and the particles in the air provide a filtering effect that warms the illumination to about 5,500K for most of the day. Starting an hour before dusk and for an hour after sunrise, the warm appearance of the sunlight is even visible to our eyes when the color temperature may dip below 4,500K, as shown in **Figure 12.1** (left.)

Because you'll be taking so many photos in daylight, you'll want to learn how to use or compensate for the brightness and contrast of sunlight, as well as how to deal with its color temperature. I'll provide some hints later in this chapter.

Incandescent/Tungsten Light

The term incandescent or tungsten illumination is usually applied to the direct descendants of Thomas Edison's original electric lamp. Such lights consist of a glass bulb that contains a vacuum, or is filled with a halogen gas, and contains a tungsten filament that is heated by an electrical current, producing photons and heat. Tungsten-halogen lamps are a variation on the basic light bulb, using a more rugged (and longer-lasting) filament that can be heated to a higher temperature, housed in a thicker glass or quartz envelope, and filled with iodine or bromine ("halogen") gases. The higher temperature allows tungsten-halogen (or quartz-halogen/quartz-iodine, depending on their construction) lamps to burn "hotter" and whiter. Although popular for automobile headlamps today, they are also popular for photographic illumination. Although incandescent illumination isn't a perfect black body radiator, it's close enough that the color temperature of such lamps can be precisely calculated and used for photography without concerns about color variation (at least, until the very end of the lamp's life).

Fluorescent Light/Other Light Sources

Fluorescent light has some advantages in terms of illumination, but some disadvantages from a photographic standpoint, including compact fluorescent lights (CFLs). This type of lamp generates light through an electro-chemical reaction that emits most of its energy as visible light, rather than heat, which is why the bulbs don't get as hot. The type of light produced varies depending on the phosphor coatings and type of gas in the tube. So, the illumination fluorescent bulbs produce can vary widely in its characteristics.

That's not great news for photographers. Different types of lamps have different "color temperatures" that can't be precisely measured in degrees Kelvin, because the light isn't produced by heating. Worse, fluorescent lamps have a discontinuous spectrum of light that can have some colors missing entirely, producing that substandard Color Rendering Index I mentioned. A particular type of tube can lack certain shades of red or other colors (see **Figure 12.1**, right), which is why fluorescent lamps and other alternative technologies such as sodium-vapor illumination can produce ghastly looking human skin tones. Their spectra can lack the reddish tones we associate with healthy skin and emphasize the blues and greens popular in horror movies.

Figure 12.1

At dawn and dusk, the color temperature of daylight may dip below 4,500K, providing this reddish rendition (left) Fluorescent lighting added a distinct greenish cast to the image (right.).

Adjusting White Balance

I showed you how to adjust white balance bracketing in <u>Chapter 8</u>. In most cases, however, the 7D II will do a good job of calculating white balance for you, so Auto can be used as your choice most of the time. Use the preset values or set a custom white balance that matches the current shooting conditions when you need to. The only really problematic light sources are likely to be fluorescents. Vendors, such as GE and Sylvania, may actually provide a figure known as the *color rendering index* (or CRI), which is a measure of how accurately a particular light source represents standard colors, using a scale of 0 (some sodium-vapor lamps) to 100 (daylight and most incandescent lamps). Daylight fluorescents and deluxe cool white fluorescents might have a CRI of about 79 to 95, which is perfectly acceptable for most photographic applications. Warm white fluorescents might have a CRI of 55. White deluxe mercury vapor lights are less suitable with a CRI of 45, while low-pressure sodium lamps can vary from CRI 0-18.

Remember that if you shoot RAW, you can specify the white balance of your image when you import it into Photoshop, Photoshop Elements, or another image editor using your preferred RAW converter. While color-balancing filters that fit on the front of the lens exist, they are primarily useful for film cameras, because film's color balance can't be tweaked as extensively or as easily as that of a sensor.

Electronic Flash Basics

Until you delve into the situation deeply enough, it might appear that serious photographers have a love/hate relationship with electronic flash. You'll often hear that flash photography is less natural looking, and that the built-in flash in most cameras should never be used as the primary source of illumination because it provides a harsh, garish look. Indeed, many "pro" cameras don't have a built-in flash at all. Available ("continuous") lighting is praised, and built-in flash photography seems to be roundly denounced.

In truth, however, the bias is against *bad* flash photography. Indeed, flash has become the studio light source of choice for pro photographers, because it's more intense (and its intensity can be varied to order by the photographer), freezes action, frees you from using a tripod (unless you want to use one to lock down a composition), and has a snappy, consistent light quality that matches daylight. (While color balance changes as the flash duration shortens, some Canon flash units can communicate to the camera the exact white balance provided for that shot.) And even pros will cede that the built-in flash of the 7D II has some important uses as an adjunct to existing light, particularly to illuminate dark shadows using a technique called *fill flash*.

But electronic flash isn't as inherently easy to use as continuous lighting. As I noted earlier, electronic flash units are more expensive, don't show you exactly what the lighting effect will be (unless you use a second source called a *modeling light* for a preview), and the exposure of electronic flash units is more difficult to calculate accurately.

Fire When Ready!

Once the capacitor is charged, the burst of light that produces the main exposure can be initiated by a signal from the 7D II that commands the internal or connected flash units to fire. External strobes can be linked to the camera in several different ways:

- **Camera mounted/hardwired external dedicated flash.** Units offered by Canon or other vendors that are compatible with Canon's lighting system can be clipped onto the accessory "hot" shoe on top of the camera or linked through a wired system such as the Canon Off Shoe Camera Cord OC-E3.

- **Wireless dedicated flash.** A compatible unit can be triggered by signals produced by a pre-flash (before the main flash burst begins), which offers two-way communication between the camera and flash unit. The triggering flash can be the 7D II's built-in unit, an external flash unit in Master mode, or a wireless non-flashing accessory, such as the Canon Speedlite Transmitter ST-E2 and new radio-controlled wireless trigger, the Speedlite Transmitter ST-E3-RT, which each do nothing but "talk" to the external flashes.

- **Wired, non-intelligent mode.** Your 7D II has a built-in PC/X connector, so you can connect non-dedicated flash units, including studio strobes, through a non-intelligent camera/flash link that sends just one piece of information, one way: it tells a connected flash to fire. There is no other exchange of information between the camera and flash. The PC/X connector can be used to link the 7D II to studio flash units, manual flash, flash units from other vendors that can use a PC cable, or even Canon brand Speedlites that you elect to connect to the 7D II in "unintelligent" mode.

◎ **Infrared/radio transmitter/receivers.** Another way to link flash units to the 7D II is through third-party wireless infrared or radio *transmitters*, like a Pocket Wizard, Radio Popper, or the Paul C. Buff CyberSync trigger. These are generally mounted on the accessory shoe of the camera, and emit a signal when the 7D II sends a command to fire through the hot shoe. The simplest of these function as a wireless PC/X connector, with no other communication between the camera and flash (other than the instruction to fire). However, sophisticated units have their own built-in controls and can send additional commands to the receivers when connected to compatible flash units. I use one to adjust the power output of my Alien Bees studio flash from the camera, without the need to walk over to the flash itself.

◎ **Simple slave connection.** In the days before intelligent wireless communication, the most common way to trigger off-camera, non-wired flash units was through a *slave* unit. These can be small external triggers connected to the remote flash (or built into the flash itself), and set off when the slave's optical sensor detects a burst initiated by the camera itself. When it "sees" the main flash (from the 7D II's built-in flash, or another flash), the slave flash units are triggered quickly enough to contribute to the same exposure. The main problem with this type of connection -- other than the lack of any intelligent communication between the camera and flash -- is that the slave may be fooled by any pre-flashes that are emitted by the other strobes, and fire too soon. Modern slave triggers have a special "digital" mode that ignores the pre-flash and fires only from the main flash burst.

How Electronic Flash Works

The bursts of light we call electronic flash are produced by a flash of photons generated by an electrical charge that is accumulated in a component called a *capacitor* and then directed through a glass tube containing xenon gas, which absorbs the energy and emits the brief flash. For the pop-up flash built into the 7D II, the full burst of light lasts about 1/1,000th of a second and provides enough illumination to shoot a subject 10 feet away at f/4 using the ISO 100 setting. In a more typical situation, you'd use ISO 200, f/5.6 to f/8 and photograph something 8 to 10 feet away. As you can see, the built-in flash is somewhat limited in range; you'll see why external flash units are often a good idea later in this chapter.

An electronic flash (whether built in or connected to the 7D II through an adapter's PC terminal or a cable plugged into a hot shoe adapter) is triggered at the instant of exposure, during a period when the sensor is fully exposed by the shutter. As I mentioned earlier in this book, the 7D II has a vertically traveling shutter that consists of two curtains. The first curtain opens and moves to the opposite side of the frame, at which point the shutter is completely open. The flash can be triggered at this point (so-called *1st curtain sync*), making the flash exposure. Then, after a delay that can vary from 30 seconds to 1/250th second (with the 7D II; other cameras may sync at a faster or slower speed), a second curtain begins moving across the sensor plane, covering up the sensor again. If the flash is triggered just before the second curtain starts to close, then *2nd curtain sync* is used. In both cases, though, a shutter speed of 1/250th second is the maximum that can be used to take a photo.

Figure 12.2 illustrates how this works. At upper left, you can see a fanciful illustration of a generic shutter (your 7D II's shutter does *not* look like this), with both curtains tightly closed. At upper right, the first curtain begins to move downward, starting to expose a narrow slit that reveals the sensor behind the shutter. At lower left, the first curtain moves downward farther until, as you can see at lower right in the figure, the sensor is fully exposed.

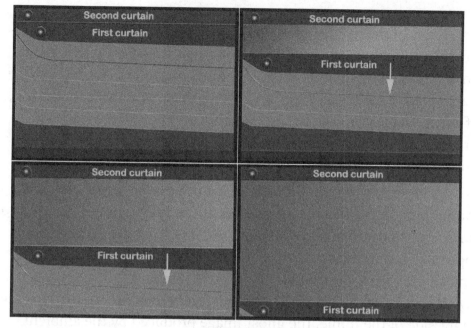

Figure 12.2

A focal plane shutter has two curtains, the upper, or front curtain, and a lower, se-cond curtain.

Ghost Images

The difference between triggering the flash when the shutter just opens, or just when it begins to close might not seem like much. But whether you use 1st curtain sync (the default setting) or 2nd curtain sync (an optional setting) can make a significant difference to your photograph *if the ambient light in your scene also contributes to the image.* You can set either of these sync modes in the Shooting 1 menu, under Flash Control and the Built-in Flash Setting and External Flash Func. Setting options.

At faster shutter speeds, particularly 1/250th second, there isn't much time for the ambient light to register, unless it is very bright. It's likely that the electronic flash will provide almost all the illumination, so 1st curtain sync or 2nd curtain sync isn't very important. However, at slower shutter speeds, or with very bright ambient light levels, there is a significant difference, particularly if your subject is moving, or the camera isn't steady.

In any of those situations, the ambient light will register as a second image accompanying the flash exposure, and if there is movement (camera or subject), that additional image will not be in the same place as the flash exposure. It will show as a ghost image and, if the movement is significant enough, as a blurred ghost image trailing in front of or behind your subject in the direction of the movement.

As I noted, when you're using 1st curtain sync, the flash's main burst goes off the instant the shutter opens fully (a pre-flash used to measure exposure in auto flash modes fires *before* the shutter opens). This produces an image of the subject on the sensor. Then, the shutter remains open for an additional period (30 seconds to 1/250th second, as I said). If your subject is moving, say, toward the right side of the frame, the ghost image produced by the ambient light will produce a blur on the right side of the original subject image, making it look as if your sharp (flash-produced) image is chasing the ghost. For those of us who grew up with lightning-fast superheroes who always left a ghost trail *behind them*, that looks unnatural (see **Figure 12.3**).

So, Canon uses 2nd curtain sync to remedy the situation. In that mode, the shutter opens, as before. The shutter remains open for its designated duration, and the ghost image forms. If your subject moves from the left side of the frame to the right side, the ghost will move from left to right, too. *Then*, about 1.5 milliseconds before the second shutter curtain closes, the flash is triggered, producing a nice, sharp flash image *ahead* of the ghost image. Voilà! We have monsieur *Speed Racer* outdriving his own trailing image. I showed you how to switch to 2nd curtain sync in Chapter 8.

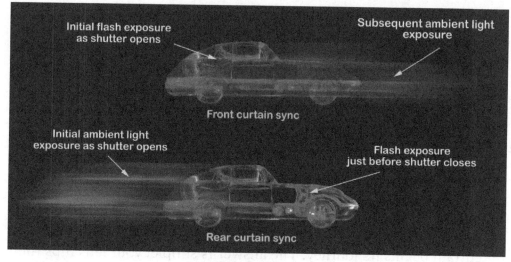

Figure 12.3

1st curtain sync produces an image that trails in front of the flash exposure (top), whereas 2nd curtain sync creates a more "natural looking" trail behind the flash image.

Avoiding Sync Speed Problems

Using a shutter speed faster than 1/250th second can cause problems. Triggering the electronic flash only when the shutter is completely open makes a lot of sense if you think about what's going on. To obtain shutter speeds faster than 1/250th second, the 7D II exposes only part of the sensor at one time, by starting the second curtain on its journey before the first curtain has completely opened, as shown in **Figure 12.4**. That effectively provides a briefer exposure as a slit, narrower than the full height of the sensor, passes over the surface of the sensor. If the flash were to fire during the time when the first and second curtains partially obscured the sensor, only the slit that was actually open would be exposed.

You'd end up with only a narrow band, representing the portion of the sensor that was exposed when the picture is taken. For shutter speeds *faster* than 1/250th second, the second curtain begins moving *before* the first curtain reaches the bottom of the frame. As a result, a moving slit, the distance between the first and second curtains, exposes one portion of the sensor at a time as it moves from the top to the bottom. **Figure 12.4** shows three views of our typical (but imaginary) focal plane shutter. At left is pictured the closed shutter; in the middle version you can see the first curtain has moved down about 1/4 of the distance from the top; and in the right-hand version, the second curtain has started to "chase" the first curtain across the frame toward the bottom.

If the flash is triggered while this slit is moving, only the exposed portion of the sensor will receive any illumination. You end up with a photo like the one shown in **Figure 12.5**. Note that a band across the bottom of the image is black. That's a shadow of the second shutter curtain, which had started to move when the flash was triggered. Sharp-eyed readers will wonder why the black band is at the *bottom* of the frame rather than at the top, where the second curtain begins its journey. The answer is simple: your lens flips the image upside down and forms it on the sensor in a reversed position. You never notice that, because the camera is smart enough to show you the pixels that make up your photo in their proper orientation. But this image flip is why, if your sensor gets dirty and you detect a spot of dust in the upper half of a test photo, if cleaning manually, you need to look for the speck in the *bottom* half of the sensor.

I generally end up with sync speed problems only when shooting in the studio, using studio flash units rather than my 7D II's built-in flash or a Canon-dedicated Speedlite. That's because if you're using either type of "smart" flash, the camera knows that a strobe is attached, and remedies any unintentional goof in shutter speed settings. If you happen to set the 7D II's shutter to a faster speed in Tv or M mode, the camera will automatically adjust the shutter speed down to 1/250th second. In Av, P, or any of the automatic modes, where the 7D II selects the shutter speed, it will never choose a shutter speed higher than 1/250th second when using flash. In P mode, shutter speed is automatically set between 1/60th to 1/250th second when using flash.

But when using a non-dedicated flash, such as a studio unit plugged into an adapter with a PC/X connector, the camera has no way of knowing that a flash is connected, so shutter speeds faster than 1/250th second can be set inadvertently. Note that the 7D II can use a feature called *high-speed sync* that allows shutter speeds faster than 1/250th second with certain external dedicated Canon flash units. When using high-speed sync, the flash fires a continuous serious of bursts at reduced power for the entire duration of the exposure, so that the illumination is able to expose the sensor as the slit moves. High-speed sync is set using the controls on the attached and powered-up compatible external flash.

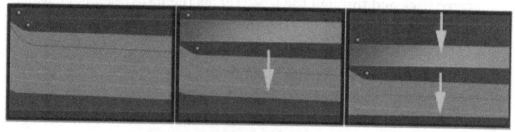

Figure 12.4

A closed shutter (left); partially open shutter as the first curtain begins to move downward (middle); only part of the sensor is exposed as the slit moves (right).

Figure 12.5

If a shutter speed faster than 1/250th second is used, you can end up photographing only a portion of the image.

Determining Exposure

Calculating the proper exposure for an electronic flash photograph is a bit more complicated than determining the settings by continuous light. The right exposure isn't simply a function of how far away your subject is (which the 7D II can figure out based on the autofocus distance that's locked in just prior to taking the picture). Various objects reflect more or less light at the same distance so, obviously, the camera needs to measure the amount of light reflected back and through the lens. Yet, as the flash itself isn't available for measuring until it's triggered, the 7D II has nothing to measure.

The solution is to fire the flash twice. The initial shot is a pre-flash that can be analyzed, then followed by a main flash that's given exactly the calculated intensity needed to provide a correct exposure. As a result, the primary flash may be longer for distant objects and shorter for closer subjects, depending on the required intensity for exposure. This through-the-lens evaluative flash exposure system, which Canon calls E-TTL II, operates whenever the pop-up internal flash is used, or you have attached a Canon dedicated flash unit to the 7D II.

Guide Numbers

Guide numbers, usually abbreviated GN, are a way of specifying the power of an electronic flash in a way that can be used to determine the correct f/stop to use at a particular shooting distance and ISO setting. In fact, before automatic flash units became prevalent, the GN was actually used to do just that. A GN is usually given as a pair of numbers for both feet and meters that represent the range at ISO 100. For example, the 7D II's built-in flash has a GN of 11/36.1 (meters/feet) at ISO 100. To calculate the correct exposure at that ISO setting, you'd divide the guide number by the distance to arrive at the appropriate f/stop.

Using the 7D II's built-in flash as an example, at ISO 100 with its GN of 39.4, if you wanted to shoot a subject at a distance of 10 feet, you'd use f/4 (Roughly 36.1 divided by 10; rounded to f/4 for simplicity's sake). At 8 feet, an f/stop of f/5.3 (round up to f/5.6) would be used. Some quick mental calculations with the GN will give you any particular electronic flash's range. You can easily see that the built-in flash would begin to peter out at about 15 feet, where you'd need an aperture of roughly f/2.8 at ISO 100. Of course, in the real world you'd probably bump the sensitivity up to a setting of ISO 400 so you could use a more practical f/5.6 at that distance.

Today, guide numbers are most useful for comparing the power of various flash units. You don't need to be a math genius to see that an electronic flash with a GN of, say, 190 would be *a lot* more powerful than your built-in flash (at ISO 100, you could use f/13 instead of f/2.8 at 15 feet).

Getting Started with the Built-In Flash

The Canon 7D II's built-in flash is a handy accessory because it is available as required, without the need to carry an external flash around with you constantly. The flash will pop up automatically when needed if you're using Scene Intelligent Auto. In other modes, you'll have to judge for yourself when flash might be useful, and flip it up yourself by pressing the Flash button on the side of the pentamirror housing. You may have to tap the shutter release to activate the button. The behavior of the internal flash varies, depending on which exposure mode you're using.

- **P.** In this mode, the 7D II fully automates the exposure process, giving you subtle fill flash effects in daylight, and fully illuminating your subject under dimmer lighting conditions. The camera selects a shutter speed from 1/60th to 1/250th second and sets an appropriate aperture.

- **Av.** In Aperture-priority mode, you set the aperture as always, and the 7D II chooses a shutter speed from 30 seconds to 1/250th second. Use this mode with care, because if the camera detects a dark background, it will use the flash to expose the main subject in the foreground, and then leave the shutter open long enough to allow the background to be exposed correctly, too. If you're not using an image-stabilized lens, you can end up with blurry ghost images even of non-moving subjects at exposures longer than 1/30th second, and if your camera is not mounted on a tripod, you'll see these blurs at exposures longer than about 1/8th second even if you are using IS.

- To disable use of a slow shutter speed with flash, access Flash Sync Speed in Av Mode in the Flash Control screen found in the Set-up 1 menu, and change from the default setting Auto to either 1/250-1/60sec. Auto or 1/250sec. (fixed), as described in Chapter 9.

- **Tv.** When using flash in Tv mode, you set the shutter speed from 30 seconds to 1/250th second, and the 7D II will choose the correct aperture for the correct flash exposure. If you accidentally set the shutter speed higher than 1/250th second, the camera will reduce it to 1/250th second when you're using the flash.

- **M/B.** In Manual or Bulb exposure modes, you select both shutter speed (30 seconds to 1/250th second) and aperture. The camera will adjust the shutter speed to 1/250th second if you try to use a faster speed with the internal flash. The E-TTL II system will provide the correct amount of exposure for your main subject at the aperture you've chosen (if the subject is within the flash's range, of course). In Bulb mode, the shutter will remain open for as long as the release button on top of the camera is held down, or the release of your remote control is activated.

Flash Range

The illumination of the 7D II's built-in flash varies with distance, focal length, and ISO sensitivity setting.

- **Distance.** The farther away your subject is from the camera, the greater the light fall-off, thanks to the inverse square law discussed earlier. Keep in mind that a subject that's twice as far away receives only one-quarter as much light, which is two f/stops' worth.

- **Focal length.** The built-in flash "covers" only a limited angle of view, which doesn't change. So, when you're using a lens that is wider than the default focal length, the frame may not be covered fully, and you'll experience dark areas, especially in the corners. As you zoom in using longer focal lengths, some of the illumination is outside the area of view and is "wasted." (This phenomenon is why some external flash units, such as the 600EX-RT, "zoom" to match the zoom setting of your lens to concentrate the available flash burst onto the actual subject area.)

⊚ **ISO setting.** The higher the ISO sensitivity, the more photons captured by the sensor. So, doubling the sensitivity from ISO 100 to 200 produces the same effect as, say, opening up your lens from f/8 to f/5.6.

Red-Eye Reduction and Autofocus Assist

When Red-Eye Reduction is turned on in the Shooting 1 menu (as described in Chapter 8), and you are using flash with any shooting mode except for Flash Off, Landscape, Sports, or Movie, the red-eye reduction lamp on the front of the camera will illuminate for about 1.5 seconds when you press down the shutter release halfway, theoretically causing your subjects' irises to contract (if they are looking toward the camera), and thereby reducing the red-eye effect in your photograph. Red-eye effects are most frequent under low light conditions, when the pupils of your subjects' eyes open to admit more light, thus providing a larger "target" for your flash's illumination to bounce back from the retinas to the sensor.

Another phenomenon you'll encounter under low light levels may be difficulty in focusing. Canon's answer to that problem is an autofocus assist beam emitted by the 7D II's built-in flash, or by any external dedicated flash unit that you may have attached to the camera (and switched on). In dim lighting conditions, the built-in flash will emit a burst of reduced-intensity flashes when you press the shutter release halfway, providing additional illumination for the autofocus system. Here are some things you need to know about the AF assist beam:

⊚ **Activation.** You must pop up the built-in flash manually using the Flash button to enable AF assist.

- **Focus mode.** The AF-assist beam will fire only if you are using One-Shot AF (single autofocus) or AI Focus AF (automatic autofocus). The beam is disabled if the camera is set to AI Servo AF (continuous autofocus) mode.

- **Distance.** The beam provides autofocus assistance only for subjects closer than roughly 13 feet from the camera. The illumination is too dim at great distances to improve autofocus performance. If you need more of an assist, an external flash such as the 580EX II and 600EX-RT can provide a focusing aid for subjects as far as 32.8 feet away.

- **Live View.** The AF-assist flash is disabled when using Live View's Live mode and Face Detection focusing modes, for both the built-in flash and external flash. However, if a Canon Speedlite with an LED light is used (such as the 580EX II or 600EX-RT), the beam will illuminate to provide autofocus assistance. The AF-Assist beam functions normally when using Quick mode autofocus in Live View.

- **Enabling/Disabling AF-assist.** You can specify how the AF-assist beam is fired using C.Fn-4, as described below.

AF-Assist with Flash Disabled

You can still use the Autofocus Assist Beam function even when you don't want the flash to contribute to the exposure by disabling flash while enabling autofocus assist, using one of the Flash Control options in the Shooting 1 menu. Just follow these steps:

1. Press the MENU button and navigate to the Shooting 1 menu.
2. Use the directional buttons to select the Flash Control entry.
3. Select Flash Firing, press SET, and choose Disable. That option disables both the built-in flash and any external dedicated flash you may have attached. However, the AF-assist beam will still fire as described earlier.
4. Press the MENU button twice to exit. (Or just tap the shutter release button.)
5. Using FE Lock and Flash Exposure Compensation

If you want to lock flash exposure for a subject that is not centered in the frame, you can use the FE Lock button (*) to lock in a specific flash exposure. Just depress and hold the shutter button halfway to lock in focus, then center the viewfinder on the subject you want to correctly expose and press the * button. The FEL (flash exposure lock) message and * icon are displayed in the viewfinder. Then, recompose your photo and press the shutter down the rest of the way to take the photo.

You can also manually add or subtract exposure to the flash exposure calculated by the 7D II when using a Creative Zone mode. The easiest way is to use the Quick Control menu. Press the Q button and navigate to the flash exposure compensation box, and rotate the Main Dial to set flash compensation.

You can also specify flash compensation using the menus, which can be easy when working with the touch screen, even though there are a few extra steps. Just press the Choose the Flash Control entry in Shooting 1 menu, then the Built-in Flash Setting, and choose Flash (icon) Exp. Comp (when Wireless is disabled.) Then use the left/right directional buttons or touch screen to enter flash exposure compensation plus or minus two f/stops. The exposure index scale on the LCD and in the viewfinder will indicate the change you've made, and a flash exposure compensation icon will appear to warn you that an adjustment has been made. As with non-flash exposure compensation, the compensation you make remains in effect for the pictures that follow, and even when you've turned the camera off, remember to cancel the flash exposure compensation adjustment by reversing the steps used to set it when you're done using it.

A third way to access flash exposure compensation is to assign that feature to the SET button, using the Custom Controls entry in the Custom Functions 3 menu, as described in Chapter 11. Thereafter, you can press the SET button when in Shooting mode, and rotate the Main Dial to adjust flash exposure compensation from the screen that pops up on the LCD. Flash exposure compensation can also be adjusted using the controls on your attached and active external flash unit. Those settings (any setting other than 0 dialed in with the external flash) will override any flash exposure compensation you've specified in the camera.

If you've enabled the Auto Lighting Optimizer in the Shooting 2 menu, as described in Chapter 8, it may cancel out any EV you've subtracted using flash exposure compensation. Disable the Auto Lighting Optimizer if you find your images are still too bright when using flash exposure compensation.

More on Flash Control Settings

I introduced the Shooting 1 menu's Flash Control settings in Chapter 8. This next section offers additional information for using the Flash Control menu. The menu includes six options (see **Figure 12.6**): Flash Firing, E-TTL II Metering, Flash Sync in AV Mode, Built-in Flash Settings, External Flash Function Settings, and External Flash C.Fn Settings.

Remember: You can access the flash control settings for both built-in and external flash directly by pressing the Flash button twice. This allows you to bypass the main menu system.

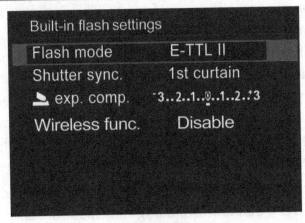

Figure 12.6
Six entries are available from the Flash Control menu.

Flash Firing

This menu entry has two options: Enable and Disable. It can be used to activate or deactivate the built-in electronic flash and any attached external electronic flash unit. When disabled, the flash cannot fire even if you accidentally elevate it, or have an accessory flash attached and turned on. However, you should keep in mind that the AF-assist beam can still be used. If you want to disable that, too, you'll need to turn it off using the entry in the AF 3 menu, discussed in Chapter 5.

Here are some applications where I always disable my flash and AF-assist beam, even though, except for Scene Intelligent Auto mode, my 7D II won't pop up the flash and fire without my intervention anyway. Some situations are too important to take chances.

- **Venues where flash is forbidden.** I've discovered that many No Photography signs actually mean "No Flash Photography," either because those who make the decisions feel that flash is distracting or they fear it may potentially damage works of art. Tourists may not understand the difference between flash and available light photography, or may be unable to set their camera to turn off the flash. One of the first phrases I learn in any foreign language is "Is it permitted to take photos if I do not use flash?" A polite request, while brandishing an advanced camera like the 7D II (which may indicate you know what you are doing), can often result in permission to shoot away.

- **Venues where flash is ineffective anyway.** We've all seen the concert goers who stand up in the last row to shoot flash pictures from 100 yards away. I tend to not tell friends that their pictures are not going to come out, because they usually show me a dismal, grainy shot (actually exposed by the dim available light) that they find satisfactory, just to prove I was wrong.

- **Venues where flash is annoying.** If I'm taking pictures in a situation where flash is permitted, but mostly supplies little more than visual pollution, I'll disable or avoid using it. Concerts or religious ceremonies may *allow* flash photography, but who needs to add to the blinding bursts when you have a camera that will take perfectly good pictures at ISO 3200? Of course, I invariably see one or two people flashing away at events where flash is not allowed, but that doesn't mean I am eager to join in the festivities.

E-TTL II Metering

The second choice in the Flash Control menu allows you to choose the type of exposure metering the 7D II uses for electronic flash. You can select the default Evaluative metering, which selectively interprets the 63 metering zones in the viewfinder to intelligently classify the scene for exposure purposes. Alternatively, you can select Average, which melds the information from all the zones together as an average exposure. You might find this mode useful for evenly lit scenes, but, in most cases, exposure won't be exactly right and you may need some flash exposure compensation adjustment.

Flash Sync Speed in AV mode

You can select the flash synchronization speed that will be used when working in Aperture-priority mode; choose from Auto (the 7D II selects the shutter speed from 30 seconds to 1/250th second) to a range embracing only the speeds from 1/250th to 1/60th second, or fixed at 1/250th second.

Normally, in Aperture-priority mode when using flash, you specify the f/stop to be locked in. The exposure is then adjusted by varying the output of the electronic flash. Because the primary exposure comes from the flash, the main effects of the shutter speed selected is on the secondary exposure from the ambient light on the scene. Your choices include:

- **Auto.** This is your best choice under most conditions. The 7D II will analyze your scene and choose a shutter speed that balances flash exposure and available light. For example, if the camera determines that a flash exposure requires an aperture of f/5.6, and then determines that the background illumination is intense enough to produce an exposure of 1/30th second at f/5.6, it might choose that slow shutter speed to provide a balanced exposure. As you might guess, the chief problem with Auto is that the 7D II can choose a shutter speed that is slow enough to cause ghost images, as discussed earlier in this chapter. Don't use Auto if the ambient light is bright and your subject is far from the camera -- that combination can lead to large f/stops and slow shutter speeds. (Use a tripod in such situations.) On the other hand, if your subject is fairly close to the camera -- 10 feet or closer -- Auto will rarely get you into trouble. (See **Figure 12.7**.)

- **1/250-1/60 sec auto.** If you want to ensure that a slow shutter speed won't be used, activate this option, to lock out shutter speeds slower than 1/60th second.

- **1/250 sec (fixed).** This setting ensures that the 7D II will always select 1/250th second. You'll end up with pitch-black backgrounds much of the time, but won't have to worry about ghost images.

Figure 12.7

At left, a shutter speed of 1/60th second was used, allowing ambient illumination to brighten the background. At right, a 1/250th second shutter speed produced a black background.

Built-in Flash Settings

There are four main choices for this menu choice, which normally appears as shown in **Figure 12.8**. You cannot select Built-in Flash Settings if an external flash is attached to the accessory shoe. A message will pop up explaining that this menu option has been

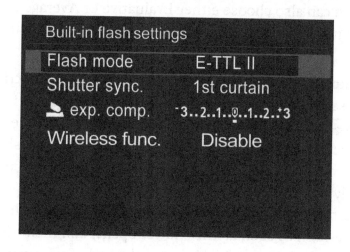

disabled.

Figure 12.8

Four entries are available from the Built-in Flash Functions menu.

However, that does not mean that you can't use an external flash; your add-on flash unit must be used off-camera and not attached to the 7D II's accessory shoe. Indeed, this menu entry has additional settings that apply when using an off-camera wireless external flash, such as Channel and Firing Group (see **Figure 12.16**), which I'll address later in this chapter in the sections on external flash. Here's a quick summary of the main Built-in Flash selections, plus additional options that appear when you change the Built-in Flash setting to wireless flash modes. I'll explain each in more detail later in this chapter. The next sections outline your choices when Flash Mode is set to E-TTL II, Manual, or MULTI.

E-TTL II

You'll leave Flash Mode at this setting most of the time. In this mode, the camera fires a pre-flash prior to the exposure, and measures the amount of light reflected to calculate the proper settings. As noted earlier, when you've selected the E-TTL II Flash mode, you can also choose either Evaluative or Average metering methods in the Flash Control menu. When Flash Mode is set to E-TTL:

- **Shutter sync.** Available only when Wireless Functions are disabled. You can choose 1st curtain sync, which fires the pre-flash used to calculate the exposure before the shutter opens, followed by the main flash as soon as the shutter is completely open. This is the default mode, and you'll generally perceive the pre-flash and main flash as a single burst. Alternatively, you can select 2nd curtain sync, which fires the pre-flash as soon as the shutter opens, and then triggers the main flash in a second burst at the end of the exposure, just before the shutter starts to close. (If the shutter speed is slow enough, you may clearly see both the pre-flash and main flash as separate bursts of light.) This action allows photographing a blurred trail of light of moving objects with sharp flash exposures at the beginning and the end of the exposure. If you have an external compatible Speedlite attached, you can also choose Hi-speed sync, which allows you to use shutter speeds faster than 1/250th second, using the External Flash Function Setting menu, described shortly.

- **Flash exposure compensation.** If you'd rather adjust flash exposure using a menu than with the ISO/Flash exposure compensation button, you can do that here. Select this option with the SET button, then dial in the amount of flash EV compensation you want using the directional buttons. The EV that was in place before you started to make your adjustment is shown as a blue indicator, so you can return to that value quickly. Use SET again to confirm your change, then tap MENU or press the MENU button twice to exit.

- ◉ **Wireless functions.** Four options are listed, from top to bottom: Disable, External:Built-in flash ratio (you can set the proportional balance between your built-in and external flash), External Flash (only), and External+ Built-in. I'm going to leave the explanation of these for the section on using the 7D II's wireless shooting capabilities.

Manual Flash

Use this setting when you want to specify exactly how much light is emitted by the flash units, and don't want the 7D II's E-TTL II exposure system to calculate the f/stop for you. When you activate this option, the two flash exposure compensation entries are replaced by internal and external flash output scales (the built-in and external flash units are represented by icons). You can select from 1/1 to 1/128th power for the built-in flash, and 1/1 to 1/164th power for the external flash. A blue indicator appears under the previous setting, and a white indicator under your new setting, a reminder that you've chosen reduced power. Click on External flash func. setting, then click ETTL and select M or Multi with the directional buttons.

When Flash Mode is set to Manual Flash, Shutter Sync and Wireless Functions entries appear, as described above. The Flash Exposure Compensation entry is replaced by a Flash Output option, which allows you to dial in a power level from 1/1 (full power) to 1/128 power. Here are some situations where you might want to use manual flash settings:

- ◎ **Close-ups.** You're shooting macro photos and the E-TTL II exposure is not precisely what you'd like. You can dial in exposure compensation, or set the output manually. Close-up photos are problematic, because the power of the built-in flash may be too much (choose 1/128 power to minimize the output), or the reflected light may not be interpreted accurately by the through-the-lens metering system. Manual flash gives you greater control.

- **Fill flash.** Although E-TTL II can be used in full daylight to provide fill flash to brighten shadows, using manual flash allows you to tweak the amount of light being emitted in precise steps. Perhaps you want just a little more illumination in the shadows to retain a dramatic lighting effect without the dark portions losing all detail. Again, you can try using exposure compensation to make this adjustment, but I prefer to use manual flash settings. (See **Figure 12.9**, left.)

- **Action stopping.** The lower the power of the flash, the shorter the effective exposure. Use 1/128th power in a darkened room (so that there is no ambient light to contribute to the exposure and cause a "ghost" image) and you can end up with a "shutter speed" that's the equivalent of 1/50,000th second! Of course, with such a minimal amount of flash power, you need to be very close to your subject. (See **Figure 12.9**, right.)

Figure 12.9

You can fine-tune fill illumination by adjusting the output of your camera's built-in flash manually (left.)At 1/128th power, the duration of the flash is very brief, producing the same effect as a fast shutter speed (right

MULTI Flash

The MULTI flash setting, available with your built-in flash and some external flash units, makes it possible to shoot cool strobo-scopic effects, with the flash firing several times in quick succession. You can use the capability to produce multiple images of moving objects, to trace movement (say, your golf swing). When you've activated MULTI flash, three new parameters appear: Flash Output, Frequency, and Flash Count. Because MULTI flash can be used with both the built-in flash or an external flash, I'll explain how to adjust each of these three parameters in the External Flash Function section which follows this one.

External Flash Function Setting

You can access this menu only when you have a compatible electronic flash attached and switched on. The settings available are shown in **Figure 12.10**. I'll list each of the available options first, and then explain how to use them in the next sections.

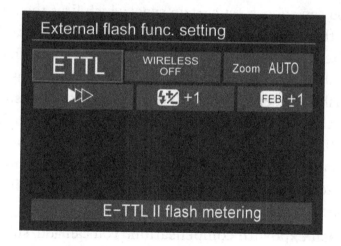

Figure 12.10

⊚ **Flash mode.** This entry allows you to set the flash mode for the external flash, from E-TTL II, Manual flash, MULTI flash, Auto External Flash Metering, and Manual External Flash Metering.

⊚ **Wireless functions.** These functions are available when using wireless flash. This setting allows you to enable or disable

437

wireless functions. You can choose Wireless: Off, Wireless: On (Optical Transmission), or Wireless: On (Radio Transmission). The last choice is shown and available only when using a radio-capable triggering device or flash, such as the 430EX III-RT or 600EX-RT.

◉ **Flash Zoom.** Some flash units can vary their coverage to better match the field of view of your lens at a particular focal length. You can allow the external flash to zoom automatically, based on information provided, or manually, using a zoom button on the flash itself. This setting is disabled when using a flash like the Canon 270EX II, which does not have zooming capability. You can select Auto, in which case the camera will tell the flash unit the focal length of the lens, or choose individual focal lengths including 24mm, 28mm, 35mm, 50mm, 70mm, 80mm, and 105mm. The 600EX-RT offers an additional setting of 200mm.

◉ **Shutter synchronization.** As with the 7D II's internal flash, you can choose 1st curtain sync, which fires the flash as soon as the shutter is completely open (this is the default mode). Alternatively, you can select 2nd curtain sync, which fires the flash as soon as the shutter opens, and then triggers a second flash at the end of the exposure, just before the shutter starts to close. If a compatible Canon flash, such as the Speedlite 430EX III or 600EX-RT is attached and turned on, you can also select High-speed sync. and shoot using shutter speeds faster than 1/250th second. HSS does not work in wireless mode.

◉ **Flash exposure compensation.** You can add/subtract exposure compensation for the external flash unit, in a range of -3 to +3 EV. Dial in the amount of flash EV compensation you want using the directional buttons. The EV that was in place before you started to make your adjustment is shown as a blue indicator, so you can return to that value quickly.

◉ **Flash exposure bracketing.** Flash Exposure Bracketing (FEB) operates similarly to ordinary exposure bracketing, providing a series of different exposures to improve your chances of getting the exact right exposure, or to provide alternative renditions for creative purposes.

If you enable wireless flash, additional options appear in this menu. I'll explain wireless flash later in this chapter:

- ⊙ **Channel.** All flashes used wirelessly can communicate on one of four channels. This setting allows you to choose which channel is used. Channels are especially helpful when you're working around other Canon photographers; each can select a different channel so one photographer's flash units don't trigger those of another photographer.

- ⊙ **Master flash.** You can enable or disable use of the external flash as the master controller for the other wireless flashes. When set to enable, the attached external flash is used as the master; when disabled, the external flash becomes a slave unit triggered by the 7D II's built-in flash.

- ⊙ **Flash Firing Group.** Multiple flash units can be assigned to a group. This choice allows specifying which groups are triggered, A/B, A/B plus C, or All. The 600EX-RT offers additional groups when using radio control mode, Groups D and E.

- ⊙ **A:B fire ratio.** If you select A/B or A/B plus C, this option appears, and allows you to set the proportionate outputs of Groups A and B, in ratios from 8:1 to 1:8 as explained in Chapter 12.

- ⊙ **Group C exposure compensation.** If you select A/B plus C, this option appears, too, allowing you to set flash exposure compensation separately for Group C flashes.

Flash Mode

Your choices for external flash mode include E-TTL II, Manual flash, which function exactly as described earlier under Built-In Flash Settings. There are three additional settings: MULTI flash, Auto External Flash Metering, and Manual External Flash Metering.

MULTI Flash

This repeating strobe effect mode includes the same Flash Output option as Manual mode, but allows you to choose Frequency from 1 to 199 flashes per elapsed second, and Flash Count for up to 30 repeating bursts. In other words, if you selected 30 Hz (cycles per second) and 30 bursts, you'd get 30 bursts within a one-second interval. Select 60 Hz instead, and the 30 bursts would take place in one-half second. (See **Figure 12.11**.)

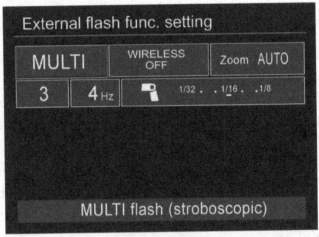

Figure 12.11

MULTI flash can be specified when using both built-in and external flash.

⊚ **Frequency/Times per second.** This figure specifies the number of bursts per second. With the built-in flash, you can choose (theoretically) 1 to 199 bursts per second. The actual number of flashes produced will be determined by your flash count (which turns off the flash after the specified number of flashes), flash output (higher output levels will deplete the available energy in your flash unit), and your shutter speed.

- ○ **Flash count/number of shots.** This setting determines the number of flashes in a given burst, and can be set from 1 to 50 flashes.

- ○ **Power level.** Adjust the output of the flash for each burst, from 1/4 to 1/128th power.

These factors work together to determine the maximum number of flashes you can string together in a single shot. The exact number will vary, depending on your settings.

Auto External Flash Metering

When you select this option, the camera does not use through-the-lens metering. Instead, it calculates the exposure based on a sensor built into the front of the flash itself. That sensor measures reflection from the subjects, using a sort of "averaging" measurement (rather than the evaluative or spot metering possible with ETTL II.) When the flash decides sufficient light has been emitted, the remaining power of the capacitor is "dumped." This is an older flash exposure system, dating back to the first autoflash units in the 1960's, and tends to underexpose a bit. There is one advantage to Auto External Flash Metering: no pre-flash is emitted, so if you are also using additional flash units with optical slaves that can't be set to ignore a pre-flash, they will be triggered at the same time as your main flash exposure.

Manual External Flash Metering

This setting just means that you cannot set the flash's functions, such as power level, using the 7D II; you'll need to use the controls on the flash itself. Consult the manual that came with your flash for instructions on making adjustments using the flash unit's buttons and dials.

High-Speed Sync

High-speed sync is a special mode that allows you to synchronize an *external* flash (but not the built-in flash) at all shutter speeds, rather than just 1/250th second and slower. The entire frame is illuminated by a series of continuous bursts as the shutter opening moves across the sensor plane, so you do *not* end up with a horizontal black band, as shown earlier in **Figure 12.5**.

HSS is especially useful in three situations, all related to problems associated with high ambient light levels:

- **Eliminate "ghosts" with moving images.** When shooting with flash, the primary source of illumination may be the flash itself. However, if there is enough available light, a secondary image may be recorded by that light (as described under "Ghost Images" earlier in this chapter). If your main subject is not moving, the secondary image may be acceptable or even desirable. Using a slow shutter speed to record the ambient light and helps illuminate dark backgrounds. But if your subject is moving, the secondary image creates a ghost image. High-speed sync gives you the ability to use a higher shutter speed. If ambient light produces a ghost image at 1/250th second, upping the shutter speed to 1/500th or 1/1,000th second may eliminate it. Of course, HSS *reduces* the amount of light the flash produces. If your subject is not close to the camera, the waning illumination of the flash may force you to use a larger f/stop to capture the flash exposure. So, while shifting from 1/250th second at f/8 to 1/500th second at f/8 *will* reduce ghost images, if you switch to 1/500th second at f/5.6 (because the flash is effectively less intense), you'll end up with the same ambient light exposure. Still, it's worth a try.

- **Improved fill flash in daylight.** The 7D II can use the built-in flash or an attached unit to fill in inky shadows -- both automatically and using manually specified power ratios, as described earlier in this chapter. However, both methods force you to use a 1/250th second (or slower) shutter speed. That limitation can cause complications.

- **In very bright surroundings,** such as beach or snow scenes, it may be difficult to get the correct exposure at 1/250th second. You might have to use f/16 or a smaller f/stop to expose a given image, even at ISO 100. If you want to use a larger f/stop for selective focus, then you encounter the second problem -- 1/250th second won't allow apertures wider than f/8 or f/5.6 under many daylight conditions at ISO 100. (See the discussion of fill flash with Aperture-priority in the next bullet.)

⊙ **If you're shooting action**, you'll probably want a shutter speed faster than 1/250th second, if at all possible under the current lighting. That's because, in fill flash situations, the ambient light (often daylight) provides the primary source of illumination. For many sports and fast-moving subjects, 1/500th second, or faster, is desirable. HSS allows you to increase your shutter speed and still avail yourself of fill flash. This assumes that your subject is close enough to your camera that the fill flash has some effect; forget about using fill and HSS with subjects a dozen feet away or farther. The flash won't be powerful enough to have much effect on the shadows.

⊙ **When using fill flash with Aperture-priority.** The difficulties of using selective focus with fill flash, mentioned earlier, become particularly acute when you switch to Av exposure mode. Selecting f/5.6, f/4, or a wider aperture when using flash is guaranteed to create problems when photographing close-up subjects, particularly at ISO settings higher than ISO 100. If you own an external flash unit, HSS may be the solution you are looking for.

If you are using a compatible flash unit, it's safe to enable high-speed sync *all the time*. That's because if you set the camera for 1/250th second or slower, the flash will fire normally at its set power output, just as if HSS were not enabled. But once you venture past 1/250th second to a faster shutter speed, the camera/flash combination is smart enough to use HSS. However, it's your responsibility to remember that you've enabled high-speed sync, and realize that as you increase the shutter speed, the effective range of the flash is reduced. At 1/1000th second, the 600EX-RT is "good" out to about two feet from the camera. (Remember, HSS does not work in wireless mode, so the flash must be attached to the camera's hot shoe.)

At 1/4000ᵗʰ second, the flash will illuminate subjects no more than about one foot from the flash/camera.

To activate HSS using the 580EX II or 600EX-RT, just follow these steps:

1. **Attach the flash.** Mount/connect the external flash on the 7D II, using the hot shoe or a cable. (HSS cannot be used in wireless mode, nor with a flash linked through the PC/X terminal.)
2. **Power up.** Turn the flash and camera on.
3. **Select HSS in the camera.** Set the External Flash Function Setting in the camera to HSS as the 7D II's sync mode.
4. **Choose Flash Control** in the Shooting 1 menu.
5. **Select External Flash Func. Setting.**
6. **Navigate to the Shutter Sync.** entry, press SET, and choose High-Speed (at the far right of the list). Press SET again to confirm.
7. **Choose HSS on the flash.** Activate HSS (FP flash) on your attached external flash. With the 580EX II, press the High-speed sync button on the back of the flash unit (it's the second from the right under the LCD). With the 600EX-RT, press Function Button 4 (Sync), located at the far right of the row of four buttons just under the LCD.
8. **Confirm HSS is active.** The HSS icon will be displayed on the flash unit's LCD (at the upper-left side with the 580EX II), and at bottom left in the 7D II's viewfinder. If you choose a shutter speed of 1/250th second or slower, the indicator will not appear in the viewfinder, as HSS will not be used at slower speeds. (See **Figure 12.12.**)
9. **View minimum/maximum shooting distance.** Choose a distance based on the maximum shown in the line at the bottom of the flash's LCD display (from 0.5 to 18 meters).
10. **Shoot.** Take the picture. To turn off HSS, press the button on the flash again. Remember that you can't use MULTI flash or Wireless flash when working with High-speed sync.

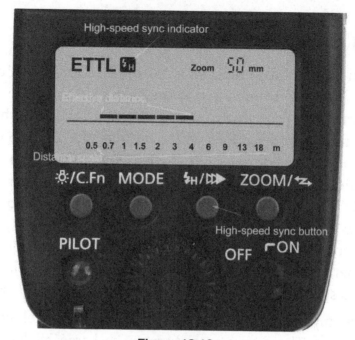

Figure 12.12

Activate High-speed sync on the flash.

External Flash Custom Function Setting

Some external Speedlites from Canon include their own list of Custom Functions, which can be used to specify things like flash metering mode and flash bracketing sequences, as well as more sophisticated features, such as modeling light/flash (if available), use of external power sources (if attached), and functions of any slave unit attached to the external flash. This menu entry allows you to set an external flash unit's Custom Functions from your 7D II's menu. The settings available in the 7D II for the Speedlite 580EX II are shown later in the section that describes that flash.

Clear External Flash Custom Function Setting

This entry allows you to zero-out any changes you've made to your external flash's Custom Functions, and return them to their factory default settings.

Using External Electronic Flash

Canon offers a broad range of accessory electronic flash units for the 7D II. They can be mounted to the flash accessory shoe, or used off-camera with a dedicated cord that plugs into the flash shoe to maintain full communications with the camera for all special features. (Non-dedicated flash units, such as studio flash, can be connected using the PC/X terminal.) They range from the Speedlite 600EX-RT and Speedlite 580EX II, which can correctly expose subjects up to 24 feet away at f/11 and ISO 200, to the 270EX, which is good out to 19 feet at f/11 and ISO 200. (You'll get greater ranges at even higher ISO settings, of course.) There are also two electronic flash units specifically for specialized close-up flash photography

I power my Speedlites with Sanyo Eneloop AA nickel metal hydride batteries. These are a special type of rechargeable battery with a feature that's ideal for electronic flash use. The Eneloop cells, unlike conventional batteries, don't self-discharge over relative short periods of time. Once charged, they can hold onto their juice for a year or more. That means you can stuff some of these into your Speedlite, along with a few spares in your camera bag, and not worry about whether the batteries have retained their power between uses. There's nothing worse than firing up your strobe after not using it for a month, and discovering that the batteries are dead.

Speedlite 600EX-RT

This flagship of the Canon accessory flash line (and most expensive at about $550) is the most powerful unit the company offers, with a GN of 197, and a manual/automatic zoom flash head that covers the full frame of lenses from 24mm wide angle to 200mm telephoto. (There's a flip-down, wide-angle diffuser that spreads the flash to cover a 14mm lens's field of view, too.) All angle specifications given by Canon refer to full-frame sensors, but this flash unit automatically converts its field of view coverage to accommodate the crop factor of the and the other 1.6X crop Canon dSLRs. The 600EX-RT shares its basic features with the discontinued (but still widely-used) 580EX II, described next, so I won't repeat them here, because the typical owner is more likely to own one of the less expensive Speedlites.

The killer feature of this unit is the new wireless two-way radio communication between the camera and this flash (or ST-E3-RT wireless controller and the flash) at distances of up to 98 feet. You can link up to 15 different flash units with radio control, using *five* groups (A, B, C, D, and E), and no line-of-sight connection is needed. (You can hide the flash under a desk or in a potted plant.) With the latest Canon cameras having a revised "intelligent" hot shoe (which includes the), a second 600EX-RT can be used to trigger a *camera* that also has a 600EX-RT mounted, from a remote location. That means you can set up multiple cameras equipped with multiple flash units to all fire simultaneously! For example, if you were shooting a wedding, you could photograph the bridal couple from two different angles, with the second camera set up on a tripod, say, behind the altar. A pro shooter might find the to be an excellent, affordable second (or third) camera to use in such situations.

The 600EX-RT maintains backward compatibility with optical transmission used by earlier cameras. However, it's a bit pricey for the average EOS owner, who is unlikely to be able to take advantage of all its features. If you're looking for a high-end flash unit and don't need radio control, I still recommend the Speedlite 580EX II (described next), which remains in the line.

Remember that with the 600EX-RT, you can't use radio control and some other features unless you own at least *two* radio-controlled Speedlites, such as a 600EX-RT or 430EX III-RT (described later) or one 600EX-RT plus the ST-E3-RT, which costs half as much. Radio control is possible only between a camera that has a radio-capable flash or ST-E3-RT in the hot shoe, and an additional radio-capable flash or ST-E3-RT.

Some 18 Custom Functions of the 600EX-RT can be set using the 's External Flash C.Fn Setting menu. Additional Personal Functions can be specified on the flash itself. The -friendly functions include:

- **C.Fn-00**   Distance indicator display (Meters/Feet)
- **C.Fn-01**   Auto power off (Enabled/Disabled)
- **C.Fn-02**   Modeling flash (Enabled-DOF preview button/Enabled-test firing button/Enabled-both buttons/Disabled)
- **C.Fn-03**   FEB Flash exposure bracketing auto cancel (Enabled/Disabled)
- **C.Fn-04**   FEB Flash exposure bracketing sequence (Metered > Decreased > Increased Exposure/Decreased > Metered > Increased Exposure)
- **C.Fn-05**   Flash metering mode (E-TTL II/E-TTL/TTL/External metering: Auto/External metering: Manual)
- **C.Fn-06**   Quickflash with continuous shot (Disabled/Enabled)
- **C.Fn-07**   Test firing with autoflash (1/32/Full power)
- **C.Fn-08**   AF-assist beam firing (Enabled/Disabled)
- **C.Fn-09**   Auto zoom adjusted for image/sensor size (Enabled/Disabled)
- **C.Fn-10**   Slave auto power off timer (60 minutes/10 minutes)
- **C.Fn-11**   Cancellation of slave unit auto power off by master unit (within 8 hours/within 1 hour)
- **C.Fn-12**   Flash recycling on external power (Use internal and external power/Use only external power)
- **C.Fn-13**   Flash exposure metering setting button (Speedlite button and dial/Speedlite dial only)
- **C.Fn-20**   Beep (Enable/Disable)
- **C.Fn-21**   Light distribution (Standard, Guide number priority, Even coverage)
- **C.Fn-22**   LCD panel illumination (On for 12 seconds, Disable, Always on)

- ⊚ **C.Fn-23**   Slave flash battery check (AF-assist beam/Flash lamp, Flash lamp only)

The Personal Functions available include the following. Note that you can set the LCD panel color to differentiate at a glance whether a given flash is functioning in Master or Slave mode.

- ⊚ **P.Fn-01**   LCD panel display contrast (Five levels of contrast)
- ⊚ **P.Fn-02**   LCD panel illumination color: Normal (Green, Orange)
- ⊚ **P.Fn-03**   LCD panel illumination color: Master (Green, Orange)
- ⊚ **P.Fn-04**   LCD panel illumination color: Slave (Green, Orange)
- ⊚ **P.Fn-05**   Color filter auto detection (Auto, Disable)
- ⊚ **P.Fn-06**   Wireless button toggle sequence (Normal > Radio > Optical, Normal < > Radio, Normal < > Optical)
- ⊚ **P.Fn-07**   Flash firing during linked shooting (Disabled, Enabled)

Speedlite 580EX II

If you were using Canon cameras prior to purchasing your 7D II, you might already own this deposed flagship of the Canon accessory flash line. It's still popular because of its relatively lower price and wide availability new or used) The 580EX II is the second-most powerful unit the company offered, with a GN of 190, and a manual/automatic zoom flash head that covers the full frame of lenses from 24mm wide angle to 105mm telephoto, as well as 14mm optics with a flip-down diffuser.

Like the 600EX-RT, this unit offers full-swivel, 180-degrees in either direction, and has its own built-in AF-assist beam and an exposure system that's compatible with the nine focus points of the . Powered by economical AA-size batteries, the unit recycles in 0.1 to 6 seconds, and can squeeze 100 to 700 flashes from a set of alkaline batteries.

The 580EX II automatically communicates white balance information to your camera, allowing it to adjust WB to match the flash output. You can even simulate a modeling light effect: When you press the depth-of-field preview button on the , the 580EX II emits a one-second burst of light that allows you to judge the flash effect. If you're using multiple flash units with Canon's wireless E-TTL system, this model can serve as a master flash that controls the slave units you've set up (more about this later) or function as a slave itself.

It's easy to access all the features of this unit, because it has a large backlit LCD panel on the back that provides information about all flash settings. There are 14 Custom Functions that can be controlled from the flash, numbered from 00 to 13. These functions are (the first setting is the default value):

- ⊙ **C.Fn-00**   Distance indicator display (Meters/Feet)
- ⊙ **C.Fn-01**   Auto power off (Enabled/Disabled)
- ⊙ **C.Fn-02**   Modeling flash (Enabled-DOF preview button/Enabled-test firing button/Enabled-both buttons/Disabled)
- ⊙ **C.Fn-03**   FEB Flash exposure bracketing auto cancel (Enabled/Disabled)
- ⊙ **C.Fn-04**   FEB Flash exposure bracketing sequence (Metered > Decreased > Increased Exposure/Decreased > Metered > Increased Exposure)
- ⊙ **C.Fn-05**   Flash metering mode (E-TTL II-E-TTL/TTL/External metering: Auto/External metering: Manual)
- ⊙ **C.Fn-06**   Quickflash with continuous shot (Disabled/Enabled)
- ⊙ **C.Fn-07**   Test firing with autoflash (1/32/Full power)
- ⊙ **C.Fn-08**   AF-assist beam firing (Enabled/Disabled)
- ⊙ **C.Fn-09**   Auto zoom adjusted for image/sensor size (Enabled/Disabled)

- ⊙ **C.Fn-10**   Slave auto power off timer (60 minutes/10 minutes)
- ⊙ **C.Fn-11**   Cancellation of slave unit auto power off by master unit (within 8 hours/within 1 hour)
- ⊙ **C.Fn-12**   Flash recycling on external power (Use internal and external power/Use only external power)
- ⊙ **C.Fn-13**   Flash exposure metering setting button (Speedlite button and dial/Speedlite dial only)

Speedlite 430EX III-RT/430EX III

This less pricey electronic flash (available for less than $300) is an affordable replacement for the 580EX II for those who don't need the beefy power of the older Speedlite. It also makes radio control wireless triggering available to those who can't afford the 600EX-RT's price tag. The 430EX III-RT has automatic and manual zoom coverage from 24mm to 105mm, and the same wide-angle pullout panel found on the 600EX RT that covers the area of a 14mm lens on a full-frame camera, and automatic conversion to the cropped frame area of the and other 1.6X crop Canon dSLRs. The 430EX III-RT also communicates white balance information with the camera, and has its own AF-assist beam. Compatible with Canon's wireless E-TTL system, it makes a good slave unit, but cannot serve as a master flash. It, too, uses AA batteries, and offers recycle times of 0.1 to 3.7 seconds for 200 to 1,400 flashes, depending on subject distance.

A second version, the Speedlite 430EX III, is also available from Canon. It can serve as an optical (non-radio) slave, but does not have radio or optical master functions. It's a good on-camera flash, but when used off-camera, it's strictly a slave unit.

This long-overdue replacement for the 430EX II has as its biggest selling point the ability to communicate either optically (as a slave) with any compatible master flash, or by radio transmission (as either master or slave) with other RT flashes, including the 600EX RT. Previously, you needed either two of the expensive

600EX RT units, or one 600EX RT and an ST-E3-RT trigger to use radio communications.

The Canon Speedlite 430EX III-RT offers a sophisticated set of features, including an LCD panel that allows you to navigate the unit's menu and view its status. These features, along with powerful output and automatic zoom means this unit has more in common with Canon's high-end Speedlites than it does with the 320EX or the 270EX II. The Speedlite 430EX III-RT is compatible with E-TTL II and earlier flash technologies. It can serve as a slave unit in an optical wireless configuration. The Speedlite 430EX III-RT has a Guide Number of 43/141 (meters/feet) at ISO 100, at 105mm focal length.

Speedlite 320EX

One of the two other most recent Canon flash units (with the Speedlite 270EX II, described next) introduced early in 2011, this $249 flash has a GN of 105. Lightweight and more pocket-sized than the 430EX III-RT, 600EX-RT, this bounceable (both horizontally and vertically) flash has some interesting features, including a built-in LED video light that can be used for shooting movies with the , or as a modeling light or even AF-assist beam when shooting with live view. Canon says that this efficient LED light can provide up to four hours of illumination with a set of AA batteries. It can be used as a wireless slave unit, and has a new flash release function that allows the shutter to be triggered remotely with a two-second delay.

Speedlite 270EX II

The Canon Speedlite 270EX II is designed to work with compatible EOS cameras utilizing E-TTL II and E-TTL automatic flash technologies. This flash unit is entirely controlled from the camera, making it as simple to use as a built-in flash. Its options can be selected and set via the camera's menu system. The 270EX II can also be used as an off-camera slave unit when controlled by a master Speedlite, transmitter unit, or a camera with an integrated Speedlite transmitter. One interesting feature of this unit is that it is also a remote control transmitter, allowing you to wirelessly release the shutter on cameras compatible with certain remote controller units. The Speedlite 270EX II has a Guide Number of 27/89 (meters/feet) at ISO 100, with the flash head pulled forward.

This $170 ultra-compact unit is Canon's entry-level Speedlite, and suitable for owners who want a simple strobe for occasional use, without sacrificing the ability to operate it as a wireless slave unit. With its modest guide number, it provides a little extra pop for fill flash applications. It has vertical bounce capabilities of up to 90 degrees, and can be switched between Tele modes to Normal (28mm full-frame coverage) at a reduced guide number of 72.

The 270EX II functions as a wireless slave unit triggered by any Canon EOS unit or flash (such as the 430EX III-RT) with a Master function. It also has the new flash release function with a two-second delay that lets you reposition the flash. There's a built-in AF-assist beam, and this 5.5-ounce, 2.6 x 2.6 x 3-inch unit is powered by just two AA-size batteries.

Close-Up Lites

Canon has offered two lites, especially suitable for close-up photography: the Macro Ring Lite MR-14EX, and Macro Twin Lite flash MT-24EX. As you might guess from their names, these lites are especially suitable for close-up, or macro photography, because they provide a relatively shadowless illumination. It's always tricky photographing small subjects up close, because there often isn't room enough between the camera lens and the subject to position lights effectively. Ring lites, in particular, especially those with their own modeling lamps to help you visualize the illumination you're going to get, mount around the lens at the camera position, and help solve many close-up lighting problems.

But, in recent years, the ring lite has gone far beyond the macro realm and is now probably even more popular as a light source for fashion and glamour photography. The right ring lite, properly used, can provide killer illumination for glamour shots, while eliminating the need to move and reset lights for those shots that lend themselves to ring lite illumination. As you, the photographer, move around your subject, the ring lite moves with you.

One of the key drawbacks to ring lites (whether used for macro or glamour photography) is that they are somewhat bulky and clumsy to use (they must be fastened around the camera lens itself, or the photographer must position the ring lite, and then shoot "through" the opening or ring). That means that you might not be moving around your subject as much as you thought and will, instead, mount the ring lite and camera on a tripod, studio stand, or other support.

Another drawback is the cost. The MR-14EX and MR-24EX close-up lites are priced in the $550 and $800 range, respectively. You have to be planning a *lot* of macro or fashion work to pay for one of those. Specialists take note. I tend to favor a third-party substitute for close-up photography, the Alien Bees ABR800 Ringflash. It's priced at about $400, and, besides, it integrates very well with my other Alien Bees studio flash units.

Wireless Evolution

For all Canon cameras prior to the introduction of the original Canon EOS 7D, the predecessor of your camera, wireless operation was an add-on option. The built-in flash of those earlier cameras was not capable of triggering any off-camera Canon Speedlite with full E-TTL exposure automation. (And, of course, cameras like EOS 5D Mark III, which do not have any built-in flash at all, were in the same boat.)

Because wireless triggering was not built into the camera itself, to control other flash units it was necessary to use either a Canon Speedlite Transmitter ST-E2 (a $250 accessory that uses hard-to-find and expensive 2CR5 batteries) or mount a "master" flash on the camera. Dedicating a flash meant sinking another $300 or more into a unit like the Speedlite 430EX III-RT, or, more recently, a 600EX-RT (at a cost north of $500) to your camera just to trigger your wireless strobes. It was especially frustrating when you did not want to use the on-camera flash to contribute to the exposure. Your "triggering" device was invariably an expensive accessory. This, of course, led to the popularity of third-party triggers, like the PocketWizard and RadioPopper product lines.

The situation has changed dramatically now that Canon models like the offer built-in wireless triggering capabilities using the built-in flash. Of course, it's not possible to cover every aspect of wireless flash in one chapter. There are too many permutations involved. For example, you can use the 7D II's built-in flash, an external flash, or the ST-E2 optical transmitter (or ST-E3-RT radio transmitter) as the master. You may have one external "slave" flash, or use several. It's possible to control all your wireless flash units as if they were one multi-headed flash, or you can allocate them into "groups" that can be managed individually. You may select one of several "channels" to communicate with your strobes (or any of multiple wireless IDs when using radio controlled units like the 600EX-RT). These are all aspects that you'll want to explore as you become used to working with the 7D II's amazing wireless capabilities.

What I hope to do in this chapter is provide the introduction to the basics that you won't find in the other guidebooks, so you can learn how to operate the 7D II's wireless capabilities quickly, and then embark on your own exploration of the possibilities. Canon has taken a giant step forward by introducing the Easy Wireless feature in the 7D II, making this "pro" feature more accessible to owners of a mid-entry-level camera like yours. You'll find more complete information in *David Busch's Guide to Canon Flash Photography*.

The following sections build on the information earlier in this chapter, and show how to take advantage of the 7D II's built-in wireless controller. While it may seem complicated at first, it really isn't. Learning the 7D II's controls doesn't take a lot of effort, and once you get the hang of it, you'll be able to make changes quickly.

Your steps may vary. This section is intended to teach you the basics of wireless flash: why to use it, how the 7D II or another dedicated flash can be used to trigger and control additional units, and what lighting ratios, channels, and groups are. I'm going to provide instructions on getting set up with wireless flash, but, depending on what flash unit you're working with (and how many you have), your specific steps may vary. The final authority on working with wireless flash has to be the manual furnished with your flash unit.

Elements of Wireless Flash

Here are some of the key concepts to electronic flash and wireless flash that I'll be describing in this chapter. Learn what these are, and you'll have gone a long way toward understanding how to use wireless flash. You need to understand the various combinations of flashes that can be used, how they can be controlled individually and together, and why you might want to use multiple and off-camera flash units. I'm going to address all these points in this section.

Flash Combinations

Your 7D II has a built-in flash unit, which can be used alone, or in combination with other, external flash units. Here's a quick summary of the permutations available to you.

- ⊙ **Built-in flash used alone.** Your built-in flash can function as the only flash illumination used to take a picture. In that mode, the flash can provide the primary illumination source (the traditional "flash photo") with the ambient light in the scene contributing little to the overall exposure. Or, the built-in flash can be used in conjunction with the scene's natural illumination to provide a balanced lighting effect. In this mode, the flash doesn't overpower the ambient light, but, instead, serves to supplement it. Finally, the built-in flash can be used as a "fill" light in scenes that are illuminated predominantly by a natural main light source, such as daylight. In this mode, the flash serves to brighten dark shadows created by the primary illumination.

- ⊙ **Built-in flash used simultaneously with off-camera flash.** You can use the off-camera flash as a *main light* and supply *fill light* from the built-in flash to produce interesting effects and pleasing portraits.

⊙ **Built-in flash used as a trigger only for off-camera flash.**
Use the 7D II's built-in wireless flash controller to command
single or multiple Speedlites for studio-like lighting effects,
without having the pop-up flash contribute to the exposure
itself.

Controlling Flash Units

There are multiple ways of controlling flash units, both through
direct or wired connections and wirelessly. Here are the primary
methods used:

⊙ **Direct connection.** The built-in flash, of course, is directly
connected to the 7D II, and triggered electronically when a
picture is taken. External flash units can also be controlled directly, either by plugging them into the accessory shoe on top
of the camera, or by linking them to a camera with a dedicated flash cord that in turn attaches to the accessory hot
shoe. When used in these modes, the camera has full communication with the flash, which can receive information
about zoom lens position, correct exposure required, and the
signals required to fire the flash. There also exist accessory
shoe adapters that provide a PC/X connection, allowing non-
dedicated strobes, such as studio flash units, to be fired by
the camera. These connections are "dumb" and convey no information other than the signal to fire.

⊙ **Dedicated wireless signals.** In this mode, external flash
units communicate with the camera through a pre-flash,
which is used to measure exposure prior to the "real" flash
burst an instant later. The pre-flash can also wirelessly send
information from the camera to the flash unit, used to adjust
zoom head position (if the flash has that), and required flash
duration to produce the desired exposure. In the case of
Canon flash units, the pre-flash information is sent and received as pulses of illumination -- much like the remote control of your television. (And, also like your TV remote, the
optical signal can bounce around the room somewhat, but

you more or less need a line-of-sight connection for the communication to work properly.)

◉ **Dedicated wireless infrared signals.** Some devices, such as the Canon ST-E2 Speedlite Transmitter, can communicate with dedicated flash units through their own infrared signals. The transmitter attaches to the accessory shoe or is connected to the accessory shoe through a dedicated cable. It was an option for wireless flash for Canon cameras prior to the EOS 7D (and later models with a built-in wireless controller), as well as for Canon cameras that have no flash unit at all (such as the EOS 1D, 1Ds, and 5D series). Although the ST-E2 costs about $470, it's still less expensive than using a unit like the 600EX -RT as a master controller, particularly when on-camera flash is not desired.

◉ **Canon and third-party IR and radio transmitters.** The 600EX-RT, 430EXIII-RT and ST-E3-RT units from Canon can communicate using radio signals as well as infrared. In addition, some excellent wireless flash controllers that use IR or radio signals to operate external flash units are available from sources like PocketWizard and RadioPopper. One advantage some of these third-party units have is the ability to dial in exposure/output adjustments from the transmitter mounted on the accessory shoe of the camera.

◉ **Optical slave units.** A relatively low-tech/low-versatility option is to use optical slave units that trigger the off-camera flash units when they detect the firing of the main flash. Slave triggers are inexpensive, but dumb: they don't allow making any adjustments to the external flash units, and are not compatible with the 7D II's E-TTL II exposure system. Moreover, you should make sure that the slave trigger responds to the *main* flash burst only, rather than a pre-flash, using a so-called *digital* mode. Otherwise, your slave units will fire before the main flash, and not contribute to the exposure.

Why Use Wireless Flash?

Canon's wireless flash system gives you a number of advantages that include the ability to use directional lighting, which can help bring out detail or emphasize certain aspects of the picture area. It also lets you operate multiple strobes; with models like the old favorite 580EX II that's as many as four flash units in each of three groups, or twelve in all (although most of us won't own 12 Canon Speedlites). With the 600EX-RT and 430EX III-RT, which also have radio control in addition to optical transmission, you can control many more flash units optically, but only 15 radio-controlled Speedlites, in five different groups.

You can set up complicated portrait or location lighting configurations. Since the two top Speedlite pumps out a lot of light for a shoe-mount flash, a set of these units can give you near studio-quality lighting. Of course, the cost of these high-end Speedlites approaches or exceeds that of some studio monolights -- but the Canon battery-powered units are more portable and don't require an external AC or DC power source.

Key Wireless Concepts

There are three key concepts you must understand before jumping into wireless flash photography: channels, groups, and flash ratios. Here is an explanation of each:

Channel controls

Canon's wireless flash system offers users the ability to determine on which of four possible channels the flash units can communicate. (The pilots, ham radio operators, or scanner listeners among you can think of the channels as individual communications frequencies.) When using optical transmission, the channels are numbered 1, 2, 3, and 4, and each flash must be assigned to one of them. Moreover, in general, each of the flash units you are working with should be assigned to the *same* channel, because the slave Speedlites will respond *only* to a master flash that is on the same channel.

When using the 600EX-RT or 430EX III-RT in radio control mode, there are 15 different channels, plus an Auto setting that allows the flash to select a channel. In addition, you can assign a four-digit Wireless Radio ID that further differentiates the communications channel your flashes use.

The channel ability is important when you're working around other photographers who are also using the same system. Photojournalists, including sports photographers, encounter this situation frequently. At any event populated by a sea of "white" lenses you'll often find photographers who are using Canon flash units triggered by Canon's own optical or (now) radio control. Third-party triggers from PocketWizard or RadioPopper are also popular, but Canon's technology remains a mainstay for many shooters.

Each photographer sets flash units to a different channel so as to not accidentally trigger other users' strobes. (At big events with more than four photographers using Canon flash and optical transmission, you may need to negotiate.) I use this capability at workshops I conduct where we have two different setups. Photographers working with one setup use a different channel than those using the other setup, and can work independently even though we're at opposite ends of the same large room.

There is less chance of a channel conflict when working with radio control and all radio-compatible Canon flash units. With 15 channels to select from, and almost 10,000 wireless radio IDs to choose from, any overlap is unlikely. (It's smart not to use a radio ID like 0000, 1111, 2222, etc. to avoid increasing the chances of conflicts. I use the last four digits of my mother-in-law's Social Security Number.) Remember that you must use either all optical or all radio transmission for all your flash units; you can't mix and match.

Groups

Canon's wireless flash system lets you designate multiple flash units in separate groups. There can be as many as three groups with the 7D II's built-in controller and earlier Speedlites like the 580EX II, labeled A, B, and C.

With the 600EX-RT, 430EX III-RT and ST-E3-RT, up to five groups (A, B, C, D, and E) can be used with as many as 15 different flash units. All the flashes in all the groups use the exact same *channel* and all respond to the same master controller, but you can set the output levels of each group separately. So, Speedlites in Group A might serve as the main light, while Speedlites in Group B might be adjusted to produce less illumination and serve as a fill light. It's convenient to be able to adjust the output of all the units within a given group simultaneously. This lets you create different styles of lighting for portraits and other shots.

It's often smart to assign flash units that will reside to the left of the camera to the A group, and flashes that will be placed to the right of the camera to the B group. It's easier to adjust the comparative power ratios because you won't have to stop and think where your groups are located. That's because the adjustment controls in the *menus* are always arranged in the same A-B-C left-to-right alignment.

For example, if your A group is used as a main light on the left, and the B group as fill on the right, you intuitively know to specify more power to the A group, and less output to the B group. Reserve the C group (if used) to some other purpose, such as background or hair lights.

Flash ratios

This ability to control the output of one flash (or set of flashes) compared to another flash or set allows you to produce lighting *ratios*. You can control the power of multiple off-camera Speedlites to adjust each unit's relative contribution to the image, for more dramatic portraits and other effects.

Which Flashes Can Be Operated Wirelessly?

A particular Speedlite can have one of two functions. It can serve as a *master* flash that's capable of triggering other compatible Canon units that are on the same channel. Or, a Speedlite can be triggered wirelessly as a *slave unit* that's activated by a *master*, with full control over exposure through the 7D II's eTTL flash system. The second function is easy: all current and many recent Canon shoe-mount flash, including the 600EX-RT, 580EX II, 430EX II, 430EX III, 430EX III-RT, 320EX, and 270EX II can be triggered wirelessly. In addition, some Speedlites and the 7D II's built-in flash have the ability to serve as a master flash.

I'm not going to discuss older flash units in this chapter; if you own one, particularly a non-Canon unit, it may or may not function as a slave. For example, the early Speedlite 380EX lacked the wireless capabilities added with later models, such as the 420EX, 430EX, and 430EX II, and 430EX III, 430EX III-RT.

Here's a quick run-down of current flash capabilities:

- **Built-in flash.** The flash built into the Canon EOS 7D II can serve as a master, triggering any of the other current flash units wirelessly. It shares that capability with the EOS 7D (which introduced wireless in-camera triggering to the Canon line), the T3i, T4i, T5i, T6i, T6s, and the Canon EOS 60D, 70D, and 80D. At this writing, all other Canon cameras with a built-in flash, introduced *prior* to the T3i, can activate external flash units wirelessly *only* when physically connected to an external flash that has master capabilities, the Canon ST-E2/ST-E3-RT transmitter, or third-party transmitters. The Canon EOS SL1/100D is a newer camera that cannot function as a master flash. 7D II's built-in flash (of course) cannot itself function as a slave unit. (It has no facility for receiving signals from a master flash.)
- **Canon Speedlite 600EX-RT.** This top of the line flash can function as a master flash when physically attached to any Canon EOS model, using either optical or radio transmission, and can be triggered wirelessly by another master flash (a 7D/60D/70D/T3i/T4i/T5i/7D II camera, another 600EX-RT or 580EX II, or the ST-E2/ST-E3-RT transmitters).
- **Canon Speedlite 580EX II.** This flash can function as a master flash when physically attached to any Canon EOS model,

and can be triggered wirelessly by an optical (not radio) transmission from another master flash (a 7D/60D/70D/T3i/T4i/T5i/7D II camera, another 580EX II, a 600EX-RT, 430EX III-RT, the ST-E2 transmitter, or ST-E3-RT transmitter in optical mode).

○ **Canon Speedlite 430EX III.** This sibling of the radio-compatible version described next cannot function as a master, but can be used as a slave when working with optical triggering technology.

○ **Canon Speedlite 430EX III-RT.** This newer flash can function as a master (in radio mode only) and as a slave when using both optical and radio technology.

○ **Canon Speedlite 430EX II.** This discontinued flash cannot function as a master, but can be triggered wirelessly by a master flash (a 7D/60D/70D/880D/T3i/T4i/T5i/^6i/T6s/7D I/II camera, a Speedlite 600EX-RT/580EX II, or the ST-E-2 and ST-E3-RT transmitters in optical mode).

○ **Canon Speedlite 320EX.** This flash can be triggered wirelessly by a master flash (a 7D/60D/70D/880D/T3i/T4i/T5i/^6i/T6s/7D I/II camera, a 600EX-RT/580EX II, or the ST-E-2 and ST-E3-RT transmitters in optical mode).

○ **Canon Speedlite 270EX II.** This flash can be triggered wirelessly by a master flash (a 7D/60D/70D/880D/T3i/T4i/T5i/T6i/T6s/7D I/II camera, a 600EX-RT/580EX II, or the ST-E-2 and ST-E3-RT transmitters in optical mode).

You can use any combination of compatible flash units in your wireless setup. The 7D II can serve as the master, or you can use an attached 600EX-RT, 580EX II, 430EX III-RT or ST-E2/ST-E3-RT as a master, with any number of 600EX-RT, 580EX II, 430EX III, 430EX III-RT, 430EX II, 320EX, or 270EX II units (or older compatible Speedlites not discussed in this chapter) as wireless slaves. I'll get you started assigning these flash to groups and channels later on.

Getting Started

Since it's necessary to set up both the camera and the strobes for wireless operation, this guide will help you with both, starting with prepping the camera and flash. To configure your equipment for wireless flash, just follow these steps. (I'm going to condense them a bit, because many of these settings have been introduced in previous chapters.)

We're going to begin by assuming that you want to use the 7D II's built-in flash as the master controller flash. If that's the case, you need to follow these steps with your external flash units first. I'm going to use the 580EX II as an example, because it's still the most widely used Canon Speedlite. You can adjust the steps for your own particular flash unit to suit:

1. **Set the wireless off-camera Speedlite to slave mode.** Any of the flash units listed earlier can be used as a slave flash. The first step is to set the off-camera flash to slave mode. The procedure differs for each individual flash model. Check your manual for exact instructions. I'll use the 580EX II as a typical example: Press the ZOOM button for two seconds until the display flashes, then rotate the control dial on the flash until the Slave indicator blinks on the LCD. Press the control dial's center button to confirm your choice.

2. **Assign a channel.** All units must use the same channel. The default channel is 1. If you need to change to a different communications channel, do so using the instructions for your particular flash unit. With the 580EX II, press the ZOOM button several times until the CH indicator flashes. Then rotate the control dial on the flash until the channel you want appears on the LCD. Press the control dial center button to confirm your choice.

3. **Assign slave to a group.** If you want to use a flash ratio to adjust the output of some slave units separately, you'll want to assign the slave flash to a group, either Group A (the default) or Group B. All units within a particular group fire at the same proportionate level. If you've set Group B to fire at

half power, *all* the Speedlites that have been assigned to Group B will fire at half power. And remember that all flash units on a particular channel are controlled by the same master flash, regardless of the group they belong to. Set the group according to the instructions for your particular flash. For the 580EX II, press the ZOOM button until the A flashes on the LCD. Then rotate the control dial on the flash to choose B. Press the control dial center button to confirm your choice.

4. **Position the off-camera flash units, with the Speedlite's wireless sensor facing the camera/master flash.** Indoors, you can position the external flash up to 33 feet from the master unit; outdoors, keep the distance to 23 feet or less. Your ability to use a flash wirelessly can depend on whether the Speedlite's sensor can receive communication from the master flash. Factors can include the direction the slave flash is pointed, and whether light can bounce off walls or other surfaces to reach the sensor. When working with the 600EX-RT's radio controls, Canon guarantees "reception" up to 98 feet from the master flash/trigger, but many shooters report no problems at distances of 150 to 200 feet (and no line-of-sight required!)

Wireless Flash Shooting

The procedures for using this mode have options for adjusting things like flash ratios. You'll work with two different menus: one that is used when the built-in flash is used as the wireless flash controller, and an alternate set of steps when an external flash mounted on the camera is used as the wireless flash controller.

Built-in Flash as Master Controller.

Just follow these steps to use the 7D II's built-in flash as the controller for off-camera flash units:

1. **Elevate built-in flash.** Start by popping up the camera's built-in flash. You can use this internal flash as a controller in two ways. It can function *in conjunction* with your remote, off-camera strobes (adding some illumination to your photos), or

set *not to flash,* and do nothing but control your external flash units. In this case, there is no illumination from your pop-up flash to contribute to the exposure). The built-in flash needs to be in the up position to use it as the 7D II's wireless flash controller either way.

2. **Enable internal flash.** Press the MENU button and navigate to the Shooting 1 menu. Choose the Flash Control entry and press the SET button. This brings up the Flash Control menu (which is at the bottom of the menu). Press the SET button to enter the Flash Control menu. Next, select the Flash Firing setting and set the camera to Enable. This activates the built-in flash, which makes wireless flash control with the 7D II possible.

3. **Confirm/Enable E-TTL II exposure.** While you can use wireless flash techniques and manual flash exposure, you're better off learning to use wireless features with the EOS 7D II set to automatic exposure. So, from the Flash Control menu, choose E-TTL II metering and select Evaluative exposure.

4. **Access wireless configuration.** In the Built-in Flash Setting menu, scroll down to Wireless Func. and press SET. **Note:** Wireless functions are not available when the camera is set to MULTI.

5. **Select wireless configuration.** In the Wireless Functions menu (see **Figure 12.13**, left), there are four choices (top to bottom): Disable, External/Internal Flash Ratio (both flashes, set proportionately), External Flash only (the built-in flash does not contribute to the exposure), and External+ Internal Flash (both flashes fire at their set levels.) The colon between the two flash icons indicates that in this mode you can set a flash *ratio* between the units. Press SET to confirm your configuration. The menu shown in **Figure 12.13**, right, appears.

6. **Choose a channel.** Scroll down to Channel, press SET, and select the channel you want to use (generally that will be Channel 1).

7. **Set flash ratio.** If you've chosen the Ratio option, scroll down to the Ratio Setting entry (it's directly under the Flash Exp.

Comp entry) and set a flash ratio between 1:1 (equal output) and 8:1 (external flash 8X the output of the internal flash, or, three stops). Only one ratios where the internal flash is *more* powerful than the external flash is possible – 1:2.

8. **Take photos.** You're all set! You can now take photos wirelessly.

9. **Exit wireless mode.** When you're finished using wireless flash, navigate to the Built-in Flash Settings in the Flash Control menu and Disable wireless flash to deactivate.

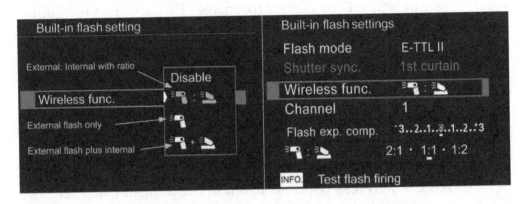

Figure 12.13

Access the wireless configuration screen (left). Choose other settings (right.)

External Flash on Camera as Master Controller.

The first step in using an external flash or controller as the master (instead of the built-in flash) is to set up one unit (either a flash or controller) as the external *master*. You can mount a Speedlite 580EX, 580EX II, 430EX III-RT (as a radio control master only), or 600EX-RT to your camera, which can serve as the master unit, transmitting E-TTL II optical signals to one or more off-camera Speedlite *slave* units. The master unit can have its flash output set to "off" so that it controls the remote units without contributing any flash output of its own to the exposure. This is useful for images where you don't want noticeable flash illumination coming in from the camera position. The next sections explain your options for setting up a master unit for fully automatic, E-TTL II exposure. Just follow these steps:

1. **Mount the external flash on the camera and turn on its power.** The external flash menus on the 7D II are not available unless a compatible flash is attached and powered up.

2. **Access External Flash Function Settings.** Press the MENU button and navigate to the Shooting 1 menu. Choose the Flash Control entry and press the SET button. This brings up the Flash Control menu (which is at the bottom of the menu). Press the SET button to enter the Flash Control menu. Next, select the Flash Firing setting and set the camera to Enable. This activates external flash.

3. **Confirm/Enable E-TTL II exposure.** From the Flash Control menu, choose E-TTL II metering and select Evaluative exposure.

4. **Select wireless configuration.** In the Flash Control menu, choose the External Flash Function Setting entry. The screen shown earlier in **Figure 12.10** appears. The Wireless option is in the center of the top row. Highlight it and press SET. Then choose Wireless: Optical Transmission, or (if you're using Canon Speedlites with radio control, Wireless: Radio Transmission. The additional options shown in **Figure 12.14** appear.

5. **Choose a channel.** Access the Channel option, and select the channel you want to use (generally that will be Channel 1).

6. **Select Flash Group.** Access the Flash Group option. Choose whether you want ALL flash to fire simultaneously at the same power level, or select A:B, A:B C to choose ratios. I'll explain ratios in more detail later.

7. **Set master flash firing.** In the Master Flash Firing entry, you can enable or disable the master flash (in which case only the slave flash units will fire.)

8. **Set flash ratio (optional).** If you've chosen a ratio setting (A:B or A:B C) scroll down to the Ratio Setting entry and set a flash ratio between 1:1 (equal output) and 8:1 (master flash group A supplying 8X the output of the slave flash group B, or, three stops). You can also select the reverse with the

Group B providing more illumination, using ratios from 1:2 to 1:8.)

9. **Take photos.** You're all set! You can now take photos wirelessly. Read the next sections for more information on Channels, Groups, and Ratios.

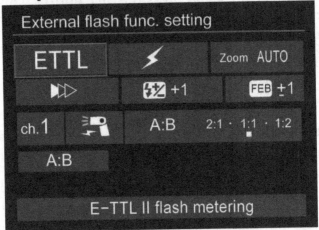

Figure 12.14

Choose other settings.

Once you've completed the steps above, your 7D II is set up to begin using wireless flash using your camera's built-in flash and one external off-camera flash. Additional options are available for the brave. I'll show you each of these one at a time. Keep in mind these two points:

- **Wireless Setting for External Flash.** As noted, you must switch your external flash from normal to wireless modes. The procedure will vary, depending on your flash unit. With the 580EX II, press and hold the ZOOM button for two seconds or longer until the display blinks. Then rotate the flash's control dial until either Master or Slave appears on the flash's LCD. Press the dial's center button to confirm your choice of Master or Slave wireless operation.

- **Sleep/No Sleep.** When the Canon Speedlite 580EX II and most other Canon units are ready to fire as a slave, the AF-assist beam will blink at one-second intervals. The unit will *not* go into a sleep mode while it is waiting to be used as a slave, but the camera will shut off at the interval you've specified in the menus.

Using a Speedlite or Transmitter as the Master in Optical Mode

You also need to tell the external flash or transmitter that it will be servicing as a master. Here are the steps to follow to set up and use a compatible Speedlite or transmitter as a camera-mounted master unit in optical triggering mode for automatic exposure.

600EX-RT

1. Press the Wireless button repeatedly until the LCD panel indicates you are in optical wireless master mode.

2. Press MODE to cycle through the ETTL, M, and Multi modes.

3. Use the menu system to control and make changes to RATIO, output, and other options on the master and slave units.

580EX II

1. Press and hold the ZOOM button to bring up the wireless options. Use the Select dial to cycle through the OFF, MASTER on, and SLAVE on options. Select and confirm MASTER on.

2. Press MODE to cycle through the ETTL, M, and Multi modes.

3. Press the ZOOM button repeatedly to cycle through the following options: Flash zoom, RATIO, CH., flash emitter ON/OFF. Use the Select dial and Select/SET button to make any changes to these options.

4. Use the Select/SET button to select and confirm the output power settings when using Manual and Multi modes, or to use FEC or FEB when in ETTL mode.

580EX

1. Slide the OFF/MASTER/SLAVE wireless switch near the base of the unit to MASTER.

2. Press MODE to cycle through the ETTL, M, and Multi modes.

3. Press the ZOOM button repeatedly to cycle through the following options: Flash zoom, RATIO, CH., flash emitter

ON/OFF. Use the Select dial and Select/SET button to make any changes to these options.

4. Use the Select/SET button to select and confirm the output power settings when using Manual and Multi modes, or to use FEC or FEB when in ETTL mode.

Using the ST-E2 Transmitter as Master

Canon's Speedlite Transmitter (ST-E2) is mounted on the camera's hot shoe and provides a way to control one or more Speedlites and/or units assigned to Groups A and B. The ST-E2 does not provide any flash output of its own and will not trigger units assigned to Group C. It has the following features and controls:

- **Transmitter.** Located on the top front of the unit, the transmitter emits E-TTL II pulses through an infrared filter.

- **AF-assist beam emitter.** Just below the transmitter, the AF-assist beam emitter works similarly to the Speedlite 430EX II and higher models.

- **Battery compartment.** The ST-E2 uses a 6.0V 2CR5 lithium battery. The battery compartment is accessed from the top of the unit.

- **Lock slider and mounting foot.** The lock slider is located on the right side of the unit when facing the front. Sliding it to the left lowers the lock pin in the mounting foot (located on the bottom of the unit) to secure it to the camera's hot shoe.

- **Back panel.** The rear of the unit features several indicators and controls:
  - **Ratio indicator.** A series of red LED lights indicating the current A:B ratio setting.
  - **Flash ratio control lamp.** A red LED that lights up when flash ratio is in use.
  - **Flash ratio setting button.** Next to the flash ratio control lamp. Press this button to activate flash ratio control.

- **Flash ratio adjustment buttons.** Two buttons with raised arrows (same color as buttons) pointing left and right. Use these to change the A:B ratio setting.

- **Channel indicator.** The channel number in use (1-4) glows red.

- **Channel selector button.** Next to the channel indicator. Press this button to select the communication channel.

- **High-speed sync (FP flash) indicator.** A red LED that glows when high-speed sync is in use.

- **High-speed sync button.** Press this button to activate/de-activate high-speed sync.

- **ETTL indicator.** A red LED that glows when E-TTL II is in use.

- **Off/On/HOLD switch.** Slide this switch to turn the unit off, on, or on with adjustments disabled (HOLD). The ST-E2 will power off after approximately 90 seconds of idle time. It will turn back on when the shutter button or test transmission button is pressed.

- **Pilot lamp/Test transmission button.** This lamp works similarly to the Speedlite pilot lamp/test buttons. The lamp glows red when ready to transmit. Press the lamp button to send a test transmission to the slave units.

- **Flash confirmation lamp.** This lamp glows green for about three seconds when the ST-E2 detects a good flash exposure.

Here are the steps to follow to set up and use the ST-E2 transmitter as a camera-mounted master unit:

1. Mount the ST-E2 unit on your 7D II.
2. Make sure both the ST-E2 unit and your camera are powered on.
3. Make sure the slave units are set to E-TTL II, assigned to the appropriate group(s), and that all units are operating on the same channel.
4. If you'd like to use set a flash ratio between Groups A and B, press the flash ratio setting button and flash ratio adjustment buttons to select the desired ratio. Press the high-speed sync button to use high-speed sync (often helpful with outdoor shooting).

Using the Speedlite 600EX-RT as Radio Master

The Speedlite 600EX-RT can serve as the master unit when mounted to your camera, transmitting radio signals to one or more off-camera Speedlite 600EX-RT slave units. The master unit can have its flash output set to "off" so that it controls the remote units without contributing any flash output of its own to the exposure. This is useful for images where you don't want noticeable flash illumination coming in from the camera position.

Here are the steps to follow to set up and use a Speedlite 600EX-RT as a camera-mounted master unit for radio wireless E-TTL II operation.

1. Mount the Speedlite 600EX-RT to your 7D II.
2. Make sure the 600EX-RT master units, slave units, and the camera are powered on.
3. Set the camera-mounted 600EX-RT to radio wireless MASTER mode. Press the Wireless button until the LCD panel indicates you are on radio wireless master mode.
4. Set the slave 600EX-RT or 430EX III-RT units to radio wireless SLAVE mode. For each 600EX-RT unit, press the Wireless button until the LCD panel indicates you are on radio

wireless slave mode. For each 430EX III-RT slaves, press the left directional key and rotate the Select dial until Slave appears on the LCD. Then press the Select button to confirm.

5. Confirm that all units are set to E-TTL II, assigned to the appropriate group(s), and that all units are operating on the same channel and ID number. The LINK lamps on all units should glow green.

Using the Speedlite 430EX III-RT as Radio Master

The Speedlite 430EX III-RT can serve as a radio master unit to trigger another 430EX III-RT or a 600EX-RT flash. Just follow these steps:

1. Press the left directional key on the Select dial. It's marked with a lightning bolt symbol.
2. Rotate the Select dial until MASTER appears on the LCD.
3. Press the Select button in the center of the Select dial.
4. Set any 600EX-RT or 430EX III-RT units that you will be using as slaves to the Slave mode.
   • For the 600EX-RT, press the Wireless button until the LCD panel indicates you are in radio wireless slave mode.
   • For any 430EX III-RT slaves, press the left directional key and rotate the Select dial until Slave appears on the LCD. Then press the Select button to confirm.
5. Repeat Step 4 for any additional Slave units.
6. When master and slaves are communicating, the LINK lamps on all units will glow green.

Using the ST-E3-RT as Radio Master

The ST-E3-RT transmitter can be mounted to the camera's hot shoe and used as a master controller to one or more slave Speedlite 600EX-RT units. The ST-E3-RT and the 600EX-RT share essentially the same radio control capabilities except that the ST-E3-RT does not produce flash, provide AF-assist, or otherwise emit light and is therefore incapable of optical wireless transmission.

The layout of the ST-E3-RT's control panel is virtually identical to the 600EX-RT. So is the menu system and operation, except that, as stated earlier, it will only operate as a radio wireless transmitter. Here are the steps to follow to set up and use the ST-E3-RT transmitter as a camera-mounted master unit for radio wireless E-TTL II operation:

1. Mount the ST-E3-RT unit on your 7D II.
2. Make sure both the ST-E3-RT unit and your camera are powered on.
3. Set the slave 600EX-RT or 430EX III-RT units to radio wireless SLAVE mode. For each 600EX-RT unit, press the Wireless button until the LCD panel indicates you are on radio wireless slave mode. For each 430EX III-RT slave, press the left directional key and rotate the Select dial until Slave appears on the LCD. Then press the Select button to confirm.
4. Confirm that all units are set to E-TTL II, assigned to the appropriate group(s), and that all units are operating on the same channel and ID number. The LINK lamps on all units should glow green.

The ST-E3-RT controls slave units as described earlier in the section, "Speedlite 600EX-RT as Radio Wireless Master Using E-TTL II."

Setting Up a Slave Flash

The whole point of working wirelessly is to have a master flash/controller trigger and adjust one or more slave flash units. So, once you've defined your master flash, the next step is to switch your remaining Speedlites into slave mode. That's done differently with each particular Canon Speedlite.

⊙ **Speedlite 600EX-RT.** Press the Wireless button repeatedly until the LCD panel indicates that the unit is in optical wireless slave mode or radio wireless slave mode. In this mode, the 600EX-RT is assigned a flash mode by the master transmitter, either a flash or ST-E2 or ST-E3-RT.

⊚ **Speedlite 580EX II.** Press and hold the ZOOM button until the wireless setting options appear. Use the Select dial and Select/SET button to select and confirm that wireless is on and in slave mode.

⊚ **Speedlite 430EX III/430EX III-RT.** For each 430EX III-RT slave, press the left directional key and rotate the Select dial until Slave appears on the LCD. Then press the Select button to confirm.

⊚ **Speedlite 430EX II.** Press and hold the ZOOM button for two seconds or more until the wireless setting options appear. Use the Select dial and Select/SET button to select and confirm that wireless is on and in slave mode.

⊚ **Speedlite 320EX.** This flash has an On/Off/Slave switch at the lower left of the back panel. In Slave mode, you can use the flash's C.Fn-10 to tell the unit to power down after either 10 or 60 minutes of idle time. That can help preserve the 320EX's batteries. The unit's C.Fn-11 can be set to allow the master transmitter to "wake" a sleeping 320EX after your choice of within 1 hour or within 8 hours. Note that the C.Fn settings of the 320EX and 270EX II (described next) can be set only while the Speedlites are connected to the camera with the hot shoe.

⊚ **Speedlite 270EX II.** This flash has an Off/Slave/On switch. If left on and idle, the 270EX II will power itself off after approximately 90 seconds. C.Fn-1 can be used to disable auto power off. As with the 320EX, in Slave mode, you can use the flash's C.Fn-10 to tell the unit to power down after either 10 or 60 minutes of idle time. The unit's C.Fn-11 can be set to allow the master transmitter to "wake" a sleeping unit after your choice of within 1 hour or within 8 hours.

More Wireless Options and Capabilities

If you're ready to immerse yourself even more deeply in wireless flash photography, the next sections will provide a little more detail on using some of the settings for ratios, channels, and groups.

Internal/External Flash Ratio Setting

Your built-in flash and your wireless flash units have their own individual *oomph* -- how much illumination they put out. This option lets you choose the relationship between these units, a *power ratio* between your built-in flash and your wireless flash units -- the relative strength of each -- as we did in Step 8 in the last section. That ability can be especially useful if you want to use the built-in flash for just a little fill light (it's not very powerful, anyway), while letting your off-camera units do the heavy work. This setting is the top choice in the Wireless Function menu, designated with icons that show an external flash and a raised camera flash.

Having the ability to vary the power of each flash unit or group of flash units wirelessly gives you greater flexibility and control. Varying the light output of each flash unit makes it possible to create specific types of lighting (such as traditional portrait lighting which frequently calls for a 3:1 lighting ratio between main light and fill light) or to use illumination to highlight one part of the photo while reducing contrast in another.

Lighting ratios determine the contrast between the main (sometimes called a "key" light) and fill light. For portraiture, usually the main light is typically placed at a 45-degree angle to the subject (although there are some variations), with the fill-in light on the opposite side or closer to the camera position. Choosing the right lighting ratio can do a lot to create a particular look or mood. For instance, a 1:1 ratio produces what's known as "flat" lighting. While this is good for copying or documentation, it's not usually as interesting for portraiture. Instead, making the main light more powerful than the fill light creates interesting shadows for more dramatic images. (See Figure **12.15**.)

Figure 12.15
More dramatic lighting ratios produce more dramatic-looking illumination.

By selecting the power ratio between the flash units, you can change the relative illumination between them. Figure **12.16** shows a series of four images with a single main flash located at a 45-degree angle off to the right and slightly behind the model. The built-in flash at the camera provided illumination to fill in the shadows on the side of the face closest to the camera. The ratio between the external and internal flash were varied using 2:1 (upper-left), 3:1 (upper-right), 4:1 (lower-left), and 5:1 (lower-right) ratios.

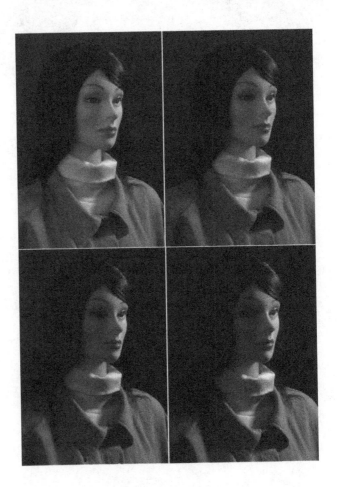

Figure 12.16

The main light (to the right and behind the model) and fill light (at the camera position) were varied using 2:1 and 3:1 (top row, left to right) as well as 4:1 and 5:1 (bottom row, left to right) ratios.

Here's how to set the lighting ratio between the internal flash and one external wireless flash unit:

1. **Choose Ratio Setting in Wireless Func. menu.** In the Built-in Flash Setting menu, highlight Wireless Func., press SET, and choose Ratio Setting. Press SET again to confirm and return to the previous menu.

2. **Access the Power Ratio entry.** Now you can set the power ratio, represented by a pair of icons corresponding to an external and internal flash unit.

3. **Set the control.** Press the SET button.

4. **Choose the desired ratio.** Then use the directional keys to choose the setting you want. Your choices range from 1:1 (the off-camera and built-in flash have equal output) to 8:1 (the off-camera flash supplies 8X output compared to the internal flash). Reversing the power proportions from 1:2 to 1:8 is also possible. Set the ratio to 4:1, for example, and the external flash will produce four times as much light as the on-camera flash, which is then used as fill illumination. For most subjects, ratios of 2:1 to 5:1 will produce the best results.

5. **Confirm.** Press SET to confirm your ratio.

Using the built-in flash only as a trigger

This setting allows you to turn off the flash output of your 7D II's built-in flash, while allowing it to emit a wireless controller flash that signals the external flash units you're working with. You'll still see a burst from your camera's built-in flash, but that burst will not contribute to the exposure. It will only be a preflash used to tell the remote/slave flash units to fire.

This is the setting to choose if you only want to use the flash controller to operate your remote flashes. It's probably the most commonly used choice when you don't want to use the internal flash for fill light, since firing the built-in flash increases the risk of red-eye effects.

Photographers prefer this mode in part because Canon's portable shoe mount flash units are much more powerful than a camera's built-in flash. They want to avoid using a light source that is directly above the lens and close to the lens, since red-eye is caused by light from the flash unit reflecting off the subject's retinas and bouncing back into the lens.

Using off-camera flash lets the photographer precisely control light direction and effect. It also makes it possible for the photographer to move around within the constraints of the flash units' ability to illuminate a scene, without worrying about getting too far from the subject for the flash unit(s) to be effective. Only the camera to subject position changes and not the light to subject position and ratio. Once you've set up the flash units relative to your subject, you can move around freely.

Here are the steps to follow when using wireless flash only (whether you're working with a single external flash, or multiple units).

1. **Choose wireless flash only.** Navigate to the Wireless Func. menu as you did earlier, but choose Wireless Flash Only (the single-flash icon in the middle of the list).

2. **Confirm.** Press the SET button to confirm the Wireless Flash Only setting.

3. **Set the Power Ratio (optional).** If you are using more than one external flash, and have assigned flash units to different groups, you can then set the power ratios between groups. (I'll explain groups later in this chapter.) If you are using only one flash, or all the flash units are assigned to the same group, you don't need to do this; setting a power ratio won't make any difference. The Firing Group entry will read "All" and the fire ratio entry will not be visible. You can only select a power ratio if you've chosen A:B in the Firing Group entry. (Remember to change the power ratio back to normal when you are finished with a session; Canon's Speedlites retain the settings you make, even after a quick battery change.)

Using Wireless and Built-in Flash

This option in the Wireless Func. screen, represented by an icon of an external unit *plus* an icon of a raised camera flash, *adds* the built-in flash to whatever wireless groups you're using. You can then use the built-in flash in conjunction with whatever firing groups you've set up. In this case you're still using the external flash units as the main sources of light, but the built-in flash can either serve to provide some extra fill (such as to illuminate the face under the brim of a hat) or to provide a second light when you only have one off-camera flash available.

It is also possible to set up a two-light portrait using an off-camera flash as a main light (about 45 degrees to the model) and the built-in flash as the fill light, as discussed earlier. Use the External/Internal Flash Ratio Setting to adjust their relative contribution to the image.

Some photographers do like to position their fill light directly above the camera and straight toward the model. The lighting ratio for such a setup would have the built-in and external strobes set to 1:1 or 2:1. Keep in mind that if using such a configuration, the light from the built-in flash is striking the subject head on and needs to be added to your calculations for the main light. In other words, setting your lighting ratio to 1:1 would actually provide a 2:1 effective lighting ratio since you would have 1 part light from the main light and 1 part light from the built-in flash illuminating one side of the subject and just 1 part light from the built-in flash illuminating the other side. Setting your lighting ratio to 2:1 would effectively provide a 3:1 lighting ratio this way. If you have set the camera to E-TTL II exposure as recommended, the lighting you choose will be automatically accounted for in the exposure selected by the camera, so no calculations are necessary by the photographer.

Working with Groups

With what you've already learned, you can shoot wirelessly using your camera's built-in flash and one or more external flash units. All these strobes will work together with the 7D II for automatic exposure using E-TTL II exposure mode. You can vary the power ratio between your built-in flash and the external units. As you become more comfortable with wireless flash photography, you can even switch the individual external flash units into manual mode, and adjust their lighting ratios manually.

But there's a lot more you can do if you've splurged and own two or more compatible external flash units (some photographers I know own five or six Speedlite 580EX II or 600EX-RT units). Canon wireless photography lets you collect individual strobes into *groups*, and control all the Speedlites within a given group together. You can operate as few as two strobes in two groups or three strobes in three groups, while controlling more units if desired. You can also have them fire at equal output settings (A+B+C mode) versus using them at different power ratios (A:B or A:B C modes). Setting each group's strobes to different power ratios gives you more control over lighting for portraiture and other uses. Canon's radio-compatible devices can communicate with up to five groups in radio mode, although you would rarely need that capability (or, more likely, not own enough flashes to distribute among five groups).This is one of the more powerful options of the EOS wireless flash system. I prefer to keep my Speedlites set to different groups normally. I can always set the power ratio to 1:1 if I want to operate the flash units all at the same power. If I change my mind and need to make adjustments, I can just change the wireless flash controller and then manipulate the different groups' output as desired.

The ST-E2 is a hot shoe mount device that offers wireless flash control for a wide variety of Canon wireless flash capable strobes and can even control flash units wirelessly for High-speed sync (HSS) photography. (HSS is described in Chapter 11.) The ST-E2 can only control three flash groups though and also can support flash exposure bracketing. Its range isn't as great as the 7D II's though.

Canon flash units that can be operated wirelessly include: 580EX II, 580EX, 550EX, 430EX III-RT, 430EX, 420EX, 320EX, 270EX II MR-14EX, and MT-24EX. The 270EX, 220EX, 380EX, and earlier Canon flash units cannot be operated wirelessly via Canon's wireless flash system. There are third-party flash units that can (such as the Sigma I use), but you must use one designed to work with Canon's wireless flash system only.

Here's how you set up groups:

1. **Determine lighting setup.** Decide whether you're using the built-in flash as part of your lighting scheme or just using the external flash units. If you do want the internal flash to contribute to the exposure, then you can scroll down in the Built-in Flash Setting entry to the External Flash/Built-in Flash Lighting Ratio Control (if you're using lighting ratios) and set that control (from 8:1 to 2:1, as noted earlier).

2. **Access lighting groups.** If you're not using the built-in flash (Wireless Func. is set to the external flash only icon), scroll down to the Firing Group entry that appears and press SET.

Select the group configuration you want. From top to bottom, the choices are as follows. I'll explain exactly what these two configurations do next:

- **All external.** Multiple external flash units functioning as one big flash.
- **A:B.** Multiple external units in two groups.

3. **Allocate flash units into groups.** You must do this at the flash unit itself. You'll need to tell each flash which group it "belongs" to, so it will respond, along with any other strobes (if any) in its group, to wireless commands directed at that particular group. The procedure for setting each flash unit's slave ID/group varies depending on what flash you are using, so consult your Speedlite's manual.

Ratio Control

By default, all the flashes in each group will fire at full power. However, for more advanced lighting setups, you can select lighting ratios.

Here's how to set the lighting ratio between the internal flash and one external wireless flash unit:

1. **Navigate to the 7D II's Flash Group selection option.** With wireless flash already activated, visit the External Speedlite Control entry in the Shooting 1 menu, navigate to the Flash Function Settings choice, Flash Functions. Navigate to the Flash Group choice at the lower left of the screen and choose SET.

2. **Choose Group Configuration.** You can select ALL, A:B, or A:B C. If you're using the 600EX-RT in radio transmission mode, you can also select Groups D and E. Press SET to confirm.

3. **Select Ratio.** If you've chosen A:B C, navigate to the A:B Ratio Control option, and select a ratio from 8:1 to 1:8. At 8:1, Group A supplies 8X output of Group B. At 1:8, the ratio is reversed.

4. **Confirm.** Press SET to confirm your ratio.

Here's how the various basic Group Configurations work:

- ⊚ **ALL.** All groups will fire at the power level set at the flash unit itself. That may be full power, or you may have set individual flashes to fire at some other power level. It's usually simpler to set your flashes at full power and allow the master to control their output.

- ⊚ **A:B.** In this configuration, you can specify the ratio of the power levels of Groups A and B, as described in Step 3 above.

- ⊚ **A:B C.** In this Group configuration, you can specify the power ratio between Groups A and B, but *not* the output of Group C flashes. Those can be controlled only using Flash Exposure Compensation, the option immediately below the A:B Power Ratio setting in **Figure 10.6.**

Choosing a Channel

Canon's wireless flash system can work on any of four channels in optical mode, so if more than one photographer is using the Canon system, each can set his gear to a different channel so they don't accidentally trigger each other's strobes. You need to be sure all of your gear is set to the same channel. Selecting a channel is done differently with each particular flash model.

The ability to operate flash units on one of four channels in optical mode isn't really important unless you're shooting in an environment where other photographers are also using the Canon wireless flash system. If the system only offered one channel, then each photographer's wireless flash controller would be firing every Canon flash set for wireless operation. By having four channels available, the photographers can coordinate their use to avoid that problem. Such situations are common at sporting events and other activities that draw a lot of shooters.

It's always a good idea to double-check your flash units before you set them up to make sure they're all set to the same channel, and this should also be one of your first troubleshooting questions if a flash doesn't fire the first time you try to use it wirelessly.

You do this as follows:

1. **Set flash units to the channel you want to use for all your groups.** Each flash unit may use its own procedure for setting that strobe's channel. Consult your Speedlite's manual for instructions. With the 580EX II, press the ZOOM button repeatedly until the CH. Indicator blinks, then rotate the control dial to select Channel 1, 2, 3, or 4. Press the control dial center button to confirm.

2. **Navigate to the 7D II's channel selection option.** In the Built-in Flash Func. Settings screen, use the directional buttons to scroll down to the Channel Setting and push the SET button.

3. **Select the channel your flashes are set to.** You can then use the up/down directional buttons to advance the channel number from 1 to 4 or back down again (you have to reverse

the directional buttons direction to get back to one; you can't just keep advancing it to get there -- it doesn't "wrap around).

4. **Double-check to make sure your flash units are set to the appropriate channel.** Your wireless flash units must be set to the same channel as the 7D II's wireless flash controller; otherwise, the Speedlites won't fire.

Flash Release Function

The Canon Speedlite 320EX and Speedlite 270EX II have a nifty feature called the Remote Release Function, which, as I write this, is completely novel in the Canon accessory flash line-up. The feature allows you to detach the Speedlite from certain EOS cameras (right now the 5DS/5DS R, 5D Mark II and Mark III, 6D, 7D, 60D, 70D, 80D, 7D, 7D II, T6i, T6s, T5i,T4i, T3i, T2i, T1i, Xsi, Xti, XT, and 2003-era original Digital), and then use a button on the flash unit as a remote control to trigger the camera from up to 16 feet away. That's right, your 320EX and 270EX II can function as a wireless re-mote control, just like the Canon RC-6, RC-5, and RC-1 infrared controls!

As you can see from the list of cameras, it works with any EOS camera that can be triggered by an IR remote. There's a (mandatory) two-second delay after you press the flash's remote release, and the flash itself does not have to fire and contribute to the exposure. An invisible infrared signal emitted by the flash triggers the camera.

To use the feature with the 7D II, use the Drive function, de-scribed earlier, and select the self-timer/infrared remote option. If you don't want the 7D II's flash to fire, make sure it's set to a mode where the flash doesn't pop up automatically. With the 320EX or 270EX II turned on and detached from the camera, position the flash so it "sees" the remote control sensor on the front of the cam-era. Press the remote release button on the side of the flash, and the camera will fire two seconds later. If you're taking a picture of your-self, this delay allows you to stash the flash out of sight and grin. The flash will not fire.

If you prefer to have the flash fire and contribute to the exposure, move the On/Off switch on the back to the middle "slave" position. In this mode, the camera itself must serve as the master, or you must have another master unit physically attached to the camera. To use the camera in master mode, use the Built-in Flash Control menu entry to activate the 7D II's master mode, as described previously. Or, you can connect a 580EX II, set to master mode, either by putting it in the accessory shoe or linked with a cable, such as the Off Camera Cord OC-E3. Alternatively, you can connect the Speedlite Transmitter ST-E2.

When you're ready, point the 320EX or 270EX II at the front of the camera/master flash within 16 feet of the camera, and press the remote control button on the side of the flash. During the two-second delay, you can then point the 320EX or 270EX II in a different direction (as is likely, because you're probably using this feature to illuminate the scene, not the camera). That's the real reason for the two-second delay, by the way: giving you the ability to reposition the "remote" release flash.

The 600EX-RT has its own remote release function, which allows you to use a slave unit to trigger your camera by remote control when using radio transmission mode. EOS cameras released since 2012 (including the 7D II) can be triggered in this way through the intelligent hot shoe, using a 600EX-RT mounted on the camera as a receiver, and the slave 600EX-RT off camera as the remote trigger. Older cameras can still be used in this mode, but you'll need to connect the on-camera 600EX-RT to the camera's N3 remote control terminal using an optional Release Cable SR-N3. (If your camera uses a different type of remote release, you're out of luck.)

Chapter 13

Introduction to Live View and Movie Making

Do you like the opening title sequence montage on *Saturday Night Live* each week? Many of the video clips were shot using the full HD movie-making capabilities and prized low-light capabilities of Canon dSLR cameras. Feature films have been shot with Canon cameras, and all manner of specialized professional video add-ons, from large electronic viewfinder "panels" to SteadyCam-style stabilization rigs, have been designed for EOS models.

Indeed, Canon models were the first to gain wide acceptance professionally for its full HD 1920 x 1080 video. Your 7D II is equipped with a headphone jack that serious videographers need to monitor audio as it's recorded (usually with an external microphone or two), an HDMI port that can output raw video files to external storage or a monitor, and both full and standard HD formats with industry-standard H.264 encoding. Your camera actually rivals the quality of some professional video capture gear -- and goes them one better because its sensor is much larger, allowing exquisite control over selective focus and depth-of-field.

Of course, this mammoth book is devoted primarily to still photography, and, as much as I would have liked to, I was unable to explain every video accessory or add-on, nor provide even a level 101 course in movie making. If you're serious about shooting video with this camera, I urge you to find a dedicated book to help you learn about A and B rolls (or their video equivalent), time codes, and other topics that are really *basics* for advanced video capture. However, in this chapter you'll find enough about movie making with the 7D II to get you started, and, I hope to spur you to further study.

Before I get into movie making, it's useful to look at live view – the still photography feature that provides a preview of the actual sensor image before you take it. Live view is what makes movie-shooting possible.

Live View

The Canon EOS 7D II has a gorgeous 3-inch LCD that can be viewed under a variety of lighting conditions and from wide-ranging angles, so you don't have to be exactly behind the display to see its live view image clearly while shooting stills or video. It offers a 100-percent view of the sensor's capture area. It's large enough to allow manual focusing, but if you want to use automatic focus, you can use the Dual Pixel CMOS AF system with both phase detection and contrast detection using the sensor. You still have to avoid pointing your 7D II at bright light sources (especially the Sun) when using live view, but the real-time preview can be used for fairly long periods without frying the sensor. (Image quality can degrade, but the camera issues a warning when the sensor starts to overheat.)

You may not have considered just what you can do with live view, but once you've played with it, you'll discover dozens of applications for this capability. Here's a list of considerations:

- **Preview your images on a TV.** Connect your 7D II to a television or monitor with the optional HDMI cable HTC-100 or stereo AV cable AVC-DC400ST, and you can preview your image on a large screen.

- **Preview remotely.** Extend the cable between the camera and TV screen, and you can preview your images some distance away from the camera.

- **Shoot from your computer.** Canon gives you the software you need to control your camera from your computer, so you can preview images and take pictures or movies without physically touching the 7D II. You'll need to install the EOS Utility to do this.

- **Shoot from tripod or handheld.** Of course, holding the camera out at arm's length to preview an image is poor technique, and will introduce a lot of camera shake. If you want to use live view for handheld images, use an image-stabilized lens and/or a high shutter speed. A tripod is a better choice if you can use one.

- ◉ **Watch your power.** Live view uses a lot of juice and will deplete your battery rapidly. Canon estimates that you can get 310 to 350 shots per battery when using live view, depending on the temperature. Expect slightly fewer exposures when using flash. The optional AC adapter is a useful accessory.

Enabling Live View

You need to take some steps before using live view (or movies). This workflow prevents you from accidentally using live view when you don't mean to, thus potentially losing a shot, and it also helps ensure that you've made all the settings necessary to successfully use the feature efficiently. Here's an overview:

- ◉ **Choose a shooting mode.** Live view works with any exposure mode available on the Mode Dial, including Scene Intelligent Auto. You can even switch from one mode to another while live view is activated.

- ◉ **Enable live view.** You'll need to activate live view by enabling Live View Shoot from the Shooting 4 menu. (See **Figure 13.1**.) I'll show you more options in the next section. (If the camera is set to Scene Intelligent Auto, which provides a reduced menu set, you'll find the options in the Shooting 3 menu.) Note that disabling live view has no effect on movie shooting.

- ◉ **Choose other live view functions.** Select from the other live view options (as described next.)

- ◉ **Select live view or movie shooting.** Rotate the Live View switch, which is concentric with the Start/Stop button to the right of the viewfinder window, to the movie camera or still camera icon.

- ◉ **Begin live viewing.** Press the Start/Stop button to enter live viewing or movie mode. Press again to exit.

- ◉ **Start capture.** Press the shutter release completely to take a picture, whether you are in live view *or* movie mode. (To start shooting movies, press the Start/Stop button when the Live

View Switch is in the Movie position.) In still mode, after image review, the 7D II returns to live viewing mode.

Shooting Menu Options

I described the Shooting 4 and 5 menu options in Chapter 8, but here's a quick recap as a refresher:

- ◉ **Live View Shooting.** Enables/disables live view shooting, and does not affect movie shooting.

- ◉ **AF method (Face+Tracking, FlexiZoneAF -- Multi, Flexi-ZoneAF -- Single).** This option lets you choose between AF with face recognition, manual zone selection, or single zone selection (all described below).

- ◉ **Continuous AF.** When enabled (the default setting), the camera will constantly refocus during live view if you've specified Face+Tracking, FlexiZoneAF--Multi, or FlexiZoneAF--Single modes. This provides faster AF when you finally take a picture, but consumes more battery power. If you want to maximize the number of possible shots, disable the continuous AF feature, at the cost of some focusing speed.

- ◉ **Grid Display.** This setting overlays Grid 1 on the screen to help you compose your image and align vertical and horizontal lines, or Grid 2, which consists of four rows of six boxes, which allows finer control over placement of images in your frame. Grid 3 adds diagonal lines.

- ◉ **Aspect Ratio.** Allows you to choose an aspect ratio from 3:2, 4:3, 16:9, or 1:1. JPEG images will be stored using the selected ratio; RAW images will be saved using the default 3:2 proportions, but the desired cropping can be restored in your image-editing software. In Custom Function 3 menu, you can choose either Masked or Outlined for LV Shooting Area Display. Selecting proportions other than the 3:2 for still images default results in a cropped image, and the live view display provides a black border on the LCD to show the limits of the image area

- **Exposure Simulation.** Allows you to choose whether the live view image mimics the exposure level of the final image, or whether the screen displays a bright image (dependent on the LCD Brightness setting you've specified in the Setup 2 menu) that may be easier to view under high ambient lighting conditions. Your choices include Enable, During DOF Preview (only), and Disable.

- **Silent LV Shooting.** Choose Mode 1 to produce a quieter shooting sound level in live view mode, with continuous shooting at up to 6 fps. Mode 2 separates the *ker* from the *clunk* sounds of the shutter tripping, with a small click as the picture is taken, and then a second quiet click when you release the shutter button. The camera ignores this setting if you're using a remote control, and defaults to Mode 1. You can also disable silent shooting.

- **Metering Timer.** Allows you to specify how long the EOS 7D Mark II's metering system will remain active before switching off, from 4, 16, or 30 seconds, plus 1, 10, or 30 minutes.

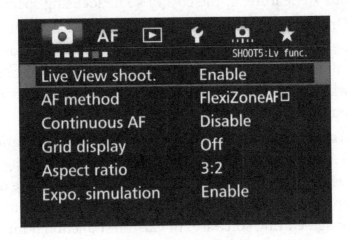

Figure 13.1

The Shooting 4 menu.

Activating Live View

Once you've enabled live view in the menu, you can continue taking pictures normally through the 7D II's viewfinder. When you're ready to activate live view, press the Start/Stop button to the left of the viewfinder. The mirror will flip up, and the sensor image will appear on the LCD. Here are some things you should keep in mind when live view is active:

- ◎ **Shooting functions don't interrupt.** You can change settings or review images normally when in Live View mode. Press the WB-Metering, DRIVE-AF, or Flash exposure compensation-ISO buttons on the top of the camera, or the Picture Control/Creative Settings button to the left of the LCD, and an overlay appears superimposed on the live view screen. You can use the Quick Control Dial and Main Dial to change those settings. You can also make adjustments to the AF Method, Drive Mode, Metering Mode, Image Quality, White Balance, Picture Style, and Auto Lighting Optimizer by pressing the Q button to the right of the LCD monitor.

- ◎ **Live view continues.** When you press the shutter release, the 7D II will take a photo, then display the image you just shot for review, as normal. When picture review is finished, the camera returns to live view mode. You can take as many consecutive shots using live view as you like, barring sensor overheating. To exit live view entirely, press the Start/Stop button.

- ◎ **Watch for overheating.** Leaving live view on for extended periods increases the temperature of the sensor, potentially causing noise or odd colors in your image. If you want to take a long exposure, turn off live view for several minutes before shooting, to allow your sensor to cool. Live view will shut off automatically after a high temperature icon warns you when things start to heat up.

- ◎ **Information display.** During live view, useful information is shown on the screen, such as battery status, Picture Style, and most of the shooting information (shutter speed, f/stop,

ISO setting, number of exposures remaining) you'd see through the viewfinder. Press the INFO. button to change the amount of information shown.

Quick Control

As mentioned above, press the Q button in live view, and you can adjust any of the values shown in the left and right hand columns that appear on the screen. Press the multi controller up/down to navigate among AF method, Drive mode, Metering Mode, Image Quality, White Balance, Picture Style, Auto Lighting Optimizer settings, and press left/right to change the settings.

Focusing in Live View

Press the AF-ON button or press the shutter button halfway to activate autofocus using the currently set live view autofocus mode. Those modes are Face Detection+Tracking, FlexiZone – Multi and FlexiZone –Single. You can also use manual focus. To change the focus mode while using live view, you can press the DRIVE-AF button and rotate the Main Dial to choose the mode you want, highlighted on the live view screen. I'll describe each of these separately.

Face Detection+Tracking Mode

This mode uses phase detection and contrast detection. The 7D II will search the frame for a human face and attempt to focus on the face. To autofocus using Face Detection+Tracking mode, follow these steps:

1. **Set lens to autofocus.** Make sure the focus switch on the lens is set to AF.
2. **Activate live view.** Press the Live View/Movie button. Select Face Detection from the Quick Control menu or the Live View Shooting menu.
3. **Face detection.** A frame will appear around a face found in the image. If only one face is detected, the frame will be green; if more than one face is found, the frame will be white and have left/right triangles flanking it. (See **Figure 13.2**.) In

that case, use the multi controller to move the frame to the face you want to use for focus. If no face is detected, the 7D II will switch to FlexiZone-Multi (described next), and you can select your focus area. Small or large faces, those partially hidden (say, by a large floppy hat, or faces that are too dark or bright may not be detected.

4. **Focus.** Press the shutter button halfway to focus the camera on the face within the positioned Face Detection frame. When focus is locked in, the AF frame will turn green and the beeper, if activated, will chime. If focus cannot be achieved, the AF frame will turn orange.

5. **Track or reframe.** Once focus is achieved, the 7D II will track the subject even if your subject moves within the frame, or you reframe your composition.

6. **Press and hold the shutter release to take the picture.** Press the shutter release all the way down to take the picture.

Figure 13.2

If multiple faces are found, the bracket can be moved among them.

FlexiZone-Multi Mode

This mode allows focusing over a wide area. In automatic selection mode, the camera selects one of 49 AF points. The 7D II can automatically select the focus *area* from up to 31 different AF positions in the frame, or any of nine different *zones* you select.

1. **Set lens to autofocus.** Make sure the focus switch on the lens is set to AF.
2. **Activate live view.** Press the Live View/Movie button.
3. **Select Automatic or Zone (Manual) Selection.** You can toggle between Automatic and Zone (Manual) Selection by pressing the SET or multi controller buttons. **In Automatic Selection mode**, the camera will select one of up to 31 focus areas without input from you. (The actual number of points available varies depending on the current aspect ratio, from 31 at 3:2 down to 21 at 16:9. White brackets appear around the area where the focus areas reside. **In Zone (Manual) Selection mode,** you can use the directional buttons to move a frame around to any of 9 different areas (three with the 16:9 aspect ratio.) If you have moved the zone out of the center, pressing the SET or multi controller buttons *does not* switch to Automatic mode; instead, either button returns the area selection to the center. If the selection *is in the center already,* pressing the SET or Trash buttons then switches to Automatic mode. This dual behavior of the SET/Trash buttons is confusing at first, but you can get used to it quickly.
4. **Select subject.** Compose the image on the LCD so the selected focus point is on the subject.
5. **Zoom in (optional.)** Press the Magnify button located to the left of the LCD monitor and the area covered by the automatically selected point or manually selected zone will be enlarged.
6. **Press the shutter release button halfway.** When focus is achieved, the AF frame turns green, and you'll hear a beep if the sound has been turned on in the Shooting 1 menu. If the camera is unable to focus, the AF point turns orange instead.

7. **Take picture.** Press the shutter release all the way down to take the picture.

FlexiZone-Single AF Mode

FlexiZone -- Single mode allows you to move the AF area around continually from one spot on the sensor to the next, rather than in area/zone "jumps." To autofocus using FlexiZone mode, follow these steps:

1. **Set lens to autofocus.** Make sure the focus switch on the lens is set to AF.
2. **Activate live view.** Press the Live View/Movie button.
3. **Choose AF point.** A focus point box will appear (when using Movie Servo AF, the box will be larger). Use the directional controls to move the AF point anywhere you like on the screen, except for the edges. Press the SET or multi controller button to move it back to the center of the screen. You can also tap the touch screen to move the AF point to that location.
4. **Select subject.** Compose the image on the LCD so the selected focus point is on the subject.
5. **Zoom in (optional.)** Press the Magnify button located to the left of the LCD monitor and the area covered by the AF point will be magnified..
6. **Press the shutter release button halfway.** When focus is achieved, the AF frame turns green, and you'll hear a beep if the sound has been turned on in the Shooting 1 menu. If the camera is unable to focus, the AF point turns orange instead.
7. **Take picture.** Press the shutter release all the way down to take the picture.

Manual Mode

Focusing manually on an LCD screen isn't as difficult as you might think, but Canon has made the process even easier by providing a magnified view. Just follow these steps to focus manually.

1. **Set lens to manual focus.** Make sure the focus switch on the lens is set to MF.
2. **Press the Magnify button.** The area of the image inside the focus frame will be magnified 5X. Press or tap Magnify again to increase the magnification to 10X. A third press will return you to the full-frame view.
3. **Move magnifying frame.** While the image is magnified, use the multi controller to move the focus frame that's superimposed on the screen to the location where you want to focus. You can press the SET or Trash button to center the focus frame in the middle of the screen.
4. **Move the magnified area.** While you're zoomed in, you can use the directional buttons to move the magnified area. A reference box at lower right shows the relative position of the zoomed area to the full frame.
5. **Focus manually.** The enlarged area is artificially sharpened to make it easier for you to see the contrast changes, and simplify focusing. When zoomed in, press the shutter release halfway and the current shutter speed and aperture are shown in orange. If no information at all appears, press the INFO. button.
6. **Use the focus ring on the lens to focus the image.** When you're satisfied, use Magnify button to cycle back.

Using Simulated Exposure

If you've activated Exposure Simulation, the LCD won't maintain a constant brightness level under varying ambient lighting conditions but will instead brighten or dim to emulate the correct exposure or over/underexposure you'll get with the current settings.

Enabling this feature also activates the histogram, which you can use to judge exposure (as explained in Chapter 4). If the histogram is not visible on the live view screen, press the INFO. button until it appears. The histogram may not display properly under very low or very high light levels, and is not available at all when you're using flash or exposures with the Bulb setting.

Basic Movie Making

The Canon EOS 7D II can shoot full HDTV movies with monaural sound (or stereo sound if you plug in an external microphone) at 1920 x 1080 resolution, or Standard HD video at 1280 x 720 resolution. VGA movies can also be shot at 640 x 480 resolution.

In some ways, the camera's movie mode is closely related to the 7D II's live view still mode. In fact, the 7D II uses live view type imaging to show you the video clip on the LCD as it is captured. Many of the functions and setting options are the same, so the information in the previous chapter will serve you well as you branch out into shooting movies with your camera.

Note: Keep in mind that in Movie mode, pressing the shutter release takes a still picture. To begin or halt movie capture, press the Start/Stop button. This differs from the procedure in live view/stills mode, in which the shutter release also takes a still picture, but the Start/Stop button activates/deactivates live view.

Before you begin capturing video, you'll want to make certain basic setup adjustments. This section will show you everything you need to know before you begin capturing video in earnest. We'll start with the two Shooting menu movie screens that become visible when the live view selector switch is rotated left to the Movie camera icon. In that mode, two new menus appear, the Shooting 4 (Movie) and Shooting 5 (Movie) menus.

Shooting 4 and 5 (Movie) Menus

Here is an introduction to the options available in the Shooting 4 and 5 (Movie) menus (see **Figure 13.3**.) Some of these have counterparts for still shooting and were explained earlier. Others are new, and I'll explain them in more detail later in this chapter. Within the Shooting (Movie) menus you'll find:

Movie Servo AF. You can enable or disable this feature, which enables the 7D to focus on the subject continuously – even if the shutter button is not held down halfway. It's a battery hog, and the constant refocusing may be undesirable if the noise is picked up by the camera's built-in microphone. To temporarily disable movie servo AF, press the Flash button, or a button you have defined with for movie servo disable using Custom Controls in the Custom Function 3 menu. After resuming movie shooting and pressing the Menu or Playback button, or changing the AF method (described next) Movie Servo AF will resume automatically. If you've disabled Movie Servo, press the shutter button or AF-ON button halfway to initiate autofocus.

- ⊚ **AF Method.** These are the same AF modes available in live view, as described earlier in this chapter.

- ⊚ **Grid Display.** The same feature described earlier under live view.

- ⊚ **Movie Recording Quality.** Choose either 1920 x 1080 (full HD) or 1280 x 720 pixels (standard HD). You can also select VGA resolution, compression method, and other parameters. I'll explain these options later in the chapter so you'll understand the sometimes-bewildering array of choices.

- ⊚ **Sound Recording.** Choose Auto, Manual, or Disable; plus enable or disable wind filter.
  - • **Auto.** The 7D II sets the audio level for you.
  - • **Manual.** Choose from 64 different sound levels. Select Rec Level and rotate the QCD while viewing the decibel meter at the bottom of the screen to choose a level that averages -12 dB for the loudest sounds.
  - • **Disable.** Shoot silently, and add voice over, narration, music, or other sound later in your movie-editing software.

You can use your 7D II's built-in microphone or plug in a stereo microphone into the 3.5mm jack on the side of the camera. An external microphone is a good idea because the built-in microphone can easily pick up camera operation, such as the autofocus motor in a lens.

- ⊚ **Wind filter.** Enable to reduce the effects of wind noise on the microphone. This also reduces low tones in the sound recording. If wind is not a problem, you'll get better quality audio with this option disabled. Even better is to use an external microphone with a wind shield.

- **Movie Servo AF speed.** This entry is available only when using FlexiZone – Single and Movie Servo AF (above) is enabled. You can choose when Movie Servo AF is active (either *always* on or *only* during shooting (which preserves battery power.) Specifying an AF Speed, from standard (0) to Slow (4.) Some lenses, such as those with STM motors, support slow focus transitions for smoother refocusing during a shot.

- **Movie Servo AF Track Sensitivity.** Allows adjusting the 7D II's tracking sensitivity from one of five levels, from Locked On to Responsive. Use this setting to tell the camera whether it should immediately track a new subject or remain on the original subject. I explain when and how to use tracking sensitivity in Chapter 5.

- **Silent LV Shooting.** Reduces the noise level, using either of two modes. Mode 1 produces a quieter shooting sound level in live view mode, and enables continuous shooting at up to 6 fps. Mode 2 separates the *ker* from the *clunk* sounds. Press the shutter release all the way, and the camera emits a small click as the picture is taken. When you release the button at least halfway, a discreet second click is heard. The camera ignores this setting if you're using a remote control, and defaults to Mode 1. Disable turns off silent shooting.

- **Metering Timer.** Specify how long the metering system remains active before switching off. You can select 4, 16, or 30 seconds, plus 1, 10, or 30 minutes. Tap the shutter release to restart the timer.

- **Time code.** Time codes are "markers" in the video stream that you can use to keep track of various positions during the editing process.

- **Silent control.** When enabled, allows you to use the directional buttons of the QCD, rather than the QCD itself, to navigate the Quick Control screen and change settings for ISO speed, sound-recording level, and other parameters (almost) silently during movie capture.

- **Shutter button function.** Allows you to specify the behaviors of the shutter button during movie shooting (see **Table 13.1.**)
- **HDMI output + LCD.** Ordinarily, when you send the video output of your 7D II to an external recording device, the camera's own LCD monitor shuts off. That No Mirroring option in this menu entry is enabled by default. If you want a simultaneous display on the camera's LCD, select Mirroring. The 7D II's LCD will show an information overlay, and the HDMI output will not. Press the INFO. button to show/hide the information overlay.

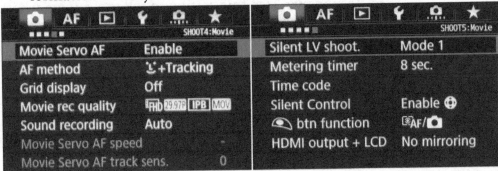

Figure 13.3

The Shooting 4 and 5 menus.

Table 13.1

Setting	Shutter Pressed Halfway	Shutter Pressed Completely
Metering/AF/Camera Icon	Metering and AF	Still photo taken
Metering/Camera Icon	Metering Only	Still photo taken
Metering/AF/Movie Camera Icon	Metering and AF	Starts/Stops Movie Capture
Metering/Movie Camera Icon	Metering Only	Starts/Stops Movie Capture

Exposure Options

When shooting movies, you can select fully automatic exposure, elect to specify exposure manually, or choose a shutter speed or aperture setting that you prefer for creative reasons. The 7D II will select an ISO speed for you automatically in all cases, generally sticking to the range ISO 100-12800. (Some oddball exceptions are applied for various combinations of exposure mode and ISO speed settings made in the Shooting 2 menu.) Exposure can be locked with the * button, and cancelled with the AF point selection button located to the right of the * button. Here are your options:

⊚ **Fully automatic exposure.** The 7D II will automatically select an appropriate exposure for you if the Mode Dial is set to Scene Intelligent Auto, P (program auto exposure), or B (bulb exposure). Note that B will not produce a bulb or time exposure; the camera defaults to P when you use the B position. The idea is to prevent you from losing video capture capabilities if you accidentally select B by mistake.

⊚ **Shutter-priority AE.** You can choose Tv on the Mode Dial, exactly as you do when shooting still photographs, and specify a shutter speed, with some limitations. The 7D II will select an appropriate aperture for you. The available shutter speeds will depend on the frame rate, primarily because you can't (logically) choose a shutter speed that is longer than the length of time needed to expose an individual frame. For example, at 30/25/24 fps, you cannot use a shutter speed longer than 1/30th second. At 60/50 fps, the longest shutter

505

speed available is 1/60th second. In all cases, shutter speeds *shorter* than 1/4000th second (1/8000th) are unavailable.

Choosing the shutter speed yourself offers two advantages. Even though each frame is captured in about 1/60th-1/30th second, slicing up the time the sensor is exposed to light allows capturing video in a much broader range of lighting conditions. Outdoors in full daylight, 1/30th second would produce an overexposure even with a very small f/stop and an ISO 100 sensitivity setting. In addition, opting for a higher shutter speed allows you to freeze action within each individual frame, reducing or eliminating blur. You might want to use 1/500th second when shooting movies of sports, or stick to 1/30th second when you want to include a little motion blur in your video for effect.

- ◉ **Aperture-priority AE.** Select Av on the Mode Dial, and you can choose an f/stop that will allow you to maximize or minimize depth-of-field, at your option, for creative effects. There is no limitation on your f/stop selection. However, you should avoid switching to a different aperture while actually capturing video, as the sudden change can provide a jarring effect.

- ◉ **Manual exposure.** Choose M on the Mode Dial and you can specify ISO speed, shutter speed, and aperture.
  - **ISO.** Press the ISO/Flash Exposure Compensation button on top of the camera to view the ISO speed setting screen. Adjust with the Main Dial. Choose Auto and the camera will select an appropriate ISO based on the shutter speed and aperture you have selected. During Manual exposure, the * button locks ISO at its current setting if you have selected Auto.
  - **Shutter speed.** Use the Main Dial to select a shutter speed, within the limitations described under Shutter-priority AE earlier.
  - **Aperture.** Use the Quick Control Dial to adjust aperture.

When choosing shutter speed or aperture, you can monitor exposure using the exposure level scale at the bottom of the LCD screen. For an additional check, you can press the INFO. button to view a live histogram.

Other Considerations

There are some additional things you need to keep in mind before you start, including exposure:

- ⊙ **You can still shoot stills.** Press the shutter release all the way down at any time while filming movies in order to capture a still photo. Movie capture will stop for about one second while a still image is captured, leaving a gap in your clip, but will resume automatically after the picture is taken. The 7D II will use the Image Quality settings you specify in the Shooting 1 menu, and will operate only in Single shooting drive mode (continuous shooting or Self-timer delays are not possible). The flash is disabled. You can also extract a 2MP, 1MP, or .3MP image from your movie clips using Zoom-Browser. Still photos are stored as separate files.

- ⊙ **Use the right card.** You'll want to use a fast memory card, preferably one with a large enough capacity to hold all the video you plan to capture. With IPB, you'll need a CF card capability of 10MB/sec or faster write speeds, and an SD card with 6MB/second write speed. For ALL-I, the recommendations jump to 30MB/sec for CF cards and 20MB/sec for SD cards. Check with your card's manufacturer to determine their nominal write speed.

- ⊙ **Final Image Simulation Preview.** Using Final Image Simulation allows you view the effects of your Picture Style, White Balance, Exposure, and other settings while you capture video.

- ⊙ **Use a fully charged battery.** Canon says that a fresh battery will allow about 90 minutes of filming at normal (non-Winter) temperatures, and around 80 minutes at temperatures of 32 degrees F.

- ⊙ **Image stabilizer uses extra power.** If your lens has an image stabilizer, it will operate at all times (not just when the shutter button is pressed halfway, which is the case with still photography) and use a considerable amount of power, reducing battery life. You can switch the IS feature off to conserve power. Mount your camera on a tripod, and you don't need IS anyway.

◎ **Silent running.** You can connect your 7D II to a television or video monitor while shooting movies, and see the video portion on the bigger screen as you shoot. However, the sound will not play -- that's a good idea, because, otherwise, you could likely get a feedback loop of sound going. The sound will be recorded properly and will magically appear during playback once shooting has concluded.

Compression, Resolution, and Frame Rates

Even intermediate movie shooters can be confused by the number of different choices for compression, resolution, and frame rates. This section will help clarify things for you.

Compression

Compression is easiest to understand, so I'll get it out of the way first. The 7D II stores files using the standard H.264/MPEG-4 codec ("coder-decoder"), but for all resolution settings except 640 x 480, you can select either ALL-I or IPB compression methods.

◎ **ALL-I (All Intraframe).** In this mode, the camera takes each individual frame that you shoot and attempts to compress it before writing the frame to your memory card. You can think of All-I compression as a series of still images, each squeezed down by discarding (hopefully) redundant information. While this compression method is not the most efficient way to reduce file size, because individual frames are stored in their entirety, the resulting files are easier to edit.

◎ **IPB (I-frame/P-frame/B-frame) Standard and Light.** This is a newer compression method that uses *interframe* compression; that is, only certain "key" frames are saved, with other frames "simulated" or interpolated from information contained in the frames that precede and succeed them. I-frames are the complete or *intraframes* (the only kind used by All-I compression); P-frames are "predicted picture" frames, which record *only the pixel changes* from the previous frame (say, a runner traveling across a fixed background); B-frames are "bi-predictive picture" frames, created by using the differences from the preceding *and* following frames. This interpolation produces image quality that is a bit lower and which requires more of your camera's DIGIC+ processing power, but file sizes are smaller.

- Video encoded using IPB must be converted, or transcoded to a format compatible with your video-editing software. The compression scheme can produce more artifacts, particularly in frames with lots of motion throughout the frame. I use this method only when the ability to shoot longer is very important.

- The 7D II offers both the Standard version, which compresses multiple frames simultaneously for greater efficiency and smaller file sizes; and a Light version available when the movie recording format is set to MP4. The latter uses a slower bit transfer rate, producing a smaller file size and greater compatibility with more playback systems.

"CLEAN" HDMI OUTPUT

Those who are more heavily involved with video will appreciate the 7D II's ability to provide 8-bit 4:2:2 output from the HDMI port. Previous Canon cameras that output a clean HDMI signal, used a 4:2:0 signal. Whilst the 7D Mk II is still recording a 4:2:0 VBR signal internally, 4:2:2 is available from an HDMI connection and can be recorded simultaneously to the internal card as well.

The video is directed through the HDMI port with embedded time code (more on time code later in this chapter) to an external monitor or recorder. You can simultaneously display the video on the color LCD as it is recorded to your memory card. You can choose whether to display the captured image and scene and camera shooting information on the LCD as you shoot. This capability allows professional videographers (or other advanced shooters) more latitude in color correction though the enhanced color space, improved monitoring during the shoot, and more versatile post-production workflow. You can, for example, synchronize the 7D II's video capture with the start/stop of the external video recorder.

In normal output mode, you can record up to 16 minutes at 235MB/minute using IPB compression before the 7D II reaches its 4GB per file limit (more on that shortly). In contrast, the larger ALL-I files will reach the 4GB limit in about five minutes at 685MB/minute. So, if you really need to capture a continuous shot in one file (say, a performance) you might want to use IPB.

The 4GB limitation is not as noxious as you might think, and you can continue capture without, in practice, an interruption. Roughly 30 seconds before the 4GB file size is reached, the elapsed shooting time/time code displayed on the LCD will begin blinking. If you continue past 4GB, a new movie file will be created automatically. This process continues until you've reached the maximum shooting time of 29 minutes, 59 seconds (established because some jurisdictions classify equipment that can capture more than 30 minutes as "camcorders" at higher tax rates). You can patch two or more clips together in editing. Note that the 7D II will not switch to your second memory card during capture even if Auto Switch Card is activated.

Resolution/Movie Recording Size

Resolution choices are a little less techie:

⊙ **1920 x 1080 (1080p).** This resolution is so-called "full HD" and is the maximum resolution displayed when using the HDTV format. Many monitors and most HD televisions can display this resolution, and you'll have the best image quality when you use it. Use this resolution for your "professional" productions, especially those you'll be editing and converting to nifty-looking DVDs. However, the top-of-the line resolution requires the most storage space, approximately 225 to

654 megabytes per minute. This means you can fit a collection of individual clips amounting to no more than about 22 minutes of recording (using ALL-I compression), or 1 hour 7 minutes (using IPB Standard) on a single 16GB memory card.

⊙ **1280 x 720.** "Standard HD" provides less resolution, and can be displayed on any monitor or television that claims HDTV compatibility. If your production will appear only on computer monitors with 1280 x 720 resolution, or on HDTVs that max out at 720p, this resolution will be fine. Don't choose this resolution in order to stretch your memory cards; it uses a 60/50 fps capture rate that streams an amount of data similar to that of 1080p shooting, so the elapsed time of your clips on a single card will be roughly the same.

⊙ **640 x 480.** This is so-called VGA resolution, suitable for display on computer monitors and, possibly, old standard definition televisions. (Remember the ones with CRT tubes instead of LCD, LED, or plasma displays?) This lower-resolution format is less demanding of your storage, too, requiring about 78 megabytes per minute capture, and providing more than three hours of individual video clips on a single 16GB card. (While you could shoot 48 minutes continuously at this rate before the 4GB ceiling is reached, you're still limited to 29 minutes 59 seconds.) Use this resolution for productions destined for display on the internet, and other similar uses.

MOV or MP4 Formats

You can select whether your output is in .MOV or .MP4 formats. MOV was developed by Apple as a format for its QuickTime movie player, and formed the basis for the development of the more recent MP4 format, which is now an industry standard. Both use lossy video compression (to save space, and can be smoothly translated from one to the other as long as the same codec (video encoder, such as H.264) was used for both. If your video is intended for Mac devices, MOV is fine, but for non-Apple devices, MP4 should be your choice.

Frame Rate

In the 7D II world, in which all video is shot using *progressive scan* with no *interlaced scan* option, frame rates are easy to choose. (Interlacing is a capture method in which even/odd numbered lines of each frame are captured alternately; with progressive scan, all the lines in a frame are captured consecutively.) Fortunately, one seemingly confusing set of alternatives can be dispensed with quickly: The 50/25 fps and 60/30 fps options can be considered as pairs of *video* oriented frame rates. The 60/30 fps rates are used only where the NTSC television standard is in place, such as North America, Japan, Korea, Mexico, and a few other places. The 50/25 frame rates are used where the PAL standard reigns, such as Europe, Russia, China, Africa, Australia, and other places. For simplicity, I'll refer just to the 60/30 frame rates in this section; if you're reading this in India, just convert to 50/25.

The third possibility is 24 fps, which is a standard frame rate used for motion pictures. Keep in mind that the rates are *nominal*. A 24 fps setting actually yields 23.976 frames per second; 30 fps gives you 29.97 actual "frames" per second.

The difference lies in the two "worlds" of motion images, film, and video. The standard frame rate for motion picture film is 24 fps, while the video rate, at least in the United States, Japan, and those other places using the NTSC standard, is 30 fps. Computer-editing software can handle either type, and convert between them. The choice between 24 fps and 30 fps is determined by what you plan to do with your video.

The short explanation is that shooting at 24 fps gives your movie a "film" look, excellent for showing fine detail. However, if your clip has moving subjects, or you pan the camera, 24 fps can produce a jerky effect called "judder." A 30 or 60 fps rate produces a home-video look that some feel is less desirable, but which is smoother and less jittery when displayed on an electronic monitor. I suggest you try both and use the frame rate that best suits your tastes and video-editing software.

You can enable/disable 24:00p recording using the entry at the bottom of the Movie Recording Quality screen.

Time Code

Advanced video shooters find SMPTE (Society of Motion Picture and Television Engineers)-compatible time codes embedded in the video files to be an invaluable reference during editing. To oversimplify a bit, the time system provides precise *hour:minute:second:frame* markers that allow identifying and synchronizing frames and audio. The time code system includes a provision for "dropping" frames to ensure that the fractional frame rate of captured video (remember that a 24 fps setting actually yields 23.976 frames per second while 30 fps capture gives you 29.97 actual "frames" per second) can be matched up with actual time spans.

As I noted in the introductions to this book and this Part, I won't be covering the most technical aspects of movie shooting (including time codes, raw HDMI streaming, etc.). If you're at the stage where you're using time codes, you don't need a primer, anyway. However, the Time Code submenu does include five options:

- ◉ **Count up.** Choose Rec Run, in which the time code counts up only when you are actually capturing video; or Free Run (also known as Time of Day), which allows the time code to run up even between shooting clips. The latter is useful when you want to synchronize clips between multiple cameras that are shooting the same event. When using Free Run, even if the cameras record at different times, you'll be able to match the video that was captured at the exact same moment during editing.

- ◉ **Start Time Setting.** Normally, the 7D II uses the camera's internal clock to specify the hours:minutes:seconds, with frames set to :00 when you begin shooting. This entry allows you to manually enter any hour:minute:second:frame of your choice, or to Reset the start time to 00:00:00:00.

- ◉ **Movie Rec. Count.** Here you can decide whether to display the elapsed time for the current clip on the LCD, or the Time Code while capturing video.

- **Movie Play Count.** This gives you the same choices during playback, allowing you to choose elapsed time or Time Code.
- **HDMI.** Here you can turn Time code embedding on or off for HDMI output.
- **Drop Frame.** As I mentioned, the 30 fps setting yields 29.97 actual frames per second, and 60 fps gives you 59.95 frames per second, causing a discrepancy between the actual time and the time code that's recorded. Choose enable and the camera will skip some time code numbers at intervals to eliminate the discrepancy. When disabled, you may notice a difference of several seconds per hour.

Silent Control

As you become more proficient at movie shooting, you'll find you're comfortable adjusting settings *during* actual capture. The Silent Control feature allows you to make these changes efficiently and, more important, in a quiet way that doesn't intrude on the shooting. Just follow these steps to work with this handy capability.

1. **Activate feature.** Choose Enable from the Shooting 5 (Movie) menu.
2. **Begin capture.** Press the Start/Stop button to begin video capture.
3. **Access adjustment screen.** Press the Q button to produce an overlay.
4. **Select parameter.** Tap the upper or lower edges of the QCD to cycle among the available settings you can adjust in P/B, Tv, Av, or M exposure modes. The selected setting will be highlighted in blue.
   - In Tv and M modes, you can adjust shutter speed.
   - In Av and M modes, you can adjust aperture.
   - In all modes except M, you can select exposure compensation.
   - The sound recording level can be adjusted in all modes.

5. **Make adjustment.** Tap the left/right surface of the inner ring to make the actual adjustment.

Playback and Editing

As a movie is being played back, a screen of options appears at the bottom of the screen, as shown in **Figure 13.3**. When the icons are shown, use the left/right cross keys to highlight one, and then press the SET button to activate that function:

- ⊚ **Exit.** Exits playback mode.
- ⊚ **Playback.** Begins playback of the movie or album. To pause playback, press the SET button again. That restores the row of icons so you can choose a function.
- ⊚ **Slow motion.** Displays the video in slow motion.
- ⊚ **First frame.** Jumps to the first frame of the video, or the first scene of an album's first video snapshot.
- ⊚ **Previous frame.** Press SET to view previous frame; hold down SET to rewind movie.
- ⊚ **Next frame.** Press SET to view next frame; hold down SET to fast forward movie.
- ⊚ **Last frame.** Jumps to last frame of the video, or the last scene of the album's last video snapshot.
- ⊚ **Edit.** Summons an editing screen (see **Figure 13.4**).
- ⊚ **Background music/volume.** Select to turn background music on/off. Rotate the main dial to adjust the volume of the background music.

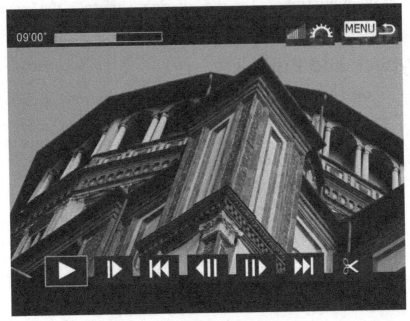

Figure 13.4

Options appear as a movie is being played back.

Figure 13.5

The editing screen allows you to snip off the beginning or end of a video clip.

While reviewing your video, you can trim from the beginning or end of your video clip by selecting the scissors symbol. The icons that appear have the following functions:

- ⊙ **Cut beginning.** Trims off all video prior to the current point.
- ⊙ **Cut end.** Removes video after the current point.
- ⊙ **Play video.** Play back your video to reach the point where you want to trim the beginning or end.
- ⊙ **Save.** Saves your video to the memory card. A screen appears offering to save the clip as a New File, or to Overwrite the existing movie with your edited clip.
- ⊙ **Exit.** Exits editing mode.
- ⊙ **Adjust volume.** Modifies the volume of the background music.

Tips for Shooting Better Video

Producing good-quality video is more complicated than just buying good equipment. There are techniques that make for gripping storytelling and a visual language the average person is very used to, but also pretty unaware of. After all, by comparison we're used to watching the best productions that television, video, and motion pictures can offer. Whether it's fair or not, our efforts are compared to what we're used to seeing produced by experts. While this book can't make you a professional videographer, there is some advice I can give you that will help you improve your results with the camera. There are a number of different things to consider when planning a video shoot, and when possible, a shooting script and storyboard can help you produce a higher quality video.

Lens Craft

I covered the use of lenses with the 7D II in more detail in <u>Chapter 7</u>, but a discussion of lens selection when shooting movies may be useful at this point. In the video world, not all lenses are created equal. The two most important considerations are depth-of-field, or the beneficial lack thereof, and zooming. I'll address each of these separately.

Depth-of-Field and Video

Have you wondered why professional videographers have gone nuts over still cameras that can also shoot video? As I've mentioned, the producers of *Saturday Night Live* could afford to have Alex Buono, their director of photography, use the niftiest, most expensive high-resolution video cameras to shoot the opening sequences of the program. Instead, Buono opted for a pair of digital SLR cameras. One thing that makes digital still cameras so attractive for video is that they have relatively large sensors, which provides improved low-light performance and results in the oddly attractive reduced depth-of-field, compared with most professional video cameras.

But wait! you say. No matter what size sensor is used to capture a full HD video frame, isn't the number of pixels in that video frame exactly the same -- 1920 x 1080 pixels? That's true -- the final resolution of the video image is precisely 1920 x 1080 pixels, whether you're capturing that frame with a point-and-shoot camera, a professional video camera, or a full-frame digital SLR like the Canon 7D II. But that's only the *final* resolution. The number of pixels used to capture each video frame varies by sensor size.

For example, your 7D II does *not* use only its central 1920 x 1080 pixels to capture a full HD video frame. If it did that, you'd have to contend with a 3.8X "crop" factor, and the field of view of, say, a 24mm wide angle would be the equivalent of a 90mm telephoto. That doesn't happen! (See Chapter 7 for a longer discussion of the effects of the so-called "crop" factor.) Instead, the 7D II captures a video frame using the proportions of a 16:9 area of its sensor, producing a negligible crop factor. Your wide-angle and telephoto lenses retain roughly their same fields of view, and you can frame and compose your video through the viewfinder normally, with only the top and bottom of the frame and a little off each side cropped off to account for the wider video aspect ratio. The roughly 15.5 million pixels used to capture the image are processed to create the 2,073,600 pixels of the final video frame. That's why the 7D II gives you such great video quality, and why your video images retain roughly the same field of view and exact same depth-of-field you get with full-frame still images.

Figure 13.6 provides a comparison of the relative size of sensors. It's a simplified view, and doesn't show the precise video capture area of any of the example sensors; I've placed black lines at the top and bottom of the full frame and APS-C sensors (using the 5D Mark III and 7D II) to show the approximate cropping used. The typical size of a professional video camera sensor is shown at lower left. The sensor the typical APS-C-sized sensor to the right of that. In comparison, the 7D II's FX image-grabber is *much* larger when compared with the sensors used in many pro video cameras and the even smaller sensors found in the typical consumer camcorder.

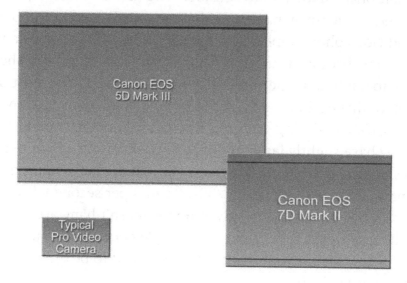

Figure 13.6

Sensor size comparison.

As I noted in Chapter 7, a larger sensor calls for the use of longer focal lengths to produce the same field of view, so, in effect, a larger sensor has reduced depth-of-field. And *that's* what makes cameras like the 7D II attractive from a creative standpoint. Less depth-of-field means greater control over the range of what's in focus. Your 7D II, with its larger sensor, has a distinct advantage over consumer camcorders in this regard, and even does a better job than many professional video cameras. With a really fast lens, such as the

Canon 85mm f/1.2 or 50mm f/1.2, some sensational selective focus effects can be achieved.

Zooming and Video

When shooting still photos, a zoom is a zoom is a zoom. The key considerations for a zoom lens used only for still photography are the maximum aperture available at each focal length ("How *fast* is this lens?), the zoom range ("How far can I zoom in or out?"), and its sharpness at any given f/stop ("Do I lose sharpness when I shoot wide open?").

When shooting video, the priorities may change, and there are two additional parameters to consider. The first two I listed, lens speed and zoom range, have roughly the same importance in both still and video photography. Zoom range gains a bit of importance in videography, because you can always/usually move closer to shoot a still photograph, but when you're zooming during a shot most of us don't have that option (or the funds to buy/rent a dolly to smoothly move the camera during capture). But, oddly enough, overall sharpness may have slightly less importance under certain conditions when shooting video. That's because the image changes in some way many times per second (24/30/60 times per second with the 7D II in NTSC mode), so any given frame doesn't hang around long enough for our eyes to pick out every single detail. You want a sharp image, of course, but your standards don't need to be quite as high when shooting video.

Here are the remaining considerations:

○ **Zoom lens maximum aperture.** The speed of the lens matters in several ways. A zoom with a relatively large maximum aperture lets you shoot in lower light levels, and a big f/stop allows you to minimize depth-of-field for selective focus. Keep in mind that the maximum aperture may change during zooming. A lens that offers an f/3.5 maximum aperture at its widest focal length may provide only f/5.6 worth of light at the telephoto position. If shooting wide open you may want to retain the same maximum aperture regardless of focal length, so depth-of-field (and, along with it, focus) will increase or decrease more predictably from shot to shot, because the *focal length* has changed (that is, going from wide-angle to tele, or the reverse), and not because the *effective aperture* has changed, too.

In that case, you'll want to use a *constant aperture* lens (sometimes called a *fixed aperture* lens, which can be interpreted two ways). Often, such lenses are Canon L lenses; with less expensive optics with a similar focal length range having a variable maximum aperture. A typical example is the EF 24-105mm f/4L IS USM zoom and EF 28-135 f/3.5-5.6 IS USM. The L lens's maximum aperture is f/4 from 24mm right up to 105mm, while its half-price cousin varies from f/3.5 at 28mm to f/5.6 at the 135mm setting.

- ◎ **Zoom range.** Use of zoom during actual capture should not be an everyday thing, unless you're shooting a kung-fu movie. However, there are effective uses for a zoom shot, particularly if it's a "long" one from extreme wide angle to extreme close-up (or vice versa). Most of the time, you'll use the zoom range to adjust the perspective of the camera *between* shots, and a longer zoom range can mean less trotting back and forth to adjust the field of view. Zoom range also comes into play when you're working with selective focus (longer focal lengths have less depth-of-field), or want to expand or compress the apparent distance between foreground and background subjects. A longer range gives you more flexibility.

- ◎ **Linearity.** Interchangeable lenses may have some drawbacks, as many photographers who have been using the video features of their digital SLRs have discovered. That's because, unless a lens is optimized for video shooting, zooming with a particular lens may not necessarily be linear. Rotating the zoom collar manually at a constant speed doesn't always produce a smooth zoom. There may be "jumps" as the elements of the lens shift around during the zoom. Keep that in mind if you plan to zoom during a shot, and are using a lens that has proved, from experience, to provide a non-linear zoom. (Unfortunately, there's no easy way to tell ahead of time whether you own a lens that is well-suited for zooming during a shot.)

Keep Things Stable and on the Level

Camera shake's enough of a problem with still photography, but it becomes even more of a nuisance when you're shooting video. The image-stabilization feature found in many Canon lenses (and some third-party optics) can help minimize this. Any of them make an excellent choice for video shooting if you're planning on going for the hand-held cinema verité look.

Just realize that while hand-held camera shots -- even image stabilized -- may be perfect if you're shooting a documentary or video that intentionally mimics traditional home movie making, in other contexts it can be disconcerting or annoying. And even IS can't work miracles. As I'll point out in the next section, it's the camera movement itself that is distracting -- not necessarily any blur in our subject matter.

If you want your video to look professional, putting the 7D II on a tripod will give you smoother, steadier video clips to work with. It will be easier to intercut shots taken from different angles (or even at different times) if everything was shot on a tripod. Cutting from a tripod shot to a hand-held shot, or even from one hand-held shot to another one that has noticeably more (or less) camera movement can call attention to what otherwise might have been a smooth cut or transition.

Remember that telephoto lenses and telephoto zoom focal lengths magnify any camera shake, even with IS, so when you're using a longer focal length, that tripod becomes an even better idea. Tripods are essential if you want to pan from side to side during a shot, dolly in and out, or track from side to side (say, you want to shoot with the camera in your kid's coaster wagon). A tripod and (for panning) a fluid head built especially for smooth video movements can add a lot of production value to your movies.

Shooting Script

A shooting script is nothing more than a coordinated plan that covers both audio and video and provides order and structure for your video when you're in planned, storytelling mode. A detailed script will cover what types of shots you're going after, what dialogue you're going to use, audio effects, transitions, and graphics. A good script needn't constrain you: as the director you are free to make changes on the spot during actual capture. But, before you change the route to your final destination, it's good to know where you were headed, and how you originally planned to get there.

When putting together your shooting script, plan for lots and lots of different shots, even if you don't think you'll need them. Only amateurish videos consist of a bunch of long, tedious shots. You'll want to vary the pace of your production by cutting among lots of different views, angles, and perspectives, so jot down your ideas for these variations when you put together your script.

If you're shooting a documentary rather than telling a story that's already been completely mapped out, the idea of using a shooting script needs to be applied more flexibly. Documentary filmmakers often have no shooting script at all. They go out, do their interviews, capture video of people, places, and events as they find them, and allow the structure of the story to take shape as they learn more about the subject of their documentary. In such cases, the movie is typically "created" during editing, as bits and pieces are assembled into the finished piece.

Storyboards

A storyboard makes a great adjunct to a detailed shooting script. It is a series of panels providing visuals of what each scene should look like. While the ones produced by Hollywood are generally of very high quality, there's nothing that says drawing skills are important for this step. Stick figures work just fine if that's the best you can do. The storyboard just helps you visualize locations, placement of actors/actresses, props and furniture, and also helps everyone involved get an idea of what you're trying to show. It also helps show how you want to frame or compose a shot. You can even shoot a series of still photos and transform them into a "storyboard" if you want, such as in **Figure 13.7**.

Figure 13.7

A storyboard is a series of simple sketches or photos to help visualize a segment of video

Storytelling in Video

Today's audience is used to fast-paced, short-scene storytelling. In order to produce interesting video for such viewers, it's important to view video storytelling as a kind of shorthand code for the more leisurely efforts print media offers. Audio and video should always be advancing the story. While it's okay to let the camera linger from time to time, it should only be for a compelling reason and only briefly.

Above all, look for movement in your scene as you shoot. You're not taking still photographs! Perhaps your ideal still picture of an old castle in Segovia, Spain might be to show the edifice in its modern-day surroundings, but a movie needs to show something *moving*, like the hang glider that soared overhead when I captured the image shown in **Figure 13.8**. The juxtaposition of old and new added an interesting contrast to the video image (and later narration). If you've seen too many travel videos that looked like they could have been assembled from a series of still photos (a "slide show" so to speak), you'll know that motion is what brings many otherwise static scenes to life.

Figure 13.8
Movies need motion to come alive.

It only takes a second or two for an establishing shot to impart the necessary information. For example, many of the scenes for a video documenting a model being photographed in a Rock and Roll music setting might be close-ups and talking heads, but an establishing shot showing the studio where the video was captured helps set the scene.

Provide variety too. If you put your shooting script together correctly, you'll be changing camera angles and perspectives often and never leave a static scene on the screen for a long period of time. (You can record a static scene for a reasonably long period and then edit in other shots that cut away and back to the longer scene with close-ups that show each person talking.)

When editing, keep transitions basic! I can't stress this one enough. Watch a television program or movie. The action "jumps" from one scene or person to the next. Fancy transitions that involve exotic "wipes," dissolves, or cross fades take too long for the average viewer and make your video ponderous.

Composition

In movie shooting, several factors restrict your composition, and impose requirements you just don't always have in still photography (although other rules of good composition do apply). Here are some of the key differences to keep in mind when composing movie frames:

⊙ **Horizontal compositions only.** Some subjects, such as basketball players and tall buildings, just lend themselves to vertical compositions. But movies are shown in horizontal format only. So if you're interviewing a local basketball star, you can end up with a worst-case situation like the one shown in **Figure 13.9**. If you want to show how tall your subject is, it's often impractical to move back far enough to show him full-length. You really can't capture a vertical composition. Tricks like getting down on the floor and shooting up at your subject can exaggerate the perspective, but aren't a perfect solution.

⊙ **Wasted space at the sides.** Moving in to frame the basketball player as outlined by the yellow box in **Figure 13.9** means that you're still forced to leave a lot of empty space on either side. (Of course, you can fill that space with other people and/or interesting stuff, but that defeats your intent of concentrating on your main subject.) So when faced with some types of subjects in a horizontal frame, you can be creative, or move in *really* tight. For example, if I was willing to give up the "height" aspect of my composition, I could have framed the shot as shown by the green box in the figure, and wasted less of the image area at either side.

⊙ **Seamless (or seamed) transitions.** Unless you're telling a picture story with a photo essay, still pictures often stand alone. But with movies, each of your compositions must relate to the shot that preceded it, and the one that follows. It can be jarring to jump from a long shot to a tight close-up unless the director -- you -- is very creative. Another common error is the "jump cut" in which successive shots vary only slightly in camera angle, making it appear that the main subject has "jumped" from one place to another. (Although everyone from French New Wave director Jean-Luc Goddard to

Guy Ritchie -- Madonna's ex -- have used jump cuts effectively in their films.) The rule of thumb is to vary the camera angle by at least 30 degrees between shots to make it appear to be seamless. Unless you prefer that your images flaunt convention and appear to be "seamy."

- **The time dimension.** Unlike still photography, with motion pictures there's a lot more emphasis on using a series of images to build on each other to tell a story. Static shots where the camera is mounted on a tripod and everything is shot from the same distance are a recipe for dull videos. Watch a television program sometime and notice how often camera shots change distances and directions. Viewers are used to this variety and have come to expect it. Professional video productions are often done with multiple cameras shooting from different angles and positions. But many professional productions are shot with just one camera and careful planning, and you can do just fine with your 7D II.

Figure 13.9

Movie shooting requires you to fit all your subjects into a horizontally oriented frame.

Here's a look at the different types of commonly used compositional tools:

- **Establishing shot.** Much like it sounds, this type of composition, as shown in **Figure 13.10**, upper left, establishes the scene and tells the viewer where the action is taking place. Let's say you're shooting a video of your offspring's move to college; the establishing shot could be a wide shot of the campus with a sign welcoming you to the school in the foreground. Another example would be for a child's birthday party; the establishing shot could be the front of the house decorated with birthday signs and streamers or a shot of the dining room table decked out with party favors and a candle-covered birthday cake. Or, in **Figure 13.10**, upper right, I wanted to show the studio where the video was shot.

- **Medium shot.** This shot is composed from about waist to head room (some space above the subject's head). It's useful for providing variety from a series of close-ups and also makes for a useful first look at a speaker. (See Figure 13.10 upper left)

- **Close-up.** The close-up, usually described as "from shirt pocket to head room," provides a good composition for someone talking directly to the camera. Although it's common to have your talking head centered in the shot, that's not a requirement. In **Figure 13.10**, middle left, the subject was offset to the right. This would allow other images, especially graphics or titles, to be superimposed in the frame in a "real" (professional) production. But the compositional technique can be used with 7D II videos, too, even if special effects are not going to be added.

- **Extreme close-up.** When I went through broadcast training back in the '70s, this shot was described as the "big talking face" shot and we were actively discouraged from employing it. Styles and tastes change over the years and now the big talking face is much more commonly used (maybe people are better looking these days?) and so this view may be appropriate. Just remember, the 7D II is capable of shooting in high-definition video and you may be playing the video on a high-def TV; be careful that you use this composition on a face that can stand up to high definition. (See **Figure 13.10**, middle right.)

- **"Two" shot.** A two shot shows a pair of subjects in one frame. They can be side by side or one in the foreground and one in the background. (See **Figure 13.10**, middle left.) This does not have to be a head to ground composition. Subjects can be standing or seated. A "three shot" is the same principle except that three people are in the frame.

- **Over-the-shoulder shot.** Long a composition of interview programs, the "Over-the-shoulder shot" uses the rear of one person's head and shoulder to serve as a frame for the other person. This puts the viewer's perspective as that of the person facing away from the camera. (See **Figure 13.10**, middle right.)

Figure 13.10

Establishing, medium, close-up, extreme close-up, two-shot, and over-the shoulder shots.

Lighting for Video

Much like in still photography, how you handle light pretty much can make or break your videography. Lighting for video can be more complicated than lighting for still photography, since both subject and camera movement are often part of the process.

Lighting for video presents several concerns. First off, you want enough illumination to create a useable video. Beyond that, you want to use light to help tell your story or increase drama. Let's take a better look at both.

Illumination

You can significantly improve the quality of your video by increasing the light falling in the scene. This is true indoors or out, by the way. While it may seem like sunlight is more than enough, it depends on how much contrast you're dealing with. If your subject is in shadow (which can help them from squinting) or wearing a ball cap, a video light can help make them look a lot better.

Lighting choices for amateur videographers are a lot better these days than they were a decade or two ago. An inexpensive incandescent video light, which will easily fit in a camera bag, can be found for $15 or $20. You can even get a good-quality LED video light for less than $100. Work lights sold at many home improvement stores can also serve as video lights since you can set the camera's white balance to correct for any color casts. You'll need to mount these lights on a tripod or other support, or, perhaps, to a bracket that fastens to the tripod socket on the bottom of the camera.

Much of the challenge depends upon whether you're just trying to add some fill-light on your subject versus trying to boost the light on an entire scene. A small video light will do just fine for the former. It won't handle the latter. Fortunately, the versatility of the 7D II comes in quite handy here. Since the camera shoots video in Auto ISO mode, it can compensate for lower lighting levels and still produce a decent image. For best results though, better lighting is necessary.

Creative Lighting

While ramping up the light intensity will produce better technical quality in your video, it won't necessarily improve the artistic quality of it. Whether we're outdoors or indoors, we're used to seeing light come from above. Videographers need to consider how they position their lights to provide even illumination while up high enough to angle shadows down low and out of sight of the camera.

When considering lighting for video, there are several factors. One is the quality of the light. It can either be hard (direct) light or soft (diffused). Hard light is good for showing detail, but can also be very harsh and unforgiving. "Softening" the light, but diffusing it somehow, can reduce the intensity of the light but make for a kinder, gentler light as well.

While mixing light sources isn't always a good idea, one approach is to combine window light with supplemental lighting. Position your subject with the window to one side and bring in either a supplemental light or a reflector to the other side for reasonably even lighting.

Lighting Styles

Some lighting styles are more heavily used than others. Some forms are used for special effects, while others are designed to be invisible. At its most basic, lighting just illuminates the scene, but when used properly it can also create drama. Let's look at some types of lighting styles:

- **Three-point lighting.** This is a basic lighting setup for one person. A main light illuminates the strong side of a person's face, while a fill light lights up the other side. A third light is then positioned above and behind the subject to light the back of the head and shoulders.

- **Flat lighting.** Use this type of lighting to provide illumination and nothing more. It calls for a variety of lights and diffusers set to raise the light level in a space enough for good video reproduction, but not to create a particular mood or emphasize a particular scene or individual. With flat lighting, you're trying to create even lighting levels throughout the video space and minimize any shadows. Generally, the lights are placed up high and angled downward (or possibly pointed straight up to bounce off of a white ceiling).

◉ **"Ghoul lighting."** This is the style of lighting used for old horror movies. The idea is to position the light down low, pointed upward. It's such an unnatural style of lighting that it makes its targets seem weird and "ghoulish."

◉ **Outdoor lighting.** While shooting outdoors may seem easier because the sun provides more light, it also presents its own problems. As a general rule of thumb, keep the sun behind you when you're shooting video outdoors, except when shooting faces (anything from a medium shot and closer) since the viewer won't want to see a squinting subject. When shooting another human this way, put the sun behind her and use a video light to balance light levels between the foreground and background. If the sun is simply too bright, position the subject in the shade and use the video light for your main illumination. Using reflectors (white board panels or aluminum foil covered cardboard panels are cheap options) can also help balance light effectively.

Audio

When it comes to making a successful video, audio quality is one of those things that separates the professionals from the amateurs. We're used to watching top-quality productions on television and in the movies, yet the average person has no idea how much effort goes in to producing what seems to be "natural" sound. Much of the sound you hear in such productions is actually recorded on carefully controlled sound stages and "sweetened" with a variety of sound effects and other recordings of "natural" sound.

Tips for Better Audio

Since recording high-quality audio is such a challenge, it's a good idea to do everything possible to maximize recording quality. Here are some ideas for improving the quality of the audio your camera records:

- **Get the camera and its microphone close to the speaker.** The farther the microphone is from the audio source, the less effective it will be in picking up that sound. While having to position the camera and its built-in microphone closer to the subject affects your lens choices and lens perspective options, it will make the most of your audio source. Of course, if you're using a very wide-angle lens, getting too close to your subject can have unflattering results, so don't take this advice too far. It's important to think carefully about what sounds you want to capture. If you're shooting video of an acoustic combo that's not using a PA system, you'll want the microphone close to them, but not so close that, say, only the lead singer or instrumentalist is picked up, while the players at either side fade off into the background.

- **Use an external microphone.** You'll recall the description of the camera's external microphone port in Chapter 2. As noted, this port accepts a stereo mini-plug from a standard external microphone, allowing you to achieve considerably higher audio quality for your movies than is possible with the camera's built-in microphones (which are disabled when an external mic is plugged in). An external microphone reduces the amount of camera-induced noise that is picked up and recorded on your audio track. (The action of the lens as it focuses can be audible when the built-in microphones are active.)

- The external microphone port can provide plug-in power for microphones that can take their power from this sort of outlet rather than from a battery in the microphone. Canon provides optional compatible microphones such as the Canon BP-512 (around $140); you also may find suitable microphones from companies such as Shure and Audio-Technica. If you are on a quest for really superior audio quality, you can even obtain a portable mixer that can plug into this jack, such as the affordable Rolls MX124 (around $150) (www.rolls.com), letting you use multiple high-quality microphones (up to four) to record your soundtrack.

- An exciting option designed specifically for still cameras like the Canon 7D II is the Beachtek DXA-SLR PRO HDSLR Audio Adapter. It's more expensive, at around $450, but has even more professional sound options and clips right onto the bottom of your camera using the tripod mounting socket.

- One advantage that a sound mixing device like the DXA-SLR PRO offers over the stock 7D II is that it adds an improved headphone output jack to your camera, so you can monitor the sound being recorded (you can also listen to your soundtrack through the headphones during playback, which is *way* better than using the 7D II's built-in speaker). The adapter has two balanced XLR microphone inputs and can also accept line input (from another audio source), and provides cool features like AGC (automatic gain control), built-in limiting, and VU meters you can use to monitor sound input.

- **Hide the microphone.** Combine the first few tips by using an external mic, and getting it as close to your subject as possible. If you're capturing a single person, you can always use a lapel microphone (described in the next section). But if you want a single mic to capture sound from multiple sources, your best bet may be to hide it somewhere in the shot. Put it behind a vase, using duct tape to fasten the microphone, and fix the mic cable out of sight (if you're not using a wireless microphone).

- **Turn off any sound makers you can.** Little things like fans and air handling units aren't obvious to the human ear, but will be picked up by the microphone. Turn off any machinery or devices that you can plus make sure cell phones are set to silent mode. Also, do what you can to minimize sounds such as wind, radio, television, or people talking in the background.

- **Make sure to record some "natural" sound.** If you're shooting video at an event of some kind, make sure you get some background sound that you can add to your audio as desired in postproduction.

- **Consider recording audio separately.** Lip-syncing is probably beyond most of the people you're going to be shooting, but there's nothing that says you can't record narration separately and add it later. It's relatively easy if you learn how to use simple software video-editing programs like iMovie (for the Macintosh) or Windows Movie Maker (for Windows PCs). Any time the speaker is off-camera, you can work with separately recorded narration rather than recording the speaker on-camera. This can produce much cleaner sound.

External Microphones

The single most important thing you can do to improve your audio quality is to use an external microphone. The 7D II's internal stereo microphones mounted on the front of the camera will do a decent job, but have some significant drawbacks, partially spelled out in the previous section:

- **Camera noise.** There are plenty of noise sources emanating from the camera, including your own breathing and rustling around as the camera shifts in your hand. Manual zooming is bound to affect your sound, and your fingers will fall directly in front of the built-in mics as you change focal lengths. An external microphone isolates the sound recording from camera noise.

- **Distance.** Anytime your 7D II is located more than 6-8 feet from your subjects or sound source, the audio will suffer. An external unit allows you to place the mic right next to your subject.

- **Improved quality.** Obviously, Canon wasn't able to install a super-expensive, super high-quality microphone, even on a $3,000 dSLR. Not all owners of the 7D II would be willing to pay the premium, especially if they didn't plan to shoot much video themselves. An external microphone will almost always be of better quality.

- **Directionality.** The 7D II's internal microphone generally records only sounds directly in front of it. An external microphone can be either of the directional type or omnidirectional, depending on whether you want to "shotgun" your sound or record more ambient sound.

You can choose from several different types of microphones, each of which has its own advantages and disadvantages. If you're serious about movie making with your 7D II, you might want to own more than one. Common configurations include:

- **Shotgun microphones.** These can be mounted directly on your 7D II, although, if the mic uses an accessory shoe mount, you'll need the optional adapter to convert the camera's shoe to a standard hot shoe. I prefer to use a bracket, which further isolates the microphone from any camera noise. One thing to keep in mind is that while the shotgun mic will generally ignore any sound coming from *behind* it, it will pick up any sound it is pointed at, even *behind* your subject. You may be capturing video and audio of someone you're interviewing in a restaurant, and not realize you're picking up the lunchtime conversation of the diners seated in the table behind your subject. Outdoors, you may record your speaker, as well as the traffic on a busy street or freeway in the background.

- **Lapel microphones.** Also called *lavalieres*, these microphones attach to the subject's clothing and pick up their voice with the best quality. You'll need a long enough cord or a wireless mic (described later). These are especially good for video interviews, so whether you're producing a documentary or grilling relatives for a family history, you'll want one of these.

- **Hand-held microphones.** If you're capturing a singer crooning a tune, or want your subject to mimic famed faux newscaster Wally Ballou, a hand-held mic may be your best choice. They serve much the same purpose as a lapel microphone, and they're more intrusive -- but that may be the point. A hand-held microphone can make a great prop for your fake newscast! The speaker can talk right into the microphone, point it at another person, or use it to record ambient sound. If your narrator is not going to appear on-camera, one of these can be an inexpensive way to improve sound.

- **Wired and wireless external microphones.** This option is the most expensive, but you get a receiver and a transmitter (both battery-powered, so you'll need to make sure you have enough batteries). The transmitter is connected to the microphone, and the receiver is connected to your 7D II. In addition to being less klutzy and enabling you to avoid having wires on view in your scene, wireless mics let you record sounds that are physically located some distance from your camera. Of course, you need to keep in mind the range of your device, and be aware of possible signal interference from other electronic components in the vicinity.

WIND NOISE REDUCTION

Always use the wind screen provided with an external microphone to reduce the effect of noise produced by even light breezes blowing over the microphone. Many mics include a low-cut filter to further reduce wind noise. However, these can also affect other sounds. You can disable the low-cut filters for some units by changing a switch on the back from L-cut (low cutoff) to Flat.

Chapter 14

Troubleshooting and Prevention

One of the nice things about modern electronic cameras like the Canon EOS 7D II is that they have fewer mechanical moving parts to fail, so they are less likely to "wear out." No film transport mechanism, no wind lever or motor drive, and no complicated mechanical linkages from camera to lens to physically stop down the lens aperture. Instead, tiny, reliable motors are built into each lens (and you lose the use of *only* that lens should something fail), and one of the few major moving parts in the camera itself is a lightweight mirror (its small size one of the results of the 7D II's 1.6X crop factor) that flips up and down with each shot.

Of course, the camera also has a moving shutter that can fail, but the shutter is built rugged enough that you can probably expect it to last 100,000 shutter cycles or more. Unless you're shooting sports in continuous mode day in and day out, the shutter on your 7D II is likely to last as long as you expect to use the camera.

The only other things on the camera that move are switches, dials, buttons, the flip-up electronic flash, and the door that slides open to allow you to remove and insert the memory card. Unless you're extraordinarily clumsy or unlucky or give your built-in flash a good whack while it is in use, there's not a lot that can go wrong mechanically with your EOS 7D II.

On the other hand, one of the chief drawbacks of modern electronic cameras is that they are modern *electronic* cameras. Your 7D II is fully dependent on two different batteries. Without them, the camera can't be used. There are numerous other electrical and electronic connections in the camera (many connected to those mechanical switches and dials), and components like the color LCD that can potentially fail or suffer damage. The camera also relies on its "operating system," or *firmware*, which can be plagued by bugs that cause unexpected behavior. Luckily, electronic components are generally more reliable and trouble-free, especially when compared to their mechanical counterparts from the pre-electronic film camera days. (Film cameras of the last 10 to 20 years have had almost as many electronic features as digital cameras, but, believe it or not, there were whole generations of film cameras that had *no* electronics or batteries.)

Digital cameras have problems unique to their breed, too; the most troublesome being the need to clean the sensor of dust and grime periodically. This chapter will show you how to diagnose problems, fix some common ills, and, importantly, learn how to avoid them in the future.

Updating Your Firmware

As I said, the firmware in your EOS 7D II is the camera's operating system, which handles everything from menu display (including fonts, colors, and the actual entries themselves), what languages are available, and even support for specific devices and features. Upgrading the firmware to a new version makes it possible to add new features while fixing some of the bugs that sneak in.

Official Firmware

Official firmware for your 7D II is given a version number that you can view by turning the power on, pressing the MENU button, and navigating to Firmware Ver. x.x.x in the Set-up 4 menu. As I write this bonus chapter, the current version is still 1.0.5. The first number in the string represents the major release number, while the second and third represent less significant upgrades and minor tweaks, respectively. I haven't actually had to do a firmware update with either camera, but I've done it many times with my other Canon cameras so I am familiar with the procedure.

Firmware upgrades are used for both cameras and certain lenses, most frequently to fix bugs in the software, and much less frequently to add or enhance features. For example, previous firmware upgrades for Canon cameras have mended things like incorrect color temperature reporting when using specific Canon Speedlites, or problems communicating with memory cards under certain conditions. The exact changes made to the firmware are generally spelled out in the firmware release announcement. You can examine the remedies provided and decide if a given firmware patch is important to you. If not, you can usually safely wait a while before going through the bother of upgrading your firmware -- at least long enough for the early adopters to report whether the bug fixes have introduced new bugs of their own. Each new firmware release incorporates the changes from previous releases, so if you skip a minor upgrade you should have no problems.

Upgrading Your Firmware

If you're computer savvy, you might wonder how your EOS 7D II is able to overwrite its own operating system -- that is, how can the existing firmware be used to load the new version on top of itself? It's a little like lifting yourself by reaching down and pulling up on your bootstraps. Not ironically, that's almost exactly what happens: At your command (when you start the upgrade process), the 7D II shifts into a special mode in which it is no longer operating from its firmware but, rather, from a small piece of software called a *bootstrap loader*, a separate, protected software program that functions only at startup or when upgrading firmware. The loader's function is to look for firmware to launch or, when directed, to copy new firmware from a memory card or your computer to the internal memory space where the old firmware is located. Once the new firmware has replaced the old, you can turn your camera off and then on again, and the updated operating system will be loaded.

Because the loader software is small in size and limited in function, there are some restrictions on what it can do. For example, the loader software isn't set up to go hunting through your memory card for the firmware file. It looks only in the top or root directory of your card, so that's where you must copy the firmware you download. Once you've determined that a new firmware update is available for your camera and that you want to install it, just follow these steps. (If you chicken out, any Canon service center can install the firmware upgrade for you.)

WARNING: Use a fully charged battery or Canon's optional ACK-E6 AC adapter kit to ensure that you'll have enough power to operate the camera for the entire upgrade. Moreover, you should not turn off the camera while your old firmware is being overwritten. Don't open the memory card door or do anything else that might disrupt operation of the 7D II while the firmware is being installed.

---

1. Download the firmware from Canon (you'll find it in the Downloads section of the Support portion of Canon's website) and place it on your computer's hard drive. The firmware is contained in a self-extracting file for either Windows or Mac OS. It will have a name such as 7D2100105.fir.

2. On your camera, format a memory card. Choose Format from the Set-up menu, and initialize the card (make sure you don't have images you want to keep before you do this!).

3. You can copy the upgrade software to the card either using a memory card reader or by connecting the camera to your computer with a USB cable and using the EOS Utility application furnished with your camera (and described in the next section). The Firmware Version entry in the Set-up 4 menu will remind you that a memory card containing the firmware is required before you can proceed.

4. Insert the memory card in the camera and then turn the camera on. With the 7D II set to any mode other than Creative Auto or Full Auto, press MENU and scroll to Firmware Ver. x.x.x in the Set-up 4 menu and press SET.

5. You'll see the current firmware version, and an option to update. Choose OK and press the SET button to begin loading the update program.

6. A confirmation screen will appear. Select OK and press SET to continue. As the Firmware Update Program loads.

7. Next, you'll get the opportunity to confirm that the version you're upgrading to is the one you want. You can press the

MENU button to cancel. (Yes, I know there are a lot of confirmation screens; Canon wants to make sure you don't upgrade your firmware by accident, or, possibly, intentionally.)

8. Finally, the very last confirmation screen is shown. Select OK, and press SET, and, I promise, the actual firmware update will really begin.

9. While the firmware updates, you'll be warned not to turn off the power switch or touch any of the 7D II's buttons.

10. When the update complete screen appears, you can turn off the EOS 7D II, remove the AC adapter, if used, and replace or recharge the battery. Then turn the camera on to boot up your camera with the new firmware update.

11. Be sure to reformat the card before returning it to regular use to remove the firmware software.

Using Direct Camera USB Link to Copy the Software

The procedure is slightly different (and a little more automated) if you choose to transfer the firmware software to the camera through a USB linkup. Follow these instructions to get started:

1. Connect the camera (with a freshly charged battery or attached to the AC Adapter) to the computer using the USB cable and turn it on.

2. Load the EOS Utility.

3. Click the Camera Settings button.

4. Select the Firmware Update option. When the Update Firmware window appears at the bottom of the EOS Utility, choose OK.

5. Follow the instructions in the dialog boxes that pop up next by pressing the SET button on the camera. (See **Figure 14.1**.)

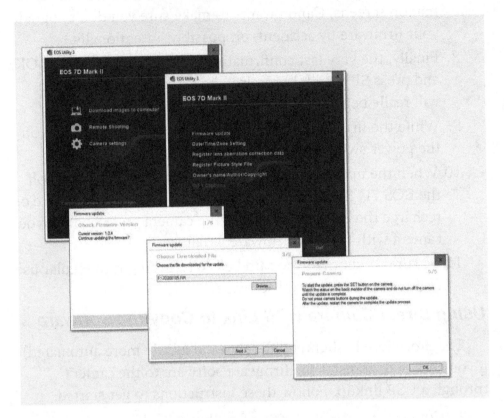

Figure 14.1

The EOS Utility can be used to update firmware.

Protecting Your LCD

The color LCD on the back of your EOS 7D II almost seems like a target for banging, scratching, and other abuse. Fortunately, it's quite rugged, and a few errant knocks are unlikely to shatter the protective cover over the LCD, and scratches won't easily mar its surface.

However, if you want to be on the safe side, there are a number of other protective products you can purchase to keep your LCD safe and, in some cases, make it a little easier to view. The simplest solution (although not always the cheapest) is to apply a plastic overlay sheet or "skin" cut to fit your LCD. These adhere either by static electricity or through a light adhesive coating that's even less clingy than stick-it notes. You can cut down overlays made for PDAs (although these can be pricey at up to $19.95 for a set of several sheets), or purchase overlays sold specifically for digital cameras. I like the GGS brand of glass protectors available on eBay and Amazon. These products will do a good job of shielding your 7D II's LCD screen from scratches and minor impacts.

Troubleshooting Memory Cards

Sometimes good memory cards go bad. Sometimes good photographers can treat their memory cards badly. It's possible that a memory card that works fine in one camera won't be recognized when inserted into another. In the worst case, you can have a card full of important photos and find that the card seems to be corrupted and you can't access any of them. Don't panic! If these scenarios sound horrific to you, there are lots of things you can do to prevent them from happening, and a variety of remedies available if they do occur. You'll want to take some time -- before disaster strikes -- to consider your options.

All Your Eggs in One Basket?

The debate about whether it's better to use one large memory card or several smaller ones has been going on since even before there were memory cards. I can remember when computer users wondered whether it was smarter to install a pair of 200MB (not *gi-gabyte*) hard drives in their computer, or if they should go for one of those new-fangled 500MB models. By the same token, a few years ago the user groups were full of proponents who insisted that you ought to use 128MB memory cards rather than the huge 512MB versions. Today, most of the arguments involve 32GB cards versus 64GB cards, and I expect that as prices for 128GB memory cards continue to drop, they'll find their way into the debate as well. Size is especially important when you're using a camera like the 7D II that captures 20-megapixel images.

Why all the fuss? Are 64GB memory cards more likely to fail than 32GB cards? Are you risking all your photos if you trust your images to a larger card? Isn't it better to use several smaller cards, so that if one fails you lose only half as many photos? Or, isn't it wiser to put all your photos onto one larger card, because the more cards you use, the better your odds of misplacing or damaging one and losing at least some pictures?

In the end, the "eggs in one basket" argument boils down to statistics, and how you happen to use your 7D II. The rationales can go both ways. If you have multiple smaller cards, you do increase your chances of something happening to one of them, so, arguably, you might be boosting the odds of losing some pictures. If all your images are important, the fact that you've lost 100 rather than 200 pictures isn't very comforting.

Also consider that the eggs/basket scenario assumes that the cards that are lost or damaged are always full. It's actually likely that your 64GB card might suffer a mishap when it's less than half-full (indeed, it's more likely that a large card won't be completely filled before it's offloaded to a computer), so you really might not lose any more shots with a single 64GB card than with multiple 16GB cards.

If you shoot photojournalist-type pictures, you probably change memory cards when they're less than completely full in order to avoid the need to do so at a crucial moment. (When I shoot sports, my cards rarely reach 80 to 90 percent of capacity before I change them.) Using multiple smaller cards means you have to change them that more often, which can be a real pain when you're taking a lot of photos. In my book, I prefer keeping all my eggs in one basket, and then making very sure that nothing happens to that basket.

There are only two really good reasons to justify limiting yourself to smaller memory cards when larger ones can be purchased at the same cost per-gigabyte. One of them is when every single picture is precious to you and the loss of any of them would be a disaster. If you're a wedding photographer, for example, and unlikely to be able to restage the nuptials if a memory card goes bad, you'll probably want to shoot no more pictures than you can afford to lose on a single card, and have an assistant ready to copy each card removed from the camera onto a backup hard drive or DVD onsite.

To be even safer, you'd want to alternate cameras or have a second photographer at least partially duplicating your coverage so your shots are distributed over several memory cards simultaneously. (Strictly speaking, the safest route of all is to beam the images to a computer as you shoot them using a Wi-Fi connection -- if you have the time.)

If none of these options are available to you, consider *interleaving* your shots. Say you don't shoot weddings, but you do go on vacation from time to time. Take 50 or so pictures on one card, or whatever number of images might fill about 25 percent of its capacity. Then, replace it with a different card and shoot about 25 percent of that card's available space. Repeat these steps with diligence (you'd have to be determined to go through this inconvenience), and, if you use four or more memory cards, you'll find your pictures from each location scattered among the different memory cards. If you lose or damage one, you'll still have *some* pictures from all the various stops on your trip on the other cards. That's more work than I like to do (I usually tote around a portable hard disk and copy the files to the drive as I go), but it's an option.

What Can Go Wrong?

There are lots of things that can go wrong with your memory card, but the ones that aren't caused by human stupidity are statistically very rare. Yes, a memory card's internal bit bin or controller can suddenly fail due to a manufacturing error or some inexplicable event caused by old age. However, if your memory card works for the first week or two that you own it, it should work forever. There's really not a lot that can wear out.

The typical memory card is rated for a Mean Time Between Failures of 1,000,000 hours of use. That's constant use 24/7 for more than 100 years! According to the manufacturers, they are good for 10,000 insertions in your camera, and should be able to retain their data (and that's without an external power source) for something on the order of 11 years. Of course, with the millions of memory cards in use, there are bound to be a few lemons here or there.

Given the reliability of solid-state memory, compared to magnetic memory, though, it's more likely that your memory problems will stem from something that you do. Memory cards are small and easy to misplace if you're not careful. For that reason, it's a good idea to keep them in their original cases or a "card safe" offered by Gepe (www.gepecardsafe.com), Pelican (www.pelican.com), and others. Always placing your memory card in a case can provide protection from the second-most common mishap that befalls memory cards: the common household laundry. If you slip a memory card in a pocket, rather than a case or your camera bag, often enough, sooner or later it's going to end up in the washing machine and probably the clothes dryer, too. There are plenty of reports of relieved digital camera owners who've laundered their memory cards and found they still worked fine, but it's not uncommon for such mistreatment to do some damage.

Memory cards can also be stomped on, accidentally bent, dropped into the ocean, chewed by pets, and otherwise rendered unusable in myriad ways. It's also possible to force a card into your 7D II's memory card slot incorrectly if you're diligent enough, doing little damage to the card itself, but damaging the contacts in the camera, eliminating its ability to read or write to any memory card. Or, if the card is formatted in your computer with a memory card reader, your 7D II may fail to recognize it. Occasionally, I've found that a memory card used in one camera would fail if used in a different camera (until I reformatted it in Windows, and then again in the camera). Every once in awhile, a card goes completely bad and -- seemingly -- can't be salvaged.

Another way to lose images is to do commonplace things with your memory card at an inopportune time. If you remove the card from the 7D II while the camera is writing images to the card, you'll lose any photos in the buffer and may damage the file structure of the card, making it difficult or impossible to retrieve the other pictures you've taken. The same thing can happen if you remove the memory card from your computer's card reader while the computer is writing to the card (say, to erase files you've already moved to your computer). You can avoid this by *not* using your computer to erase files on a memory card but, instead, always reformatting the card in your 7D II before you use it again.

What Can You Do?

Pay attention: If you're having problems, the *first* thing you should do is *stop* using that memory card. Don't take any more pictures. Don't do anything with the card until you've figured out what's wrong. Your second line of defense (your first line is to be sufficiently careful with your cards that you avoid problems in the first place) is to *do no harm* that hasn't already been done. Read the rest of this section and then, if necessary, decide on a course of action (such as using a data recovery service or software described later) before you risk damaging the data on your card further.

Now that you've calmed down, the first thing to check is whether you've actually inserted a card in the camera. If you've set the camera in the Shooting menu so that Shoot w/o Card has been turned on, it's entirely possible (although not particularly plausible) that you've been snapping away with no memory card to store the pictures to, which can lead to massive disappointment later on. Of course, the No Memory Card message appears on the LCD when the camera is powered up, and it is superimposed on the review image after every shot, but maybe you're inattentive, aren't using picture review, or have purchased one of those LCD fold-up hoods mentioned earlier in this chapter. You can avoid all this by turning the Release Shutter w/o Card feature off in the Shooting 1 menu and leaving it off.

Things get more exciting when the card itself is put in jeopardy. If you lose a card, there's not a lot you can do other than take a picture of a similar card and print up some Have You Seen This Lost Flash Memory? flyers to post on utility poles all around town.

If all you care about is reusing the card, and have resigned yourself to losing the pictures, try reformatting the card in your camera. You may find that reformatting removes the corrupted data and restores your card to health. Sometimes I've had success reformatting a card in my computer using a memory card reader (this is normally a no-no because your operating system doesn't understand the needs of your 7D II), and *then* reformatting again in the camera.

If your memory card is not behaving properly, and you *do* want to recover your images, things get a little more complicated. If your pictures are very valuable, either to you or to others (for example, a wedding), you can always turn to professional data recovery firms. Be prepared to pay hundreds of dollars to get your pictures back, but these pros often do an amazing job. You wouldn't want them working on your memory card on behalf of the police if you'd tried to erase some incriminating pictures. There are many firms of this type, and I've never used them myself, so I can't offer a recommendation. Use a Google search to turn up a ton of them. I use a software program called RescuePro, which came free with one of my SanDisk memory cards.

A more reasonable approach is to try special data recovery software you can install on your computer and use to attempt to resurrect your "lost" images yourself. They may not actually be gone completely. Perhaps your memory card's "table of contents" is jumbled, or only a few pictures are damaged in such a way that your camera and computer can't read some or any of the pictures on the card. Some of the available software was written specifically to reconstruct lost pictures, while other utilities are more general-purpose applications that can be used with any media, including floppy disks and hard disk drives. They have names like OnTrack, Photo Rescue 2, Digital Image Recovery, MediaRecover, Image Recall, and the aptly named Recover My Photos. You'll find a comprehensive list and links, as well as some picture-recovery tips at www.ultimateslr.com/memory-card-recovery.php.

Usually, once you've recovered any images on a memory card, reformatted it, and returned it to service, it will function reliably for the rest of its useful life. However, if you find a particular card going bad more than once, you'll almost certainly want to stop using it forever. See if you can get it replaced by the manufacturer, if you can, but, in the case of memory card failures, the third time is never the charm.

Cleaning Your Sensor

There's no avoiding dust. No matter how careful you are, some of it is going to settle on your camera and on the mounts of your lenses, eventually making its way inside your camera to settle in the mirror chamber. As you take photos, the mirror flipping up and down causes the dust to become airborne and eventually make its way past the shutter curtain to come to rest on the anti-aliasing filter atop your sensor. There, dust and particles can show up in every single picture you take at a small enough aperture to bring the foreign matter into sharp focus. No matter how careful you are and how cleanly you work, eventually you will get some of this dust on your camera's sensor.

Fortunately, one of the EOS 7D II's most useful features is the automatic sensor cleaning system that reduces or eliminates the need to clean your camera's sensor manually. Canon has applied anti-static coatings to the sensor and other portions of the camera body interior to counter charge build-ups that attract dust. A separate filter over the sensor vibrates ultrasonically each time the 7D II is powered on or off, shaking loose any dust.

Although the automatic sensor cleaning feature operates when you power the camera up or turn it off, you can activate it at any time. Choose Sensor Cleaning from the Set-up 3 menu, and select Clean Now. If you'd rather turn the feature on or off, choose Auto Cleaning instead, and then choose either Enable or Disable with the directional buttons. Press SET, then press the MENU button to return to the Set-up 3 menu.

If some dust does collect on your sensor, you can often map it out of your images (making it invisible) using software techniques with the Dust Delete Data feature in the Shooting 3 menu. Operation of this feature is described in Chapter 8. Of course, even with the EOS 7D II's automatic sensor cleaning/dust resistance features, you may still be required to manually clean your sensor from time to time. This section explains the phenomenon and provides some tips on minimizing dust and eliminating it when it begins to affect your shots.

Dust the FAQs, Ma'am

Here are some of the most frequently asked questions about sensor dust issues.

Q. I see tiny specks in my viewfinder. Do I have dust on my sensor?

A. If you see sharp, well-defined specks, they are clinging to the underside of your focus screen and not on your sensor. They have absolutely no effect on your photographs, and are merely annoying or distracting.

Q. I can see dust on my mirror. How can I remove it?

A. Like focus screen dust, any artifacts that have settled on your mirror won't affect your photos. You can often remove dust on the mirror or focus screen with a bulb air blower, which will loosen it and whisk it away. Stubborn dust on the focus screen can sometimes be gently flicked away with a soft brush designed for cleaning lenses. I don't recommend brushing the mirror or touching it in any way. The mirror is a special front-surface-silvered optical device (unlike conventional mirrors, which are silvered on the back side of a piece of glass or plastic) and can be easily scratched. If you can't blow mirror dust off, it's best to just forget about it. You can't see it in the viewfinder, anyway.

Q. **I see a bright spot in the same place in all of my photos. Is that sensor dust?**

A. You've probably got either a "hot" pixel or one that is permanently "stuck" due to a defect in the sensor. A hot pixel is one that shows up as a bright spot only during long exposures as the sensor warms. A pixel stuck in the "on" position always appears in the image. Both show up as bright red, green, or blue pixels, usually surrounded by a small cluster of other improperly illuminated pixels, caused by the camera's interpolating the hot or stuck pixel into its surroundings, as shown in **Figure 14.2**. A stuck pixel can also be permanently dark. Either kind is likely to show up when they contrast with plain, evenly colored areas of your image.

- Finding one or two hot or stuck pixels in your sensor is unfortunately fairly common. They can be "removed" by telling the 7D II to ignore them through a simple process called *pixel mapping*. If the bad pixels become bothersome, Canon can remap your sensor's pixels with a quick trip to a service center.
- Bad pixels can also show up on your camera's color LCD panel, but, unless they are abundant, the wisest course is to just ignore them.

Q. **I see an irregular out-of-focus blob in the same place in my photos. Is that sensor dust?**

A. Yes. Sensor contaminants can take the form of tiny spots, larger blobs, or even curvy lines if they are caused by minuscule fibers that have settled on the sensor. They'll appear out of focus because they aren't actually on the sensor surface but, rather, a fraction of a millimeter above it on the filter that covers the sensor. The smaller the f/stop used, the more in-focus the dust becomes. At large apertures, it may not be visible at all.

Q. **I never see any dust on my sensor. What's all the fuss about?**

A. Those who never have dust problems with their EOS 7D II fall into one of four categories: those for whom the camera's automatic dust removal features are working well; those who seldom change their lenses and have clean working habits that minimize the amount of dust that invades their cameras in the first place; those who simply don't notice the dust (often because they don't shoot many macro photos or other pictures using the small f/stops that makes dust evident in their images); and those who are very, very lucky.

Figure 14.2

A stuck pixel is surrounded by improperly interpolated pixels created by the 7D II's demosaicing algorithm.

Identifying and Dealing with Dust

Sensor dust is less of a problem than it might be because it shows up only under certain circumstances. Indeed, you might have dust on your sensor right now and not be aware if it. The dust doesn't actually settle on the sensor itself, but, rather, on a protective filter a very tiny distance above the sensor, subjecting it to the phenomenon of *depth-of-focus*. Depth-of-focus is the distance the focal plane can be moved and still render an object in sharp focus. At f/2.8 to f/5.6 or even smaller, sensor dust, particularly if small, is likely to be outside the range of depth-of-focus and blur into an unnoticeable dot.

However, if you're shooting at f/16 to f/22 or smaller, those dust motes suddenly pop into focus. Forget about trying to spot them by peering directly at your sensor with the shutter open and the lens removed. The period at the end of this sentence, about .33mm in diameter, could block a group of pixels measuring 40 x 40 pixels (160 pixels in all!). Dust spots that are even smaller than that can easily show up in your images if you're shooting large, empty areas that are light colored. Dust motes are most likely to show up in the sky, as in **Figure 14.3**, or in white backgrounds of your seamless product shots and are less likely to be a problem in images that contain lots of dark areas and detail.

To see if you have dust on your sensor, take a few test shots of a plain, blank surface (such as a piece of paper or a cloudless sky) at small f/stops, such as f/22, and a few wide open. Open Photoshop, copy several shots into a single document in separate layers, then flip back and forth between layers to see if any spots you see are present in all layers. You may have to boost contrast and sharpness to make the dust easier to spot.

Figure 14.3

Only the dust spots in the sky are apparent in this shot.

Avoiding Dust

Of course, the easiest way to protect your sensor from dust is to prevent it from settling on the sensor in the first place. Some Canon lenses come with rubberized seals around the lens mounts that help keep dust from infiltrating, but you'll find that dust will still find a way to get inside. Here are my tips for eliminating the problem before it begins.

- **Clean environment.** Avoid working in dusty areas if you can do so. Hah! Serious photographers will take this one with a grain of salt, because it usually makes sense to go where the pictures are. Only a few of us are so paranoid about sensor dust (considering that it is so easily removed) that we'll avoid moderately grimy locations just to protect something that is, when you get down to it, just a tool. If you find a great picture opportunity at a raging fire, during a sandstorm, or while surrounded by dust clouds, you might hesitate to take the picture, but, with a little caution (don't remove your lens in these situations, and clean the camera afterwards!) you can still shoot. However, it still makes sense to store your camera in a clean environment. One place cameras and lenses pick up a lot of dust is inside a camera bag. Clean your bag from time to time, and you can avoid problems.

- **Clean lenses.** There are a few paranoid types that avoid swapping lenses in order to minimize the chance of dust getting inside their cameras. It makes more sense just to use a blower or brush to dust off the rear lens mount of the replacement lens first, so you won't be introducing dust into your camera simply by attaching a new, dusty lens. Do this before you remove the lens from your camera, and then avoid stirring up dust before making the exchange.

- **Work fast.** Minimize the time your camera is lens-less and exposed to dust. That means having your replacement lens ready and dusted off, and a place to set down the old lens as soon as it is removed, so you can quickly attach the new lens.

- **Let gravity help you.** Face the camera downward when the lens is detached so any dust in the mirror box will tend to fall away from the sensor. Turn your back to any breezes, indoor forced air vents, fans, or other sources of dust to minimize infiltration.

- **Protect the lens you just removed.** Once you've attached the new lens, quickly put the end cap on the one you just removed to reduce the dust that might fall on it.

- **Clean out the vestibule.** From time to time, remove the lens while in a relatively dust-free environment and use a blower bulb like the one shown in **Figure 14.4** (*not* compressed air or a vacuum hose, please!) to clean out the mirror box area. A blower bulb is generally safer than a can of compressed air, or a strong positive/negative airflow, which can tend to drive dust further into nooks and crannies.

- **Be prepared.** If you're embarking on an important shooting session, it's a good idea to clean your sensor *now*, rather than come home with hundreds or thousands of images with dust spots caused by flecks that were sitting on your sensor before you even started.

- **Clone out existing spots in your image editor.** Photoshop and other editors have a clone tool or healing brush you can use to copy pixels from surrounding areas over the dust spot or dead pixel. This process can be tedious, especially if you have lots of dust spots and/or lots of images to be corrected. The advantage is that this sort of manual fix-it probably will do the least damage to the rest of your photo. Only the cloned pixels will be affected.

- **Use filtration in your image editor.** A semi-smart filter like Photoshop's Dust & Scratches filter can remove dust and other artifacts by selectively blurring areas that the plug-in decides represent dust spots. This method can work well if you have many dust spots, because you won't need to patch them manually. However, any automated method like this has the possibility of blurring areas of your image that you didn't intend to soften.

Figure 14.4
Use a robust air bulb for cleaning your sensor.

Sensor Cleaning

Those new to the concept of sensor dust actually hesitate before deciding to clean their camera themselves. Isn't it a better idea to pack up your 7D II and send it to a Canon service center so their crack technical staff can do the job for you? Or, at the very least, shouldn't you delegate the task to the friendly folks at your local camera store (if you're lucky, you have one nearby)?

Of course, if you choose to let someone else clean your sensor, they will be using methods that are more or less identical to the techniques you would use yourself. None of these techniques are difficult, and the only difference between their cleaning and your cleaning is that they might have done it dozens or hundreds of times. If you're careful, you can do just as good a job.

Of course vendors like Canon won't tell you this, but it's not because they don't trust you. It's not that difficult for a real goofball to mess up his camera by hurrying or taking a shortcut. Perhaps the person uses the "Bulb" method of holding the shutter open and a finger slips, allowing the shutter curtain to close on top of a sensor cleaning brush. Or, someone tries to clean the sensor using masking tape, and ends up with goo all over its surface. If Canon recommended *any* method that's mildly risky, someone would do it wrong, and then the company would face lawsuits from those who'd contend they did it exactly in the way the vendor suggested, so the ruined camera is not their fault. If you visit Canon's website, you'll find this recommendation: "If the image sensor needs cleaning, we recommend having it cleaned at a Canon service center, as it is a very delicate component."

You can see that vendors like Canon tend to be conservative in their recommendations, and, in doing so, make it seem as if sensor cleaning is more daunting and dangerous than it really is. Some vendors recommend only dust-off cleaning, through the use of reasonably gentle blasts of air, while condemning more serious scrubbing with swabs and cleaning fluids. However, these cleaning kits for the exact types of cleaning they recommended against are for sale in Japan only, where, apparently, your average photographer is more dexterous than those of us in the rest of the world. These kits are similar to those used by official repair staff to clean your sensor if you decide to send your camera in for a dust-up.

As I noted, sensors can be affected by dust particles that are much smaller than you might be able to spot visually on the surface of your lens. The filters that cover sensors tend to be fairly hard compared to optical glass. Cleaning the 22.3mm x 14.9mm sensor in your Canon 7D II within the tight confines of the mirror box can call for a steady hand and careful touch. If your sensor's filter becomes scratched through inept cleaning, you can't simply remove it yourself and replace it with a new one.

There are three basic kinds of cleaning processes that can be used to remove dusty and sticky stuff that settles on your dSLR's sensor. All of these must be performed with the shutter locked open. I'll describe these methods and provide instructions for locking the shutter later in this section.

- **Air cleaning.** This process involves squirting blasts of air inside your camera with the shutter locked open. This works well for dust that's not clinging stubbornly to your sensor.
- **Brushing.** A soft, very fine brush is passed across the surface of the sensor's filter, dislodging mildly persistent dust particles and sweeping them off the imager.
- **Liquid cleaning.** A soft swab dipped in a cleaning solution such as ethanol is used to wipe the sensor filter, removing more obstinate particles.

Placing the Shutter in the Locked and Fully Upright Position for Cleaning

Make sure you're using a fully charged battery or the optional AC Adapter Kit ACK-E18.

1. Remove the lens from the camera and then turn the camera on.
2. Set the EOS 7D II to any one of the non-fully automatic modes.

3. You'll find the Clean Manually menu choice in the Set-up 3 menu under Sensor Cleaning. Press the SET button.

4. Select OK and press SET again. The mirror will flip up and the shutter will open.

5. Use one of the methods described below to remove dust and grime from your sensor. Be careful not to accidentally switch the power off or open the memory card or battery compartment doors as you work. If that happens, the shutter may be damaged if it closes onto your cleaning tool.

6. When you're finished, turn the power off, replace your lens, and switch your camera back on.

Air Cleaning

Your first attempts at cleaning your sensor should always involve gentle blasts of air. Many times, you'll be able to dislodge dust spots, which will fall off the sensor and, with luck, out of the mirror box. Attempt one of the other methods only when you've already tried air cleaning and it didn't remove all the dust.

Here are some tips for doing air cleaning:

*   **Use a clean, powerful air bulb.** Your best bet is bulb cleaners designed for the job, like the Giottos Rocket. Smaller bulbs, like those air bulbs with a brush attached sometimes sold for lens cleaning or weak nasal aspirators, may not provide sufficient air or a strong enough blast to do much good.

*   **Hold the EOS 7D II upside down.** Then look up into the mirror box as you squirt your air blasts, increasing the odds that gravity will help pull the expelled dust downward, away from the sensor. You may have to use some imagination in positioning yourself.

*   **Never use air canisters.** The propellant inside these cans can permanently coat your sensor if you tilt the can while spraying. It's not worth taking a chance.

*   **Avoid air compressors.** Super-strong blasts of air are likely to force dust under the sensor filter.

Brush Cleaning

If your dust is a little more stubborn and can't be dislodged by air alone, you may want to try a brush, charged with static electricity, which can pick off dust spots by electrical attraction. One good, but expensive, option is the Arctic Butterfly sold at www.visible-dust.com. A motor built into the brush is used to "flutter" the tip for a few seconds prior to cleaning (see **Figure 14.5**, left), charging the brush's anti-static properties. Then, the motor is turned off (**Figure 14.5**, right) and the brush tip is passed above the surface of the sensor. (It's not necessary to touch the sensor.) The dust is attracted to the brush and removed by another quick flutter once you've removed the brush from the mirror chamber. A cheaper, inanimate, sensor cleaning brush can be purchased from a variety of sources. You need a 16mm version. It can be stroked across the short dimension of your T6i/T6s's sensor.

Ordinary artist's brushes are much too coarse and stiff and have fibers that are tangled or can come loose and settle on your sensor. A good sensor brush's fibers are resilient and described as "thinner than a human hair." Brush cleaning is done with a dry brush by gently swiping across the surface of the sensor filter with the tip. The dust particles are attracted to the brush particles and cling to them. You should clean the brush with compressed air before and after each use, and store it in an appropriate air-tight container between applications to keep it clean and dust-free. Although these special brushes are expensive, one should last you a long time.

Figure 14.5

A proper brush like this Arctic Butterfly is required for dusting off your sensor.

Liquid Cleaning

Unfortunately, you'll often encounter really stubborn dust spots that can't be removed with a blast of air or flick of a brush. These spots may be combined with some grease or a liquid that causes them to stick to the sensor filter's surface. In such cases, liquid cleaning with a swab may be necessary. During my first clumsy attempts to clean my own sensor, I accidentally got my blower bulb tip too close to the sensor, and some sort of deposit from the tip of the bulb ended up on the sensor. I panicked until I discovered that liquid cleaning did a good job of removing whatever it was that took up residence on my sensor.

You can make your own swabs out of pieces of plastic (some use fast food restaurant knives, with the tip cut at an angle to the proper size) covered with a soft cloth or Pec-Pad, as shown in **Figure 14.6**. However, if you've got the bucks to spend, you can't go wrong with good-quality commercial sensor cleaning swabs, such as those sold by Photographic Solutions, Inc. (www.photosol.com).

You want a sturdy swab that won't bend or break so you can apply gentle pressure to the swab as you wipe the sensor surface. Use the swab with methanol (as pure as you can get it, particularly medical grade; other ingredients can leave a residue), or the Eclipse solution also sold by Photographic Solutions. Eclipse is actually quite a bit purer than even medical-grade methanol. A couple drops of solution should be enough, unless you have a spot that's extremely difficult to remove. In that case, you may need to use extra solution on the swab to help "soak" the dirt off.

Once you overcome your nervousness at touching your 7D II's sensor, the process is easy. You'll wipe continuously with the swab in one direction, then flip it over and wipe in the other direction. You need to completely wipe the entire surface; otherwise, you may end up depositing the dust you collect at the far end of your stroke. Wipe; don't rub.

If you want a close-up look at your sensor to make sure the dust has been removed, you can pay $50-$100 for a special sensor "microscope" with an illuminator. Or, you can do like I do and work with a plain old Carson MiniBrite PO-55 illuminated 5X magnifier, as seen in **Figure 14.7**. It has a built-in LED and, held a few inches from the lens mount with the lens removed from your 7D II, provides a sharp, close-up view of the sensor, with enough contrast to reveal any dust that remains. You can read more about this great device at `http://dslrguides.com/carson`.

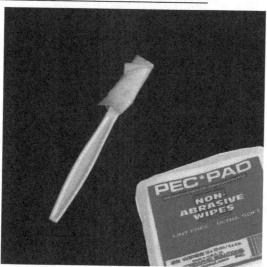

Figure 14.6

Carefully wrap a Pec-Pad around the swab.

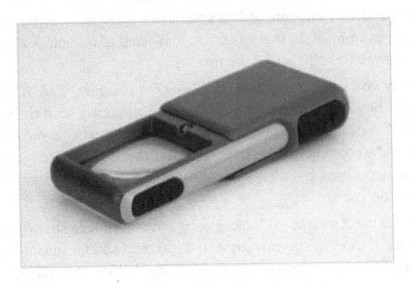

Figure 14.7

An illuminated magnifier like this Carson MiniBrite PO-55 can be used as a 'scope to view your sensor.

Printed in July 2021
by Rotomail Italia S.p.A., Vignate (MI) - Italy